SFT Lexicon

Spiritual Freedom Technique

by

Jen Ward

ISBN-13: 978-0-9994954-5-2

ISBN-10: 0-9994954-5-3

2018: ORIGINAL EDITION

SFT Tapping: Spiritual Freedom Technique

See Yourself Reflected in Every Miracle.

People keep calling the taps I offer EFT taps. It never has been accurate. EFT stands for emotional freedom taps. That is an introduction to what I do. The emotions are rooted in the astral plane, which is a more subtle vibration than this physical world. When most people cross over, they merely cross over to the astral plane, which is very similar to the physical plane.

I tap into issues that are also rooted in the causal plane and the mental plane of existence as well as the physical and astral plane. The causal and mental realms are even more refined than the vibratory rate of the astral plane. The causal plane lies closer to the astral plane. It is where a person's Akashic records are stored. Everything that one will ever experience is stored in files on the causal plane. "Above" that is the mental plane. It is where all mental information is held. People who are really smart but not very aware feel most comfortable on this level.

When we dream, we visit these other levels of consciousness. Most people merely go to the astral plane. It is similar to the physical plane but may seem distorted and elongated. The layout is different than the physical as well. When people are on the causal plane in a dream, they may show up in a different time period. They may also have a dream of looking through photos. They are really looking at their own memories or causal records. When they are seeing geometric shapes or mathematical equations in a dream, it is indicative of being on the mental plane.

Beyond the mental plane is the pure soul plane. One must drop the ego to be present here. That is why it is so difficult to be present in this vibratory rate. It is beyond the duality of yin and yang. On the soul plane, love is more of a nothingness, a peaceful calm. If one is having reactions, fears or issues, they are all research as to what needs to be released so one can get to the ultimate state of awakening, the soul plane.

It is our goal as spiritual beings to remember our true purpose. Our true purpose as spiritual beings is to consciously operate from the soul plane while still maintaining a physical body. This is what enlightenment is: To be conscious of all aspects of ourselves. THIS IS WHAT MY SFT TAPS DO. It is profound. Those who understand the spiritual goal of gaining awareness from the soul plane are very grateful for these taps and my assistance.

They now realize that spiritual freedom does not happen by giving your proxy to someone outside of yourself. Spiritual freedom can be as simplistic as pushing through the resistance of doing the taps that I post because they don't just address physical or emotional issues. They address issues on these levels but they also address all the experiences that happen on the causal and mental realm as well. They bypass the ego's meddling in our own awakening and put it back into perspective as a helpful tool as opposed to a limitation.

The taps I share are about you no longer giving pieces of yourself away. It is about you collecting back to yourself every wonderful aspect of your beautiful essence that you have dispersed through the illusion of time and space, to stretch your awareness from beyond the farthest star and to see your beautiful wonderment reflected in every single miracle. That is what awaits you with awakening. Godspeed.

TABLE OF CONTENTS

Introduction

The Purest Spiritual Teaching

Every spiritual teaching that has come to man to free him of the limitations of conditioning has failed. The carrier of the truth passes on and the truth is used in turn to trap humanity at a deeper level rather than free them. If only there was a means to prevent this. The taps that I post are the answer because they empower the individual instead of asking them to promise their loyalty to that of another key individual. The purity of these taps is that they preclude one from giving their power away, even and especially, to me.

They address taking one's power back from all takers and all power mongers. If someone was prone to abuse power and was teaching others the taps, the taps would prevent that person from being able to take from others purely by the nature of the taps. They are a key exercise in teaching humans their empowerment after having their abilities shut down in them for so long.

The taps are the equivalent of physical therapy for a broken body. They are physical therapy for omniscient beings that have been told they are worthless. In a couple generations, after the taps become a common activity, they will no longer be necessary. Humans will just be able to shift conditions with their intentions. But for now, they are as effective as teaching spiritual beings to walk again.

So perhaps, the purest spiritual teaching is a non-teaching with no dogma and no guidelines except to empower one's self as much as possible by doing the taps that I post. Of course, I can assist on an energetic level and do. Everyone who uses the taps that I post is being assisted by me. I know when a new breakthrough is happening with people doing my taps because I feel the effects physically. Sometimes I just need to drop out of the physical body and sleep. But it is done without the distraction of exchange or ego gratification. It is simply done for the benefit of giving to and uplifting humanity.

As each one individual is freed of their personal mire, all of humanity is freed. Every person, creature, blade of grass and stone. So perhaps the reason why every spiritual sage failed in delivering truth to the masses and now perhaps watching in hindsight, was because they all came in male form. Perhaps the current wave of empowerment for women is a reflection of the message of truth being delivered to this world through the embodiment of the expansiveness of the female capacity to love. Perhaps the current message reflects higher consciousness simply due to the nature of female energy.

It is true male energy is different than female energy. Male energy is driven, competitive and contained. Female energy is expansive, benevolent and compassionate with a deep awareness of the subtleties of truth. Perhaps, truth being delivered through a female embodiment with no need of adulation or worship is the cure for the ills of man. Perhaps, the female empowerment on a sub-cellular level in all beings is what indeed is the remedy to awakening the slumbering man.

The more I write, create taps, study the makeup of the world from a naive point of view and assist people, the more I feel a receptivity to what I do. As I feel the receptivity in people trying and sharing the taps, I feel an expansion in the consciousness of culture. It is a good thing that politicians are blatant liars and cheats. It shows their inability to hide their true nature anymore. The nature of man and the nature of politics have not changed. The individuals have changed. They are now wise to the ills of man. It is ugly and can be scary to see them. But it is also empowering to know what one is dealing with.

I have been and may continue to get assaulted and insulted along the way. I never set out in this life to be an instrument to awaken humanity. I just wanted to fall in love and have a big family. But the more I am immersed in the joy of outflowing, the more I am empowered in assisting others. This compels me to assist more. Even the attacks, assaults and disappointments from loved ones cannot squelch my desire to free others, for in seeing others reclaim their joy, I see joy and hope reflected in all nature. Even the songbirds and trees enjoy the new found expansion in consciousness. There is an enthusiasm in life even if it has not reached all humans yet.

Instructions:

Say each statement **three** times out loud while *continuously* tapping on the top of your head at the crown chakra, and say it a fourth time while tapping on your chest at the heart chakra. Say each word deliberately. They are not just words but a vibration that you are initiating to shift energy. Pause after each word. Say it in a commanding but even tone, not as a question. You are not asking for permission. You are gaining awareness and empowerment. Forgo saying it in a **singsong** tone or with bravado. These are both sabotages of the mind to weaken the strength of the vibration of the command. Say them all. If you allow yourself to choose which ones are relevant, you are putting the wolf in charge of the gate. The harder they are to get through, the more **relevant** they are to you. You are supported by your greater self in doing these.

Gain Pure Abundance

(Say each statement three times out loud while continuously tapping on the top of your head at the crown chakra and say it a fourth time while tapping on your chest at the heart chakra. Say each word deliberately. They are not just words but a vibration that you are initiating to shift energy. Pause after each word. Say it in a commanding but even tone, not as a question. Forgo saying it in a singsong tone or with bravado. Say them all.)

"I release converting my abundance to problems; in all moments."

"I release converting my abundance to lack; in all moments."

"I release converting my abundance to loneliness; in all moments."

"I release converting my abundance to dis-ease; in all moments."

"I release converting my abundance to drama; in all moments."

"I release converting my abundance to complaints; in all moments."

"I release converting my abundance to apathy; in all moments."

"I release converting my abundance to unworthiness; in all moments."

"I release converting my abundance to failure; in all moments."

"I release converting my abundance to self doubt; in all moments."

"I release converting my abundance to sabotage; in all moments."

"I release converting my abundance to depression; in all moments."

"I release converting my abundance to anger; in all moments."

"I release converting my abundance to judgment; in all moments."

"I release converting my abundance to helplessness; in all moments."

"I convert all problems back to abundance; in all moments."

"I convert all lack back to abundance; in all moments."

"I convert all loneliness back to abundance; in all moments."

"I convert all dis-ease back to abundance; in all moments."

"I convert all drama back to abundance; in all moments."

"I convert all complaints back to abundance; in all moments."

"I convert all apathy back to abundance; in all moments."

"I convert all unworthiness back to abundance; in all moments."

"I convert all failure back to abundance; in all moments."

"I convert all self doubt back to abundance; in all moments."

"I convert all sabotage back to abundance; in all moments."

"I convert all depression back to abundance; in all moments."

"I convert all anger back to abundance; in all moments."

"I convert all judgment back to abundance; in all moments."

"I convert all helplessness back to abundance; in all moments."

"I collect and embrace abundance in all forms; in all moments."

"I am centered and empowered in abundance; in all moments."

"I resonate and emanate abundance; in all moments."

Release the Connection to Abusers

When dogs have been kept in a cage for a long time, it is difficult for them to come out. When they have been abused over a period of time, they naturally cower. This happens with people as well.

I can tell when someone has been abused. The internal cowering translates to the next life. It takes a lot of love and nurturing to undo the effect of abuse. It is easy to attract someone else to come in and take the role of an abuser if your energy says that you are used to being abused.

These taps can be a shortcut to release those energetic signals that say one is comfortable with abuse.

(Say each statement three times while tapping on your head and say it a fourth time while tapping on your chest.)

"I release attracting the abusers; in all moments."

"I recant all vows and agreements between myself and all the abusers; in all moments."

"I remove all curses between myself and all the abusers; in all moments."

"I remove all blessings between myself and all the abusers; in all moments."

"I dissolve all karmic ties between myself and all the abusers; in all moments."

"I remove all the pain, burden, limitations and programming that all abusers have put on me; in all moments."

"I remove all the pain, burden and limitations that I have put on all the abusers; in all moments."

"I take back all the joy, love, abundance, freedom, health, success, security, companionship, peace, life and wholeness that all abusers have taken from me; in all moments."

"I give back all the joy, love, abundance, freedom, life and wholeness that I have taken from all abusers; in all moments."

"I release resonating with all abusers; in all moments."

"I release emanating with all abusers; in all moments."

"I remove all abusers from my sound frequency; in all moments."

"I remove all abusers from my light body; in all moments."

"I shift my paradigm from all abusers to joy, love, abundance, freedom, life, peace and wholeness; in all moments."

"I am centered in joy, love, abundance, freedom, life, peace and wholeness; in all moments."

Addiction

(Say each statement three times out loud while continuously tapping on the top of your head at the crown chakra and say it a fourth time while tapping on your chest.)

"I release storing trauma and sadness in my body; in all moments."

"I send all energy matrices into the light and sound that compromise my free will; in all moments."

"I command all complex energy matrices that compromise my free will to be escorted into the light and sound; in all moments."

"I release poisoning myself; in all moments."

"I release punishing myself; in all moments."

"I release inflicting drama upon myself; in all moments."

"I release creating a nightmare out of my life; in all moments."

"I gain the strength to be empowered and unencumbered; in all moments."

"I release creating distractions from my joy; in all moments."

"I release depending on crutches; in all moments.'"

"I release being stuck in 'hunt and gather' mode; in all moments."

"I release hating myself; in all moments."

"I release the trauma of being born; in all moments."

"I release mourning my tribe; in all moments."

"I release the trauma of being separated from my tribe; in all moments."

"I release being stuck in the past; in all moments."

"I recant all vows and agreements between myself and all addictions; in all moments."

"I dissolve all karmic ties between myself and all addictions; in all moments."

"I shift my paradigm from addiction to joy, love, abundance and freedom; in all moments."

"I am centered and empowered in joy, love, abundance, freedom and wholeness; in all moments."

Dealing with Alcoholism

(Say each statement three times out loud while continuously tapping on the top of your head at the crown chakra and say it a fourth time while tapping on your chest.)

"I declare myself a surrogate for _____ in doing these taps; in all moments."

"I also declare myself a surrogate for our family in doing these taps; in all moments."

"I release being pickled in alcohol; in all moments."

"I release using alcohol as a crutch; in all moments."

"I release being in denial about alcohol; in all moments."

"I release lashing out due to alcohol; in all moments."

"I release being crippled into ineffectiveness by alcohol; in all moments."

"I release defending alcohol; in all moments."

"I convert all the energy I use to drink into effectiveness; in all moments."

"I release being obsessed with alcohol; in all moments."

"I release the genetic propensity to drink too much; in all moments."

"I strip all illusion off of drinking; in all moments."

"I remove all masks, walls and armor from alcohol; in all moments."

"I remove all masks, walls and armor of overdrinking from my beingness; in all moments."

"I remove all engrams of alcohol from my beingness; in all moments."

"I remove the claws of alcohol from my beingness; in all moments."

"I remove all vivaxes between myself and alcohol; in all moments."

"I remove all tentacles between myself and alcohol; in all moments."

"I remove all programming and conditioning that alcohol has put on me; in all moments."

"I send all energy matrices that crave alcohol into the light and sound; in all moments."

"I command all complex energy matrices that crave alcohol to be escorted into the light and sound; in all moments."

"I send all energy matrices that benefit from a state of stupor to be escorted into the light and sound; in all moments."

"I command all complex energy matrices that benefit from a state of stupor to be escorted into the light and sound; in all moments."

"I recant all vows and agreements between myself and alcohol; in all moments."

"I send all energy matrices into the light and sound that impersonate me; in all moments."

"I command all complex energy matrices that impersonate me to be escorted into the light and sound; in all moments."

"I send all energy matrices into the light and sound that impersonate love, truth, integrity or God; in all moments."

"I command all complex energy matrices that impersonate love, truth, integrity or God to be escorted into the light and sound; in all moments."

"I send all energy matrices into the light and sound that impersonate my loved ones; in all moments."

"I command all complex energy matrices that impersonate my loved ones to be escorted into the light and sound; in all moments."

"I send all energy matrices into the light and sound that impersonate righteousness; in all moments."

"I command all complex energy matrices that impersonate righteousness to be escorted into the light and sound; in all moments."

"I send all energy matrices into the light and sound that hide where the alpha and the omega intersect; in all moments."

"I command all complex energy matrices that hide where the alpha and the omega intersect to be escorted into the light and sound; in all moments."

"I remove all curses between myself and alcohol; in all moments."

"I remove all blessings between myself and alcohol; in all moments."

"I sever all strings and cords between myself and alcohol; in all moments."

"I release taking solace in alcohol; in all moments."

"I release identifying with alcoholism; in all moments."

"I dissolve all karmic ties between myself and alcohol; in all moments."

"I remove all the pain, burden and limitations that alcohol has put on me; in all moments."

"I remove all the pain, burden and limitations that I have put on all others due to alcohol; in all moments."

"I remove all the fear, futility and unworthiness that alcohol has put on me; in all moments."

"I remove all the fear, futility and unworthiness that I have put on all others due to alcohol; in all moments."

"I remove all the ignorance, paralysis and illusion of separateness that alcohol has put on me; in all moments."

"I remove all the ignorance, paralysis and illusion of separateness that I have put on all others due to alcohol; in all moments."

"I take back all that alcohol has taken from me; in all moments."

"I give back to all others all that that I have taken from them due to alcohol; in all moments."

"I withdraw all my energy and support from alcohol; in all moments."

"I collapse and dissolve all psychic attractions to alcohol; in all moments."

"I dissipate all of alcoholism by converting it back into divine love; in all moments."

"I release resonating with alcohol; in all moments."

"I release emanating with alcohol; in all moments."

"I extract all alcohol from my sound frequency; in all moments."

"I extract all alcohol from my light emanation; in all moments."

"I extract all alcohol from my whole beingness; in all moments."

"I shift my paradigm from alcoholism to acquiescent calm; in all moments."

"I transcend all alcohol; in all moments."

"I am centered and empowered in an acquiescent calm; in all moments."

"I resonate, emanate, and am interconnected with all life in an acquiescent calm; in all moments."

Demons of Addiction

(Say each statement three times out loud while continuously tapping on the top of your head at the crown chakra and say it a fourth time while tapping on your heart chakra.)

"I release harboring demons; in all moments."

"I release sympathizing with my demons; in all moments."

"I release feeding my demons; in all moments."

"I release giving power over to my demons; in all moments."

"I release creating demons; in all moments."

"I release the fear of my own demons; in all moments."

"I release giving my demons superhuman strength; in all moments."

"I release the belief that my demons are evil spirits; in all moments."

"I release confusing my demons with demonic possession in all moments."

"I exorcise my demons; in all moments."

"I release owning the demons; in all moments."

"I release being enslaved to the demons; in all moments."

"I recant all vows and agreements between myself and the demons; in all moments."

"I remove all blessings and curses between myself and the demons; in all moments."

"I sever all strings and cords between myself and the demons; in all moments."

"I break all chains between myself and the demons; in all moments."

"I dissolve all karmic ties between myself and the demons; in all moments."

"I remove all the fear, guilt, pain, burden, limitations, anger, greed, lust, jealousy and engrams that the demons have put on me; in all moments."

"I take back all the joy, love, abundance, freedom, health, success, security, companionship, peace, life, wholeness, beauty, enthusiasm, contentment, spirituality, enlightenment and confidence that the demons have taken from me; in all moments."

"I withdraw all my energy from the demons; in all moments."

"I collapse and disintegrate the demons into divine love; in all moments."

"I repair and fortify the Wei chi of all my bodies; in all moments."

"I align all my bodies; in all moments."

"I release resonating with the demons; in all moments."

"I release emanating with the demons; in all moments."

"I extract all the demons from my sound frequency and dissolve them into divine love; in all moments."

"I extract all the demons from my light body and dissolve them into divine love; in all moments."

"I shift my paradigm from the demons to joy, love, abundance, freedom, health, success, security, companionship, peace, life, wholeness, beauty, enthusiasm, contentment, spirituality, enlightenment and confidence; in all moments."

"I transcend the demons; in all moments."

"I am centered and empowered in divine love; in all moments."

"I remove and dissolve everything from my essence that is not divine love; in all moments."

"I resonate and emanate divine love; in all moments."

Taps to Remove All Cravings

Cravings for food, porn, video games, a need to be validated, needed or to feel important, a need for drama, being a victim, addictions and so much more are all cravings to be loved. Instead of working on a superficial level, these taps work deep within. Use your self-discipline to do these taps and let the cravings fall away.

(Say each statement three times while tapping on your head and say it a fourth time while tapping on your chest.)

"I declare myself a surrogate for humanity in doing these taps; in all moments."

"I release looking for something to crave; in all moments."

"I release looking for a problem to solve; in all moments."

"I release filtering out the joy; in all moments."

"I release looking for a void to fill; in all moments."

"I release confusing cravings for love; in all moments."

"I release using cravings to nurture myself; in all moments."

"I release using cravings as a crutch; in all moments."

"I release keeping cravings as pets; in all moments."

"I release being enslaved to cravings; in all moments."

"I eliminate the first cause in regards to all cravings; in all moments."

"I eliminate the first cause that moved me away from pure contentment; in all moments."

"I remove all vivaxes between myself and all cravings; in all moments."

"I remove the claws of all cravings from my beingness; in all moments."

"I remove all tentacles between myself and all cravings; in all moments."

"I dig out the roots of all cravings from my beingness; in all moments."

"I remove all programming and conditioning that all cravings have put on me; in all moments."

"I remove all engrams of all cravings from my beingness; in all moments."

"I send all energy matrices of all cravings into the light; in all moments."

"I withdraw all my energy from all cravings; in all moments."

"I strip all illusion off of all cravings; in all moments."

"I command all complex energy matrices of cravings to be escorted into the light and sound; in all moments."

"I recant all vows and agreements between myself and all cravings; in all moments."

"I remove all curses between myself and all cravings; in all moments."

"I remove all blessings between myself and all cravings; in all moments."

"I sever all strings and cords between myself and all cravings; in all moments."

"I dissolve all karmic ties between myself and all cravings; in all moments."

"I remove all the pain, burden and limitations that all cravings have put on me; in all moments."

"I remove all the pain, burden and limitations that I have put on all others due to cravings; in all moments."

"I remove all the fear, futility and unworthiness that all cravings have put on me; in all moments."

"I remove all the fear, futility and unworthiness that I have put on all others due to cravings; in all moments."

"I remove all the helplessness, weakness and illusion of separateness that all cravings have put on me; in all moments."

"I remove all the helplessness, weakness and illusion of separateness that I have put on all others due to cravings; in all moments."

"I take back all that cravings have taken from me; in all moments."

"I give back to all others all that I have taken from them due to cravings; in all moments."

"I remove all masks, walls and armor from all cravings; in all moments."

"I collapse and dissolve all cravings; in all moments."

"I release resonating with cravings; in all moments."

"I release emanating with cravings; in all moments."

"I extract all cravings from my sound frequency; in all moments."

"I extract all cravings from my light emanation; in all moments."

"I extract all cravings from all 32 layers of my auric field; in all moments."

"I extract all cravings from my whole beingness; in all moments."

"I shift my paradigm from all cravings to complete perpetual contentment; in all moments."

"I transcend all cravings; in all moments."

"I am centered and empowered in complete perpetual contentment; in all moments."

"I resonate and emanate complete perpetual contentment; in all moments."

"I am interconnected with all life in complete perpetual contentment; in all moments."

A Truth Revealed and Taps to End Smoking

In the private sessions, new things are revealed that have never occurred to anyone but resonate with absolute truth. Last night, a deeper cause for smoking was revealed. Take away the hypnotizing advertisements, the peer pressure and the addictive chemicals that cigarettes are laced with, why do some people continue to smoke? Also, aside from the susceptibility of some people to the aforementioned things, why are some people more destined to smoke?

Last night, during the group session, I tuned into one of the participant's reason for smoking. I saw their past life record of being very close to the campfire. It was a dangerous existence and the fire meant safety from wild animals, safety from freezing to death and security of having the whole clan gathered around. To some people, this experience was so exhilarating that they inadvertently try to recreate it through the act of smoking.

When they feel their lungs fill up with smoke, it gives them a sense of that feeling of hovering over a fire or security in a closed confine with the smoke of a fire. The primal urge for comfort and security is recreated because to be so close to a fire meant that there was imminent danger.

If you are predisposed to smoke and tried everything to quit, try these taps to see if they help.

(Say each statement three times out loud while continuously tapping on the top of your head at the crown chakra and say it a fourth time while tapping on your chest at the heart chakra.)

"I release using smoking to tap into past life security; in all moments."

"I release mourning true security; in all moments."

"I release confusing smoking with security; in all moments."

"I release using smoking to tap into past life safety; in all moments."

"I release mourning true safety; in all moments."

"I release confusing smoking with safety; in all moments."

"I release using smoking to tap into past life connectedness; in all moments."

"I release mourning true connectedness; in all moments."

"I release confusing smoking with connectedness; in all moments."

"I release using smoking to connect with my tribe; in all moments."

"I release mourning a connection with my tribe; in all moments."

"I release confusing smoking with being connected with my tribe; in all moments."

"I release using smoking to tap into past life adventure; in all moments."

"I release mourning true adventure; in all moments."

"I release confusing smoking with adventure; in all moments."

"I release using smoking to feel love; in all moments."

"I release mourning love; in all moments."

"I release confusing smoking with love; in all moments."

"I release using smoking to return to a simpler time; in all moments."

"I remove all primal promptings to inhale smoke; in all moments."

"I am secure, safe, connected, have adventure and am loved all with clear and open lungs; in all moments."

"I shift my paradigm to clear and open lungs; in all moments."

"I am centered and empowered in clear and open lungs; in all moments."

If you start coughing as you do these, it is a sign that you are clearing out deep issues from the lungs and your whole body. You don't have to smoke presently to benefit from these.

Sugar Addiction

(Say each statement three times out loud while continuously tapping on the top of your head at the crown chakra and say it a fourth time while tapping on your chest at the heart chakra.)

"I release craving sugar; in all moments."

"I release associating sugar with love; in all moments."

"I release craving love; in all moments."

"I fill the void with divine, sweet love; in all moments."

"I accept and process the sweetness of life; in all moments."

"I send all energy matrices into the light and sound that cause me to crave sugar; in all moments."

"I command all complex energy matrices that cause me to crave sugar to be escorted into the light and sound; in all moments."

"I dissipate all cravings; in all moments."

"I dissipate the primal need to hunt and gather; in all moments."

"I release using craving sweets to feed the need to hunt and gather; in all moments."

"I disconnect craving sweets with the primal need to hunt and gather; in all moments."

"I remove all associations between sugar and hunting and gathering; in all moments."

"I release hunting and gathering to feel productive; in all moments."

"I remove all engrams of hunting and gathering; in all moments."

"I remove all engrams and triggers that associate sugar with love and survival; in all moments."

"I am centered, loved and productive; in all moments."

Worksheet for Addictions

You can use this as a template to release yourself from anything that seems to be overtaking your time and attention. Some suggestions: Food, drugs, alcohol, sweets, porn, a habit, television, video games, reoccurring thoughts, a person, sex, money or gambling.

(Say each statement three times out loud while continuously tapping on the top of your head at the crown chakra and say it a fourth time while tapping on your chest at the heart chakra.)

"I release being addicted to _____; in all moments."

"I release confusing _____ for family; in all moments."

"I release confusing _____ for friendship; in all moments."

"I shatter the illusion of _____; in all moments."

"I release using _____ as a crutch; in all moments."

"I release replacing my joy with _____; in all moments."

"I release replacing love with _____; in all moments."

"I release inhibiting my own creativity by _____; in all moments."

"I release trading in my abundance to _____; in all moments."

"I release choosing _____ over freedom; in all moments."

"I release confusing _____ for reality; in all moments."

"I release choosing _____ over reality; in all moments."

"I release using _____ as a security blanket; in all moments."

"I release allowing _____ to dumb down my consciousness; in all moments."

"I release choosing _____ over adventure; in all moments."

"I release choosing _____ over life; in all moments."

"I release lowering my vibration to the level of _____; in all moments."

"I release being manipulated by _____; in all moments."

"I remove all tentacles between myself and _____; in all moments."

"I remove all blessings between myself and _____; in all moments."

"I remove all curses between myself and _____; in all moments."

"I remove all vivaxes between myself and _____; in all moments."

"I sever all strings and cords between myself and _____; in all moments."

"I shift my paradigm from _____ to joy, love, abundance, freedom, health, success, security, companionship, peace, life and wholeness; in all moments."

The Adopted Child

Many children who are adopted have residual feelings of rejection. I have facilitated sessions where the clients were affected by emotional issues that they picked up in utero. A fetus knows what its mother is feeling about it. It is important for a mother to send loving thoughts to the baby regardless if she is going to keep it or put it up for adoption. A baby can feel rejection before it is born, especially if the mother was not happy about the prospect of being pregnant.

People who are adopted may romanticize their birth parents. They may want to be reunited with them. In some rare cases this may happen, but in most cases, the longing for them seems moot. It really isn't. Birth parents can love their children from afar. Adopted children can accept that love and try to see it as a plus element instead of a loss.

When we look at our lives with a broader brush, we can realize that our parents may only be our parents this one lifetime and that whomever we are with is the person the Universe arranged for us to be with.

We are not inherently unlovable when we are adopted; we are merely experiencing a situation that is meant to strengthen our internal relationship with love.

(Say each statement three times out loud while continuously tapping on the top of your head at the crown chakra and say it a fourth time while tapping on your chest.)

"I release the guilt and trauma of being adopted; in all moments."

"I release the void that being adopted created; in all moments."

"I release the chaos and confusion that was stored in utero; in all moments."

"I release feeling unworthy; in all moments."

"I untangle the emotional and mental confusion around the concept of mother; in all moments."

"I release feeling abandoned; in all moments."

"I release the belief I was abandoned; in all moments."

"I release rejecting the intangible love; in all moments."

"I accept the love from my birth parents through inner channels; in all moments."

"I release being disappointed in my parents; in all moments."

"I release invalidating my parents; in all moments."

"I release feeling cheated out of parents; in all moments."

"I accept the love of my parents; in all moments."

"I shift my paradigm from feeling deficient to belonging; in all moments."

"I shift my paradigm from feeling empty to belonging; in all moments."

"I am centered and empowered in belonging; in all moments."

"I resonate, emanate and am interconnected with all life in belonging; in all moments."

Release Traits of an Adult Child of an Alcoholic

(Say each statement three times while tapping on your head and say it a fourth time while tapping on your chest.)

"I release isolating in all moments."

"I release being afraid of people and authority figures; in all moments."

"I release seeking approval; in all moments."

"I release losing my identity; in all moments."

"I release being frightened by angry people; in all moments."

"I release being frightened by any personal criticism; in all moments."

"I release marrying alcoholism; in all moments."

"I sever all association or gravitation to alcoholism; in all moments."

"I release living from the vantage point of victims; in all moments."

"I release being attracted by the weakness in my close relationships; in all moments."

"I release using concern for others to distract from self-care; in all moments."

"I release using concern for others to distract from my own issues; in all moments."

"I release being enthralled in an over-concern for others; in all moments."

"I release basing my self-esteem on the approval of others; in all moments."

"I release an overdeveloped sense of responsibility; in all moments."

"I release being concerned with others rather than myself; in all moments."

"I release overlooking my own faults; in all moments."

"I release feeling guilty for standing up for myself; in all moments."

"I release giving in to others; in all moments."

"I release being compelled to give to others; in all moments."

"I release being addicted to excitement; in all moments."

"I release confusing love and pity; in all moments."

"I release the tendency to 'love' people I can 'pity' or 'rescue'; in all moments."

"I release stuffing my feelings; in all moments."

"I untangle the energy of a traumatic childhood; in all moments."

"I release all the trauma from my whole beingness; in all moments."

"I release using numbness to avoid the pain; in all moments."

"I release the fear of feeling pain; in all moments."

"I release all physical, emotional and mental anguish; in all moments."

"I remove all memories of childhood trauma; in all moments."

"I awaken my ability to discern the truth; in all moments."

"I awaken my ability to self-advocate; in all moments."

"I awaken my ability to self-nurture; in all moments."

"I awaken the incredibly healing ability to love myself; in all moments."

"I release judging myself harshly; in all moments."

"I release having low self-esteem; in all moments."

"I release being dependent on others; in all moments."

"I release being afraid of abandonment; in all moments."

"I release holding on to unhealthy relationships to avoid feeling abandoned; in all moments."

"I release living with sick people to avoid loneliness or abandonment; in all moments."

"I extract all of alcoholism from my whole beingness; in all moments"

Reverse the Aging Process

Technique to Rejuvenate Your Endocrine System

In contemplation, pinpoint a certain time in a younger version of you when you can remember being present, aware, grateful and productive. Look at that version of you and get a sense of remembering what it was like to be that you. In a very focused way, overlay that version of you onto you in the present. Overlay it on you, be totally focused on that version of you and allow it to sink into you.

Careful. DO NOT DO THIS IN THE OPPOSITE. Do not overlay yourself on top of the younger version of you. There may be a natural tendency to do that. But do not visit the present you into the past for this particular technique. Bring that version of you into the present.

When you have the younger version of you overlaid on top of you, visualize securing it to you in some way. Either clip it around the edges, or glue it on top or just hold it in place. See it bulky on top of you but hold tight to the younger version of you. You can even perceive the present you moving around underneath trying to break through. Allow the younger you to prevail.

Hold the younger version over the present version of you until there is no more struggle. Hold down until all the thicknesses are smoothed out and all the lumps are gone. Allow the present you to disintegrate. Be only aware of the younger you in its place.

Shift your attention back into the present and look out of your body through the new set of younger eyes. Feel a sense of youth and empowerment. Forgo talking about or focusing on anything that the old you would have focused on or talked about. Retrain your dialogue to match the younger you.

(Say each statement three times out loud while continuously tapping on the top of your head at the crown chakra and say it a fourth time while tapping on your chest.)

"I release aging out of habit; in all moments."

"I lengthen and repair all my telomeres; in all moments."

"I release telling myself I am getting old; in all moments."

"I release the fear of aging; in all moments."

"I release shutting down my faculties; in all moments."

"I release gauging my health by my age; in all moments."

"I reverse the aging process; in all moments."

"I regenerate every cell of my essence; in all moments."

"I repair all functions of my body; in all moments."

"I remove all engrams of aging; in all moments."

"I wash my energy in youthful exuberance; in all moments."

"I am centered and empowered in youthful exuberance; in all moments."

Allergies

(Say each statement three times out loud while continuously tapping on the top of your head at the crown chakra and say it a fourth time while tapping on your chest.)

"I release living a fruitless existence; in all moments."

"I release sucking in the sand; in all moments."

"I release sucking in the particles of my labor; in all moments."

"I release dying unfulfilled; in all moments."

"I release sucking in despair; in all moments."

"I release all the discouragement that courses through my body; in all moments."

"I release being fed up; in all moments."

"I release being inundated with despair; in all moments."

"I free all channels of my body from despair; in all moments."

"I release being poisoned by my environment; in all moments."

"I release the monotony of an unfulfilled life; in all moments."

"I cleanse my essence of despair; in all moments."

"I cleanse my essence of hopelessness; in all moments."

"I cleanse my essence of convention; in all moments."

"I ignite exuberance into my existence; in all moments."

"I release tolerating the intolerable; in all moments."

"I cleanse my essence of monotony; in all moments."

"I ingest all things of my empowerment; in all moments."

"I disarm everything that causes reactions in my body; in all moments."

"My body is impervious to reacting to the mundane; in all moments."

"I strengthen my constitution; in all moments."

"I am centered and empowered in non-reactionary body functions; in all moments."

Alternative Therapy

Life is therapy.

In doing ANYTHING besides stewing in your thoughts, you are healing yourself and others. It is not as difficult as the mind makes it out to be. The mind is sometimes the prison warden and by doing simple, easy to manage things, you are slipping past its keen watchful eye of self-contempt.

- Go do something you love.
- Talk to others who are lonely.
- Go bond with nature.
- Remember what you used to do for fun and put a new spin on it.
- Pour love into the earth through gardening.
- Take in a stray.
- Rescue plants from the department stores.
- Overcome limitations.
- Challenge fears.
- Change your thoughts.
- Change your clothes.
- Clean something up.
- Create something.
- Restore something.

Aneurism

(Say each statement three times out loud while continuously tapping on the top of your head at the crown chakra and say it a fourth time while tapping on your chest.)

"I remove all the issues stored up in my arteries; in all moments."

"I remove all the issues that cling to the walls of my arteries; in all moments."

"I release being clingy; in all moments."

"I release hoarding or collecting; in all moments."

"I release feeling unsafe; in all moments."

"I flush out all my pathways; in all moments."

"I strengthen and fortify with resilience all my inner walls; in all moments."

"I heal and repair all my inner walls and pathways; in all moments."

"I strengthen all my blood vessels; in all moments."

"I smooth all the energy in my pathways; in all moments."

"I remove all inconsistencies in my pathways; in all moments."

"I dissipate all the anger into calm; in all moments."

"I convert all anguish into peace; in all moments."

"I release looming towards death; in all moments."

"I regenerate every aspect of my essence with exuberance and self-respect; in all moments."

"I scour and rebalance all my cells with the purity my love; in all moments."

"I immerse myself in the exuberance of pure love; in all moments."

The Angel of Death

Did you ever have a real tough boss that you were terrified of, but when you got more mature, you began to like? Maybe a mutual respect grew between you. Anyone reading this is able to develop that type of relationship with the Angel of Death.

In past times, people were real superstitious and created much fear around death. Maybe they created this faceless terrifying being out of their fear. I had one client who was terrified to cross over because she was afraid of seeing the Angel of Death. I have had clients terrified of glimpsing the Angel of Death because it meant that he would be visiting.

(Say each statement three times out loud while continuously tapping on the top of your head at the crown chakra and say it a fourth time while tapping on your chest.)

"I release the belief that the Angel of Death is evil; in all moments."

"I release my fear of the Angel of Death; in all moments."

"I release the fear of death; in all moments."

"I release the belief that death is coming for me; in all moments."

"I release expecting a visit from the Angel of Death; in all moments."

"I recant all vows and agreements between myself and the Angel of Death; in all moments."

"I remove all curses between myself and the Angel of Death; in all moments."

"I remove all blessings between myself and the Angel of Death; in all moments."

"I dissolve all karmic ties between myself and the Angel of Death; in all moments."

"I remove all the pain, burden and limitations that the Angel of Death has put on me; in all moments."

"I take back all the joy, love, abundance, freedom, health, success, life and wholeness that the Angel of Death has taken from me; in all moments."

"I withdraw all my energy from the Angel of Death; in all moments."

"I shift my paradigm from the Angel of Death, to love, light and healing; in all moments."

"I transcend the Angel of Death; in all moments."

"I release resonating with the Angel of Death; in all moments."

"I release emanating with the Angel of Death; in all moments."

"I remove all of the Angel of Death from my sound frequency; in all moments."

"I remove all of the Angel of Death from my light body; in all moments."

"I am centered and empowered in love, light and healing; in all moments."

Releasing Anger Marathon

Why just manage anger? Why not release it?

(Say each statement three times out loud while continuously tapping on the top of your head at the crown chakra and say it a fourth time while tapping on your chest.)

"I release using anger as a crutch; in all moments."

"I release using anger as an anchor; in all moments."

"I release confusing anger for strength; in all moments."

"I release the belief that anger is empowering; in all moments."

"I release identifying with anger; in all moments."

"I release being married to anger; in all moments."

"I release worshiping anger; in all moments."

"I release being a conduit for anger; in all moments."

"I release inflicting anger on others; in all moments."

"I release the fear of being nothing; in all moments."

"I release the fear of being nothing without anger; in all moments."

"I release the belief that I am nothing without anger; in all moments."

"I release using anger as a means of avoidance; in all moments."

"I release confusing anger as my soul mate; in all moments."

"I release being a pawn for anger; in all moments."

"I release using anger to plug up the void; in all moments."

"I release being sacrificed to anger; in all moments."

"I release the belief that female energy is weak; in all moments."

"I release using anger to empower female energy; in all moments."

"I release immersing anger into female energy; in all moments."

"I release being in love with anger; in all moments."

"I release befriending anger; in all moments."

"I release being proud of anger; in all moments."

"I release using anger to feel empowered; in all moments."

"I release being a mouthpiece for anger; in all moments."

"I release the fear of releasing anger; in all moments."

"I release using anger to stuff down the pain and emotions; in all moments."

"I release the fear of vomiting up the pain and emotions; in all moments."

"I release targeting others with the anger; in all moments."

"I release needing a target or excuse to release anger; in all moments."

"I release allowing anger to define me; in all moments."

"I disarm all anger; in all moments."

"I release identifying with anger; in all moments."

"I compile all the anger into an undefined state; in all moments."

"I dissolve all anger into the purity of divine love; in all moments."

"I melt away all the pain and its accommodating emotions; in all moments."

"I send all energy matrices into the light and sound that hold me in anger; in all moments."

"I command all complex energy matrices that hold me in anger to be escorted into the light and sound; in all moments."

"I express myself in the fluidity and receptiveness of divine love; in all moments."

"I am centered and empowered in divine love; in all moments."

"I resonate, emanate and am connected with all life in divine love; in all moments."

"I recant all vows and agreements between myself and anger; in all moments."

"I remove all curses between myself and anger; in all moments."

"I remove all blessings between myself and anger; in all moments."

"I release advocating anger; in all moments."

"I release perpetuating anger; in all moments."

"I release justifying anger; in all moments."

"I remove all blessings between myself and anger; in all moments."

"I release using anger to validate myself; in all moments."

"I sever all strings and cords between myself and anger; in all moments."

"I nullify my allegiance with anger; in all moments."

"I dissolve all karmic ties between myself and anger; in all moments."

"I remove all the pain, burden, limitations and engrams that anger has put on me; in all moments."

"I remove all the pain, burden, limitations and engrams that I have put on all others due to anger; in all moments."

"I take back all the joy, love, abundance, freedom, health, success, security, companionship, peace, life, wholeness, beauty, enthusiasm, contentment, spirituality, enlightenment, confidence, family, intellect and the ability to discern that anger has taken from me; in all moments."

"I give back all the joy, love, abundance, freedom, health, success, security, companionship, peace, life, wholeness, beauty, enthusiasm, contentment, spirituality, enlightenment, confidence, family, intellect and the ability to discern that I have taken from all others due to anger; in all moments."

"I withdraw all my energy from anger in both the microcosm and the macrocosm; in all moments."

"I release resonating with anger; in all moments."

"I release emanating with anger; in all moments."

"I extract all anger from my sound frequency; in all moments."

"I extract all anger from my light emanation; in all moments."

"I shift my paradigm from anger to joy, love, abundance, freedom, health, success, security, companionship, peace, life, wholeness, beauty, enthusiasm, contentment, spirituality, enlightenment, confidence, family, intellect and the ability to discern; in all moments."

"I transcend anger; in all moments."

"I repair and fortify the Wei chi of my spiritual beingness; in all moments."

"I am centered and empowered in divine love; in all moments."

Releasing Displaced Anger

All anger is displaced.

One day, I found myself driving in a very impoverished part of town. The streets were so narrow that it created a single lane so that oncoming traffic was blocked. I was stopped to ask a pedestrian for directions. As I did this, a car came around the corner and couldn't get past me. I finished up the exchange so I could get out of the driver's way. It was not soon enough for her.

The driver unleashed such a wrath on me that did not match the infraction that I had committed. It was so ruthless and toxic that I felt that I was being used by her as a vessel to extract deep pain from her beingness. With compassion for her and her plight, I sent it into the light and was free of it.

Recently, I have found myself pretty angry about a couple things that have been bumps in the road in dealing with others. It causes a reaction in me of feeling invalidated by others and thinking that I don't

Jen Ward

matter. But this woman has stuck in my mind as an example of someone in pain. When I get angry with someone for something that is smaller than my reaction, I know I am projecting an old pain onto my dynamics with them. This happens a lot.

People get angry at the wrong person all the time. They are fighting an old battle that never got resolved. It is time to get unstuck from old paradigms.

(Say each statement three times out loud while continuously tapping on the top of your head at the crown chakra and say it a fourth time while tapping on your chest at the heart chakra.)

"I release being angry; in all moments."

"I release the pain, trauma and frustration of being wronged; in all moments."

"I extract and dissolve all displaced anger; in all moments."

"I release revisited old battles; in all moments."

"I release the anguish of feeling defeated; in all moments."

"I release reliving past defeat; in all moments."

"I release projecting past battles onto present situations; in all moments."

"I release seeking revenge; in all moments."

"I release being a professional victim; in all moments."

"I diffuse my inner powder keg; in all moments."

"I convert all angst, pain and frustration into the resolve of divine love; in all moments."

"I remove all the engrams that past battles have put on me; in all moments."

"I release being pulled into past battles; in all moments."

"I remove all vivaxes and tentacles between myself and past battles; in all moments."

"I send all energy matrices into the light that pull me into past battles; in all moments."

"I send all energy matrices into the light that engulf me in anger; in all moments."

"I release identifying with anger; in all moments."

"I collapse and dissolve all portals, wormholes and passageways between myself and anger; in all moments."

"I shift my paradigm from anger and past battles to the calm of the present moment; in all moments."

"I am centered and empowered in the calm of the present moment; in all moments."

Release the Apathy

(Say each statement three times out loud while continuously tapping on the top of your head at the crown chakra and say it a fourth time while tapping on your chest.)

"I release confining myself to four walls; in all moments."

"I release being a couch potato; in all moments."

"I release just waiting this life out; in all moments."

"I release giving up; in all moments."

"I release sleeping to escape; in all moments."

"I release eating for entertainment; in all moments."

"I release just taking up space; in all moments."

"I release wishing my life away; in all moments."

"I release getting all my enjoyment out of entertainment devices; in all moments."

"I release the aversion to being outside; in all moments."

"I release feeling exposed by being outside; in all moments."

"I reawaken my zest for life; in all moments."

"I shift my paradigm from apathy to a zest for living; in all moments."

"I transcend all apathy; in all moments."

"I am centered and empowered in a zest for living; in all moments."

Appeasing Others

(Say each statement three times out loud while continuously tapping on the top of your head at the crown chakra, and say it a fourth time while tapping on your chest at the heart chakra.)

"I release coming out of my center to please others; in a moments."

"I release trying to please someone else; in all moments."

"I release wearing the anxiety of someone else; in all moments."

"I release tapping into negative currents of energy; in all moments."

"I release being pulled into negative streams of energy; in all moments."

"I release running around to accommodate others; in all moments."

"I release being manipulated out of my joy; in all moments."

"I release sacrificing my joy to appeasing others; in all moments."

"I release reliving a past memory; in all moments."

"I release sieving away my peace and resolve; in all moments."

"I release looking for joy, love, abundance, freedom and wholeness outside of myself; in all moments."

"I release being worn down; in all life moments."

"I calm down my energy; in all moments."

"I move through my day with peace and gratitude; in all moments."

"I resonate and emanate with peace and gratitude; in all moments."

Arthritis

(Say each statement three times while tapping on your head and say it a fourth time while tapping on your chest.)

"I release feeling decrepit and old; in all moments."

"I release being dehydrated; in all moments."

"I release losing my flexibility; in all moments."

"I release losing my natural fluids; in all moments."

"I release the trauma of decomposing; in all moments."

"I release the trauma of not leaving the physical body after death; in all moments."

"I release recreating my decomposition; in all moments."

"I release using up my natural emollients; in all moments."

"I release constricting my natural tissue; in all moments."

"I return flexibility throughout my body; in all moments."

"I release being worked to the bone; in all moments."

"I remove all engrams of being worked to the bone; in all moments."

"I remove the sludge of emotional issues stored in and around my bones; in all moments."

"I remove the sludge of emotional issues stored in and around my muscle bellies; in all moments."

"I release recoiling my muscle fibers; in all moments."

"I elongate my muscle fibers; in all moments."

"I elongate my muscle bellies; in all moments."

"I release the belief that I must degenerate; in all moments."

"I release degenerating out of habit; in all moments."

"I release the need to do what is expected of me; in all moments."

"I release aging because it is expected of me; in all moments."

"I release mimicking the degeneration of others; in all moments."

"I lubricate all my joints; in all moments."

"I release depleting my bone density; in all moments."

"I refortify the density of my bones with empowerment; in all moments."

"I regenerate the density of my bones and joints; in all moments."

"I release feeling rusty; in all moments."

"I release calling myself old; in all moments."

"I release saying negative things about myself; in all moments."

"I release the genetic propensity to have joint issues; in all moments."

"I remove the propensity for arthritic joints from my DNA; in all moments."

"I release owning degeneration, aging or disease; in all moments."

"I put distance between myself and degeneration, aging and disease; in all moments."

"I regenerate; in all moments."

"I remove all blockages to having dense, healthy lubricated bones and joints; in all moments."

"I am centered and empowered in having dense, healthy, lubricated bones and joints; in all moments."

Autoimmune Disorders

(Say each statement three times while tapping on your head and say it a fourth time while tapping on your chest.)

"I release blaming myself; in all moments."

"I release punishing myself; in all moments."

"I remove all systemic guilt; in all moments."

"I release the genetic propensity to punish myself; in all moments."

"I remove systemic guilt and shame; in all moments."

"I remove all guilt and shame from my parasympathetic nervous system; in all moments."

"I release turning on myself; in all moments."

"I recant all vows of self-deprecation; in all moments."

"I release diminishing myself; in all moments."

"I release defacing myself; in all moments."

"I remove all engrams of suffering; in all moments."

"I release recreating suffering in my current body; in all moments."

"I release suffering out of habit; in all moments."

"I disconnect all associations between aging and suffering; in all moments."

"I remove all guilt and shame from my endocrine system; in all moments."

"I remove all self-deprecation from my endocrine system; in all moments."

"I release inadvertently programming my endocrine system to punish me; in all moments."

"I disconnect all tendencies between punishing myself and my environment; in all moments."

"I remove all ethnic propensity to punish myself; in all moments."

"I exonerate myself of all transgressions I have inflicted on any ethnicity; in all moments."

"I dissipate the physical, emotional, causal and mental need to punish myself; in all moments."

"I release feeling at a disadvantage for my current gender, race and age; in all moments."

Releasing the Aversion to Color

Color represents different things. To deny color is to deny your own essence. Green is vitality, pink is emotional balance, orange is healing, blue is mental balance, purple is healthy imagination and yellow is spirituality. They all intertwine and interweave in such a beautiful array to express how dynamic we are!

Energy comes in all colors. If you have an aversion to a particular color, may I suggest that you wear it and get comfortable with it until you uncover the correlation that you are avoiding by not wearing it. For example, red is the color of blood so if you don't like red, it may uncover an aversion to spilling your blood or death. Yellow may be identified with urine. Green may be identified with mucous. It may also be an aversion to opening up a particular chakra that is being used as a storage tank for negative energy.

(Say each statement three times while tapping on your head and say it a fourth time while tapping on your chest.)

"I release the aversion to color; in all moments."

"I release being stuck in mourning (Shiva); in all moments."

"I release the belief that color is immodest; in all moments."

"I release defining color as arrogant or disrespectful; in all moments."

"I release the belief that colors are disrespectful to God; in all moments."

"I shift my paradigm from black and white to color; in all moments."

"I am centered in a colorful array of joy, love, abundance, freedom and wholeness; in all moments."

"I release the trauma of spilling my blood; in all moments."

"I release associating red with dying; in all moments."

"I release associating red with losing my baby; in all moments."

"I release the aversion to my sexuality; in all moments."

"I release my aversion to red; in all moments."

"I release my aversion to orange; in all moments."

"I release my aversion to yellow; in all moments."

"I release my aversion to green; in all moments."

"I release my aversion to blue; in all moments."

"I release my aversion to purple; in all moments."

Awaken

(Say each statement three times out loud while continuously tapping on the top of your head at the crown chakra and say it a fourth time while tapping on your chest at the heart chakra.)

"I shake off the dross; in all moments."

"I slough off old consciousness; in all moments."

"I smooth down all engrams of the old consciousness; in all moments."

"I release all obstacles, fears and obstacles to manifesting the New Earth; in all moments."

"I release all habitual opinions, beliefs and doubts; in all moments."

"I release working for the old status quo; in all moments."

"I release betting on the wrong horse; in all moments."

"I release being a resistance to the New Earth to have to overcome; in all moments."

"I release coming to the party late; in all moments."

"I release the belief that I am lagging behind and missed something; in all moments."

"I release the fear of having to subscribe to something; in all moments."

"I release the belief that I need to subscribe to something to partake; in all moments."

"I release assigning old engrams to new consciousness; in all moments."

"I release coming from mind instead of heart; in all moments."

"I open my heart to new consciousness; in all moments."

"I take back the reigns from the mind; in all moments."

"I shift my paradigm from the old consciousness to new consciousness; in all moments."

"I am centered and empowered in new consciousness; in all moments."

Awakening

(Say each statement three times while tapping on your head and say it a fourth time while tapping on your chest.)

"I do these taps for myself and as a surrogate for humanity; in all moments."

"I remove all curses that have been put on me; in all moments."

"I remove all blessings that have turned into curses; in all moments."

"I remove all spells that have been put on me; in all moments."

"I dissipate all psychic energy that has influenced me; in all moments."

"I remove all programing and conditioning that has been put on me; in all moments."

"I release subtly being swayed off the path of love; in all moments."

"I release deviating from my highest truth; in all moments."

"I release believing the systemic lies; in all moments."

"I reinstate the ability to discern truth; in all moments."

"I release being a pawn for ignoble intentions; in all moments."

"I nullify all contracts and relationships with all individuals and groups that have been using me or harming others; in all moments."

"I recant all vows and agreements between myself and all others; in all moments."

"I recant all vows and agreements between myself and all ignoble groups and intentions; in all moments."

"I release sacrificing myself or martyring myself; in all moments."

"I release allowing my loving and trusting nature to be used to enslave me; in all moments."

"I release being pitted against my brethren; in all moments."

"I release being influenced by anything; in all moments."

"I tap into direct knowingness and reinstate my greatest exponential purpose; in all moments."

"I release worshiping monetary wealth; in all moments."

"I release worshiping those with monetary wealth or status; in all moments."

"I release giving myself away; in all moments."

"I recollect all my energies from all those who have taken from me; in all moments."

"I defragment myself; in all moments."

"I make myself whole; in all moments."

"I repair and fortify my energy field; in all moments."

"I align all my bodies; in all moments."

"I release struggling between the ebb and the flow of life; in all moments."

"I release churning in dangerous waters; in all moments."

"I shift my paradigm from struggling to thriving; in all moments."

"I release wallowing in self indulgence; in all moments."

"I shift my paradigm from being a taker to being a giver; in all moments."

"I am centered and empowered in divine love; in all moments."

"I open my heart chakra with the purity of divine love; in all moments."

"I reinstate the balance between the yin and yang individually and collectively; in all moments."

"I pour perpetual, exponential divine love into all members of humanity; in all moments."

"I dissipate all the ills of man; in all moments."

"I release using the false understanding of humility to grovel in a stupor of ineffectiveness; in all moments."

"I remove all crutches and excuses from realizing my empowerment; in all moments."

"I release demi-godding humans; in all moments."

"I release the systemic genocide of all species at the hands of human ignorance; in all moments."

"I release perpetuating dissent through gossip, complaints, ignorance and greed; in all moments."

"I extract all self righteousness from my sound frequency and light emanation; in all moments."

"I release perpetuating gloom and doom in any form of agreeing with it; in all moments."

"I strip off all mass illusion and deceit; in all moments."

"I transcend linear existence; in all moments."

"I release being enslaved to matter, energy, space or time; in all moments."

"I awaken all my subtle sense; in all moments."

"I remove all engrams that limit me from realizing my greatest empowerment; in all moments."

"I remove all schisms and imbalances in my sound frequency and light emanation; in all moments."

"I transcend the limitations of the third dimension; in all moments."

"I release demonizing those with a noble intention; in all moments."

"I release the fear of being separated from my consciousness; in all moments."

"I resonate, emanate and am interconnected with all life in the purity and sanctity of divine love; in all moments."

"I reconnect with those who support and help me perpetuate my highest purpose; in all moments."

"I reinstate my female empowerment; in all moments."

"I thrive in the purest expression of Universal peace; in all moments."

"I live, move and express my highest purpose as a sacred contributor to Universal peace and the empowerment of all; in all moments."

"I release being distracted from anything that does not support the empowerment of all; in all moments."

"I dissipate all that does not support or contribute to Universal peace and empowerment; in all moments."

"I awaken; in all moments."

Enlightening the Masses

Recently, I facilitated a session with a woman who felt it was her passion to educate everyone against the ills of the controlling factions. She would do anything she could to lead others to the truth. What she did not realize was in past lives she was the one that had controlled others. Her gifts and talents were used to suppress the lives of others. This was a point of contention that she was trying to undo in the present life. It was less about her trying to uplift humanity and more about trying to undo the times when she suppressed the freedom of others.

A past life of hers opened up to reveal when this issue played out in real time. She was a very intelligent young officer in a cavalry outpost. Their mission was to clear away Indians so that settlers could move in. She was able to use her skills to help her company make better ground with their mission. This directly resulted in the death and displacement of many Indians.

When I revealed this lifetime to my client, it resonated as truth to her. One of her special projects in this lifetime was highlighting the plight of the Native Americans. Now she understood why. In that past lifetime, she died disillusioned defending the fort. She was disheartened by her part in the genocide and died because she couldn't defend her position wholeheartedly any more.

Here are the taps that we used to release the angst of this connection within her:

"I release using my gifts and talents to advance mass control; in all moments."

"I release taking part in genocide; in all moments."

"I release the guilt and trauma of controlling the masses; in all moments."

"I recant all vows and agreements between myself and mass control; in all moments."

"I remove all curses between myself and mass control; in all moments."

"I release being enslaved to mass control; in all moments."

"I dissolve all karmic ties between myself and mass control; in all moments."

"I remove all the pain, burden and limitations that partaking in mass control has put on me; in all moments."

"I remove all the pain, burden and limitations that I have put on all others by partaking in mass control; in all moments."

"I withdraw all my energy, talents and gifts from mass control; in all moments."

"I take back all the Joy, Love, Abundance, Freedom, Life and Wholeness that mass control has taken from me; in all moments."

"I give back to all others all the Joy, Love, Abundance, Freedom, Life and Wholeness that I have taken from them via mass control; in all moments.

"I release resonating with mass control; in all moments."

"I release emanating with mass control; in all moments."

"I remove all mass control from my sound frequency; in all moments."

"I remove all mass control from my light body; in all moments."

"I shift my paradigm from mass control to Joy, Love, Abundance, Freedom, Life and Wholeness; in all moments."

Many of those who are adamant at exposing those who reign power over the masses are trying to release their own history of abusing power at the mercy of the vulnerable. By doing this series of taps, one can release themselves of the angst that is involved in enlightening the masses.

Stop Breaking Your Back

Have you ever been with someone who treats you like you don't matter? They talk about you to others, take you for granted and blame you for things that are not your fault? If your back is hurting, maybe that is what you are doing to it. Pain and feigning weakness are its only defense. Be kinder to your back, and it may surprise you how strong it is.

(Say each statement three times out loud while continuously tapping on the top of your head at the crown chakra and say it a fourth time while tapping on your chest.)

"I release telling my back that it's broken; in all moments."

"I release telling others that my back is broken; in all moments."

"I release telling others that my back is aching; in all moments."

"I release the belief that my back is weak; in all moments."

"I release desecrating my back; in all moments."

"I release giving my back trouble; in all moments."

"I release using my back as a pack animal; in all moments."

"I release betraying my back; in all moments."

"I remove all the pain and hopelessness from my back; in all moments."

"I remove all the weakness and unworthiness from my back; in all moments."

"I remove all the emotional issues stored in my back; in all moments."

"I release blaming my back; in all moments."

"I release making my back rigid; in all moments."

"I release overburdening my back; in all moments."

"I release ignoring my back's needs; in all moments."

"I release minimizing my back's contribution; in all moments."

"I release hurting my back; in all moments."

"I release invalidating my back; in all moments."

"I extract all the fear stored in my back; in all moments."

"I release being stabbed in the back; in all moments."

"I remove all the weapons from my back; in all moments."

"I remove all the schisms from my back; in all moments."

"I heal all causal wounds in my back; in all moments."

"I remove all scar tissue from the vertebrae of my spine; in all moments."

"I release fusing the vertebrae of my spine together; in all moments."

"I repair and fortify the structure of my spine; in all moments."

"I repair and fortify the resiliency of my spine; in all moments."

"I repair and fortify the Wei Chi of my back; in all moments."

"I restore confidence into my back; in all moments."

"I restore strength back into my back; in all moments."

"I restore productivity to my back; in all moments."

"I restore optimism back into my back; in all moments."

"I release sabotaging my back; in all moments."

"I release discouraging my back; in all moments."

"I recalibrate the stride of health back into my back; in all moments."

"I reintegrate empowerment and effectiveness into my back; in all moments."

"I reclaim all aspects of a powerful, healthy back; in all moments."

"I take back all the empowerment of my back; in all moments."

"I make my back whole; in all moments."

"I pour fluid gratitude into my back; in all moments."

"I pour joy, love, abundance, healing, life and strength into my back; in all moments."

"I make space in this world for a happy, healthy back; in all moments."

"I remove all blockages to exuding a strong, healthy, flexible back; in all moments."

"I stretch my capacity to exude a strong, healthy, flexible back; in all moments."

"I am centered and empowered in a strong, healthy, flexible back; in all moments."

"I exude vitality through a strong, healthy, flexible back; in all moments."

Be in the Moment

The moment is where genius is. It's not in the mental realms.

Passion is not rooted in the emotions. Passion is drawn from the moment.

We can't have an energy shortage. We ARE, and everything IS, energy.

Energy is harvested in the moment.

Creativity is tapped in the moment.

Fear is an indication that one is not in the moment.

All answers are gleaned from the moment.

Getting answers from the moment is tapping into direct knowing.

People confuse truth with opinions.

Opinions are rooted in the mental realm; truth is beyond the mind and is connected to by being in the moment.

There is a primal fear that people will lose themselves if they are in the moment.

Most practices can prevent what they try to attain when they are a distraction from being in the moment.

All the disciplines of meditation, prayer and contemplation are an attempt to connect to the divine through the moment. These taps do just that.

(Say each statement three times while tapping on your head and say it a fourth time while tapping on your chest.)

"I release avoiding the moment; in all moments."

"I release allowing thought to prevent me from immersing in the moment; in all moments."

"I release allowing feelings to prevent me from immersing in the moment; in all moments."

"I release allowing experiences to prevent me from immersing in the moment; in all moments."

"I release allowing fear to prevent me from immersing in the moment; in all moments."

"I release using beliefs to avoid being in the moment; in all moments."

"I release using physicality to avoid being in the moment; in all moments."

"I release using expectations to avoid being in the moment; in all moments."

"I release using time to prevent me from being in the moment; in all moments."

"I release using space to prevent me from being in the moment; in all moments."

"I release using matter to avoid being in the moment; in all moments."

"I tap into direct knowingness by being in the moment; in all moments."

"I release using energy to avoid being in the moment; in all moments."

"I release making it difficult to be in the moment; in all moments."

"I release being enslaved to avoid being in the moment; in all moments."

"I remove all vivaxes between myself and avoiding the moment; in all moments."

"I remove all tentacles between myself and avoiding the moment; in all moments."

"I remove the claws of avoiding the moment from my beingness; in all moments."

"I remove all programming and conditioning to avoid the moment; in all moments."

"I release confusing being in the moment with being separated from my consciousness; in all moments."

"I release the fear of losing myself in the moment; in all moments."

"I release confusing being in the moment with being nothing; in all moments."

"I wipe out all engrams that avoid the moment; in all moments."

"I send all energy matrices into the light and sound that cause me to avoid being in the moment; in all moments."

"I command all complex energy matrices that cause me to avoid being in the moment, to be escorted into the light and sound; in all moments."

"I strip all illusion off of avoiding being in the moment; in all moments."

"I remove all masks, walls, and armor from avoiding being in the moment; in all moments."

"I withdraw all my energy from avoiding being in the moment; in all moments."

"I nullify all contracts between myself and avoiding being in the moment; in all moments."

"I nullify all contracts between myself and anyone or anything that causes me to avoid being in the moment; in all moments."

"I recant all vows and agreements between myself and avoiding being in the moment; in all moments."

"I remove all curses between myself and avoiding being in the moment; in all moments."

"I remove all blessings between myself and avoiding being in the moment; in all moments."

"I sever all strings, cords and wires between myself and avoiding being in the moment; in all moments."

"I dissolve all karmic ties between myself and avoiding being in the moment; in all moments."

"I remove all the pain, burden and limitations that avoiding being in the moment has put on me; in all moments."

"I remove all the fear, futility and unworthiness that avoiding being in the moment has put on me; in all moments."

"I remove all the false humility and illusion of separateness that avoiding being in the moment has put on me; in all moments."

"I take back all that avoiding the moment has taken from me; in all moments."

"I collapse and dissolve all portals and passageways to avoiding being in the moment; in all moments."

"I collapse and dissolve avoiding being in the moment; in all moments."

"I release resonating with avoiding being in the moment; in all moments."

"I release emanating with avoiding being in the moment; in all moments."

"I extract all of avoiding being in the moment from my sound frequency; in all moments."

"I extract all of avoiding being in the moment from my light emanation; in all moments."

"I extract all of avoiding being in the moment from my whole beingness; in all moments."

"I shift my paradigm from avoiding being in the moment to the perpetual moment of my empowerment; in all moments."

"I transcend avoiding being in the moment; in all moments."

"I make space in this world to be in the perpetual moment of my empowerment; in all moments."

"I remove all blockages to being in the perpetual moment of my empowerment; in all moments."

"I stretch my capacity to be in the perpetual moment of my empowerment; in all moments."

"I am centered and empowered in being in the perpetual moment of my empowerment; in all moments."

"I resonate, emanate and am interconnected to all life in the perpetual moment of my empowerment; in all moments."

Being from Another Planet / Feeling Like You Don't Belong

Some people truly feel like they don't belong on earth.

Some people are not comfortable in their skin.

Some people feel like they don't fit in.

Some people don't like their body. These taps are for them and everyone else.

(Say each statement three times out loud while continuously tapping on the top of your head at the crown chakra, and say it a fourth time while tapping on your chest at the heart chakra. Say each word deliberately. They are not just words but a vibration that you are initiating to shift energy. Pause after each word. Say it in a commanding but even tone, not as a question. Forgo saying it in a singsong tone or with bravado. Say them all.)

"I release the trauma of being grounded on Earth; in all moments."

"I release resenting Earth; in all moments."

"I release feeling like an alien on Earth; in all moments."

"I release the belief that I don't belong on Earth; in all moments."

"I release the trauma of being abandoned on Earth; in all moments."

"I release rejecting Earth; in all moments."

"I release waiting to be saved; in all moments."

"I release hating my Earth body; in all moments."

"I release rejecting my Earth body; in all moments."

"I release the trauma of losing my tail; in all moments."

"I release mourning my tail; in all moments."

"I release having trouble balancing without my tail; in all moments."

"I release feeling like a stranger to humans; in all moments."

"I release the inability to interact with humans; in all moments."

"I release feeling suffocated in this human body; in all moments."

"I release the trauma of losing my wings; in all moments."

"I release grounding myself; in all moments."

"I declare myself a surrogate for humanity in doing these taps; in all moments."

"I release the belief that I am limited to the human body; in all moments."

"I release negating all but the physical interaction; in all moments."

"I release rejecting the reality of my imagination; in all moments."

"I release being locked down in the physical body; in all moments."

"I release rejecting my intangible self; in all moments."

"I release vacillating between vulnerability and superiority in the physical body; in all moments."

"I release denying my true self; in all moments."

"I release the primal need to conquer; in all moments."

"I release the belief that humans are superior to other species; in all moments."

"I release using superiority as a form of denial; in all moments."

"I release the fear of my own vulnerability; in all moments."

"I remove all the self-induced prophecy of the negative force; in all moments."

"I release feeling vulnerable in energy to a negative force; in all moments."

"I release manifesting a negative force; in all moments."

"I withdraw all my energy from anything negative that I have created; in all moments."

"I collapse and dissolve all negative creations that I have created; in all moments."

"I withdraw all my energy from all others' negative creations that I have supported; in all moments."

"I collapse and dissolve the negative aspects that I have supported in all others' negative creations; in all moments."

"I remove all vivaxes between myself and the human body; in all moments."

"I remove all vivaxes between myself and physical existence; in all moments."

"I release being led around by the nose by physical existence; in all moments."

"I remove all tentacles between myself and physical existence; in all moments."

"I remove the claws of physical existence from my beingness; in all moments."

"I release being enslaved to physical existence; in all moments."

"I release being diminished by physical existence; in all moments."

"I remove all programming and conditioning that physical existence has put on me; in all moments."

"I remove all engrams that physical existence has put on me; in all moments."

"I send all energy matrices into the light and sound that trap me in physical existence; in all moments."

"I send all energy matrices into the light and sound that prevent me from seeing my omniscience; in all moments."

"I send all energy matrices into the light and sound that prevent me from knowing my omnipotence; in all moments."

"I send all energy matrices into the light and sound that prevent me from being omnipresent; in all moments."

"I recant all vows and agreements between myself and physical existence; in all moments."

"I remove all curses between myself and physical existence; in all moments."

"I remove all blessings between myself and physical existence; in all moments."

"I sever all strings, cords and wires between myself and physical existence; in all moments."

"I dissolve all karmic ties between myself and physical existence; in all moments."

"I withdraw all my energy from physical existence; in all moments."

"I strip all illusion off of physical existence; in all moments."

"I remove all masks, walls and armor from physical existence; in all moments."

"I remove all the pain, burden and limitations that physical existence has put on me; in all moments."

"I remove all the pain, burden and limitations that I have put on all others due to physical existence; in all moments."

"I remove all the fear, futility, helplessness and unworthiness that physical existence has put on me; in all moments."

"I remove all the fear, futility, helplessness and unworthiness that I have put on all others due to physical existence; in all moments."

"I remove the illusion of separateness that physical existence has put on me; in all moments."

"I remove the illusion of separateness that I have put on all others due to physical existence; in all moments."

"I take back all the joy, love, abundance, freedom, health and wholeness that physical existence has taken from me; in all moments."

"I give back to all others all the joy, love, abundance, freedom, health, and wholeness that I have taken from them due to physical existence; in all moments."

"I release resonating with physical existence; in all moments."

"I release emanating with physical existence; in all moments."

"I strip off all illusion that physical existence has put on me; in all moments."

"I strip off all illusion that I have put on all others due to physical existence; in all moments."

"I remove all the masks, walls and armor that physical existence has put on me; in all moments."

"I remove all masks, walls and armor that I have put on all others due to physical existence; in all moments."

"I extract all of physical existence from my sound frequency; in all moments."

"I extract all of physical existence from my light emanation; in all moments."

"I shift my paradigm from physical existence to joy, love, abundance, freedom, empowerment and wholeness; in all moments."

"I shift humanity's paradigm from physical existence to joy, love, abundance, freedom, empowerment and wholeness; in all moments."

"I transcend physical existence; in all moments."

"Humanity transcends physical existence; in all moments."

"I am centered and empowered in joy, love, abundance, freedom, health and wholeness; in all moments."

"Humanity is centered and empowered in joy, love, abundance, freedom, health and wholeness; in all moments."

"I resonate and emanate joy, love, abundance, freedom, health and wholeness within myself and to all others; in all moments."

"Humanity resonates, emanates, and is interconnected in joy, love, abundance, freedom, health and wholeness; in all moments."

Release the Glass Ceiling of Being Gay

Recently, I facilitated a private remote healing session with a young, gay male. He is very talented and creative, a genius perhaps, but he began sabotaging himself. He began not applying his gifts and being distracted by social issues. I tuned into his energy and his root chakra was very blocked. I was also picking up on a truth that he wouldn't even admit to himself.

The thought that came through like this: *Why should I even try? No matter how successful I become, I am still going to be gay.*

This was not conscious. But when I told him what his energy told me, he felt it was a deep truth he was holding. He is very confident and self-assured, but the societal opinions held about being gay were still affecting him subliminally, in all different ways. As I led him through the following taps, he broke down and released this primal hurt.

Here are the taps: (Say each statement three times out loud while tapping on your head and say it a fourth time while tapping on your chest.)

"I release feeling shame and persecution; in all moments."

"I remove and dissolve all the persecution stored in every orifice of my beingness; in all moments."

"I shatter the glass ceiling of being gay on my joy; in all moments."

"I shatter the glass ceiling of being gay on my love; in all moments."

"I shatter the glass ceiling of being gay on my abundance; in all moments."

"I shatter the glass ceiling of being gay on my freedom; in all moments."

"I shatter the glass ceiling of being gay on my health; in all moments."

"I shatter the glass ceiling of being gay on my success; in all moments."

"I shatter the glass ceiling of being gay on my confidence; in all moments."

"I shatter the glass ceiling of being gay on my companionship; in all moments."

"I shatter the glass ceiling of being gay on my creativity; in all moments."

"I shatter the glass ceiling of being gay on my peace; in all moments."

"I shatter the glass ceiling of being gay on my life; in all moments."

"I shatter the glass ceiling of being gay on my importance; in all moments."

"I shatter the glass ceiling of being gay on my sexuality; in all moments."

"I shatter the glass ceiling of being gay on my wholeness; in all moments."

"I shatter the glass ceiling of being gay on my beauty; in all moments."

"I shatter the glass ceiling of being gay on my enthusiasm; in all moments."

"I shatter the glass ceiling of being gay on my contentment; in all moments."

"I repair and fortify my wei chi; in all moments."

"I am centered and empowered in divine love; in all moments."

Please do these taps. There are so many pockets of injustice that we release when we look at the issues that others struggle with as part of our own plight. That is compassion as an art form. Please do these taps to hone compassion as a skill.

Being Nice

You know how someone who is over-nice is irritating? It is because those who can perceive in subtle energies can see the hypocrisy or the deception behind it. The person is lying to either themselves or others because they are denying themselves the various responses that being an exponential person allows.

We think of being nice as the highest good. But it can be a prison of its own. A lot of damage can be done to someone and to others by the compulsion to be nice. Anything that is done to excess is a deviation from personal freedom.

(Say each statement three times out loud while tapping on your head and say it a fourth time while tapping on your chest.)

"I release being galvanized in 'nice'; in all moments."

"I release being paralyzed in 'nice'; in all moments."

"I release using being nice as a form of denial; in all moments."

"I release the trauma that I am hiding by being nice; in all moments."

"I release wasting all my energy being nice; in all moments."

"I release manipulating others by being nice; in all moments."

"I release the belief that nice is the highest action; in all moments."

"I release being programmed to be nice; in all moments."

"I release all 'nice' programming, conditioning and engrams; in all moments."

"I release being trapped in being nice; in all moments."

"I release defining nice as being holy; in all moments."

"I release using nice to be superior; in all moments."

"I release being enslaved to being nice; in all moments."

"I recant all vows and agreement between myself and being nice; in all moments."

"I remove all curses and blessings between myself and being nice; in all moments."

"I sever all strings and cords between myself and being nice; in all moments."

"I dissolve all karmic ties between myself and being nice; in all moments."

"I send all energy matrices into the light that ensconce me in being nice; in all moments."

"I remove all vivaxes between myself and being nice; in all moments."

"I remove all tentacles between myself and being nice; in all moments."

"I strip all illusion off of being nice; in all moments."

"I transcend being nice; in all moments."

"I shift my paradigm from nice to authentic; in all moments."

"I remove all nice from my sound frequency; in all moments."

"I remove all nice from my light body; in all moments."

"I release resonating with being nice; in all moments."

"I release emanating with being nice; in all moments."

"I shatter the glass ceiling of being nice; in all moments."

"I am centered and empowered in divine love; in all moments."

Being Shamed

(Say each statement three times out loud while continuously tapping on the top of your head at the crown chakra, and say it a fourth time while tapping on your chest.)

"I release being manipulated by society; in all moments."

"I release being shamed in anyway; in all moments."

"I release being an enabler of shame; in all moments."

"I remove all engrams of being humiliated or ashamed; in a moments."

"I remove all engrams of being embarrassed; in all moments."

"I release belittling others to feel superior; in all moments."

"I release being belittled so others could feel superior; in all moments."

"I release taking it on the shin; in all moments."

"I release taking it in stride; in all moments."

"I release being a scapegoat; in all moments."

"I release using others as a scapegoat; in all moments."

"I release being used by others to work out their issues; in all moments."

"I release using others to work out my issues on; in all moments."

"I hold others accountable for their violation of me; in all moments."

"I hold myself accountable; in all moments."

"I am centered and empowered in accountability; in all moments."

Being Stubborn

There are some ornery characters on earth. They are so loving at the core but have piled on the pain life after life. Now, when it is time to get themselves free, they are so wounded and defensive that they won't allow any of the good things in. They are afraid to trust, they are afraid to love and they are afraid to have.

Life has given them the whole "bait and switch" one too many times when it comes to receiving the fruits of living. They are afraid they are going to be duped once again. They blame life for withholding the things that they themselves are afraid to accept.

If this sounds even slightly familiar, here are some SFT Taps that might be helpful. (Say each statement three times while tapping on your head and say it a fourth time while tapping on your chest.)

"I release saying 'F@%K You' to life; in all moments."

"I release saying 'F@%K You' to love; in all moments."

"I release saying 'F@%K You' to joy; in all moments."

"I release saying 'F@%K You' to abundance; in all moments."

"I release saying 'F@%K You' to my loved ones; in all moments."

"I release saying 'F@%K You' to my gifts; in all moments."

"I release saying 'F@%K You' to relationships; in all moments."

"I release saying 'F@%K You' to potential life partners; in all moments."

"I release saying 'F@%K You' to my guides; in all moments."

"I release saying 'F@%K You' to God; in all moments."

"I release saying 'F@%K You' to myself; in all moments."

"I release saying 'F@%k You' to enlightenment/transcendence/nirvana; in all moments."

"I shift my paradigm from 'F@%k You' to acceptance; in all moments."

Bladder Issues

I recently was asked by a client who had a great session with me but had one gnawing issue with her bladder remaining. She asked me to tune in and see if I picked up something that would help. This is what came through to assist her.

"There is a resistance there for you. See how you lost your enthusiasm? It feels like a life of dehydrating in the desert. The fear of losing your life fluids, fear of losing your life force." I told her to do these taps:

(Say each statement three times while tapping on your head and say it a fourth time while tapping on your chest.)

"I release the trauma of being dehydrated; in all moments."

"I release being dehydrated; in all moments."

"I release confusing eliminating my bladder with losing my life force; in all moments."

"I release confusing eliminating my bladder with death; in all moments."

"I release confusing eliminating my bladder with loss of control; in all moments."

"I release the fear of loss of control; in all moments."

"I release holding my bladder in protest of surrendering; in all moments."

"I disconnect the connection between relieving my bladder and vulnerability; in all moments."

"I release confusing an empty bladder with vulnerability; in all moments."

"I release the trauma of bleeding out; in all moments."

"I release the trauma of having my intestines ripped out; in all moments."

"I release trying to hold it together; in all moments."

"I release trying to hold it all in; in all moments."

"I release feeling hopeless; in all moments."

"I restore elasticity to my bladder; in all moments."

"I release reliving a slow death; in all moments."

"I release being focused on aging; in all moments."

"I release confusing aging with bleeding out; in all moments."

"I release confusing urinating with bleeding out; in all moments."

"I maintain my continence; in all moments."

"I release the fear of being empty; in all moments."

The client responded shortly after that she felt a powerful shift and still feels the issue is working itself out. She was very grateful and humble.

Powerful Technique to Reestablish Health/Taps for All Body Parts

The reason why so many people are in pain or disease is that their different body parts are all feeling invalidated and they are screaming out for attention. They are doing their best to be validated amongst all the clamoring of all the other body parts. Think of it as a roomful of type "A" personalities vying for top billing.

Here are taps to validate all your body parts at once and get them working on the same page. Please enjoy.

(Say each statement three times out loud while continuously tapping on the top of your head at the crown chakra and say it a fourth time while tapping on your chest.)

"I release ignoring any of my body parts; in all moments."

"I release invalidating my body parts; in all moments."

"I release treating my body parts as scapegoats; in all moments."

"I release treating my body parts as disposable; in all moments."

"I release storing unworthiness in my body parts; in all moments."

"I remove all implements that are shoved in my body parts; in all moments."

"I remove all the memories of fatal wounds from my body parts; in all moments."

"I heal all the wounds of all my body parts; in all moments."

"I release all schisms between my body parts; in all moments."

"I release my body parts working against each other; in all moments."

"I release any of my body parts going rogue; in all moments."

"I remove all the anger from all my body parts; in all moments."

"I remove all the feelings of rejection and abandonment from all my body parts; in all moments."

"I remove all vivaxes between all my body parts and pain and dis-ease; in all moments."

"I remove all tentacles between all my body parts and pain and dis-ease; in all moments."

"I remove the claws of pain and dis-ease from all my body parts; in all moments."

"I remove the memory of failing from all my body parts; in all moments."

"I remove all programming and conditioning that pain and dis-ease have put on my body parts; in all moments."

"I remove all engrams that pain and dis-ease have put on my body parts; in all moments."

"I send all energy matrices into the light and sound that diminish the performance of any or all of my body parts; in all moments."

"I command all complex energy matrices to recognize themselves as that; in all moments."

"I command all complex energy matrices that have entrapped any or all of my body parts to be escorted into the light and sound; in all moments."

"I send all energy matrices into the light and sound that immerse any or all of my body parts in pain or dis-ease; in all moments."

"I recant all vows and agreements between any or all of my body parts and pain or dis-ease; in all moments."

"I remove all curses between any or all of my body parts and both pain or dis-ease; in all moments."

"I remove all blessings between any or all of my body parts and both pain or dis-ease; in all moments."

"I sever all strings and cords between any and all of my body parts and both pain or dis-ease; in all moments."

"I dissolve all karmic ties between any or all of my body parts and pain and dis-ease; in all moments."

"I remove all the pain, burden, limitations and illusion of separateness that both pain or dis-ease have put on any or all of my body parts; in all moments."

"I take back all the good that pain or dis-ease has taken from any or all of my body parts; in all moments."

"I take back all the joy, love, abundance, freedom, health and wholeness that both pain or dis-ease have taken from any or all of my body parts; in all moments."

"I remove all the pain and dis-ease from all 32 layers of all my body parts' auric field; in all moments."

"All my body parts withdraw all their energy from pain and dis-ease; in all moments."

"All my body parts repair and fortify their Wei chi; in all moments."

"My body parts strip all illusion off of both pain and dis-ease; in all moments."

"My body parts remove all masks, walls and armor from both pain and disease; in all moments."

"My body parts collapse and dissolve all of both pain and dis-ease; in all moments."

"My body parts release resonating with either pain or dis-ease; in all moments."

"My body parts release emanating with either pain or dis-ease; in all moments."

"All my body parts extract all of both pain and dis-ease from their sound frequency; in all moments."

"All my body parts extract all of both pain and dis-ease from their light emanation; in all moments."

"All my body parts transcend both pain and dis-ease; in all moments."

"I pour perpetual gratitude and love into all my body parts; in all moments."

"All my body parts are in a gracious symbiotic relationship with all other body parts; in all moments."

"All my body parts are centered and empowered in joy and optimal health; in all moments."

"I am centered and empowered in joy and optimal health; in all moments."

"I and all my body parts resonate and emanate joy and optimal health; in all moments."

Compassion for Your Body Parts

The reason for disease that trumps all others is treating the body like an inanimate object with no feelings. This is wrong and barbaric. Every component of our body has consciousness. This means that it cares about surviving.

- It feels rejection,
- it gets overwhelmed,
- cries in pain,
- wants to be validated,
- to be loved,
- to do a good job
- and it wants to be appreciated.
- It also wants its love felt and its contribution acknowledged.
- The body parts have similar reactions to being ignored and invalidated that you do.
- It shuts down,
- acts out,
- screams out,
- feigns sickness,
- gives up,
- hides,
- mopes,
- sabotages the ingrate,
- sabotages others,
- holds resentment,
- builds up anger,
- drags along for attention,
- sabotages others,
- tries harder,
- exhausts itself.

So when body parts are being invalidated by us and suffering, instead of pouring love, kindness and compassion into them, we...

- Complain about them,
- cut them out,
- poison,
- eradicate them with radiation,
- mutilate them,
- blame them for the whole system being out of whack,
- talk about how they aren't functioning,
- continue to demoralize them,
- curse them for our misgivings.

I have such compassion for a body. Self-worth is a tough one but the way a group of cells holds together with all the ingratitude and ignorant practices that are thrown at it is amazing. Everybody is an unsung hero in my books. When someone is complaining about something their body has failed at, I talk silently with their body and give them compassion for what they have to endure at the hands of ignorance.

Body parts are living, breathing, contributing organisms just like all aspects of nature are functioning individuals working in agreement with the ecosystem that it is a part of. For optimal health, everyone should start thinking of their body as a community of souls working for a common goal instead of thinking of it as one overlord being served by the minions. In doing so, you give so much of yourself voice and reason. This creates fluidity in the functioning of your body systems rather than stagnant pools of energy that cause dissension or disease in the whole.

Worksheet for Body Parts / Taps for Health

What is the part of your body that is overtaxed the most? Is it your heart or liver? Maybe it is your nervous system or you have stomach issues. Whichever it is, use these taps to bring some ease to your issues with it. Put in the area of the body that brings the most dis-ease. Or do the taps for the body as a whole.

(Say each statement three times while tapping on your head and say it a fourth time while tapping on your chest.)

"I release neglecting my _____; in all moments."

"I release overtaxing my _____; in all moments."

"I release betraying my _____; in all moments."

"I release the genetic propensity to hold dis-ease in my_____ in all moments."

"I release wearing dis-ease in my _____ as a badge of honor; in all moments."

"I release using pain in my _____ to maintain a sense of belonging; in all moments."

"I release using pain in my _____ as an excuse to nurture myself; in all moments."

"I release using pain in my _____ to feel connected to a loved one; in all moments."

"I recant all vows and agreements between myself and my _____; in all moments."

"I remove all curses between myself and my _____; in all moments."

"I remove all the pain burden and limitations my _____has put on me; in all moments."

"I remove all the pain burden and limitations that I have put on my _____; in all moments."

"I take back all the joy, love, abundance, freedom, health, life and wholeness that my _____ has taken from me; in all moments."

"I give back all the joy, love, abundance, freedom, health, life and wholeness that I have taken from my _____; in all moments."

"I shift my paradigm from dis-ease to health; in all moments."

"I am centered in joy, love, abundance, freedom, health, life and wholeness; in all moments."

Once one experiences that health is a choice, what else do they need to know to empower themselves? Once someone takes back their health, they realize how empowered they are. No longer are they enslaved to fate. It is a great freedom.

Empower Your Physical Body

So much of sickness and disease is caused by the physical body being invalidated. Pain is its only present form of communication.

(Say each statement three times out loud while tapping on the top of your head at the crown chakra and say it a fourth time while tapping on your chest at the heart chakra.)

"I release not being able to stomach life; in all moments."

"I release abusing my stomach; in all moments."

"I release gorging on problems; in all moments."

"I release feeding myself fear; in all moments."

"I release being blinded to truth; in all moments."

"I release wearing blinders; in all moments."

"I release being long in the tooth; in all moments."

"I release breaking my neck for others; in all moments."

"I release bending over backwards for others; in all moments."

"I release running on empty; in all moments."

"I release shooting myself in the foot; in all moments."

"I release telling my heart that it's broken; in all moments."

"I release telling my ass that it's busted; in all moments."

"I release binding myself up; in all moments."

"I release having a limp wrist; in all moments."

"I release using my finger to curse others; in all moments."

"I release storing the trauma of dying in my adrenal glands; in all moments."

"I release storing mental aberrations in my peace; in all moments."

"I release telling myself that I am sad; in all moments."

"I release telling myself that I am sick; in all moments."

"I release focusing on dis-ease as a form of denial; in all moments."

"I release telling myself that I am old; in all moments."

"I release using age as an excuse; in all moments."

"I release telling my body that it is inadequate; in all moments."

"I release using my body to harbor unworthiness; in all moments."

"I release telling my body that it's unattractive; in all moments."

"I release blaming my body; in all moments."

"I release using my hormones to be a bitch; in all moments."

"I release using gender to put a glass ceiling on myself; in all moments."

"I release using my gender to bow out of certain experiences; in all moments."

"I remove all vivaxes between myself and my physical body; in all moments."

"I remove all tentacles between myself and the physical body; in all moments."

"I shatter all glass ceilings on the physical body; in all moments."

"I release interfering with my physical body reflecting my true splendor; in all moments."

"I release interfering with the natural cadence of the physical body; in all moments."

"I remove all programming and conditioning that I have put on the physical body; in all moments."

"I release diminishing the body to the lowest common denominator; in all moments."

"I remove all limited engrams from the physical body; in all moments."

"I send all energy matrices into the light and sound that limit the physical body; in all moments."

"I command all complex energy matrices that limit the physical body to be escorted into the light and sound; in all moments."

"I send all energy matrices into the light and sound that program the physical body for dis-ease in all moments."

"I command all complex energy matrices that program the physical body for dis-ease to be escorted into the light and sound; in all moments."

"I nullify all contracts that limit the physical body; in all moments."

"I recant all vows and agreements between myself and the physical body; in all moments."

"I release worshiping the physical body; in all moments."

"I release deferring to the physical body; in all moments."

"I release diminishing the physical body; in all moments."

"I release underestimating the physical body; in all moments."

"I release ignoring the physical body; in all moments."

"I release cutting off two-way communication with the physical body; in all moments."

"I validate every cell of my beingness; in all moments."

"I recant all curses between myself and the physical body; in all moments."

"I remove all blessings between myself and the physical body; in all moments."

"I sever all strings and cords between myself and the physical body; in all moments."

"I release staying entrenched in the physical body out of fear of death; in all moments."

"I release the fear of being separated from my consciousness; in all moments."

"I dissolve all karmic ties between myself and the physical body; in all moments."

"I remove all the pain, burden and limitations that I have put on the physical body; in all moments."

"I remove all the fear, futility and unworthiness that I have put on the physical body; in all moments."

"I remove all the sickness, dis-ease and illusion of separateness that I have put on the physical body; in all moments."

"I give back to the physical body all that I have withheld from it; in all moments."

"I strip all illusion off of the physical body; in all moments."

"I align the physical body with my highest purpose; in all moments."

"I infuse joy, love and abundance into every cell of my physical body; in all moments."

"I infuse freedom, health and wholeness into every cell of my physical body; in all moments."

"My physical body is centered and empowered in the divinity of optimal health; in all moments."

Fortifying Bone Density with Self-Love

Recently, I facilitated a private remote session with an 83-year-old woman. It was easy to scan her body and realize what her main issue was. Her bones were very thin. On her left side, they were alarmingly depleted in the hip region.

The issue was with people taking from her. She is such a nurturing person, and she was actually energetically leaking from her own bones to give to others. It made me wonder about a correlation between older people and hip fractures.

I know that women store a lot of emotional issues in their pelvic bowl. I am also wondering if their nurturing nature, at all costs, depletes them physically. I am betting that more older women experience hip fractures than older men.

I was getting the understanding that bone density is directly related to how one gives of themselves. There needs to be a balance between giving and receiving. If one is not capable of receiving, it could leave them weak and frail in a very real way.

(Say each statement three times out loud while tapping on your head and say it a fourth time while tapping on you chest.)

"I release attracting takers; in all moments."

"I release being attracted to takers; in all moments."

"I release using takers as a way to sabotage myself; in all moments."

"I release using takers to railroad myself; in all moments."

"I send all energy matrices into the light and sound that draw me to takers; in all moments."

"I recant all vows and agreements between myself and all takers; in all moments."

"I remove all curses between myself and all takers; in all moments."

"I sever all strings and cords between myself and all takers; in all moments."

"I dissolve all karmic ties between myself and all takers; in all moments."

"I remove all the pain, burden, limitations and engrams that all takers have put on me; in all moments."

"I take back all the joy, love, abundance, freedom, health, success, security, companionship, creativity, peace, life, wholeness, beauty, enthusiasm, contentment, spirituality, enlightenment and confidence that all takers have taken from me; in all moments."

"I withdraw all my energy from all takers; in all moments."

"I release resonating with all takers; in all moments."

"I release emanating with all takers; in all moments."

"I remove all takers from my sound frequency; in all moments."

"I remove all takers from my light body; in all moments."

"I shift my paradigm from all takers to joy, love, abundance, freedom, health, success, security, companionship, creativity, peace, life, wholeness, beauty, enthusiasm, contentment, spirituality, enlightenment and confidence; in all moments."

"I transcend all takers; in all moments."

"I make space in this world for self love; in all moments."

"I remove all blockages to self love; in all moments."

"I stretch my capacity to accept self love; in all moments."

"I infuse and saturate my sound frequency with self love; in all moments."

"I imbue and permeate all of my light body with self love; in all moments."

"I am centered and empowered in self love; in all moments."

"I resonate and emanate with self love; in all moments."

Brain and Nervous System Function

(Say each statement three times while tapping on the head and say it a fourth time while tapping on your chest.)

"I remove all barriers to my brain receiving high levels of oxygen; in all moments."

"I remove all blockages to my brain receiving higher consciousness; in all moments."

"I rewire my brain to optimal awareness; in all moments."

"I rewire my body to optimal function; in all moments."

"I reconnect my brain and body for optimal cohesion; in all moments."

"I repair my myelin sheaths; in all moments."

"I rewire my brain-body connection to higher awareness; in all moments."

"I flood my brain and body with oxygen; in all moments."

"I flood my brain and body with the vibration of everything it is lacking; in all moments."

"I satiate all my brain and body's requirements on all levels; in all moments."

"I flood my brain and body with gratitude; in all moments."

"I flood my brain and body with optimal awareness; in all moments."

"I flood my whole essence with the vibration of higher consciousness; in all moments."

Eradicate Lumpy Breasts

(Say each statement three times while tapping on your head and say it a fourth time while tapping on your chest.)

"I release storing shame in my breasts; in all moments."

"I release the trauma of being fondled; in all moments."

"I release being stripped of my dignity; in all moments."

"I release the trauma of being passed around; in all moments."

"I release the trauma of having my baby ripped from my breast; in all moments."

"I release hating my breast; in all moments."

"I release confusing my breast with being unsafe; in all moments."

"I release the trauma of mothering the child of my abuser; in all moments."

"I release the conflict between loving my child and hating its father; in all moments."

"I soften all my lymph nodes; in all moments."

"I drain all my lymph nodes; in all moments."

"I restore fluidity to my lymphatic system; in all moments."

"I drain all issues out of my lymphatic system; in all moments."

"I release the belief that having breasts are a disadvantage; in all moments."

"I embrace the empowering nature of my female energy; in all moments."

"I repair and fortify the empowering properties of my breasts; in all moments."

"I release rejecting my breasts; in all moments."

"I remove all programming and conditioning in regard to my breasts; in all moments."

"I remove all engrams in my breasts; in all moments."

"I release harnessing my breasts to appease others; in all moments."

"I remove all judgment that I have internalized in my breasts; in all moments."

"I infuse my breasts with joy, love, abundance, freedom and wholeness; in all moments."

Broken Childhood

Let's face it. Not everyone has had a happy childhood. Some of us have come into a lonely, loveless life where nurturing and kindness was something we watched happen to others from afar. Some of us are still numb from the experience. Some of us have not been able to gain the momentum in life that those who have been treasured have to their advantage.

There are great techniques to change the script of what we endured at the mercy of the world. A good technique is to visualize yourself as an angel of light and go to the baby that you once were. Pour incredible love into yourself in baby form. Give yourself all the encouragement and nurturing that was withheld from you. Return often to the child the baby grows into and comfort yourself in those lonely, scary moments that you have endured.

You can also tap into earlier lifetimes when you were loved. Realize that this lifetime is only one experience and it does not define the totality of who you are.

Also, try doing these taps: (Say each statement three times while tapping on your head and say it a fourth time while tapping on your chest.)

"I release the trauma of being born; in all moments."

"I release the trauma of being molested; in all moments."

"I release the trauma of losing my innocence; in all moments."

"I release mourning my innocence; in all moments."

"I release being a scapegoat; in all moments."

"I release being the black sheep; in all moments."

"I release the belief that my parents hate me; in all moments."

"I release the belief that I am unlovable; in all moments."

"I release being numb; in all moments."

"I release the belief that I am damaged; in all moments."

"I release defining my childhood as unhappy; in all moments."

"I release being shattered; in all moments."

"I make myself whole; in all moments."

"I heal all my wounds; in all moments."

"I shift the paradigm of my childhood to joy, love, abundance, security, peace and wholeness; in all moments."

"I am loved, nurtured and valued; in all moments."

A Cure for Worrying about Cancer

Cancer is emotional energy that becomes so stagnant and heavy that is manifests as a physical presence. Cutting and burning it out is such a drastic measure. It is necessary for some, but what if you could address the issues creating the problem in the body too?

People who recover from cancer also have a fear of it coming back. This exercise, will address all the subtle issues that go with the diagnosis, the treatment and the recovery.

Use the Energetic Cleanse on page 111 or download the Energetic Cleanse here: https://www.jenward.com/energetic-cleanse-sign-up-form/ and complete the exercise with all the taps on the sheet. Put one word in all the blanks on the page and do every single tap for that issue. Don't do only the ones you want to do because your ego will trick you into thinking that you don't need to do them.

Here is the short list of taps to do on the issue. Add yours to the list:

- Cancer
- Treatment
- The diagnosis
- Western medicine
- The doctors
- Arrogant doctors
- Unkind doctors
- Chemotherapy
- Surgery
- Insensitive people
- Toxic people
- Being unappreciated
- Being dumped on
- Avoidance
- Shame
- Being overwhelmed

- Taking ownership of cancer
- Succumbing to cancer
- Commiserating with someone with cancer
- The hospital stay
- The unknown
- Other patients
- Being minimized by cancer
- Complacency
- Genetic propensity for cancer
- Issues stored in the DNA
- Using cancer to feel special
- Using cancer to opt out in some way
- Using cancer to connect with loved one
- Using cancer to get sympathy
- Self-neglect
- Unworthiness
- Cursing yourself
- Expecting to get cancer
- Letting others down
- Using cancer as an excuse
- Being polite
- Being afraid to say no
- Self-deprivation
- Self-deprecation
- Self-loathing
- Shock and dismay
- Celebrating cancer
- The pink ribbon campaign
- Fear of cancer
- Psychic energy of cancer
- Losing a loved one to cancer
- The normalization of cancer
- Accepting cancer
- Indulging in sympathy and drama
- Leukemia
- Emphysema
- Acidic PH levels
- Carcinoma
- Radiation
- Lymphoma
- Tumors
- Hodgkin
- Sarcoma

- Breast cancer
- Ovarian cancer

Any other issues that come up while doing these taps, add them to the list and do them as well. If you have a loved one who is diagnosed with cancer and you wish to help them, you can do these taps as a surrogate for them. What is empowering for the family is to do the taps together to help a family member. It can turn the energy wasted in sadness and frustration to encouraging wellness.

Wellness Awareness (Taps "C" Word)

I don't like to say the "c" word. I have this philosophy that words are vibrations and that we all are vibrations. People use that word a lot now. They didn't used to. Now, they make races for it and wear colors to celebrate overcoming it, but I see it all as treating the concept of it as something acceptable. It is not acceptable. It is a violation to the body, spirit and society.

It is a black mark on history that we would allow our environment to be so toxic that we weaken our bodies with poisons. It is our bubonic plague. To meet it with such complacency is preposterous to me. The fact that we don't use every means possible to eradicate it because it might interfere with the profit margin for the very rich is an insult to humanity. It is silly to me that we honor people who overcome the "c" (which is a great thing) as a cloaking device to accept the state of affairs as is.

We have the greatest minds, resources and technology available on the planet right now and if it was a priority to purify our environment of toxins, it would happen. But it is more profitable to research ways to dodge a bullet instead of raising the standards and quality of life for all. Hospitals, care centers and research facilities are a big commodity. Research centers are really finding ways to help the body coexist with the poisons that we all know are a byproduct of our gluttonous needs and wants. What really needs to happen is to adopt cleaner ways--NOT to assist the body to function in a compromised capacity while force feeding it insidious toxins.

It is insane that those of us who adopt alternative means to cleanse the body are considered the crackpots. We work diligently to eradicate every toxic feeling, experience and thought that might cling to an ingested toxin and create an abnormal presence in the body. It is preposterous to me that this is the process that society objects to.

It seems silly to me that those of us who hold a higher intention for the physicality of man are considered rogue. How strange that those who merely get by and serve others simply because we know the blueprint and care, are scoffed at and treated like the ones with an agenda. Yes. The agenda is to serve, to enlighten and uplift. When have those qualities been attributed to a big business lately besides through sound bytes? Just saying.

So keep wearing pink ribbons and looking for a magic cure. I am certain Bigfoot has it buried away somewhere. Please don't be offended. Also please don't mind if I don't join the bandwagon. A wise person told me once that animals don't realize that roads are dangerous. They are born with roads in their world and accept them as part of the landscape. Please forgive me for not accepting the "c" word as part of my landscape. In my Universe, the world is free of such highways.

In my private sessions, I have created taps for people to make more space in this world for the things that they want like love, abundance and health. So when I see and hear campaigns for cancer awareness, I wonder if I am the only one who perceives this as a means to make illness more of a mainstay into our consciousness.

Is there a way to celebrate survivors of illness without losing that original message in a barrage of ribbons, races and parades? To me, the original message is getting lost and it seems like society is advocating cancer. I understand the emotional component of the fight but that also gets lost in the national campaigns that, to me, feel like a celebration of a disease.

I don't want to be aware of cancer. I like the word wellness. Why can't people be made aware of wellness checkups without imprinting an insidious word and disease in our every day verbiage? Brainwashing and conditioning are achieved with repetition of a desired result. To hear the word cancer every day in any content feels like it is creating a complacency with hearing it instead of a means of eradicating it.

Here are some taps to assist:

(Say each statement three times while tapping on the head and say it a fourth time while tapping on the chest.)

"I eradicate cancer; in all moments."

"I release endorsing cancer; in all moments."

"I recant all vows and agreements between myself and cancer; in all moments."

"I remove all curses between myself and cancer; in all moments."

"I dissolve all karmic ties between myself and cancer; in all moments."

"I release my fear of cancer; in all moments."

"I release my genetic propensity to have cancer; in all moments."

"I remove all the pain, burden and limitations that cancer has taken from me; in all moments."

"I take back all the joy, love, abundance, freedom, life and wholeness that cancer has taken from me; in all moments."

"I release resonating with cancer; in all moments."

"I release emanating with cancer; in all moments."

"I remove all cancer from my sound frequency; in all moments."

"I remove all cancer from my light body; in all moments."

"I shift my paradigm from cancer to joy, love, abundance, freedom, health, life and wholeness; in all moments."

Can't pink go back to being just an innocent color that we wrap our baby daughters in?

Candida

(Say each statement three times while tapping on you head and say it a fourth time while tapping on your chest.)

"I flush all excess sugar out of my body; in all moments."

"I release growing unhealthy yeast in my body; in all moments."

"I shift my body's paradigm from acidic to alkaline; in all moments."

"I convert all acidic conditions to a balanced natural state; in all moments."

"I flush all unhealthy yeast out of my body; in all moments."

"I saturate my being with the alkaline state of divine love; in all moments."

"I release using candida to punish myself; in all moments."

"I release corroding by inner mechanisms with candida; in all moments."

"I breathe healthy, nurturing empowerment into my essence; in all moments."

"I dry up all inner dampness; in all moments."

"I warm myself from within; in all moments."

"I soothe my whole essence; in all moments."

Carpal Tunnel

(Say each statement three times while tapping on your head and say it a fourth time while tapping on your chest.)

"I release being enslaved; in all moments."

"I release being shackled at the wrists; in all moments."

"I release being shackled to a job; in all moments."

"I release associating work with being enslaved; in all moments."

"I release twisting the energy in my limbs; in all moments."

"I release entwining being emotionally disgruntled in my physical body; in all moments."

"I remove all engrams of being enslaved; in all moments."

"I remove all engrams of being shackled; in all moments."

"I release feeling trapped in a job; in all moments."

"I release being under pressure; in all moments."

"I release the trauma of wielding a weapon; in all moments."

"I release confusing work with going to battle; in all moments."

"I remove all engrams of going to battle; in all moments."

"I lay down my sword and shield; in all moments."

"I exonerate myself for all kills; in all moments."

"I clean the slate; in all moments."

"I command my limbs to function; in all moments."

"I operate in a pain free vessel; in all moments."

"I am centered and empowered in a guilt free, pain free domain; in all moments."

Have the Experiences That You Have Been Missing

The chakras are real working apertures. People think of their chakras as either open or closed, but there are 32 layers of the auric field, so all 32 layers must be open for a chakra to be fully effective. Also, if all 32 layers are not all aligned, it can make the opening smaller or almost completely covered with the other layers of the auric field. These taps are to remedy this.

One truth that was revealed in a session was that that little pouch of fat underneath the belly button is caused because the second chakra is closed or misaligned. Also, the reason that people have a hard time leaving the body is that the layers of the crown chakra are misaligned. The reason that people aren't connected to the earth is because the earth star chakra, (the one below the feet), is misaligned or closed.

If someone has tried everything to be healthy, get fit, regain balance, regain sexual prowess or have spiritual experiences to no avail, these taps may be the cure.

(Say each statement three times out loud while continuously tapping on the top of your head at the crown chakra and say it a fourth time while tapping on your chest.)

"We declare ourselves surrogates for humanity in doing these taps; in all moments."

"We unjar all 32 layers of our heart chakra; in all moments."

"We open up all 32 layers of our heart chakra; in all moments."

"We align all 32 layers of our heart chakra; in all moments."

"We send all energy matrices into the light and sound that cause us to close our heart chakra; in all moments."

"We send all energy matrices into the light and sound that cause us to misalign any layers of our heart chakra; in all moments."

"We unjar all 32 layers of our earth star chakra; in all moments."

"We open up all 32 layers of our earth star chakra; in all moments."

"We align all 32 layers of our earth star chakra; in all moments."

"We send all energy matrices into the light and sound that cause us to close our earth star chakra; in all moments."

"We send all energy matrices into the light and sound that cause us to misalign any layers of our earth star chakra; in all moments."

"We unjar all 32 layers of our eighth (soul star) chakra; in all moments."

"We open all 32 layers of our eighth (soul star) chakra; in all moments."

"We align all 32 layers of our eighth (soul star) chakra; in all moments."

"We send all energy matrices into the light and sound that cause us to close any layers of our eighth (soul star) chakra; in all moments."

"We send all energy matrices into the light and sound that cause us to misalign any layers of our eighth (soul star) chakra; in all moments."

"We unjar all 32 layers of our root chakra; in all moments."

"We open up all 32 layers of our root chakra; in all moments."

"We align all 32 layers of our root chakra; in all moments."

"We send all energy matrices into the light and sound that cause us to close any of the layers of our root chakra; in all moments."

"We send all energy matrices into the light and sound that cause us to misalign any of the layers of our root chakra; in all moments."

"We unjar all 32 layers of our crown chakra; in all moments."

"We open up all 32 layers of our crown chakra; in all moments."

"We align all 32 layers of our crown chakra; in all moments."

"We send all energy matrices into the light and sound that cause us to close any layers of our crown chakra; in all moments."

"We send all energy matrices into the light and sound that cause us to misalign any layers of our crown chakra; in all moments."

"We unjar all 32 layers of the sacral chakra; in all moments."

"We open up all 32 layers of the sacral chakra; in all moments."

"We align all 32 layers of the sacral chakra; in all moments."

"We send all energy matrices into the light and sound that cause us to close any layers of the sacral chakra; in all moments."

"We send all energy matrices into the light and sound that cause us to misalign any layers of the sacral chakra; in all moments."

"We unjar all 32 layers of our third eye; in all moments."

"We open up all 32 layers of our third eye; in all moments."

"We align all 32 layers of our third eye; in all moments."

"We send all energy matrices into the light and sound that cause us to close any layers of our third eye; in all moments."

"We send all energy matrices into the light and sound that cause us to misalign any layers of our third eye; in all moments."

"We unjar all 32 layers of the solar plexus; in all moments."

"We open up all 32 layers of the solar plexus; in all moments."

"We align all 32 layers of the solar plexus; in all moments."

"We send all energy matrices into the light and sound that cause us to close any layers of the solar plexus; in all moments."

"We send all energy matrices into the light and sound that cause us to misalign any layers of the solar plexus; in all moments."

"We unjar all 32 layers of our throat chakra; in all moments."

"We open all 32 layers of our throat chakra; in all moments."

"We align all 32 layers of our throat chakra; in all moments."

"We send all energy matrices into the light and sound that cause us to close any layers of our throat chakra; in all moments."

"We send all energy matrices into the light and sound that cause us to misalign any layers of our throat chakra; in all moments."

Stop Resisting Change

(Say each statement three times out loud while continuously tapping on the top of your head at the crown chakra and say it a fourth time while tapping on your chest.)

"I release resisting change; in all moments."

"I release the fear of change; in all moments."

"I release confusing change with death; in all moments."

"I release confusing moving on with crossing over; in all moments."

"I release the trauma of crossing over; in all moments."

"I release the fear of losing myself; in all moments."

"I release the belief that I lose myself in crossing over; in all moments."

"I release the fear of being separated from all I hold dear; in all moments."

"I release confusing change with losing what I hold dear; in all moments."

"I release using old consciousness as a crutch; in all moments."

"I release nesting in old consciousness; in all moments."

"I release avoiding change to keep a loved one company in old consciousness; in all moments."

"I release confusing change with abandonment; in all moments."

"I shift my paradigm from defining change as losing to realize it as gaining; in all moments."

"I let go of old consciousness with celebration and exuberance; in all moments."

"I am centered and empowered in the fluidity of change; in all moments."

Releasing the Fear of Change

It is human nature to want things to stay the same. We equivocate the lack of change with security. But the nature of life is fluid and it is our nature to be fluid. I noticed an interesting phenomenon in the grocery store one day. It hit me like a truth. There are people of all ages at the supermarket and it is a great place to do a field study on life. What I noticed was that the people who were more fluid in their body seemed to be more flexible in their thoughts as well.

Even in very older people, the ones that were still moving around on their own seemed to be more flexible in their beliefs and tolerances. It made me realize that yoga and other forms of flexibility training are great for the mental body as well as the physical body. And if one is rigid in their thoughts, it shows up in a rigidity in their body. Fear of change shows up in so many ways. Here are some taps to assist.

(Say each statement three times while tapping on your head and say it a fourth time while tapping on your chest.)

"I release the fear of change; in all moments."

"I release equivocating change as being usurped from my life; in all moments."

"I release the fear of the unknown; in all moments."

"I release the unknown triggering being defeated in battle; in all moments."

"I release equating change with life and death scenarios; in all moments."

"I release the fear of death; in all moments."

"I release confusing change for death; in all moments."

"I release the fear of the future; in all moments."

"I release fixating on death; in all moments."

"I release being rigid; in all moments."

"I release quantifying change as a lack of control; in all moments."

"I shift my paradigm from rigidity to change; in all moments."

The more that we are able to say yes to the small changes, the more we are able to stay centered and accept the big changes.

Release Chaos

Chaos is a fear-based state that interferes with atoms moving towards realizing more love.

(Say each statement three times while tapping on your head and say it a fourth time while tapping on your chest.)

"We release confusing random action for chaos; in all moments."

"We release the fear of chaos; in all moments."

"We release the fear of random action; in all moments."

"We release giving up our freedom to avoid chaos; in all moments."

"We release being jarred out of the moment by chaos; in all moments."

"We release being enslaved to chaos; in all moments."

"We release being paralyzed in inaction by chaos; in all moments."

"We release being veered from living our purpose by chaos; in all moments."

"We release being knocked off balance by chaos; in all moments."

"We remove all vivaxes between ourselves and chaos; in all moments."

"We remove all tentacles between ourselves and chaos; in all moments."

"We remove the claws of chaos from our beingness; in all moments."

"We remove all programming and conditioning that chaos has put on us; in all moments."

"We remove all engrams that chaos has put on us; in all moments."

"We send all energy matrices into the light and sound that immerse us in chaos; in all moments."

"We command all complex energy matrices that immerse us in chaos to be escorted into the light and sound; in all moments."

"We send all energy matrices into the light and sound that compile the pain body; in all moments."

"We command all complex energy matrices that compile the pain body to be escorted into the light and sound; in all moments."

"We send all energy matrices of chaos into the light and sound that propagate the pain body; in all moments."

"We command all complex energy matrices of chaos that propagate the pain body to be escorted into the light and sound; in all moments."

"We strip all illusion off of chaos; in all moments."

"We recant all vows and agreements between ourselves and chaos; in all moments."

"We remove all curses between ourselves and chaos; in all moments."

"We remove all blessings between ourselves and chaos; in all moments."

"We release confusing chaos with living our purpose; in all moments."

"We release using chaos to quantify our worth; in all moments."

"We sever all strings, cords and wires between ourselves and chaos; in all moments."

"We dissolve all karmic ties between ourselves and chaos; in all moments."

"We remove all masks, walls and armor from chaos; in all moments."

"We withdraw all our energy and support from chaos; in all moments."

"We remove all the pain, burden and limitations that chaos has put on us; in all moments."

"We remove all the pain, burden and limitations that we have put on all others due to chaos; in all moments."

"We remove all the fear, futility and unworthiness that chaos has put on us; in all moments."

"We remove all the fear, futility and unworthiness that we have put on all others due to chaos; in all moments."

"We remove all the paralysis, dis-ease, shackles and illusion of separateness that chaos has put on us; in all moments."

"We remove all the paralysis, dis-ease, shackles and illusion of separateness that we have put on all others due to chaos; in all moments."

"We take back all that chaos has taken from us; in all moments."

"We give back to all others all that we have taken from them due to chaos; in all moments."

"We collapse and dissolve all chaos; in all moments."

"We release resonating or emanating with chaos; in all moments."

"We extract all chaos from our sound frequency and the universal sound frequency; in all moments."

"We extract all chaos from our light emanation and the universal light emanation; in all moments."

"We extract all chaos from our whole beingness and the whole universal beingness; in all moments."

"We shift our paradigm and the universal paradigm from chaos to synergetic, random action; in all moments."

"We are individually and universally centered and empowered in synergetic, random action; in all moments."

"We individually and universally resonate, emanate and are interconnected with all life in synergetic, random action; in all moments."

Children of All Ages

(Say each statement three times while tapping on your head and say it a fourth time while tapping on your chest.)

"I release the fear of falling asleep; in all moments."

"I release the fear of monsters; in all moments."

"I dissolve all monsters with my kindness; in all moments."

"I am invisible to all bullies; in all moments."

"I release being overwhelmed; in all moments."

"I release feeling silly; in all moments."

"I release making excuses; in all moments."

"I release the belief that I need excuses; in all moments."

"I release apologizing for no reason; in all moments."

"I release trying to please everyone; in all moments."

"I am off-duty; in all moments."

"I am not responsible; in all moments."

"I am exonerated; in all moments."

"I am guilt-free; in all moments."

"I heal all animals; in all moments."

"I free all animals; in all moments."

"I comfort all children; in all moments."

"I release being poisoned; in all moments."

"All engrams of being poisoned are removed; in all moments."

"My body is healed and whole; in all moments."

Taps to Conceive a Healthy Baby

Here is to getting pregnant if you want to! You will forget after you get pregnant that these taps helped you, so…you are welcome!

(Say each statement three times while tapping on your head and say a fourth time while tapping on you chest.)

"I flush my uterus clean; in all moments."

"I remove all emotional issues in regards to conceiving; in all moments."

"I remove all issues hindering the conception of my baby; in all moments."

"I remove all stress from the process of conceiving; in all moments."

"I remove all blockages from my fallopian tubes; in all moments."

"I flush clean my kidneys; in all moments."

"I flush clean my liver; in all moments."

"I flush clean my heart; in all moments."

"I flush clean our DNA; in all moments."

"I flush clean our chromosomes; in all moments."

"I remove all desperation to conceive; in all moments."

"I remove the fear of not conceiving; in all moments."

"I remove all selfish motives in regards to conceiving; in all moments."

"I extract all need and want from the process of conceiving; in all moments."

"I release all unworthiness in regards to conceiving; in all moments."

"I empower the sperm; in all moments."

"I empower the egg; in all moments."

"I make space in my womb for the sperm to fertilize the egg; in all moments."

"I remove all blockages to the sperm fertilizing the egg; in all moments."

"I stretch the capacity for the sperm to fertilize the egg; in all moments."

"I make space in my womb for the egg to accept the sperm; in all moments."

"I remove all blockages to the egg accepting the sperm; in all moments."

"I stretch the egg's capacity to accept the sperm; in all moments."

"The sperm is centered and empowered in fertilizing the egg; in all moments."

"The egg is centered and empowered in accepting the sperm; in all moments."

"I make space in this world to conceive, gestate and give birth to a healthy baby; in all moments."

"I remove all blockages to conceiving, gestating and giving birth to a healthy baby; in all moments."

"I stretch my capacity to conceive, gestate and give birth to a healthy baby; in all moments."

"I am centered and empowered in conceiving, gestating and giving birth to a healthy baby; in all moments."

"I resonate and emanate in confidence in conceiving, gestating and giving birth to a healthy baby; in all moments."

Releasing a Parent's Angst

There is great responsibility in being a parent. It is a parent's unspoken fear that they will let their child down in some way or another. A prevalent fear is that one won't be able to keep their child safe. Thoughts around their children are so horrific that parents spend a lot of energy battling to keep them dormant. The underlying fear is that the parent will draw negative scenarios to their life by their thoughts. This creates a mind loop that becomes a person's private battle.

In past times, the mortality rate was much higher and personal security was much lower. What most people may not realize is that when they have irrational fears, it is because it is something that they may have already experienced in a previous life. It isn't really irrational. It is a memory. Knowing a fear is a memory may help people because they realize that they don't need to be experienced again. When one lets go of a past memory, instead of trying to suppress a thought, it can be emotionally freeing.

(Say each statement three times while tapping on your head and say it a fourth time while tapping on your chest.)

"I release the fear of tragedy happening to my children; in all moments."

"I release the fear of someone taking my children; in all moments."

"I release the fear of not being able to protect my children; in all moments."

"I release the fear of being separated from my children; in all moments."

"I release the fear of disappointing my children; in all moments."

"I release the guilt and trauma of killing my children; in all moments."

"I release the trauma of watching my children die; in all moments."

"I release the guilt and trauma of causing my children die; in all moments."

"I release being betrayed by my children; in all moments."

"I shift my paradigm from fearing for my children to joy, love, abundance, freedom, health, success, security, companionship, peace, life and wholeness; in all moments."

Cholesterol

Think about the little pig who built his house out of brick. He was the safe one. Plaque in the body is a natural way to protect ourselves from the world that will harm us. Laying down plaque is a way of building up walls.

(Say each statement three times while tapping on your head and say it a fourth time while tapping on your chest.)

"I release storing emotional issues in my blood; in all moments."

"I remove all issues from my blood; in all moments."

"I release feeling unsafe; in all moments."

"I release confusing fatty foods with feeling safe; in all moments."

"I release craving fatty foods to feel safe; in all moments."

"I purify my blood; in all moments."

"I release having blood poisoning; in all moments."

"I remove all engrams of blood poisoning; in all moments."

"I release forming inner walls of protection; in all moments."

"I crumble down the inner walls of protection; in all moments."

"I remove all the layers of plaque from my body; in all moments."

"I release the need to fortify walls of protection; in all moments."

"I feel safe and secure on all levels; in all moments."

"I am safe and secure on all levels; in all moments."

"I release the primal craving for meat; in all moments."

"I remove myself from the hunt and gather mode; in all moments."

"I release associating eating meat with conquering the enemy; in all moments."

"I release eating heavy meat to feel safe; in all moments."

"I release eating heavy meat to feel important; in all moments."

"I release packing on pounds to feel safe; in all moments."

"I release gaining weight as a form of avoidance; in all moments."

"I release all emotional issues stored in my lungs; in all moments."

"I am repulsed by smoking; in all moments."

"I heal my lungs and body of the damage smoking has done; in all moments."

"I release aging out of habit; in all moments."

"I release degenerating with age; in all moments."

"I drop out of the conformity of time and Western beliefs; in all moments."

"I heal my body on all levels; in all moments."

l

three times out loud while continuously tapping on the top of your head at the
it a fourth time while tapping on your chest.)

others; in all moments."

"I release glamorizing others; in all moments."

"I release comparing myself to others; in all moments."

"I release gauging my worth against the backdrop of others; in all moments."

"I release categorizing anyone's worth using a physical syllabus; in all moments."

"I remove all engrams of jealousy; in all moments."

"I remove all engrams of competing; in all moments."

"I release the primal urge to compete; in all moments."

"I release creating hostility in my interactions; in all moments."

"I release feeling or believing that I am justified; in all moments."

"I release selling my soul for wisps of illusion; in all moments."

"I reflect the purity of my soul; in all moments."

"I express myself through the purity of my soul; in all moments."

"I deal in integrity and my language is truth; in all moments."

"I have benevolence for all; in all moments."

"I am centered and empowered in integrity and truth; in all moments."

Communications

Truth and love resonate at similar frequencies. The reason there is not more love in the world is because there is so little truth. As follows, the reason there is so little love in relationships is because there is so little truth. The amount of love in a relationship is equal and synonymous in some ways to the amount of truth in a relationship.

(Say each statement three times while tapping on your head and say it a fourth time while tapping on your chest.)

"I release saying what I don't mean; in all moments."

"I release hearing only what I want to hear; in all moments."

"I release being sabotaged by preconceived notions; in all moments."

"I release being sabotaged by my own mind; in all moments."

"I release being held captive by my own mind; in all moments."

"I release being led by the reptilian brain; in all moments."

"I release reverting to primal mode; in all moments."

"I release reverting to reactionary mode; in all moments."

"I release tangling the energy of my communications; in all moments."

"I untangle the energy of my communications; in all moments."

"I release lying; in all moments."

"I release the fear of hearing the truth; in all moments."

"I release protecting the ego in regards to hearing truth; in all moments."

"I release the fear of seeing myself in a different light; in all moments."

"I release lying to myself; in all moments."

"I dissipate all the psychic energy that interferes with my clarity of speech; in all moments."

"I dissipate all the psychic energy that interferes with my clarity of thought; in all moments."

"I dissipate all the psychic energy that interferes with the clarity of my communications; in all moments."

"I remove all the mind loops that have entrenched me; in all moments."

"I remove all the drama that has kept me stuck; in all moments."

"I release wasting my energy on complaining; in all moments."

"I release wasting my energy on gossip; in all moments."

"I dissipate all the whirlpool of energies I have created with gossip and drama; in all moments."

"I release engaging others in psychic whirlpools of energy; in all moments."

"I clear up all miscommunications; in all moments."

"I release 'dropping the ball' when someone is speaking with me; in all moments."

"I release the fear of speaking my truth; in all moments."

"I remove all obstacles to speaking my truth; in all moments."

"I release being polite; in all moments."

"I remove all programming and conditioning that prevent clear communications; in all moments."

"I release confusing rudeness as truth; in all moments."

"I release confusing passive communication for kindness; in all moments."

"I expose all truth in a kind and loving way; in all moments."

"I free all truths in a kind and loving way; in all moments."

"I speak only truth; in all moments."

"I openly receive and accept truth; in all moments."

"I awaken to all truths; in all moments."

"I make space in the world for clear communications; in all moments."

"I remove all blockages to clear communications; in all moments."

"I expand my capacity to continually engage in clear communications; in all moments."

"I am centered and empowered in clear communications; in all moments."

"I resonate, emanate and am interconnected to all life in engaging in clear communications; in all moments."

"I resonate, emanate and am interconnected to all life in giving and receiving clear communications; in all moments."

Competition

Many of us have this outmoded belief that we only succeed at the expense of others. It is ingrained from past lives when we were pitted against each other in life or death scenarios. We have learned to believe that we have to outdo others.

The truth is, when one person is uplifted, it uplifts all. When we try to hold back our gifts, we actually hold ourselves back. When we uplift others, we are uplifted by that very act.

Here are some taps to assist with this issue: (Say each statement three times while tapping on the head and a fourth time while tapping on your chest.)

"I release the fear of sharing my gifts; in all moments."

"I release the fear of being martyred; in all moments."

"I release the belief that life is a competition; in all moments."

"I release competing with others; in all moments."

"I release the aversion to sharing my gifts; in all moments."

"I release dimming myself so others can shine; in all moments."

"I release diminishing the gifts of others; in all moments."

"I strip all illusion off my gifts; in all moments."

"I nullify all contracts that work to diminish me; in all moments."

"I release withholding my gifts; in all moments."

"I make space in this world to share my gifts; in all moments."

"I remove all blockages to sharing my gifts; in all moments."

"I stretch my capacity to share my gifts; in all moments."

"I am centered and empowered in sharing my gifts; in all moments."

"I resonate, emanate, and am interconnected with all life in sharing my gifts; in all moments."

Changing Your Comfort Zone

In a recent remote session, my client was grappling with the issue of abuse. An interesting epiphany came to light. Overall, she was comfortable with being abused. It isn't that she liked it. But it was what she was familiar with. Being abused, as an experience, was like a comfortable pair of shoes.

I realized that this was true of many negative experiences like poverty, unhappiness, illness, slavery and failure.

Here are some taps to assist: (Say each statement three times out loud while tapping on the top of your head at the crown chakra and say it a fourth time while tapping on your chest at the heart chakra.)

"I release being comfortable with abuse; in all moments."

"I shift my paradigm from abuse to wholeness; in all moments."

"I release being comfortable with poverty; in all moments."

"I shift my paradigm from poverty to wealth; in all moments."

"I release being comfortable with unhappiness; in all moments."

"I shift my paradigm from unhappiness to joy; in all moments."

"I release being comfortable with illness; in all moments."

"I shift my paradigm from illness to health; in all moments."

"I release being comfortable with slavery; in all moments."

"I shift my paradigm from slavery to freedom; in all moments."

"I release being comfortable with failure; in all moments."

"I shift my paradigm from failure to success; in all moments."

Control Freak

(Say each statement three times out loud while tapping on the top of your head at the crown chakra and say it a fourth time while tapping on your chest at the heart chakra.)

"I release confusing control for empowerment; in all moments."

"I remove the genetic propensity to control; in all moments."

"I release micromanaging the Universe; in all moments."

"I release the notion that I could ever fail; in all moments."

"I release compartmentalizing the Universe into pass or fail; in all moments."

"I balance my parasympathetic with my sympathetic nervous systems; in all moments."

"I repair and fortify the Wei chi on the symbiotic relationship between my parasympathetic and sympathetic nervous system; in all moments."

"I shift my paradigm from control to empowerment; in all moments."

"I relinquish control to surrender; in all moments."

"I surrender to divine love; in all moments."

"I am centered and empowered in divine love; in all moments."

Forgo Control

Do you know why so many people feel they need to maintain control? Because at a primal level, control is what is relinquished when we die. So many people associate control as feigning off death.

(Say each statement three times out loud while continuously tapping on the top of your head at the crown chakra and say it a fourth time while tapping on your chest at the heart chakra.)

"I release using control to feign off death; in all moments."

"I release confusing losing control with death; in all moments."

"I release associating losing control with death; in all moments."

"I release using control as a crutch; in all moments."

"I release using control as a security blanket; in all moments."

"I release micromanaging the Universe; in all moments."

"I release using control to feel safe; in all moments."

"I relinquish control; in all moments."

"I surrender the illusion of control; in all moments."

"I surrender to the Universe; in all moments."

"I am centered and empowered in trusting the Universe; in all moments."

Creativity

(Say each statement three times while tapping on your head and say it a fourth time while tapping on your chest.)

"I am centered and empowered in inspiration; in all moments."

"I acknowledge and validate my daydreams; in all moments."

"I shift my paradigm from boredom to ingenuity; in all moments."

"I maintain the vantage point of childlike wonder; in all moments."

"I continue to always try; in all moments."

"I release conforming to a 9 to 5 existence; in all moments."

"I follow my heart; in all moments."

"I transcend time; in all moments."

"I listen to my creative cycles; in all moments."

"I transform difficulties into opportunities; in all moments."

"I love my creations and then move on; in all moments."

"I breathe life into the constructs of my creations; in all moments."

"I am both humble and proud; in all moments."

"I embrace new ways to embrace myself; in all moments."

"I contemplate each move; in all moments."

"I see each situation from exponential vantage points; in all moments."

"I shatter all limitations and glass ceilings; in all moments."

"I perceive from my subtle senses; in all moments."

"I perceive the world from multiple dimensions; in all moments."

"I embrace and create new experiences; in all moments."

"I reinvent my creations and start from scratch; in all moments."

"I love everyone and everything; in all moments."

Crohn's Disease

(Say each statement three times while tapping on your head and say it a fourth time while tapping on your chest.)

"I release the trauma of being wounded in battle; in all moments."

"I release being killed in battle; in all moments."

"I remove the pain and anguish of being pierced with a sword; in all moments."

"I heal all intestinal wounds; in all moments."

"I release the trauma of being gorged; in all moments."

"I release the trauma of being hunted down; in all moments."

"I release the trauma of being eaten; in all moments."

"I release losing my guts; in all moments."

"I release dying in terror; in all moments."

"I remove all the terror stored in my body; in all moments."

"I remove all engrams of dying in terror; in all moments."

"I remove all engrams of dying in battle; in all moments."

"I release being sodomized; in all moments."

"I remove all engrams of being sodomized; in all moments."

"I release existing in squalor; in all moments."

"I release eating putrid food; in all moments."

"I remove all engrams of eating putrid food; in all moments."

"I remove all engrams of existing in squalor; in all moments."

"I remove all mold from my body; in all moments."

"I heal all wounds; in all moments."

"I realign all my bodies; in all moments."

"I pour well-being, calm and optimal health through my essence; in all moments."

"I am centered and empowered in optimal health; in all moments."

"I resonate, emanate and am interconnected with all life in optimal health; in all moments."

Demons

These energies are responsible for addictions, compulsive behavior, a taste for violence, greed, mental unbalance and more. Please do these taps to cleanse humanity and know that you will be benefiting yourself, relationships and loved ones in the process. See doing these taps as a personal gift to humanity and then mark this day as a pivotal advancement to peace and love prevailing on earth.

(Say each statement three times while tapping on your head and say it a fourth time while tapping on your chest.)

"We declare ourselves surrogates for humanity in doing these taps; in all moments."

"We release being manipulated by demons; in all moments."

"We release being deceived by demons; in all moments."

"We release the genetic propensity to accept demons; in all moments."

"We release being suckered by demons; in all moments."

"We release using demons as a crutch; in all moments."

"We take back our free will and ability to discern from all demons; in all moments."

"We release being controlled by demons; in all moments."

"We release being stuck in the primal mode of fear; in all moments."

"We release being shackled to demons; in all moments."

"We release being afraid of demons; in all moments."

"We release being enslaved to demons; in all moments."

"We release being enslaved by demons; in all moments."

"We nullify all contracts between ourselves and all demons; in all moments."

"We release systemic all allegiance to demons; in all moments."

"We remove all vivaxes between ourselves and all demons; in all moments."

"We remove all tentacles between ourselves and all demons; in all moments."

"We remove the claws of all demons from our beingness; in all moments."

"We release being ruled by demons; in all moments."

"We remove all programming and conditioning that all demons have put on us; in all moments."

"We remove all engrams of all demons; in all moments."

"We send all energy matrices of all demons into the light and sound; in all moments."

"We command all complex energy matrices of all demons to be escorted into the light and sound; in all moments."

"We send all energy matrices into the light and sound that perpetuate fear of demons; in all moments."

"We command all complex energy matrices that perpetuate fear of demons to be escorted into the light and sound; in all moments."

"We recant all vows and agreements between ourselves and all demons; in all moments."

"We strip all illusion off of all demons; in all moments."

"We remove all masks, walls and armor from all demons; in all moments."

"We shatter all glass ceilings that all demons have put on us; in all moments."

"We eliminate the first cause in regards to all demons; in all moments."

"We remove all curses between ourselves and all demons; in all moments."

"We remove all blessings between ourselves and all demons; in all moments."

"We strip all illusion off of all demons; in all moments."

"We withdraw all our energy from all demons; in all moments."

"We remove all the pain, burden and limitations that all demons have put on us; in all moments."

"We remove all the fear, futility and unworthiness that all demons have put on us; in all moments."

"We remove all the apathy, indifference and devastation that all demons have put on us; in all moments."

"We remove all the rejection, abandonment and illusion of separateness that all demons have put on us; in all moments."

"We remove all that we have put on all others due to demons; in all moments."

"We take back all that demons have taken from us; in all moments."

"We give back all that we have taken from all others due to demons; in all moments."

"We collapse and dissolve all demons; in all moments."

"We release resonating or emanating with demons; in all moments."

"We extract all demons from our sound frequency; in all moments."

"We extract all demons from our light emanation; in all moments."

"We extract all demons from all 32 layers of our auric field; in all moments."

"We extract all demons from our whole beingness; in all moments."

"We abolish all demons as a construct; in all moments."

"We shift our paradigm from all demons to love and acceptance; in all moments."

"We transcend all demons; in all moments."

"We are centered and empowered in universal love and spiritual freedom; in all moments."

"We resonate, emanate and are interconnected with all life in universal love and spiritual freedom; in all moments."

Addressing Symptoms of Depression

(Say each statement three times while tapping on your head and say it a fourth time while tapping on your chest.)

"I release being sad; in all moments."

"I release feeling hopeless; in all moments."

"I fill myself with purpose; in all moments."

"I shift my paradigm into optimism; in all moments."

"I exonerate myself; in all moments."

"I am worthy; in all moments."

"I am competent; in all moments."

"I release feeling helpless; in all moments."

"I embrace my empowerment; in all moments."

"I engage in activities that interest me; in all moments."

"I enjoy many hobbies and activities; in all moments."

"I recharge all my endocrine processes; in all moments."

"I balance my serotonin levels; in all moments."

"I untangle all confusion; in all moments."

"I recharge all my chakras; in all moments."

"I feed energy into all my endocrine functions; in all moments."

"I am active and present in life; in all moments."

"I am decisive and cognitive; in all moments."

"I regulate my sleep patterns; in all moments."

"I regulate my appetite; in all moments."

"I release all obsessive thoughts; in all moments."

"I release fixating on death; in all moments."

"I release being irritable; in all moments."

"I remove all engrams that entrench me in negativity; in all moments."

"I sever all ties with those who have crossed by their own volition; in all moments."

"I dissipate all psychic energies that encourage suicide; in all moments."

"I infuse my whole being with golden rays of happiness; in all moments."

"I convert all stagnant energy into the loving state of optimal health; in all moments."

"I dry up all symptoms that distract me from perpetual ease and bliss; in all moments."

"I am centered and empowered in a perpetual state of the joyous grace of gratitude; in all moments."

Cyclical Depression

Sometimes people get depressed during certain parts of the year. They have no explanation for it. It feels like there is some ominous kind of trigger like the changing of the seasons. But knowing it is looming, doesn't help deal with it. It could be triggered by the holidays approaching or getting less light in the day which is called Seasonal Affective Disorder.

May I suggest a deeper solution?

Some of us may be mourning a past life where we were having a pleasant day-to-day existence and were killed or pulled into slavery or imprisonment at a certain time of year. The change in the seasons could trigger an unconscious memory of a past state of mourning. It feels like this is a time in the cycle of the year when being conquered, in general, happened more than at other times.

If this is an issue that you deal with, you may want to try these taps: (Say each statement three times while tapping on your head and say it a fourth time while tapping on your chest.)

"I release mourning the loss of my freedom; in all moments."

"I release mourning my life; in all moments."

"I release the belief that I am missing out; in all moments."

"I release lamenting the future; in all moments."

"I release being enslaved to loss; in all moments."

"I release the belief that life is imprisonment; in all moments."

"I release defining this season with sadness; in all moments."

"I shift my paradigm to joy, love, abundance and freedom; in all moments."

"I am centered and satisfied in divine love; in all moments."

Undoing Holiday Blues

There are some people who don't feel "on board" with the holidays. It is a sensation of not having the same feeling that everyone else does and not understanding why. This discomfort could be compared somewhat to hanging out with two people who are in love and being the odd man out. The feeling can range from slight dread, to a total disconnect and depression.

There are so many reasons for this. A tragedy may have happened at this time of the year that gets conjured up by the holidays (present life or past); also, feelings of lack get triggered. Some start to take inventory on their life around this time and it may come up short.

Whether it is a small matter or one of great dread, here is a compilation of taps from different sessions to assist you in feeling more joy, love, abundance, freedom and wholeness at the holidays and always. Hopefully, they will be self-explanatory.

(Say each statement three times while tapping on your head and say it a fourth time while tapping on your chest.)

"I release hating the holidays in all moments."

"I release feeling lonely on the holidays; in all moments."

"I release associating the holidays with trauma; in all moments."

"I release the dread triggered by the holidays; in all moments."

"I release the belief that God hates me; in all moments."

"I release the belief that I am separate from God; in all moments."

"I release the belief that God has abandoned me; in all moments."

"I release feeling separate from life; in all moments."

"I release associating holidays with loss; in all moments."

"I release associating the holidays with unworthiness; in all moments."

"I release associating the fear of being 'called out' with the holidays; in all moments."

"I release all shame that is triggered by the holidays; in all moments."

"I release depending on others for my joy; in all moments."

"I remove all that is not joy, love, and abundance from my holidays; in all moments."

"I make space in this world for a joyous holidays; in all moments."

"I remove all blockages to having a joyous holiday; in all moments."

"I stretch my capacity to have a joyous holiday; in all moments."

"I am centered in joy, love, abundance and freedom; in all moments."

If you are in a funk, please do these taps. You don't have to believe in anything to have them work. If you know someone else in a funk today, please share these taps with them. Maybe they will do it because they care about you and it may help their quality of life in some way.

The Devil

What if these invisible factors that have been preventing us from being our most exuberant self were throwbacks from past lives? In past lives and in some present religions, the fear of the devil can paralyze people in fear. Here are taps to address a deep-seated fear that can literally hold someone in hell.

(Say each statement three times while tapping on your head and say it a fourth time while tapping on your chest.)

"I release being in sympathy with the Devil; in all moments."

"I release working for the Devil; in all moments."

"I release the belief that I am damned; in all moments."

"I release the trauma of being sacrificed; in all moments."

"I release the belief that God has forsaken me; in all moments."

"I release cursing God; in all moments."

"I recant all vows and agreements between myself and the Devil; in all moments."

"I remove all curses between myself and the Devil; in all moments."

"I dissolve all karmic ties between myself and the Devil; in all moments."

"I remove all the pain, burden and limitations that the Devil has put on me; in all moments."

"I take back all the joy, love, abundance, freedom, health, success, security, companionship, peace, life, beauty, enthusiasm and contentment that the devil has taken from me; in all moments."

"I release doing the Devil's bidding; in all moments."

"I release resonating with the Devil; in all moments."

"I release emanating with the Devil; in all moments."

"I remove all of the Devil from my sound frequency in all moments."

"I remove all of the Devil from my light body; in all moments."

"I shift my paradigm from the Devil to joy, love, abundance, freedom, health, success, security, companionship, peace, life, beauty, enthusiasm and contentment; in all moments."

"I am centered and empowered in Divine Love; in all moments."

Digestive Disorders

(Say each statement three times while tapping on your head and say it a fourth time while tapping on your chest.)

"I release the inability to stomach life; in all moments."

"I release being gutted; in all moments."

"I release eating putrid foods; in all moments."

"I release eating garbage to survive; in all moments."

"I release having my organs shut down; in all moments."

"I release shutting down my energy; in all moments."

"I release starving to death; in all moments."

"I release being used to starving; in all moments."

"I release losing my ability to process food; in all moments."

"I release registering food as an intrusion; in all moments."

"I release all the chaos in my organs; in all moments."

"I remove all the trauma stored in my digestive system; in all moments."

"I remove all miscommunication from my different organs; in all moments."

"I release infighting amongst my organs; in all moments."

"I release the confusing messages my organs are receiving; in all moments."

"I reinstate congruency within my digestive system; in all moments."

"All my organs work in agreement; in all moments."

"I open up my digestive system to receive food; in all moments."

"All organs of my digestive system work together at optimal level; in all moments."

Divorce

If you are going through the process of divorce, you may want to try these taps. It doesn't have to be so hard.

(Say each statement three times while tapping on your head and say it a fourth time while tapping on your chest.)

"I release confusing divorce with going to battle; in all moments."

"I release creating conflict to separate from my spouse; in all moments."

"I release using hate to separate from my spouse; in all moments."

"I release using conflict to justify my freedom; in all moments."

"I release creating drama to depart from the marriage; in all moments."

"I release demonizing my spouse to validate myself; in all moments."

"I release using the children as leverage; in all moments."

"I release using shared interests as leverage; in all moments."

"I release hating my spouse; in all moments."

"I release staying with my spouse out of desperation to avoid loneliness; in all moments."

"I release the fear of being alone; in all moments."

"I release the fear of being abandoned; in all moments."

"I release equivocating divorce with being abandoned; in all moments."

"I release allowing divorce to derail my life; in all moments."

"I release allowing divorce to consume the narrative; in all moments."

"I release defining divorce as an absence of love; in all moments."

"I release falling out of the love; in all moments."

"I stay in love with my ex-spouse; in all moments."

Cut the Drama

(Say each statement three times out loud while continuously tapping on the top of your head at the crown chakra and say it a fourth time while tapping on your chest.)

"I release being pulled into drama; in all moments."

"I release choosing drama; in all moments."

"I remove all vivaxes between myself and the drama; in all moments."

"I remove all tentacles between myself and the drama; in all moments."

"I remove the claws of drama from my beingness; in all moments."

"I send all energy matrices into the light that immerse me in drama; in all moments."

"We remove all interference in my empowerment; in all moments."

"I release coarsening my vibration with my choice of words; in all moments."

"I release coarsening my vibration with my thoughts; in all moments."

"I release coarsening my vibration with feelings; in all moments."

"I release coarsening my vibration with the memories I choose; in all moments."

"I release coarsening my vibration with the choices I make; in all moments."

"I release coarsening my vibration with the agreements I make; in all moments."

"I release coarsening my vibration with the experiences I choose; in all moments."

"I release weakening my boundaries with the things that I share; in all moments."

"I release giving away my power in ignorance; in all moments."

"I release coarsening my vibration with ignorance; in all moments."

"I release coarsening my vibration with denial; in all moments."

"I release coarsening my vibration with linear thinking; in all moments."

"I release gnawing on the bone of personal issues; in all moments."

"I release thrashing around for survival; in all moments."

"I am centered empowered and at peace; in all moments."

"I surrender to and am buoyed by the love; in all moments."

Pull Yourself Out of the Drama

(Say each statement three times out loud while continuously tapping on the top of your head at the crown chakra and say it a fourth time while tapping on your chest at the heart chakra.)

"I release being immersed in problems; in all moments."

"I shift my vantage point to have an overview of all issues; in all moments."

"I release being immersed in disease; in all moments."

"I shift my vantage point to have an overview of all health concerns; in all moments."

"I release being immersed in drama; in all moments."

"I shift my vantage point to have an overview of all relationships; in all moments."

"I release being immersed in debt; in all moments."

"I shift my vantage point to have an overview financial obligations; in all moments."

"I release being immersed in sadness; in all moments."

"I shift my vantage point to have an overview of all emotional issues; in all moments."

"I release being immersed in failure; in all moments."

"I shift my vantage point to have an overview of all opportunities; in all moments."

"I release being immersed in insecurity; in all moments."

"I shift my vantage point to have an overview of all issues of security; in all moments."

"I release being immersed in control; in all moments."

"I shift my vantage point to have an overview of freedom; in all moments."

"I perpetually stay in a balanced state of grace; in all moments."

"I am centered and empowered in a balanced state of grace; in all moments."

Drug Addiction

(Say each statement three times while tapping on your head and say it a fourth time while tapping on your chest.)

"I declare myself a surrogate for humanity in doing these taps; in all moments."

"We gift all those with addictions the strength to transcend them; in all moments."

"We strip all denial off of the world in dealing with drugs, opioids and addictions; in all moments."

"We release allowing drugs and addictions to run the world; in all moments."

"We dissipate the systemic indifference that allows drugs, opioids and addictions to flourish; in all moments."

"We remove all masks, walls and armor off of all drugs, opioids and addictions; in all moments."

"We release the burden of being saddled with drugs, opioids and addictions; in all moments."

"We release allowing drugs, opioids and addictions to take our children; in all moments."

"We release allowing drugs, opioids and addictions to diminish our quality of life; in all moments."

"We release passively watching while drugs, opioids and addictions hold the world hostage; in all moments."

"We strip all illusion off of drugs, opioids and addictions; in all moments."

"We release allowing drugs, opioids and addictions to pull us into their psychic grip; in all moments."

"We release being indifferent or apathetic to drugs, opioids and addictions; in all moments."

"We release being separated from our humanity by drugs, opioids and addictions; in all moments."

"We release being manipulated by drugs, opioids and addictions; in all moments."

"We break up the cluster of power mongers that use drugs, opioids and addictions to reign; in all moments."

"We release being plummeted into ignorance by drugs, opioids and addictions; in all moments."

"We release enabling drugs, opioids and addictions; in all moments."

"We release being stripped of our progressiveness by drugs, opioids and addictions; in all moments."

"We release being complacent with drugs, opioids and addictions; in all moments."

"We release ever empowering drugs, opioids and addictions in any way; in all moments."

"We eliminate the first cause in the creation of drugs, opioids and addictions; in all moments."

"We release being enamored with drugs, opioids and addictions; in all moments."

"We strip all illusion and defenses off those who perpetuate drugs, opioids and addictions to control others; in all moments."

"We release converting our empowerment to complacency of drugs, opioids and addictions; in all moments."

"We release being enslaved to drugs, opioids and addictions; in all moments."

"We release diminishing ourselves by using drugs, opioids and addictions; in all moments."

"We remove all vivaxes between ourselves and drugs, opioids and addictions; in all moments."

"We remove all tentacles between ourselves and drugs, opioids and addictions; in all moments."

"We withdraw all our energy from all drugs, opioids and addictions; in all moments."

"We collapse and dissolve all portals to drugs, opioids and addictions; in all moments."

"We remove all programming and conditioning that drugs, opioids and addictions have put on us; in all moments."

"We remove all individual and universal engrams of drugs, opioids and addictions; in all moments."

"We release worshiping drugs, opioids and addictions; in all moments."

"We release allowing drugs, opioids and addictions to rob us of our voice; in all moments."

"We release feeding drugs, opioids and addictions with adulation or fear; in all moments."

"We send all energy matrices into the light and sound that enable drugs, opioids and addictions; in all moments."

"We command all complex energy matrices that enable drugs, opioids and addictions to be escorted into the light and sound; in all moments."

"We send all energy matrices into the light and sound that allow drugs, opioids and addictions to grip individuals; in all moments."

"We command all complex energy matrices that allow drugs, opioids and addictions to grip individuals to be escorted into the light and sound; in all moments."

"We send all energy matrices into the light and sound that prevent us from eliminating drugs, opioids and addictions; in all moments."

"We command all complex energy matrices that prevent us from eliminating drugs, opioids and addictions to be escorted into the light and sound; in all moments."

"We recant all vows and agreements between ourselves and drugs, opioids and addictions; in all moments."

"We remove all curses between ourselves and all drugs, opioids and addictions; in all moments."

"We remove all blessings between ourselves and all drugs, opioids and addictions; in all moments."

"We remove the perceived payoff of using drugs, opioids, and addictions; in all moments."

"We sever all strings, cords and psychic connection between ourselves and all drugs, opioids and addictions; in all moments."

"We dissolve all karmic ties between ourselves and all drugs, opioids and addictions; in all moments."

"We remove all the pain, burden, limitations, fear, futility, unworthiness and illusion of separateness that drugs, opioids and addictions have put on us; in all moments."

"We bury drugs, opioids and addictions in their own ignoble intentions; in all moments."

"We remove all muscle memory that causes us to defer to drugs, opioids and addictions; in all moments."

"We dismantle all energy grids between ourselves and all drugs, opioids and addictions; in all moments."

"We take back all the joy, love, abundance, freedom, health, success, security, companionship, creativity, peace, life, wholeness, beauty, enthusiasm, contentment, spirituality, enlightenment, confidence, the ability to discern and empowerment that drugs, opioids and addictions have taken from us; in all moments."

"We strip drugs, opioids and addictions of their girth; in all moments."

"We strip drugs, opioids and addictions of their illusions of grandeur; in all moments."

"We disarm drugs, opioids and addictions from manipulating our children; in all moments."

"We crumble all constructs created by drugs, opioids and addictions; in all moments."

"We nullify all contracts with all drugs, opioids and addictions; in all moments."

"We strip all illusion off of all mandates of drugs, opioids and addictions; in all moments."

"We eliminate the first cause in all mandates of drugs, opioids and addictions; in all moments."

"We hold an open portal for universal strength, freedom and empowerment of individuals; in all moments."

"We release confusing drugs, opioids and addictions with a rite of passage; in all moments."

"We release confusing drugs, opioids and addictions with salvation; in all moments."

"We release resonating or emanating with drugs, opioids and addictions; in all moments."

"We extract all of drugs, opioids and addictions from our individual and universal sound frequency; in all moments."

"We extract all of drugs, opioids and addictions from our individual and universal light emanation; in all moments."

"We extract all of drugs, opioids and addictions from all 32 layers of our individual and universal aura; in all moments."

"We extract all of drugs, opioids and addictions from our whole beingness; in all moments."

"We shift our paradigm from drugs, opioids and addictions to individual and universal joy, love, abundance, freedom, health, peace, strength and empowerment; in all moments."

"We transcend drugs, opioids and addictions; in all moments."

"We are centered and empowered in individual and universal joy, love, abundance, freedom health, peace, strength and empowerment; in all moments."

"We infuse individual and universal joy, love, abundance, freedom, health, peace, strength and empowerment into our sound frequency; in all moments."

"We imbue individual and universal joy, love, abundance, freedom, health, peace, strength and empowerment into our light emanation; in all moments."

"We resonate, emanate and are interconnected to all life in individual and universal joy, love, abundance, freedom, health, peace, strength and empowerment; in all moments."

The Answer on Drug Use…Intention

Recently, I facilitated a private remote session with a regular client. She is struggling with the moral and physiological issue of smoking marijuana. I had to cancel a previous session with her because she was high at the time. She was really confused as to why it was an issue. I tried to explain to her why I did not want to facilitate a session with her if she was committed to smoking marijuana.

When I am doing energy work, I am so receptive and open. I have to be so acute in my awareness and at the same time protect myself from foreign energies. When someone indulges in smoking, drinking, rich foods or drugs, many times, it is foreign energies that are compelling one to indulge. It is like being home and having all the doors and windows of your house open where anyone can walk in. Before I do work with anyone, they need to have the intention of closing all their windows and doors. Otherwise, the point of me helping is moot. It would be like trying to convert a gang of thugs.

She had a sincere question as to why marijuana was not good for her to have. I had no answer for her really except that it pokes holes in one's energy field and I don't feel comfortable working with anyone who is actively participating. But to her, smoking marijuana was spiritual. In her session, I received the answer she needed.

In her past lives, I saw her using herbs in a spiritual ritual. I saw her smoking the peace pipe and I saw her drinking an ambrosia in an ancient Aztec-like culture. These drugs took her to a spiritually higher consciousness. It was a good memory that she relived by smoking marijuana in the present.

But then I saw the marijuana of the present and how it is used to subjugate the masses. I saw the drug trade, sex trafficking, the buying and selling of guns to dangerous militia groups all funded and run by the money made in drug sales. I saw people being literally led down a beautiful wooded path that felt spiritual and wonderful but as it went on longer and grew wider, it became a tarred-over, smelly mining road. It just kept going and going and the people that were on it were too tired to go back but realized that they were walking to a wasteland. That is where drug use literally takes people.

So I received the answer to my client's question, "Why were drugs okay in past life experiences but not okay in the present climate?" The answer is intention. In the past, the smoking of a drug took the client to a higher vibration where she could connect with her spiritual self. In the present, smoking marijuana led her to a lie because she was not led anywhere good in the smoking of it. She was merely pacified while she denied expressing her own greatness. It was not medicinal for her. It was a crutch.

Where recreational drugs lead now is a cesspool. The consciousness of a person these days is that they can get beyond their own limitations much more easily without indulging in the lie that drugs are helping them. People will argue this with me but they are being duped. I see the illusion of where drugs empty the person out in the other worlds. It is very low in the worlds of God. Very low. I would never stop there even to get a drink except if I was helping someone who was trapped there, which I was.

The woman felt that she had demons. That was her excuse to give away her power. She had no demons. The energy she felt was stagnant energy within her creating a personification of itself and lying to her. It was dead energy that she gave life to with her fear and her beliefs. It was time for her to do some inner dusting and take back her power.

(Say each statement three times out loud while continuously tapping on the top of your head at the crown chakra and say it a fourth time while tapping on your heart chakra.)

"I release harboring demons; in all moments."

"I release sympathizing with my demons; in all moments."

"I release feeding my demons; in all moments."

"I release giving power over to my demons; in all moments."

"I release creating demons; in all moments."

"I release the fear of my own demons; in all moments."

"I release giving my demons superhuman strength; in all moments."

"I release the belief that my demons are evil spirits; in all moments."

"I release confusing my demons with demonic possession in all moments."

"I exorcise my demons; in all moments."

"I release owning the demons; in all moments."

"I release being enslaved to the demons; in all moments."

"I recant all vows and agreements between myself and the demons; in all moments."

"I remove all blessings and curses between myself and the demons; in all moments."

"I sever all strings and cords between myself and the demons; in all moments."

"I break all chains between myself and the demons; in all moments."

"I dissolve all karmic ties between myself and the demons; in all moments."

"I remove all the fear, guilt, pain, burden, limitations, anger, greed, lust, jealousy and engrams that the demons have put on me; in all moments."

"I take back all the joy, love, abundance, freedom, health, success, security, companionship, peace, life, wholeness, beauty, enthusiasm, contentment, spirituality, enlightenment and confidence that the demons have taken from me; in all moments."

"I withdraw all my energy from the demons; in all moments."

"I collapse and disintegrate the demons into divine love; in all moments."

"I repair and fortify the Wei chi of all my bodies; in all moments."

"I align all my bodies; in all moments."

"I release resonating with the demons; in all moments."

"I release emanating with the demons; in all moments."

"I extract all the demons from my sound frequency and dissolve them into divine love; in all moments."

"I extract all the demons from my light body and dissolve them into divine love; in all moments."

"I shift my paradigm from the demons to joy, love, abundance, freedom, health, success, security, companionship, peace, life, wholeness, beauty, enthusiasm, contentment, spirituality, enlightenment and confidence; in all moments."

"I transcend the demons; in all moments."

"I am centered and empowered in divine love; in all moments."

"I remove and dissolve everything from my beingness that is not divine love; in all moments."

"I resonate and emanate divine love; in all moments."

Restore the Earth to Its Wonder

(Say each statement three times out loud while continuously tapping on the top of your head at the crown chakra and say it a fourth time while tapping on your chest.)

"I declare myself a surrogate for the Earth in doing these taps; in all moments."

"I release being energetically raped; in all moments."

"I release burning out of control; in all moments."

"I release being stripped of all resources; in all moments."

"I release being devoid of love; in all moments."

"I release struggling to maintain my balance; in all moments."

"I release letting all my inhabitants down; in all moments."

"I release being poisoned; in all moments."

"I release being plagued by power and dis-ease; in all moments."

"I release breaking out in rashes of war; in all moments."

"I release being drained of my life force; in all moments."

"I release being humiliated and abused; in all moments."

"I release being a scapegoat; in all moments."

"I release allowing my energy to be pissed away; in all moments."

"I take back all the energy that has been taken from me; in all moments."

"I repair all the layers of my auric field; in all moments."

"I release being enslaved; in all moments."

"I remove all curses and blessings that have been put on me; in all moments."

"I recant all vows and agreements between myself and being diminished; in all moments."

"I remove all vivaxes between myself and being diminished; in all moments."

"I remove all tentacles between myself and being diminished; in all moments."

"I remove the claws of control from my beingness; in all moments."

"I send all energy matrices into the light and sound that diminish me; in all moments."

"I sever all strings and cords between myself and being diminished; in all moments."

"I align all my bodies; in all moments."

"I dissolve all karmic ties between myself and being diminished; in all moments."

"I withdraw all my energy from being diminished; in all moments."

"I remove all the pain, burden, limitations, and illusion of separateness that being diminished has put on me; in all moments."

"I transcend being diminished; in all moments."

"I extract all of being diminished from both my sound frequency and light emanation; in all moments."

"I infuse joy, love, abundance, into both my sound frequency and light emanation; in all moments."

"I infuse freedom, peace, and wholeness into my sound frequency and light emanation; in all moments."

"I strip all illusion off of being diminished; in all moments."

"I remove all masks, walls, and armor from all those who diminish; in all moments."

"I put out all fires with divine love; in all moments."

"I drench myself with divine love; in all moments."

"I am centered, empowered, and saturated in divine love; in all moments."

"I hold my stance in divine love; in all moments."

"I repair and fortify my Wei chi; in all moments."

"I release hiding my empowerment; in all moments."

"I perpetuate my empowerment; in all moments."

"I maintain the charge of empowerment and divine love through my beingness; in all moments."

Desecrating Earth

(Say each statement three times out loud while continuously tapping on the top of your head and say it a fourth time while tapping on your chest.)

"I release desecrating Gaia; in all moments."

"I release condoning the desecrating of Gaia; in all moments."

"I release the trauma of my first life on earth; in all moments."

"I release treating the earth like a hostile world; in all moments."

"I release being stranded amongst the barbarians; in all moments."

"I release the trauma of being abandoned on a loveless world; in all moments."

"I release hating earth; in all moments."

"I release treating the earth like it's an evil stepmother; in all moments."

"I release desecrating the earth; in all moments."

"I release the devastating isolation of being left to inbreed amongst the barbarians; in all moments."

"I release mourning my home planet; in all moments."

"I release creating negative experiences to conjure up the vibration of my home planet; in all moments."

"I release mourning my tail; in all moments."

"I release feeling helpless without my tail; in all moments."

"I release waiting to be rescued; in all moments."

"I shift my paradigm from resenting earth to respecting and appreciating Gaia; in all moments."

"I heal all resentment of the earth with my love and respect for Gaia; in all moments."

"I heal the earth with my purity and sanctity of my love; in all moments."

"I am centered and empowered in my love and respect for Gaia; in all moments."

"I hold a loving intention for the wellbeing of earth and all its loving inhabitants; in all moments."

Earth Abusers

We can no longer watch from a distance as greed whittles away our quality of life on earth. The beast is at the door. If you are feeling sick inside as you watch greed and ignorance eat up natural resources then you owe it to your peace of mind to do these taps. We owe it to future generations.

You are empowered by the intention here. These taps are addressing a real threat at a deep energetic level. I was awakened from a deep slumber to write and share these. It is not too late. This is a way of finally stepping up to the plate in the comfort of your own home and making your intentions count for something. It doesn't matter if you don't believe they work, feel silly, are overwhelmed by the length or get confused. DO THESE TAPS.

Do just one or two if that is all you can do, but then come back to them. Play a game with yourself. Do one on each commercial of your favorite show. It is time you realize that you don't have the luxury of complacency. Beauty, trust, security, nature and hope will perhaps die unless you do these. Manifest your higher purpose. You can't afford to be complacent or wait for someone else to do something about it. IT IS UP TO YOU. This is your world.

(Say them out loud if you can and say them slowly. Don't run through them. Pause before the phrase, "in all moments." Say each statement three times while tapping on your head and say them a fourth time while tapping on your chest.)

"I declare myself a surrogate for the Earth and world inhabitants in doing these taps; in all moments."

"We gift all Earth Abusers with the sensitivities of an empath to know their every transgression; in all moments."

"We strip all denial off of the world in consuming fossil fuels; in all moments."

"We release allowing Earth Abusers to poison the planet; in all moments."

"We release allowing Earth Abusers to wield power; in all moments."

"We dissipate the systemic indifference that allows Earth Abusers to reign; in all moments."

"We release being pacified or lied to by Earth Abusers; in all moments."

"We remove all masks, walls, and armor from Earth Abusers; in all moments."

"We release the burden of being limited to Earth Abusers; in all moments."

"We release allowing Earth Abusers to maintain a position of the elite; in all moments."

"We release allowing Earth Abusers to poison the earth; in all moments."

"We release allowing Earth Abusers to take away our freedoms; in all moments."

"We release allowing Earth Abusers to segregate us into the haves and have-nots in all moments."

"We release allowing Earth Abusers to decide out worthiness; in all moments."

"We release allowing Earth Abusers to use us to feel powerful; in all moments."

"We release allowing Earth Abusers to play God with our personal freedoms; in all moments."

"We release passively watching while Earth Abusers hold the world hostage; in all moments."

"We release sitting by and watching Earth Abusers dismantle inalienable rights; in all moments."

"We strip all illusion off of Earth Abusers; in all moments."

"We give back to Earth Abusers all the transgressions they have inflicted upon others; in all moments."

"We release allowing Earth Abusers to profit in any financial way from raping the land; in all moments."

"We release allowing Earth Abusers to strip our quality of life; in all moments."

"We release being indifferent or apathetic to Earth Abusers; in all moments."

"We release allowing Earth Abusers to erode our sacred land; in all moments."

"We release being separated from our humanity by Earth Abusers; in all moments."

"We release allowing Earth Abusers to use us to continue to abuse the earth; in all moments."

"We release being manipulated by Earth Abusers; in all moments."

"We break up the cluster of power mongers that abuse the earth; in all moments."

"We release being ignorant to Earth Abusers; in all moments."

"We release Earth Abusers from being allowed to manipulate the masses; in all moments."

"We release denying our responsibilities in dealing with Earth Abusers; in all moments."

"We release denying our responsibility in caring for the Earth; in all moments."

"We release enabling Earth Abusers; in all moments."

"We release being stripped of our progressiveness by Earth Abusers; in all moments."

"We release being complacent with Earth Abusers; in all moments."

"We release diminishing ourselves to allow Earth Abusers the benefit of the doubt; in all moments."

"We release allowing Earth Abusers to fly under the radar; in all moments."

"We release ever empowering Earth Abusers in any way; in all moments."

"We eliminate the first cause in empowering Earth Abusers; in all moments."

"We release being swayed by Earth Abusers; in all moments."

"We release being bought off by Earth Abusers; in all moments."

"We stop the onslaught of power mucking done by Earth Abusers; in all moments."

"We strip all illusion and defenses off those who use Earth Abusers to control others; in all moments."

"We release converting our empowerment to loyalty to Earth Abusers; in all moments."

"We release being enslaved to Earth Abusers; in all moments."

"We release diminishing Earth to empower Earth Abusers; in all moments."

"We remove all vivaxes between Earth and all Earth Abusers; in all moments."

"We remove all tentacles between ourselves and all Earth Abusers; in all moments."

"We remove all our energy and support from all Earth Abusers; in all moments."

"We collapse and dissolve Earth Abusers' ability to minimize or diminish the Earth; in all moments."

"We remove all programming and conditioning that allow Earth Abusers to rape the Earth; in all moments."

"We remove all individual and universal engrams of Earth Abusers from the Earth; in all moments."

"We break all energy grids between Earth and all Earth abusers; in all moments."

"We release indulging Earth Abusers; in all moments."

"We release allowing Earth Abusers to rob us of our purity of home; in all moments."

"We release allowing Earth Abusers to diminish Earth; in all moments."

"We send all energy matrices into the light and sound that enable Earth Abusers; in all moments."

"We release allowing Earth Abusers to play victim; in all moments."

"We command all complex energy matrices that enable Earth Abusers to be escorted into the light and sound; in all moments."

"We send all energy matrices into the light and sound that allow Earth Abusers to abuse the Earth; in all moments."

"We command all complex energy matrices that allow Earth Abusers to abuse the Earth to be escorted into the light and sound; in all moments."

"We send all energy matrices into the light and sound that prevent us from dealing with Earth Abusers; in all moments."

"We command all complex energy matrices that prevent us from dealing with Earth Abusers to be escorted into the light and sound; in all moments."

"We release allowing Earth Abusers to use us to abuse the earth; in all moments."

"We recant all vows and agreements between the Earth and all Earth Abusers; in all moments."

"We remove all curses between the Earth and all Earth Abusers; in all moments."

"We remove all blessings between the Earth and all Earth Abusers; in all moments."

"We sever all strings, cords and wires between the Earth and Earth Abusers; in all moments."

"We dissolve all karmic ties between the Earth and Earth Abusers; in all moments."

"We remove all the pain, burden, limitations, fear, futility, unworthiness and illusion of separateness that Earth Abusers have put on the Earth; in all moments."

"We give back to Earth Abusers all the pain, burden, limitations, fear, futility, unworthiness and illusion of separateness that they have put on the Earth; in all moments."

"We take back all the joy, love, abundance, freedom, health, success, security, companionship, creativity, peace, life, wholeness, beauty, enthusiasm, contentment, spirituality, enlightenment, confidence, the ability to discern and empowerment that Earth Abusers have taken from Earth; in all moments."

"We strip Earth Abusers of all ignoble intentions; in all moments."

"We strip Earth Abusers of all illusions of grandeur; in all moments."

"We crumble all constructs mandated by Earth Abusers; in all moments."

"We nullify all contracts between the Earth and Earth Abusers; in all moments."

"We strip all illusion off of the mandates of Earth Abusers; in all moments."

"We eliminate the first cause in enabling Earth Abusers; in all moments."

"We hold an open portal for universal empowerment of Earth; in all moments."

"We hold an open portal for universal peace; in all moments."

"We hold an open portal for a clean Earth; in all moments."

"We release being locked in agreement with Earth Abusers; in all moments."

"We release the belief that Earth Abusers are empowered; in all moments."

We release Earth being raped by Earth Abusers; in all moments."

We relinquish the ruthless pursuit of Earth Abusers; in all moments."

We release Earth resonating or emanating with Earth Abusers; in all moments."

We extract all of Earth Abusers from the Earth's sound frequency; in all moments."

We extract all of Earth Abusers from the Earth's light emanation; in all moments."

We extract all of Earth Abusers from all 32 layers of the Earth's aura; in all moments."

We extract all of Earth Abusers from the Earth's whole beingness; in all moments."

We shift our paradigm from Earth Abusers to Universal individual empowerment and peace on Earth; in all moments."

We transcend all Earth Abusers; in all moments."

We are centered and committed to peace on Earth; in all moments."

We infuse peace on Earth into our sound frequency; in all moments."

We imbue peace on Earth into our light emanation; in all moments."

We resonate, emanate and are interconnected to all life in peace on Earth; in all moments."

Eating Disorders

A client came to me recently. She was distraught about being told she needed a root canal. She really didn't want to get one. She started to tell me that the issue started when she was younger and she would purge. I immediately felt the pain and shame she was holding.

There are two different energetic experiences happening with eating disorders. When someone purges, there is so much incredible pain inside of them that there is no room for anything else. When someone is purging, they are trying to extract the pain. I have had many clients who have not had eating disorders but still have dreams or inner experiences of throwing up thick ugly tar like substance after their private session. They are purging their own pain.

The other experience with eating disorders is that there is a huge abyss within the person that they are trying to plug up with food. Sometimes they will also use other things to try to plug it up like drugs, alcohol, shopping, smoking or people. When people can't be alone with themselves and need to find something to entertain them, that is sometimes a sign that they are feeding a void.

With this particular client, I got the image of her baby teeth. I was shown that the pain we were releasing for her was stored in her physical body in her first molars. When I told her this, she confirmed that molestation started when she was three years old. As a baby, she processed the emotional pain of being molested into the physical pain of cutting her first molars. This is how emotional pain and physical pain became tangled and confused within her.

I led her through the following taps. After doing the first one, she felt incredibly lighter. After doing a few of them, she cried out joyfully saying that she didn't need a root canal at all. She felt the intense experience lift from her. For her, the thought of having a root canal was triggering the experience of being molested. This is part of what was released in her session.

(Say each statement three times while tapping on your head and say it a fourth time while tapping on your chest.)

"I release feeding the pain; in all moments."

"I remove the pain; in all moments."

"I recant all vows and agreements between myself and the pain; in all moments."

"I remove all curses between myself and the pain; in all moments."

"I dissolve all karmic ties between myself and the pain; in all moments."

"I remove all the shame, burden and limitations that pain has put on me; in all moments."

"I withdraw all my energy from the pain; in all moments."

"I take back all the joy, love, abundance, freedom, health, success, security, companionship, peace, life and wholeness that the pain has taken from me; in all moments."

"I release resonating with the pain; in all moments."

"I release emanating with the pain; in all moments."

"I remove all the pain from my sound frequency; in all moments."

"I remove all the pain from my light body; in all moments."

"I shift my paradigm from pain to joy, love, abundance, freedom, health, success, security, companionship, peace, life and wholeness that the pain has taken from me; in all moments."

"I am centered and empowered in divine love; in all moments."

If you purge, you are going to want to do these. If you binge or indulge in excesses, you are going to want to go through the whole list a second time and switch out the word "void" for "pain." And if you are really feeling freed up from this exercise, you may want to do it a third time and put the word "shame" where the word "pain" is used.

An Aversion to Eating

Some people have an aversion to eating. I have uncovered a few of the reasons in my private remote sessions. One of my clients was a food tester for royalty and was poisoned to death. One client's spouse put rat poison in their food and died miserably. One client had to eat rotten food in squalor to survive. Another client starved to death with a whole group of people, so she felt guilty about eating anything at all.

Our body image is so skewed because we are more than a physical body. We have an astral body that is very similar to the physical. Some people can get a sense of it when they look at themselves. You know how there are times when you look in the mirror and you just look so beautiful? This is you seeing the energetic light and love just pouring through yourself. When you look in the mirror and you look distorted or big, you are looking at your astral body and believing it is your physical body. You can do this because you are looking at yourself through your astral eyes.

I know someone who felt so vulnerable in group settings that as a little girl, she made herself really huge just so she could be seen. She ended up manifesting a huge physical body for herself. It was not quite the effect that she'd hoped for since the huge presence made her even more invisible to attention.

The body is fluid like a river in the sense that it changes continuously depending on the thoughts and feelings fed to it. If people could realize that they do more good in the world and for themselves by simply changing their thoughts, we would truly have a grassroots revolution.

Here are some taps for people who have an aversion to eating: (Say each statement three times out loud while continuously tapping on the top of your head at the crown chakra and say it a fourth time while tapping on your chest.)

"I release the fear and trauma of being poisoned; in all moments."

"I release the pain and anguish of being poisoned to death; in all moments."

"I release the trauma of having to survive on squalor; in all moments."

"I release the disgust of eating rotting garbage; in all moments."

"I release the guilt of eating when so many have gone hungry; in all moments."

"I release trying to starve myself out; in all moments."

"I release hating food; in all moments."

"I release hating myself; in all moments."

"I release punishing myself; in all moments."

"I release wanting to disappear; in all moments."

"I release trying to starve myself out; in all moments."

"I release trying to punish others by starving; in all moments."

"I release using starving myself to communicate my pain; in all moments."

"I release feeling out of control; in all moments."

"I release being starved for attention; in all moments."

"I release being starved to be heard; in all moments."

"I recant my vow of martyrdom; in all moments."

"I release being a martyr; in all moments."

"I release mourning a past life; in all moments."

"I release feeling trapped in an experience; in all moments."

"I release using physical and emotional drama to stand out; in all moments."

"I release starving to be validated; in all moments."

There are so many varying factors to why we do what we do. May these taps give people a clue as to what motivates them on a subliminal level.

The Ego Is What Creates All Unhappiness

(Say each statement three times while tapping on your head and say it a fourth time while tapping on your chest.)

"I release being browbeaten by the ego; in all moments."

"I release being led around by the ego; in all moments."

"I shatter all glass ceilings of the ego; in all moments."

"I release confusing the mechanical workings of the ego with my own empowered sheen; in all moments."

"I release enjoying the trappings of the ego; in all moments."

"I release being betrayed by the ego; in all moments."

"I release deferring to the ego; in all moments."

"I nullify all contracts with the ego; in all moments."

"I eliminate the first cause in enabling the ego; in all moments."

"I release being subjugated by the ego; in all moments."

"I remove all shackles of the ego; in all moments."

"I release worshiping the ego; in all moments."

"I release confusing the ego for God; in all moments."

"I release donning unworthiness to honor God; in all moments."

"I release the belief that God wants me subjugated; in all moments."

"I transcend the ego; in all moments."

"I am centered and empowered in transcending the ego; in all moments."

"I resonate, emanate, and am interconnected with all life in transcending the ego; in all moments."

Energetic Ponzi Schemes

All of society is paralyzed in layers and layers of Ponzi schemes. Everything that puts a label on us is a form of a Ponzi scheme. They are things that not only do we unwittingly give all our energy to, we are also saddled with the issues of the members of that group as well. We give all of ourselves to these groups and they saddle us with the burden of responsibility. All we receive back is the mere minimum to keep us complacent.

We see this reflected in our schools, government, monetary system and even our mental concept of God. Even our sexuality has the dynamic of a Ponzi scheme where the prettier ones get more accolades and the wallflowers are diminished. So many people bow out of their family responsibility, jobs and even society as an innate compulsion to free themselves of the Ponzi schemes that are breaking the spirit of their individuality.

Doing this exercise is an easier way to free ourselves than bowing out of society. (Say each statement three times out loud while continuously tapping on the top of your head at the crown chakra and say it a fourth time while tapping on your chest.)

"We declare ourselves surrogates for all Souls in doing these taps; in all moments."

"We release being vested in Ponzi schemes; in all moments."

"We release being bonded to lies by Ponzi schemes; in all moments."

"We release converting sacred intentions to Ponzi schemes; in all moments."

"We remove all the torture that Ponzi schemes have put on us; in all moments."

"We release being entrenched in Ponzi schemes; in all moments."

"We release starting new Ponzi schemes; in all moments."

Jen Ward

"We remove all vivaxes between ourselves and all Ponzi schemes; in all moments."

"We remove all tentacles between ourselves and all Ponzi schemes; in all moments."

"We release being subjugated by any Ponzi scheme; in all moments."

"We remove the hands of all Ponzi schemes from our beingness; in all moments."

"We remove all programming and conditioning that all Ponzi schemes have put on us; in all moments."

"We remove all engrams of all Ponzi schemes; in all moments."

"We release being coerced back into Ponzi schemes; in all moments."

"We nullify all contracts with all Ponzi schemes; in all moments."

"We withdraw all our energy from all Ponzi schemes; in all moments."

"We collapse and dissolve all Ponzi schemes; in all moments."

"We send all energy matrices of all Ponzi schemes into the light and sound; in all moments."

"We command all complex energy matrices of all Ponzi schemes to be escorted into the light and sound; in all moments."

"We strip all illusion off of all Ponzi schemes; in all moments."

"We remove all masks, walls, and armor off of all Ponzi schemes; in all moments."

"We release healing Ponzi schemes with fear and doubt; in all moments."

"We recant all vows and agreements between ourselves and all Ponzi schemes; in all moments."

"We release all loyalty to all Ponzi schemes; in all moments."

"We remove all curses between ourselves and all Ponzi schemes; in all moments."

"We remove all blessings between ourselves and all Ponzi schemes; in all moments."

"We sever all strings, cords, and wires between ourselves and all Ponzi schemes; in all moments."

"We dissolve all karmic ties between ourselves and all Ponzi schemes; in all moments."

"We eliminate the first cause in regards to all Ponzi schemes; in all moments."

"We eliminate the first cause in regards to each Ponzi scheme; in all moments."

"We remove all the pain, burden and limitations that all Ponzi schemes have put on us and all others; in all moments."

"We remove all the fear, futility and unworthiness that all Ponzi schemes have put on us and all others; in all moments."

"We remove all apathy, indifference and denial that all Ponzi schemes have put on us and all others; in all moments."

"We remove all shackles and illusion of separateness that all Ponzi schemes have put on us and all others; in all moments."

"We take back ALL that all Ponzi schemes have taken from us and all others; in all moments."

102

"We give back to all others all that all Ponzi schemes have taken from them; in all moments."

"We release resonating with all Ponzi schemes; in all moments."

"We release emanating with all Ponzi schemes; in all moments."

"We extract all Ponzi schemes from our sound frequency and the universal sound frequency; in all moments."

"We extract all Ponzi schemes from our light emanation and the universal light emanation; in all moments."

"We extract all Ponzi schemes from our whole beingness and the whole universe; in all moments."

"We shift our paradigm from all Ponzi schemes to universal exponential joy, love, abundance and freedom; in all moments."

"We transcend all Ponzi schemes; in all moments."

"We are centered and empowered in universal exponential joy, love, abundance and freedom; in all moments."

"We resonate, emanate, and are interconnected with all souls in universal, exponential joy, love, abundance and freedom; in all moments."

Energetic Vitamin

Do you know why affirmations don't always work? Because as one says the affirmation, the mind is going a mile a minute reminding them of all the instances of the opposite. For example, if someone uses the affirmation, "I am abundant," the mind will remind itself of all the bills and problems to refute the affirmation.

A way to bypass the mind's discernment is to not deal with the issues as if you are dealing with the physical body. The mind only controls what it understands. In metaphysical terms, we are not a solid form. We are a frequency of sound and an emanation of light. The mind does not know how to refute when we work in light and sound. It is above its pay scale.

These taps are meant to add to the quality of your essence without the mind knowing how to negate it. Enjoy these. These are like taking a positive vitamin and gushing it right into your energy field. These taps you can do daily.

(Say each statement three times out loud while tapping on your head and say it a fourth time while tapping on your chest.)

"I resonate with joy, love, abundance, freedom, health, success, security, companionship, creativity, peace, life, wholeness, beauty, enthusiasm, contentment and confidence; in all moments."

"I emanate with joy, love, abundance, freedom, health, success, security, companionship, creativity, peace, life, wholeness, beauty, enthusiasm, contentment and confidence; in all moments."

"I infuse joy, love, abundance, freedom, health, success, security, companionship, creativity, peace, life, wholeness, beauty, enthusiasm, contentment and confidence into my sound frequency; in all moments."

"I imbue joy, love, abundance, freedom, health, success, security, companionship, creativity, peace, life, wholeness, beauty, enthusiasm, contentment and confidence into my light body; in all moments."

Print these out. Keep them in your wallet. Post them on your wall. Start your day with them. Do them before you go to a meeting. Do them before you go to a family event. Make them a daily routine. Do them as a sacred prayer to honor yourself because you are worthy, and you deserve to realize that you are already all of these.

Energy Drained

(Say each statement three times out loud while continuously tapping on the top of your head and say it a fourth time while tapping on your chest.)

"I release being drained of my energy; in all moments."

"I release giving up my life force willingly; in all moments."

"I release the belief that empowerment is futile; in all moments."

"I release being manipulated out of my energy; in all moments."

"I release exchanging my energy for a mere stroke of the ego; in all moments."

"I release giving up my energy to be in complacency; in all moments."

"I release choosing complacency over empowerment; in all moments."

"I dry up the connection between myself and all the sources that drain me; in all moments."

"I take back all my energy from all the sources that have drained me; in all moments."

"I release being susceptible to those who feed off me; in all moments."

"I release giving away my energy; in all moments."

"I release martyring myself; in all moments."

"I strip all illusion off of all sources that drain energy; in all moments."

"I release being a helpless muse; in all moments."

"I shift my paradigm from being a helpless muse to being empowered and aware; in all moments."

"I am centered and empowered in being empowered and aware; in all moments."

Repairing One's Energy Field

In a client's first session, I usually assist them in repairing their energy field. The outer edge of one's energy field has a protective "skin" that contains one's electromagnetic charge. Many people have their outer layer ripped open or even shredded due to trauma.

When this occurs, their energy is not contained and it dissipates. To me, they feel like a deflated mylar balloon. Someone with a broken wei chi may feel uncomfortable when people are standing close and may feel ineffective in certain ways. Someone whose wei chi is in tact may have a more dynamic presence.

Here are a couple of taps to fix one's energy field. If someone is sensitive to feeling their energy, they may get a sense of feeling filled or grounded shortly afterwards. (Say each statement three times while tapping your head and say it a fourth time while tapping the chest)

"I repair and fortify the wei chi of all my bodies; in all moments."

"I repair and heal all 32 layers of my auric field; in all moments."

"I align all my bodies; in all moments."

"I am centered in divine love; in all moments."

I recently facilitated a session with a client whose wei chi I had helped repair in a previous session. It felt compromised again. It only took asking them a couple questions to realize why. They had smoked weed since our last session. People think there is no consequence to recreational drugs, but they do break the integrity of the energy field leaving people susceptible and more easily influenced.

Energy Grids

(Say each statement three times while tapping on your head and say it a fourth time while tapping on your chest.)

"I declare myself a surrogate for all the inhabitants of the world in doing these taps; in all moments."

"I break all energy grids between myself and war; in all moments."

"I free humanity of all power grids of war; in all moments."

"I break all energy grids between myself and poverty; in all moments."

"I free humanity of all power grids of poverty; in all moments."

"I break all energy grids between myself and slavery; in all moments."

"I free humanity of all power grids of slavery; in all moments."

"I break all energy grids between myself and lack; in all moments."

"I free humanity of all power grids of lack; in all moments."

"I break all energy grids between myself and fossil fuels; in all moments."

"I free humanity of all power grids of fossil fuels; in all moments."

"I break all energy grids between myself and ignorance; in all moments."

"I free humanity of all power grids of ignorance; in all moments."

"I break all energy grids between myself and power; in all moments."

"I free humanity of all power grids of power; in all moments."

"I break all energy grids between myself and power mongers; in all moments."

"I free humanity of all power grids of power mongers; in all moments."

"I break all energy grids between myself and pollution; in all moments."

"I free humanity of all power grids of pollution; in all moments."

"I break all energy grids between myself and cultural clash; in all moments."

"I free humanity of all power grids of cultural clash; in all moments."

"I break all energy grids between myself and unworthiness; in all moments."

"I free humanity of all power grids of unworthiness; in all moments."

"I break all energy grids between myself and worship of monetary wealth; in all moments."

"I free humanity of all power grids of worship of monetary wealth; in all moments."

"I break all energy grids between myself and apathy; in all moments."

"I free humanity of all power grids of apathy; in all moments."

"I break all energy grids between myself and linear existence; in all moments."

"I free humanity of all power grids of linear existence; in all moments."

"I break all energy grids between myself and third dimensional limitations; in all moments."

"I free humanity of all power grids of third dimensional limitations; in all moments."

"I break all energy grids between myself and inequality; in all moments."

"I free humanity of all power grids of inequality; in all moments."

"I break all energy grids between myself and arrogance; in all moments."

"I free humanity of all power grids of arrogance; in all moments."

"I break all energy grids between myself and illusion; in all moments."

"I free humanity of all power grids of illusion; in all moments."

"I break all energy grids between myself and limitations; in all moments."

"I free humanity of all power grids of limitations; in all moments."

"I break all energy grids between myself and illness; in all moments."

"I free humanity of all power grids of illness; in all moments."

"I break all energy grids between myself and degeneration; in all moments."

"I free humanity of all power grids of degeneration; in all moments."

"I break all energy grids between myself and crime; in all moments."

"I free humanity of all power grids of crime; in all moments."

"I break all energy grids between myself and addiction; in all moments."

"I free humanity of all power grids of addiction; in all moments."

"I break all energy grids between myself and primal mode; in all moments."

"I free humanity of all power grids of primal mode; in all moments."

"I break all energy grids between myself and big business; in all moments."

"I free humanity of all power grids of big business; in all moments."

"I break all energy grids between myself and control; in all moments."

"I free humanity of all power grids of control; in all moments."

Energy Vampires

Energy vampires are more prevalent than just the people who hold us hostage by making us listen to their problems. They are the situations that we get caught up in and feel helpless to control. They are long meetings, long-winded bosses, people who move very slowly and deliberately in line because they feel validated on some level by holding us up. They are those individuals who so painstakingly want a bit of our attention but don't seem to be aware enough or able to reciprocate.

They are the long phone calls, the barrage of businesses savvy at getting our attention, they are the misguided well-doers that want to make certain we do what is morally right in their minds. They are also those who know how to pull at our heartstrings and simply anyone or anything that leaves us feeling a little depleted or less fulfilled. Who hasn't gone out shopping and come home just exhausted beyond all rationale? Who hasn't wanted to donate to a cause and felt like they lost a little piece of themselves in the process?

It's time to get all your energy back and put yourself together.

I know the tendency is to do the ones that sound interesting. But this is a whole protocol that works to comb through all aspects of the issue. Simply doing the ones you like is not as effective as doing them all. The mind has many ways to sabotage.

(Say each statement three times while tapping on your head and say it a fourth time while tapping on your chest.)

"I release being energetically raped; in all moments."

"I release energetically raping others; in all moments."

"I release being an energy vampire; in all moments."

"I release falling prey to energy vampires; in all moments."

"I release being at the mercy of energy vampires; in all moments."

"I release the fear of saying no; in all moments."

"I release the fear of offending; in all moments."

"I release the need to keep up appearances; in all moments."

"I see through the facade of all energy vampires; in all moments."

"I recant all vows and agreements between myself and all energy vampires; in all moments."

"I remove all curses between myself and all energy vampires; in all moments."

"I dissolve all karmic ties between myself and all energy vampires; in all moments."

"I remove all the pain, burden, limitations and weakness that all energy vampires have put on me; in all moments."

"I remove all the pain, burden, limitations and weakness I have put on all others as an energy vampire; in all moments."

"I take back all the joy, love, abundance, freedom, health, success, security, companionship, creativity, peace, life, wholeness and enthusiasm that all energy vampires have taken from me; in all moments."

"I withdraw all my energy from all energy vampires; in all moments."

"I give back all that I have taken from all others as an energy vampire; in all moments."

"I repair and fortify my Wei chi; in all moments."

"I remove all energy vampires from my sound frequency; in all moments."

"I remove all energy vampires from my light body; in all moments."

"I release resonating with energy vampires; in all moments."

"I release emanating with energy vampires; in all moments."

"I shift my paradigm from all energy vampires to joy, love, abundance, freedom, life, wholeness and enthusiasm; in all moments."

"I am centered and empowered in divine light, love, sound, healing, health, joy, beauty, abundance, freedom and enthusiasm; in all moments."

There are so many who are naive to the energetic interactions at play in life. That is okay. Some things are best left NOT scrutinized. But here is a golden opportunity to stay pleasantly ignorant of the ugly underbelly of society while still benefiting from the efforts of others. This is a great opportunity. May many see it as such and feel the shift in their level of energy.

Your Energetic Flu Shot

(Say each statement three times out loud while continuously tapping on the top of your head at the crown chakra and say it a fourth time while tapping on your heart chakra.)

"I release being susceptible to getting the flu; in all moments."

"I release allowing my will to be worn down; in all moments."

"I release the belief that getting the flu is inevitable; in all moments."

"I release being in agreement with getting the flu; in all moments."

"I release getting the flu so that I can take a break; in all moments."

"I release needing to get the flu to nurture myself; in all moments."

"I release using the flu to create a sense of connectedness with others; in all moments."

"I release listening to the promotions of the flu; in all moments."

"I release empowering sickness by getting the flu; in all moments."

"I release getting the flu as an excuse; in all moments."

"I release feeling validated by getting the flu; in all moments."

"I validate, nurture and encourage my white blood cells; in all moments."

"I validate, nurture and encourage every cell of my beingness; in all moments."

"I am centered and empowered in refusing the flu; in all moments."

"I am centered and empowered in optimal health; in all moments."

"I infuse optimal health into my sound frequency; in all moments."

"I imbue optimal health into my light body; in all moments."

"I resonate and emanate optimal health; in all moments."

Release Being an Energy Generator for Others

There are many people who perceive beyond the physical limitations of what is considered the norm. They may not even be able to articulate it. But they know that something exists beyond the illusion of this world. It may feel uncomfortable and foreboding. Because there is no way to convey what they are experiencing in this reality, they are deemed crazy. They may keep such awareness to themselves as a means to blend and NOT be considered crazy.

For those who deal with this private hell, I understand. You are not crazy. You are just toggling one or two realities at the same time. It is not your fault and you are not wrong. Please do this exercise and see if it brings comfort. I see you here and in all dimensions. You are the warriors and the great minds that you believe yourselves to be. It is just not showing up in this reality yet.

Be patient with others. They are doing their best to deal with their own issues that they can't totally grasp. Denying other realities and greater truths seems to be their coping mechanism. Have patience with them and hold on to your truth. As distorted and perverted as it is perceived here, it has value. You have value. You matter.

(Say each statement three times out loud while continuously tapping on the top of your head at the crown chakra and say it a fourth time while tapping on your chest.)

"I declare myself a surrogate for all beings in all dimensions and realities in doing these taps; in all moments."

"We release being bred to be an energy generator; in all moments."

"We release being enslaved to being energy generators; in all moments."

"We release being raped of our individuality; in all moments."

"We release the fear of the horizon beyond being an energy generator; in all moments."

"We release the fear of our own freedom; in all moments."

"We release confusing being an energy generator with security; in all moments."

"We release buying false security with our energy; in all moments."

"We remove all vivaxes between ourselves and being an energy generator; in all moments."

"We remove all tentacles between ourselves and being an energy generator; in all moments."

"We remove the claws of being an energy generator from our beingness; in all moments."

"We remove all programming and conditioning that being an energy generator has put on us; in all moments."

"We remove all engrams that being an energy generator has put on us; in all moments."

"We remove all the illusion that being an energy generator has put on us; in all moments."

"We shatter all glass ceilings that being an energy generator has put on us; in all moments."

"We send all energy matrices into the light and sound that support us being an energy generator; in all moments."

"We command all complex energy matrices that propagate us being energy generators to be escorted into the light and sound; in all moments."

"We recant all vows and agreements between ourselves and being an energy generator; in all moments."

"We remove all curses between ourselves and being an energy generator; in all moments."

"We remove all blessings between ourselves and being an energy generator; in all moments."

"We sever all strings, cords and wires between ourselves and being an energy generator; in all moments."

"We dissolve all karmic ties between ourselves and being an energy generator; in all moments."

"We remove all the pain, burden, limitations and illusion of separateness that being energy generators has put on us; in all moments."

"We remove all the fear, futility and unworthiness that being an energy generator has put on us; in all moments."

"We take back all that being an energy generator has taken from us; in all moments."

"We withdraw all our energy from being an energy generator; in all moments."

"We strip all illusion off of being an energy generator; in all moments."

"We remove all masks, walls and armor from being an energy generator; in all moments."

"We close and dissolve all portals, wormholes and passageways between ourselves and being an energy generator; in all moments."

"We collapse and dissolve being energy generators; in all moments."

"We release resonating with being energy generators; in all moments."

"We release emanating with being energy generators; in all moments."

"We extract all of being energy generators from our sound frequency; in all moments."

"We extract all of being energy generators from our light emanation; in all moments."

"We extract all of being energy generators from our whole beingness; in all moments."

"We shift our paradigm from being energy generators to exponential freedom; in all moments."

"We transcend being energy generators; in all moments."

"We are centered and empowered in exponential freedom; in all moments."

"We infuse exponential joy, love, abundance, freedom, and wholeness into our sound frequency; in all moments."

"We infuse exponential joy, love, abundance, freedom and wholeness into our light emanation; in all moments."

The Energetic Cleanse

Think of something that annoys you or you have been obsessing over. It can be a job, person, task, relationship, global issue or a habit. After you name the issue, say each statement out loud three times while tapping on the top of your head, and say it a fourth time while tapping on your chest.

"All engrams of _____ are removed; in all moments."

"All vivaxes with _____ are removed; in all moments."

"All tentacles of _____ are removed; in all moments."

"All my energy is withdrawn from _____; in all moments."

"All dependency on _____ is released; in all moments."

"Feeling beholden to _____ is eliminated; in all moments."

"All vows and agreements with_____ are recanted; in all moments."

"All contracts with_____ are nullified; in all moments."

"All curses with _____ are removed; in all moments."

"All blessing with _____ are removed; in all moments."

"All strings and cords with _____ are severed; in all moments."

"All karmic ties with _____ are dissolved; in all moments."

"All the pain, burden, limitations and engrams that _____ has inflicted are removed; in all moments."

"All the pain, burden, limitations and engrams that have been caused due to _____ are removed; in all moments."

"All that was taken from _____ is returned; in all moments."

"All the joy, love, abundance, freedom, health, success, security, companionship, creativity, peace, life, wholeness, beauty, enthusiasm, contentment, spirituality, enlightenment, and confidence that _____ has taken is returned; in all moments."

"Resonating with _____ is released; in all moments."

"Emanating with _____ is released; in all moments."

"All of _____ is removed from my sound frequency; in all moments."

"All of _____ is removed from my light emanation; in all moments."

"My paradigm is shifted from _____ to Joy, Love, Abundance, Freedom, Health, Success, Security, Companionship, Creativity, Peace, Life, Wholeness, Beauty, Enthusiasm, Contentment, Spirituality, Enlightenment, and Confidence; in all moments."

"All illusion is stripped from _____; in all moments."

"The first cause of enabling _____ is eliminated; in all moments."

"All masks, walls and armor are removed from _____; in all moments."

"All masks, walls, and armor that were implemented due to _____ are removed; in all moments."

"All energy matrixes of _____ are sent into the Light and Sound; in all moments."

"All complex energy matrices of _____ are escorted into the Light and Sound; in all moments."

"All portals to _____ are collapsed and dissolved; in all moments."

"All of _____ is transcended; in all moments."

"The Wei Chi of all bodies is repaired; in all moments."

"All bodies are aligned; in all moments."

"All are centered and empowered in Divine Love; in all moments."

Cleaning the Slate of All Old Engrams

Most people don't realize it, but we are not existing in the third dimension anymore. We have transcended to the fifth dimension. We did so without much fanfare or the need for a mass exodus by souls who aren't able to handle the shift. They are being coddled in a way because they were allowed to bring their baggage from the lower states of consciousness with them until they are able to let go of it on their own. It is much kinder this way than to have it ripped away in a stringent upgrade.

There is evidence of the shift in consciousness in subtle ways. Fear, war and power plays aren't able to sweep people up as they once did. Sure we are being given a great show of posturing, but humans don't have the stomach for war in the fifth dimension. Kindness and thoughtfulness are starting to prevail and people are starting to think for themselves once again. We can now see more clearly behind ignoble intentions without being duped.

The biggest shift though is the ability to manifest great, wonderful things with intentions. That is why what I do in shifting people is so effortless and drastic. It is because I am actually just removing the illusions that humans hold as a crutch until they get used to the vibration of the fifth dimension.

Everyone is at a greater state of consciousness than they realize. They are just being shifted slowly so as not to shock their system. It is like easing your toe into the water to get used to the temperature as opposed to diving in.

People have brought all their ideas, concepts and even archaic beliefs to the fifth dimension like a security blanket until they feel comfortable giving them up. The thing is they don't realize it because they have also brought the controlling elements of their comfort items as well.

A client who does the tapping exercises religiously had a dream experience to illustrate what is happening. In the inner worlds, she was driving really fast and efficiently. (This represents her ability to accept the freedom of the fifth dimension.) Everywhere she drove she had to zip around all people's belongings that were strewn in the street. (This is their personal baggage they brought with them.) It didn't slow her down and everyone was pleasant enough, but the belongings did block the streets.

She was then stopped by the police. They accused her of having a weapon. She had a smooth oval object in her hand but it was not a gun. They tried to arrest her but she argued for her rights. They did confiscate the object though. When she got to the police station to retrieve it, she opened it up and it had essential oils inside.

The oval object represented truth. The police were the old engrams of fear and intimidation that were universally established. People hadn't only brought their personal baggage with them to the fifth dimension. They had also brought universal concepts that were really limiting. Our old ways of demonizing others are an illusion and very tiresome for those who of us who have outgrown them. But these universal engrams need to be dissipated by the collective for all to be free.

I had a similar experience of being demonized last night. I was awakened to the authorities asking about me. They used an old name I used to go by and put the word "dead" on the end. There was mass confusion out in the street. People were being released from their old state of consciousness. They were becoming free of third dimension limitations. But it was not presented that way. "Officials" were talking loud and implying that it was a bad accident and it was my fault. No one would charge me or say it to me, but they made a point of having everyone believe I was guilty of causing a horrendous crime. They used innuendos, implications and indirect comments to intimidate.

This plays out in my daily life. As careful and as kind as I can be watching my thoughts and intentions, I am still disliked by many and demonized in an ethereal way. It is the way it always has been for those who hold the intention of freeing humanity in any subtle way.

Many of you may see this happen in your own life. Don't fall for it. Here's to dealing with those old collective engrams and finally eliminating them. They are made of old consciousness, fear and ignoble intentions. It's time to dissipate them so that humanity can enjoy the pristine purity and freedom of the fifth dimension.

(Say each statement three times while tapping on your head and say it a fourth time while tapping on your chest. Then go on to the next.)

"I declare myself a surrogate for the collective in doing these taps; in all moments."

"We strip all denial off of the world in immersing itself in old engrams; in all moments."

"We release allowing engrams to enslave humanity; in all moments."

"We dissipate the dark psychic energy that uses engrams to enslave the world; in all moments."

"We remove all masks, walls, and armor off engrams; in all moments."

"We expose all power mongers who use engrams to limit humanity; in all moments."

"We release allowing old engrams to exist; in all moments."

"We release allowing old engrams to strip society of its humanity; in all moments."

"We protect all individuals from being swallowed up in old engrams; in all moments."

"We stop old engrams from pimping out humanity; in all moments."

"We stop engrams from lining the pockets of the power mongers; in all moments."

"We stop engrams from seeming legit; in all moments."

"We release allowing engrams to squelch our freedom; in all moments."

"We release passively watching while engrams flourish in the fifth dimension; in all moments."

"We strip all illusion off of all engrams; in all moments."

"We release being duped by engrams; in all moments."

"We release being separated from our humanity by old engrams; in all moments."

"We release being manipulated by engrams; in all moments."

"We release deferring to engrams; in all moments."

"We release allowing engrams to frame our perception of reality; in all moments."

"We release allowing engrams to shove an agenda down our throat; in all moments."

"We dissolve all engrams of greed and deceit; in all moments."

"We release being kept ignorant to engrams; in all moments."

"We release adulating engrams; in all moments."

"We release endorsing engrams; in all moments."

"We release being stripped of our freedom by engrams; in all moments."

"We release having our individuality diminished by engrams; in all moments."

"We release being complacent in perceiving engrams; in all moments."

"We release having our humanity gutted by engrams; in all moments."

"We release being squelched into a hellish existence by engrams; in all moments."

"We eliminate the first cause in the creation or mandating of engrams; in all moments."

"We release all psychic energies of engrams; in all moments."

"We strip all illusion and defenses off those who manipulate using engrams; in all moments."

"We release converting our sacred devotion to Source into deference to engrams; in all moments."

"We release being enslaved to engrams; in all moments."

"We release diminishing ourselves by allowing engrams to exist; in all moments."

"We remove all vivaxes between ourselves and all engrams; in all moments."

"We remove all tentacles between ourselves and all engrams; in all moments."

"We withdraw all our energy from all engrams; in all moments."

"We release being naïve to engrams; in all moments."

"We collapse and dissolve all engrams; in all moments."

"We remove all programming and conditioning that engrams have put on us; in all moments."

"We remove all individual and universal engrams from our whole beingness; in all moments."

"We remove all controlling devices that engrams have put on us; in all moments."

"We release allowing engrams to induce us to fear or hatred; in all moments."

"We release allowing engrams to rob us of our voice, dignity or freedom; in all moments."

"We release the belief that engrams are inevitable; in all moments."

"We send all energy matrices into the light and sound that formulate or enable engrams; in all moments."

"We command all complex energy matrices that formulate or enable engrams to be escorted into the light and sound; in all moments."

"We send all energy matrices into the light and sound that make engrams; in all moments."

"We command all complex energy matrices that make up engrams to be escorted into the light and sound; in all moments."

"We send all energy matrices into the light and sound that perpetuate the ignoble intentions of engrams; in all moments."

"We command all complex energy matrices that perpetuate the ignoble intentions of engrams to be escorted into the light and sound; in all moments."

"We release being deceived by engrams; in all moments."

"We nullify all contacts with all engrams; in all moments."

"We recant all vows and agreements between ourselves and all engrams; in all moments."

"We remove all curses between ourselves and all engrams; in all moments."

"We remove all curses that engrams have put on the world; in all moments."

"We remove all blessings between ourselves and all engrams; in all moments."

"We remove all payoffs to perpetrating engrams; in all moments."

"We sever all strings, cords and psychic connection between ourselves and all engrams; in all moments."

"We sever all strings, cords and psychic connection between ourselves all those who support engrams; in all moments."

"We dissipate all psychic streams of energy that allow engrams to go unchecked; in all moments."

"We dissolve all karmic ties between ourselves and all engrams; in all moments."

"We remove all the pain, burden, limitations, fear, futility, unworthiness, anger, abandonment, rejection and illusion of separateness that all engrams have put on us; in all moments."

"We bury all engrams in the weight of their own ignoble intentions; in all moments."

"We paralyze the machine that mandates engrams; in all moments."

"We remove all muscle memory of all engrams; in all moments."

"We break all energy grids between ourselves and all engrams; in all moments."

"We take back all the joy, love, abundance, freedom, health, success, security, companionship, creativity, peace, life, wholeness, beauty, enthusiasm, contentment, spirituality, enlightenment, confidence, the ability to discern, individuality and empowerment that all engrams have taken from us; in all moments."

"We disarm the ability of engrams to desecrate humanity; in all moments."

"We disarm the ability of all engrams to enslave humanity; in all moments."

"We disarm the ability of all engrams to immerse us in lower consciousness; in all moments."

"We strip all engrams of their illusion; in all moments."

"We strip all engrams of their authority; in all moments."

"We disarm all engrams from the ability to dwindle our quality of life; in all moments."

"We eliminate the first cause in engrams tainting civil liberties; in all moments."

"We crumble and dissolve all constructs created by engrams; in all moments."

"We nullify all contracts with the constructs of engrams; in all moments."

"We strip all illusion off those who benefit from engrams; in all moments."

"We eliminate the first cause in all the mandates of engrams; in all moments."

"We hold open all portals for higher consciousness and Universal freedom in all; in all moments."

"We release confusing old engrams with truth; in all moments."

"We release confusing engrams as an inevitable solution; in all moments."

"We release resonating or emanating with old engrams; in all moments."

"We extract all engrams from our individual and universal sound frequency; in all moments."

"We extract all engrams from our individual and universal light emanation; in all moments."

"We extract all engrams from all 32 layers of our individual and universal aura; in all moments."

"We extract all engrams from our whole beingness; in all moments."

"We blast pure divine love into all aspects of the world that engrams have tainted; in all moments."

"We shift our paradigm from engrams to the higher consciousness of individual and universal joy, love, abundance, freedom, health, peace, strength, empowerment and integrity; in all moments."

"We transcend engrams; in all moments."

"We make space in the world for universal higher consciousness; in all moments."

"We remove all blockages to universal higher consciousness; in all moments."

"We stretch our capacity to fathom and embrace universal higher consciousness; in all moments."

"We are centered and empowered in the higher consciousness of universal peace and freedom; in all moments."

"We infuse the higher consciousness of universal peace and freedom into our sound frequency; in all moments."

"We imbue the higher consciousness of universal peace and freedom into our light emanation; in all moments."

"We resonate, emanate and are interconnected to all life in the higher consciousness of universal peace and freedom; in all moments."

As I finish writing this, I become physically ill and dizzy. I have to run to the bathroom and lay down after they are shared. If it was easy to break through all the resistance to higher consciousness, we would all be enjoying a more evolved state and be free of illness and despair. Please break through the resistance to doing this exercise. The payoff for humanity and earth is immeasurable.

Enhancing Western Medicine Or Dealing with Diagnosis

If someone is dealing with medical issues, here is a technique to assist in boosting the ability to heal. Benefit from everything that Western medicine has to offer without giving over your power, being scared about an outcome, being compartmentalized into a statistic or being compromised in any way. These taps are in no way a critique of Western medicine. They are releasing those undercurrents of fear and doubt deep beneath the surface.

(Say each statement three times out loud while continuously tapping on the top of your head at the crown chakra and say it a fourth time while tapping on your heart chakra.)

"I release agreeing to a diagnosis; in all moments."

"I release the genetic propensity to resonate with a diagnosis; in all moments."

"I release being bullied into a diagnosis; in all moments."

"I release the fear of speaking my truth; in all moments."

"I release worshiping doctors; in all moments."

"I release being a statistic; in all moments."

"I release choosing dis-ease out of fear of seeming different; in all moments."

"I release choosing dis-ease to belong; in all moments."

"I release the belief that dis-ease is inevitable; in all moments."

"I release accepting a diagnosis; in all moments."

"I release falling in line with a diagnosis; in all moments."

"I release resonating with a diagnosis; in all moments."

"I release emanating with a diagnosis; in all moments."

"I reject a diagnosis; in all moments."

"I remove all the energy that causes me to resonate with the diagnosis; in all moments."

"I release giving my power to Western medicine; in all moments."

"I release being imprisoned within my body; in all moments."

"I remove all crippling beliefs; in all moments."

"I release being boxed in by Western medicine; in all moments."

"I shatter all glass ceilings of Western medicine; in all moments."

"I recant all vows and agreements between myself and Western medicine; in all moments."

"I remove all curses between myself and Western medicine; in all moments."

"I remove all blessings between myself and Western medicine; in all moments."

"I sever all strings and cords between myself and Western medicine; in all moments."

"I dissolve all karmic ties between myself and Western medicine; in all moments."

"I withdraw all my energy from Western medicine; in all moments."

"I take back my power from Western medicine in all moments."

"I remove all the pain, burden, limitations, diagnosis, disease and engrams that Western medicine has put on me; in all moments."

"I take back all the joy, love, abundance, freedom, health, life and wholeness that Western medicine has taken from me; in all moments."

"I release resonating with Western medicine; in all moments."

"I release emanating with Western medicine; in all moments."

"I extract all of Western medicine from my sound frequency; in all moments."

"I extract all of Western medicine from my light body; in all moments."

"I enhance my own ability to spontaneously heal; in all moments."

"I shift my paradigm from Western medicine to my own ability to spontaneously heal; in all moments."

"I transcend Western medicine; in all moments."

"I am centered and empowered in my own ability to spontaneously heal; in all moments."

"I recharge and ignite all energy systems in my beingness; in all moments."

"I connect all energy systems in my beingness; in all moments."

"I repair and fortify the Wei chi of all my bodies; in all moments."

"I repair and fortify the Wei chi of all the energy systems in my beingness; in all moments."

"I align all my bodies; in all moments."

"I plug in all the energy systems of my beingness into all my bodies; in all moments."

"I make space in this world to have optimal health; in all moments."

"I remove all blockages to being in optimal health; in all moments."

"I stretch my capacity to be in optimal health; in all moments."

"I am centered and empowered in optimal health; in all moments."

"I infuse optimal health into my sound frequency; in all moments."

"I imbue optimal health into my light body; in all moments."

"I resonate and emanate optimal health; in all moments."

Entities

(Say each statement three times while tapping on your head and say it a fourth time while tapping on your chest.)

"I remove all curses that have been put on me; in all moments."

"I send all energy matrices that are attached to me into the light and sound; in all moments."

"I command all complex energy matrices that are attached to me to be escorted into the light and sound; in all moments."

"I blow all energies that are trying to influence me out of my energy field and cause them to recoil from the force of my love; in all moments."

"I repair and fortify the Wei chi of all my bodies; in all moments."

"I seal and heal all 32 layers of my auric field with the purity of divine love; in all moments."

"I am impervious to the influences of all unworthy intentions; in all moments."

"I am centered, empowered and protected in the sanctity of divine love; in all moments."

"I refuse access to all unworthy intentions; in all moments."

"I wither away all tentacles that use fear to breach the integrity of my essence; in all moments."

"I am impervious to all attacks; in all moments."

Equality Marathon

Want to do some good?

(Say each statement three times out loud while tapping on the top of your head at the crown chakra and say it a fourth time while tapping on your chest at the heart chakra.)

"I declare myself a surrogate for humanity in doing these taps; in all moments."

"I release anyone being invalidated because of their race; in all moments."

"I release anyone being invalidated because of their ethnicity; in all moments."

"I release anyone being invalidated because of their religion; in all moments."

"I release anyone being invalidated because of the color of their skin; in all moments."

"I release anyone being invalidated because of their sex; in all moments."

"I release anyone being invalidated because of their beliefs; in all moments."

"I release anyone being invalidated because of their occupation; in all moments."

"I release anyone being invalidated because of their level of education; in all moments."

"I release anyone being invalidated because of their intelligence level; in all moments."

"I release anyone being invalidated because of their level of development; in all moments."

"I release anyone being invalidated because of their level of their sexual orientation; in all moments."

"I release anyone being invalidated because of their physical appearance or weight; in all moments."

"I release anyone being targeted because of their race; in all moments."

"I release anyone being targeted because of their ethnicity; in all moments."

"I release anyone being targeted because of their religion; in all moments."

"I release anyone being targeted because of the color of their skin; in all moments."

"I release anyone being targeted because of their sex; in all moments."

"I release anyone being targeted because of their beliefs; in all moments."

"I release anyone being targeted because of their occupation; in all moments."

"I release anyone being targeted because of their level of education; in all moments."

"I release anyone being targeted because of their intelligence level; in all moments."

"I release anyone being targeted because of their level of development; in all moments."

"I release anyone being targeted because of their sexual orientation; in all moments."

"I release anyone being targeted because of their physical appearance or weight; in all moments."

"I release anyone feeling unworthy because of their race; in all moments."

"I release anyone feeling unworthy because of their ethnicity; in all moments."

"I release anyone feeling unworthy because of their religion; in all moments."

"I release anyone feeling unworthy because of the color of their skin; in all moments."

"I release anyone feeling unworthy because of their sex; in all moments."

"I release anyone feeling unworthy because of their beliefs; in all moments."

"I release anyone feeling unworthy because of their occupation; in all moments."

"I release anyone feeling unworthy because of their level of education; in all moments."

"I release anyone feeling unworthy because of their intelligence; in all moments."

"I release anyone feeling unworthy because of their level of development; in all moments."

"I release anyone feeling unworthy because of their sexual orientation; in all moments."

"I release anyone feeling unworthy because of the level of their physical appearance or weight; in all moments."

"I remove all the trauma and injustice that has been put on everyone because of their race; in all moments."

"I remove all the trauma and injustice that has been put on everyone because of their ethnicity; in all moments."

"I remove all the trauma and injustice that has been put on everyone because of their religion; in all moments."

"I remove all the trauma and injustice that has been put on everyone because of their skin color; in all moments."

"I remove all the trauma and injustice that has been put on everyone because of their sex; in all moments."

"I remove all the trauma and injustice that has been put on everyone because of their beliefs; in all moments."

"I remove all the trauma and injustice that has been put on everyone because of their occupation; in all moments."

"I remove all the trauma and injustice that has been put on everyone because of their level of education; in all moments."

"I remove all the trauma and injustice that has been put on everyone because of their level of intelligence; in all moments."

"I remove all the trauma and injustice that has been put on everyone because of their level of development; in all moments."

"I remove all the trauma and injustice that has been put on everyone because of their sexual orientation; in all moments."

"I remove all the trauma and injustice that has been put on everyone because of their physical appearance or weight; in all moments."

"I treat everyone as the spark of divinity that they are; in all moments."

"I release trying to subjugate anyone; in all moments."

"I release feeling superior to anyone; in all moments."

"I am centered and empowered in justice, equality, respect and love for all; in all moments."

Be Proud of Your Ethnicity

(Say each statement three times while tapping on your head and say it a fourth time while tapping on your chest.)

"I release the guilt and shame of being of mixed-race; in all moments."

"I release feeling like a mistake; in all moments."

"I release the belief that I am a mistake; in all moments."

"I release believing my parents; in all moments."

"I remove all the conflict within me caused by being mixed-race; in all moments."

"I release crying alone in the dark; in all moments."

"I release feeling inferior; in all moments."

"I release the belief that I am inferior; in all moments."

"I release allowing my ethnicity to interfere with my joy; in all moments."

"I release allowing my ethnicity to interfere with my love; in all moments."

"I release allowing my ethnicity to interfere with my abundance; in all moments."

"I release allowing my ethnicity to interfere with my freedom; in all moments."

"I release allowing my ethnicity to interfere with my success; in all moments."

"I release allowing my ethnicity to interfere with my security; in all moments."

"I release allowing my ethnicity to interfere with my companionship; in all moments."

"I release allowing my ethnicity to interfere with my creativity; in all moments."

"I release allowing my ethnicity to interfere with my peace; in all moments."

"I release allowing my ethnicity to interfere with my life; in all moments."

"I release allowing my ethnicity to interfere with my wholeness; in all moments."

"I release allowing my ethnicity to interfere with my beauty; in all moments."

"I release allowing my ethnicity to interfere with my enthusiasm; in all moments."

"I release allowing my ethnicity to interfere with my contentment; in all moments."

"I release allowing my ethnicity to interfere with my spirituality; in all moments."

"I release allowing my ethnicity to interfere with my enlightenment; in all moments."

"I release allowing my ethnicity to interfere with my confidence; in all moments."

"I release allowing my ethnicity to interfere with my family; in all moments."

"I release allowing my ethnicity to interfere with my intellect; in all moments."

"I release allowing my ethnicity to interfere with my ability to discern; in all moments."

"I release allowing my ethnicity to interfere with my empowerment; in all moments."

"I embrace all the unique facets of my ethnicity; in all moments."

"I release using my ethnicity as an excuse; in all moments."

"I release using my ethnicity as a crutch; in all moments."

"I release wearing my ethnicity like a banner; in all moments."

"I remove all masks, walls, and armor that my ethnicity has put on me; in all moments."

"I release the propensity to defend my ethnicity; in all moments."

"I am centered and empowered in the beauty and uniqueness of my ethnicity; in all moments."

"I resonate, emanate, and am interconnected with all life in the beauty and uniqueness of my ethnicity; in all moments."

Taps You Can Do Every Day

(Say each statement three times out loud while continuously tapping on the top of your head at the crown chakra and say it a fourth time while tapping on your chest.)

"Slim this body down; in all moments."

"Regenerate this nervous system; in all moments."

"Tighten this skin; in all moments."

"Open this heart; in all moments."

"Flatten this stomach; in all moments."

"Melt all this fat; in all moments."

"Nourish and open this mind; in all moments."

"Let down those guards; in all moments."

"Remove those masks; in all moments."

"Take off that armor; in all moments."

"Repair all natural boundaries; in all moments."

"Replenish this pool of enthusiasm; in all moments."

"Open up these inner channels; in all moments."

"Connect to this higher wisdom; in all moments."

"Bypass that ego; in all moments."

"Tone this muscle mass; in all moments."

"Flex this skeletal structure; in all moments."

"Empty these intestines; in all moments."

"Scrape clean and open these passageways; in all moments."

"Rejuvenate this whole system; in all moments."

"Make this experience healthy and happy; in all moments."

"Be free and happy; in all moments."

Exonerate Yourself

(Say each statement three times out loud while tapping on the top of your head at the crown chakra and say it a fourth time while tapping on your chest at the heart chakra.)

"I mend all the hearts that I have broken; in all moments."

"I bring hearing to all those that I have caused to go deaf; in all moments."

"I repair the vision of all those that I have blinded; in all moments."

"I enable all those that I have cut down at the pass; in all moments."

"I re-knit all the bones that I have broken; in all moments."

"I heal all the wounds that I have inflicted; in all moments."

"I repair all the lives that I have disheveled; in all moments."

"I undo all the miscarriages of justice that I have birthed; in all moments."

"I redirect all the lives that I have coached into indifference back into enthusiasm; in all moments."

"I grant freedom to all those I have enslaved; in all moments."

"I let go the grip on all those that I have held in judgment; in all moments."

"I open all the minds that I have closed; in all moments."

"I set back on the path all those I have caused to lose their way; in all moments."

"I am centered and empowered in the healing act of the liberation of all souls; in all moments."

Exorcism

Releasing negative influences doesn't need to be scary. Being afraid is merely removing issues from the low vantage point of the emotions or astral plane. Removing the energies from the detached state of these taps from a higher vantage point can free someone of influences, cravings and negative qualities. Being afraid and commanding a lot of drama around any issue is merely an indulgence of the ego.

(Say this statement three times out loud while continuously tapping on the top of your head at the crown chakra and say it a fourth time while tapping on your chest at the heart chakra.)

"I send all energy matrices of hate into the light and sound; in all moments."

"I command all complex energy matrices of hate to be escorted into the light and sound; in all moments."

"I send all energy matrices of fear into the light and sound; in all moments."

"I command all complex energy matrices of fear to be escorted into the light and sound; in all moments."

"I send all energy matrices of want into the light and sound; in all moments."

"I command all complex energy matrices of want to be escorted into the light and sound; in all moments."

"I send all energy matrices of need into the light and sound; in all moments."

"I command all complex energy matrices of need to be escorted into the light and sound; in all moments."

"I send all energy of lust into the light and sound; in all moments."

"I command all complex energy matrices of lust to be escorted into the light and sound; in all moments."

"I send all energy matrices of cravings into the light and sound; in all moments."

"I command all complex energy matrices of cravings to be escorted into the light and sound; in all moments."

"I send all energy matrices of greed into the light and sound; in all moments."

"I command all complex energy matrices of greed to be escorted into the light and sound; in all moments."

"I send all energy matrices of deceit into the light and sound; in all moments."

"I command all complex energy matrices of deceit to be escorted into the light and sound; in all moments."

"I send all energy matrices of denial into the light and sound; in all moments."

"I command all complex energy matrices of denial to be escorted into the light and sound; in all moments."

"I send all energy matrices of apathy into the light and sound; in all moments."

"I command all complex energy matrices of apathy to be escorted into the light and sound; in all moments."

"I send all energy matrices of power into the light and sound; in all moments."

"I command all complex energy matrices of power to be escorted into the light and sound; in all moments."

"I send all energy matrices of being victim into the light and sound; in all moments."

"I command all complex energy matrices of being victim to be escorted into the light and sound; in all moments."

"I send all energy matrices of ignorance into the light and sound; in all moments."

"I command all complex energy matrices of ignorance to be escorted into the light and sound; in all moments."

"I send all energy matrices of jealousy into the light and sound; in all moments."

"I command all complex energy matrices of jealousy to be escorted into the light and sound; in all moments."

"I send all energy matrices of disease into the light and sound; in all moments."

"I command all complex energy matrices of disease to be escorted into the light and sound; in all moments."

"I send all energy matrices of arrogance into the light and sound; in all moments."

"I command all complex energy matrices of arrogance to be escorted into the light and sound; in all moments."

"I send all energy matrices of entitlement into the light and sound; in all moments."

"I command all complex energy matrices of entitlement to be escorted into the light and sound; in all moments."

Energetic Exorcism

Please do the world a favor and do these taps. Even if you don't understand how it works. If you are feeling alone, sad, or overwhelmed, doing these taps will help bring peace.

(Say each statement three times out loud while tapping on the top of your head at the crown chakra and say it a fourth time while tapping on your chest at the heart chakra.)

"We declare ourselves surrogates for Spirit Guides everywhere in doing these taps; in all moments."

"We command all complex energy matrices that show up as evil in the world to be escorted into the light and sound; in all moments."

"We command all complex energy matrices that create division in the world to be escorted into the light and sound; in all moments."

"We command all complex energy matrices that cause dis-ease in the world to be escorted into the light and sound; in all moments."

"We command all complex energy matrices that serve power in the world to be escorted into the light and sound; in all moments."

"We command all complex energy matrices that enslave the masses to be escorted into the light and sound; in all moments."

"We command all complex energy matrices that desecrate the Earth to be escorted into the light and sound; in all moments."

"We command all complex energy matrices that diminish female energy to be escorted into the light and sound; in all moments."

"We command all complex energy matrices that pollute the world to be escorted into the light and sound; in all moments."

"We command all complex energy matrices that trap the world in the third dimension to be escorted into the light and sound; in all moments."

"We command all complex energy matrices that refuse to transcend to be escorted into the light and sound; in all moments."

"We command all complex energy matrices that grip the world in fear to be escorted into the light and sound; in all moments."

"We command all complex energy matrices that enthrall the world in materialism to be escorted into the light and sound; in all moments."

"We command all complex energy matrices that contaminate the universal sound frequency to be escorted into the light and sound; in all moments."

"We command all complex energy matrices that contribute to creating an egocentric world to be escorted into the light and sound; in all moments."

"We command all complex energy matrices that push an agenda to be escorted into the light and sound; in all moments."

"We command all complex energy matrices that contaminate the universal light emanation to be escorted into the light and sound; in all moments."

"We command all complex energy matrices that are indifferent to nature to be escorted into the light and sound; in all moments."

"We command all complex energy matrices that breed contempt through self-righteousness to be escorted into the light and sound; in all moments."

"We command all complex energy matrices that perpetuate ignorance in the world to be escorted into the light and sound; in all moments."

"We command all complex energy matrices that perpetuate the illusion of separateness in the world to be escorted into the light and sound; in all moments."

"We command all complex energy matrices that perpetuate anything but love in the world to be escorted into the light and sound; in all moments."

"We command all complex energy matrices that cause the world to forget their true essence to be escorted into the light and sound; in all moments."

"We command all complex energy matrices that perpetuate futility in the world to be escorted into the light and sound; in all moments."

"We command all complex energy matrices that perpetuate unworthiness in the world to be escorted into the light and sound; in all moments."

"We command all complex energy matrices that shroud the world in illusion to be escorted into the light and sound; in all moments."

"We command all complex energy matrices that blind the world to truth to be escorted into the light and sound; in all moments."

"We command all complex energy matrices that immerse the world in denial to be escorted into the light and sound; in all moments."

"We command all complex energy matrices that try to immerse the world in darkness to be escorted into the light and sound; in all moments."

"We command all complex energy matrices that cause the beings of the world to recoil from the love to be escorted into the light and sound; in all moments."

Expand Exponentially

(Say each statement three times out loud while continuously tapping on the top of your head at the crown chakra and say it a fourth time while tapping on your chest.)

"Exponential joy is funneled into my energy system; in all moments."

"Exponential love is funneled into my energy system; in all moments."

"Exponential abundance is funneled into my energy system; in all moments."

"Exponential freedom is funneled into my energy system; in all moments."

"Exponential health is funneled into my energy system; in all moments."

"Exponential success is funneled into my energy system; in all moments."

"Exponential worthiness is funneled into my energy system; in all moments."

"Exponential companionship is funneled into my energy system; in all moments."

"Exponential confidence is funneled into my energy system; in all moments."

"Exponential creativity is funneled into my energy system; in all moments."

"Exponential peace is funneled into my energy system; in all moments."

"Exponential enthusiasm is funneled into my energy system; in all moments."

"Exponential beauty is funneled into my energy system; in all moments."

"Exponential contentment is funneled into my energy system; in all moments."

"Exponential enlightenment is funneled into my energy system; in all moments."

"Exponential awareness is funneled into my energy system; in all moments."

Expanding Consciousness

(Say each statement three times while tapping continuously on your head and say it a fourth time while continuously tapping on your chest.)

"I release being ungrateful; in all moments."

"I release negating inanimate life; in all moments."

"I release dismissing inanimate life; in all moments."

"I release compartmentalizing life; in all moments."

"I remove the dividing line between animate and inanimate life; in all moments."

"I release enslaving inanimate life; in all moments."

"I release all indifference to inanimate life; in all moments."

"I make space in this world to respect inanimate life; in all moments."

"I remove all blockages to respecting inanimate life; in all moments."

"I stretch my capacity to respect inanimate life; in all moments."

"I am centered and empowered in respecting inanimate life; in all moments."

"I resonate, emanate, and am interconnected with all life in respecting inanimate life; in all moments."

"I remove all indifference to inanimate life; in all moments."

"I remove all bigotry towards inanimate life; in all moments."

"I release cursing inanimate life; in all moments."

"I remove all negative vortexes between myself and inanimate life; in all moments."

"I nullify all contracts that enslave inanimate life; in all moments."

"I eliminate the first cause in diminishing inanimate life; in all moments."

"I strip all illusion off of diminishing inanimate life; in all moments."

"I remove all masks, walls, and armor that diminishing inanimate life has put on me; in all moments."

"I release seeing my physicality as inanimate; in all moments."

"I release seeing trees as inanimate; in all moments."

"I release feeling superior over inanimate life; in all moments."

"I release the belief that I am inferior to inanimate life; in all moments."

"I awaken to the consciousness of inanimate life; in all moments."

Falling to One's Death

We forget that hospitals, wheelchairs and painkillers are a relatively modern invention. In the past, when we fell or broke a limb, we lay there mangled and twisting, writhing in pain until someone put us out of our misery or death came to us. These memories still surface when we are confronted with health issues. They are the hiccups of past torments making their way to the surface for validation. They need not be permanent.

If past issues are acknowledged and the body is validated, we can move through them quite quickly. See? It is not always something settling into us. Most times, it is something devastating trying to leave. That is the purpose of the taps, to acknowledge the pain quickly and to help it pass through.

One of my first clients was terrified of birds. It sounds silly to some. But the image that I saw was of her as a young Native American man. He was climbing on the rocks of a cliff to access eggs in the nests. He lost his footing and fell to his demise, but death wasn't swift. He lay there watching the vultures circle as he got weaker. They did not wait for him to die before they moved in and started picking at his flesh. They made their first strikes at the moist areas where the blood drained out--the intestines and the eyeballs. This was how my client left that life. Here are some of the taps that I led her through:

(Say each statement three times while tapping on your head and say it a fourth time while tapping on your chest.)

"I release the pain and trauma of falling to my death; in all moments."

"I release the fear of heights; in all moments."

"I release the horror of being eaten alive; in all moments."

"I release the fear of being eaten by birds/dogs/cats/natives (whatever it is); in all moments."

"I untangle the limbs of my body; in all moments."

"I untangle the energy of my body; in all moments."

"I release mingling my sense of adventure with fear; in all moments."

"I release allowing fear to over ride my sense of adventure; in all moments."

"I release feeling helpless and abandoned; in all moments."

"I release the belief that I am helpless and abandoned; in all moments."

"I shift my paradigm from helpless and abandoned, to empowered and free; in all moments."

"I am centered in joy, love, abundance, freedom, health, success, adventure and wholeness; in all moments."

We are only as brave as the strongest memory of our deepest fear. When we understand that we are empowered by taking a nonreactive stance to unconscious triggers, we can just address them without being blindsided by emotional reactions. We don't even have to fully understand the emotional reaction to address them head on. Our own resistance to addressing them then becomes a sabotage because the taps work easily and effectively.

Fatigue

(Say each statement three times out loud while continuously tapping on the top of your head at the crown chakra and say it a fourth time while tapping on your chest.)

"I release being drained of my energy; in all moments."

"I release giving up my life force willingly; in all moments."

"I release the belief that empowerment is futile; in all moments."

"I release being manipulated out of my energy; in all moments."

"I release exchanging my energy for a mere stroke of the ego; in all moments."

"I release giving up my energy to be in complacency; in all moments."

"I release choosing complacency over empowerment; in all moments."

"I dry up the connection between myself and all the sources that drain me; in all moments."

"I take back all my energy from all the sources that have drained me; in all moments."

"I release being susceptible to those who feed off me; in all moments."

"I release giving away my energy; in all moments."

"I release martyring myself; in all moments."

"I strip all illusion off of all sources that drain energy; in all moments."

"I release being a helpless muse; in all moments."

"I shift my paradigm from being a helpless muse to being empowered and aware; in all moments."

"I am centered and empowered in being empowered and aware; in all moments."

Tiredness

Being stuck in past traumas is something that is stored in the endocrine system and causes tiredness and weakness in the present lifetime.

(Say each statement three times while tapping on your head and say it a fourth time while tapping on your chest.)

"I release the trauma of dying of an infectious disease; in all moments."

"I release the fear of dying of a contagious disease; in all moments."

"I release the trauma of being decapitated; in all moments."

"I release the trauma of being hung; in all moments."

"I release the trauma of being sacrificed; in all moments."

"I release the trauma of being tortured to death; in all moments."

"I release the trauma of being burned alive; in all moments."

"I release the trauma of being murdered; in all moments."

"I release the trauma of dying in childbirth; in all moments."

"I release the trauma of dying in war; in all moments."

"I release the trauma of bleeding out my life force; in all moments."

"I release the fear of being decapitated; in all moments."

"I release adding fear to my essence; in all moments."

"I dry up all space for terrorism in my essence; in all moments."

"I remove all fear from my essence; in all moments."

"I remove all old engrams of victimization and exploitation from my essence; in all moments."

"I repair and fortify the Wei chi of all my bodies; in all moments."

"I align all my bodies; in all moments."

"I dissolve anything that is not divine love from my essence; in all moments."

"I infuse perpetual and infinite joy, love, abundance, freedom, health, success, security, creativity, peace, life, wholeness, beauty, enthusiasm, enlightenment and accountability into my essence; in all moments."

"I am centered and empowered in divine love; in all moments."

Releasing Fear Marathon

Love is the opposite of fear. Where there is love, there is no fear. There are many primal experiences that many of us are afraid of. If we can release their grip on us, it will automatically make room for more love. Love is our natural state. The fear moves in to squelch out the love. Here is to releasing big chunks of fear so that one can return to the natural state of love.

(Say each statement out loud while tapping on your head and say it a fourth time while tapping on your chest.)

"I release the fear of dying; in all moments."

"I release the fear of being separated from my consciousness; in all moments."

"I release the fear of plunging to my death; in all moments."

"I release the fear of being tortured; in all moments."

"I release the fear of being decapitated; in all moments."

"I release the fear of hanging; in all moments."

"I release the fear of drowning; in all moments."

"I release the fear of being held under the water; in all moments."

"I release the fear of being buried alive; in all moments."

"I release the fear of being humiliated; in all moments."

"I release the fear of being sacrificed; in all moments."

"I release the fear of spiders; in all moments."

"I release the fear of being raped; in all moments."

"I release the fear of losing my children; in all moments."

"I release the fear of being abandoned; in all moments."

"I release the fear of abandoning my loved ones; in all moments."

"I release the fear of being suffocated; in all moments."

"I release the fear of the Angel of Death; in all moments."

"I release the fear of going to hell; in all moments."

"I release the fear of being betrayed; in all moments."

"I release the fear of running for my life; in all moments."

"I release the fear of starving to death; in all moments."

"I release the fear of the world ending; in all moments."

"I release the fear of going to war; in all moments."

"I release the fear of being singled out in a crowd; in all moments."

"I release the fear of speaking my truth; in all moments."

"I release the fear of being crippled; in all moments."

"I release the fear of being different; in all moments."

"I release the fear of dying; in all moments."

"I release the fear of being alone; in all moments."

"I release the fear of snakes; in all moments."

"I release the fear of being eaten alive; in all moments."

"I release the fear of losing my home; in all moments."

"I release the fear of being a nothing; in all moments."

"I release the fear of being invisible; in all moments."

"I release the fear of being a ghost; in all moments."

"I release the fear of disappointing God; in all moments."

"I release the fear of being a failure; in all moments."

"I release the fear of being stupid; in all moments."

"I release the fear of being disfigured; in all moments."

"I release the fear of cats/dogs; in all moments

"I release the fear of the government; in all moments."

"I release the fear of alien invasion; in all moments."

"I release the fear of foreigners; in all moments."

"I release the fear of being enslaved; in all moments."

"I release the fear of being murdered; in all moments."

"I release the fear of losing my mind; in all moments."

"I release the fear of growing old; in all moments."

"I release the fear of being helpless; in all moments."

"I release the fear of making a mistake; in all moments."

"I release the fear of causing others their lives; in all moments."

"I release the fear of responsibility; in all moments."

"I release the fear of marriage; in all moments."

"I release the fear of ceremonies; in all moments."

"I release the fear of being shanghai'd; in all moments."

"I release the fear of being passed around; in all moments."

"I release the fear of being lost; in all moments."

"I release the fear of the dark; in all moments."

"I release the fear of being possessed; in all moments."

"I release the fear of being mutilated; in all moments."

"I release the fear of losing a limb; in all moments."

"I release the fear of authority; in all moments."

"I release the fear of losing power; in all moments."

"I release the fear of being buried alive; in all moments."

"I release the fear of ghosts; in all moments."

"I release the fear of being born; in all moments."

"I release the fear of governing parties; in all moments."

"I release the fear of religious factions; in all moments."

"I release the fear of dying; in all moments."

This list is just scratching the surface. It is a good way to get a sense of what past traumas have been experienced by the ones that cause a greater reaction. In seeing the vastness of the list, one can understand why the love gets pushed out. May all who do these feel a shift in their own ability to embrace the love.

Fear of Death

(Say each statement three times out loud while continuously tapping on the top of your head at the crown chakra and say it a fourth time while tapping on your chest.)

"I untangle my sound frequency; in all moments.

"I release confusing my body for a prison cell; in all moments."

"I release trapping myself in my body; in all moments."

"I release confusing leaving my body with death; in all moments."

"I releasing confusing freedom for death; in all moments."

"I send all energy matrices into the light that cause me to confuse freedom for death; in all moments."

"I remove all vortexes between freedom and death; in all moments."

"I remove all tentacles between freedom and death; in all moments."

"I remove the claws of death from freedom; in all moments."

"I release needing to die to have freedom; in all moments."

"I remove all engrams that correlate freedom with dying; in all moments."

"I release correlating travel with death; in all moments."

"I release the fear of traveling; in all moments."

"I release associating travel with hardships; in all moments."

"I remove all vortexes between travel and hardships; in all moments."

"I remove all tentacles between travel and hardships; in all moments."

"I send all energy matrices into the light that induce hardships during travel; in all moments."

"I remove the claws of hardship from travel; in all moments."

"I release being forced to travel; in all moments."

"I release confusing travel for being usurped from my home; in all moments."

"I release the fear of change; in all moments."

"I release confusing change for death; in all moments."

"I remove all vortexes between change and death; in all moments."

"I remove all tentacles between change and death; in all moments."

"I release the belief that change only comes through death; in all moments."

"I release begging for death; in all moments."

"I remove all misconceptions about death; in all moments."

"I release my love-hate with death; in all moments."

"I remove all vortexes between myself and death; in all moments."

"I remove all vivaxes between myself and death; in all moments."

"I remove all tentacles between myself and death; in all moments."

"I remove all preconceived notions that I have about death; in all moments."

"I release associating death with pain; in all moments."

"I release the fear of being separated from my consciousness upon death; in all moments."

"I release staying with the physical body upon death; in all moments."

"I release the trauma of not crossing over after death; in all moments."

"I remove all engrams of an unpleasant death; in all moments."

"I release losing my way upon death; in all moments."

"I send all energy matrices into he light that support or perpetuate the fear of death; in all moments."

"I recant all vows and agreements between myself and death; in all moments."

"I release the belief that death is inevitable; in all moments."

"I shatter the glass ceiling of death; in all moments."

"I remove all curses between myself and death; in all moments."

"I remove all blessings between myself and death; in all moments."

"I sever all strings and cords between myself and death; in all moments."

"I dissolve all karmic ties between myself and death; in all moments."

"I remove all the pain, burden, limitation, and illusion of separateness that death has put on me; in all moments."

"I take back all the good that death has taken from me; in all moments."

"I withdraw all my energy from death; in all moments."

"I release challenging death; in all moments."

"I release using death to prove my bravado; in all moments."

"I strip all illusion off of death; in all moments."

"I remove all masks, wall, and armor from death; in all moments."

"I release resonating with death; in all moments."

"I release emanating with death; in all moments."

"I extract all of death from my sound frequency; in all moments."

"I extract all of death from my light emanation; in all moments."

"I shift my paradigm from death to enlightenment; in all moments."

"I transcend death; in all moments.""

"I am centered and empowered in enlightenment; in all moments."

"I anchor my consciousness in universal joy; in all moments."

"I anchor my consciousness in universal love; in all moments."

"I anchor my consciousness in universal abundance; in all moments."

"I anchor my consciousness in universal freedom; in all moments."

"I anchor my consciousness in universal health; in all moments."

"I anchor my consciousness in universal success; in all moments."

"I anchor my consciousness in universal security; in all moments."

"I anchor my consciousness in universal companionship; in all moments."

"I anchor my consciousness in universal peace; in all moments."

"I anchor my consciousness in universal life; in all moments."

"I anchor my consciousness in universal wholeness; in all moments."

"I anchor my consciousness in universal beauty; in all moments."

"I anchor my consciousness in universal enthusiasm; in all moments."

"I anchor my consciousness in universal contentment; in all moments."

"I anchor my consciousness in universal enlightenment; in all moments."

"I anchor my consciousness in universal truth; in all moments."

"I anchor my consciousness in universal confidence; in all moments."

"I anchor my consciousness in universal empowerment; in all moments."

Fear of Speaking

In many of my sessions, the clients have suffered an incredible trauma simply because they spoke truth. I have seen people tortured in ways that are unfathomable because they showed leadership qualities and stood apart in the crowd. This threatened the ruling lord of the land. There have been endless corrupt governing parties in the past.

How that shows up in this lifetime is that people are afraid to speak up. They had not pulled back the conscious memory of being tortured but the reaction is so strong in them that it may make sense.

Here are some taps to alleviate the reaction: (Say each statement three times while tapping the top of your head and say it a fourth time while tapping on your chest.)

"I release the trauma of being martyred; in all moments."

"I release the trauma of being tortured; in all moments."

"I recant my vow of silence; in all moments."

"I recant my vow of martyrdom; in all moments."

"I release the fear of speaking; in all moments."

"I release the fear of sharing my truth; in all moments."

"I release the fear of being tortured; in all moments."

"I release the fear of being martyred; in all moments."

If someone is being affected by debilitating inability to express themselves, these may help.

Release the Fear of Travel

In past lives, many of us were ousted from our homes by violence or natural disaster. The plight of the current refugees was once ours. Those who remember obliquely in their past what this felt like, have compassion for these sweet souls and refuse to demonize them as we all once were.

Those who are hell bent on the notion of living only one life are only afforded the compassion of what they have accrued in one birth cycle. Can you see how this is a black eye on compassion since compassion is seeing your own plight walking in another set of shoes?

Here are some taps to free your own soul. In doing so, perhaps you will unwind the entanglement of all of humanity.

(Say each statement three times out loud while continuously tapping on the top of your head at the crown chakra and say it a fourth time while tapping on your chest.)

"I release the fear of travel; in all moments."

"I release allowing current events to instill fear in me; in all moments."

"I release giving my fate over to fear; in all moments."

"I release confusing travel with the trauma of being usurped from my home; in all moments."

"I release dreading travel; in all moments."

"I release correlating travel with negative excavations; in all moments."

"I release the fear of never returning from travel; in all moments."

"I release the trauma of dying on an odyssey or quest; in all moments."

"I release the guilt and trauma of leaving loved ones behind; in all moments."

"I release the fear of abandoning those I love; in all moments."

"I release confusing travel for abandoning; in all moments."

"I remove all guilt surrounding travel; in all moments."

"I release all association between travel and being forced to leave; in all moments."

"I release confusing travel with losing freewill; in all moments."

"I remove all negative engrams that traveling reveals; in all moments."

"I shift my paradigm from dreading travel to looking forward to it; in all moments."

"I shift my paradigm from being distracted during travel to staying in the moment; in all moments."

"I enjoy the flexibility and freedom of travel; in all moments."

"I enjoy the happy return from all travels; in all moments."

"I am centered and empowered in the love and freedom of travel; in all moments."

Disappointment

(Say each statement three times out loud while tapping on the top of your head at the crown chakra and say it a fourth time while tapping on your chest at the heart chakra.)

"I release being disappointed by life; in all moments."

"I release being disappointed by others; in all moments."

"I release expecting to be disappointed; in all moments."

"I release having disappointment be a mainstay; in all moments."

"I release being married to disappointment; in all moments."

"I release carrying disappointment around; in all moments."

"I release the fear of disappointing others; in all moments."

"I send all energy matrices into the light and sound that set me up to disappoint others; in all moments."

"I send all energy matrices into the light and sound that set me up to be disappointed; in all moments."

"I command all complex energy matrices that set me up to disappoint others to be escorted into the light and sound; in all moments."

"I command all complex energy matrices that set me up to be disappointed to be escorted into the light and sound; in all moments."

"I remove all vivaxes between myself and disappointment; in all moments."

"I remove all tentacles between myself and disappointment; in all moments."

"I remove the claws of disappointment from my beingness; in all moments."

"I nullify all contracts between myself and disappointment; in all moments."

"I recant all vows and agreements between myself and disappointment; in all moments."

"I remove all curses between myself and disappointment; in all moments."

"I remove all blessings between myself and disappointment; in all moments."

"I remove all strings, cords and wires between myself and disappointment; in all moments."

"I dissolve all karmic ties between myself and disappointment; in all moments."

"I remove all the pain, burden and limitations that disappointment has put on me; in all moments."

"I remove all the pain, burden and limitations that I have put on all others due to disappointment; in all moments."

"I remove all the fear, futility and unworthiness that disappointment has put on me; in all moments."

"I remove all the fear, futility and unworthiness that I have put on all others due to disappointment; in all moments."

"I remove all the ignorance, blindness to spiritual law and illusion of separateness that disappointment has put on me; in all moments."

"I remove all the ignorance, blindness to spiritual law and illusion of separateness that I have put on all others due to disappointment; in all moments."

"I take back all that disappointment has taken from me; in all moments."

"I give back to all others all that I have taken from them due to disappointment; in all moments."

"I withdraw all my energy from disappointment; in all moments."

"I strip all illusion off of disappointment; in all moments."

"I remove all masks, walls and armor from disappointment; in all moments."

"I permanently close all portals and passageways to disappointment; in all moments."

"I collapse and dissolve disappointment; in all moments."

"I release resonating with disappointment; in all moments."

"I release emanating with disappointment; in all moments."

"I extract all disappointment from my sound frequency; in all moments."

"I extract all disappointment from my light emanation; in all moments."

"I shift my paradigm from disappointment to universal joy, love, abundance, freedom and wholeness; in all moments."

"I transcend disappointment; in all moments."

"I am centered and empowered in universal joy, love, abundance, freedom and wholeness; in all moments."

"I make space in this world for universal contentment; in all moments."

"I remove all blockages to universal contentment; in all moments."

"I stretch the universe's capacity to embrace universal contentment; in all moments."

"I send all energy matrices into the light and sound that interfere with universal contentment; in all moments."

"I command all complex energy matrices that interfere with universal contentment, to be escorted into the light and sound; in all moments."

"I resonate and emanate with universal contentment; in all moments."

Discouragement

(Say each statement three times while tapping on your head and say it a fourth time while tapping on your chest.)

"I release feeling like a failure; in all moments."

"I release feeling like I never get ahead; in all moments."

"I release the belief that I am moving backwards; in all moments."

"I release the fear of never getting ahead; in all moments."

"I release the belief I am a failure; in all moments."

"I release the belief that I will never get ahead; in all moments."

"I release the feeling and belief that nothing ever changes; in all moments."

"I release feeling stuck; in all moments."

"I release being discouraged; in all moments."

"I release being blind to the big picture; in all moments."

"I see the expansion of consciousness; in all moments."

"I embrace the expansion of consciousness; in all moments."

"I release all conditioning that linear enslavement has put on me; in all moments."

"I flush out all negative program and reactions; in all moments."

"I accept my freedom; in all moments."

"I acclimate to the expansiveness of consciousness; in all moments."

"I awaken to the expansiveness of exponential love; in all moments."

Feeling Disconnected

Very recently, I facilitated a private remote session with a new client. Her good friend has been having sessions with me and she has seen the profound shift in her friend so she was receptive to my work. This helps because of how deep the sessions work. The more of a trust factor that I have with the client, the more profound a shift that can happen. When setting up the session, she said that she had no real issues except for dealing with an ex partner she was going to be meeting with. Of course, I realized that that was not the case. It never is that simple.

As soon as we connected, I realized how receptive she was. I perceived a deep loneliness in her. She also facilitated energy work in the form of massage therapy but when she was taught to allow the clients' issues to flow into the earth to release through her feet, she was merely jamming it all into her body. She was not energetically following through. So she was jam-packed with a lot of issues of her own and all of her clients. At the beginning of the session, she felt like iron.

The reason this happened came through later in the session. It touched on a current theme that ran through her lifetimes. It was a profound insight for her to realize and it made a certain sense to her when it was revealed. She had lost both her legs during a past life, so the ingrained memory or habit of that (what I call an engram) was preventing the energy from flowing down her legs and into the ground. There was a disconnect between her and the earth. These taps helped.

"I release feeling disconnected from the earth; in all moments."

"I connect to the earth; in all moments."

"I recycle all energy back into love by perpetually pouring it into the earth; in all moments."

As I led her through instructions how to do the taps, she had a very difficult time doing them. The instructions are to say each statement three times while tapping on your head and say it a fourth time while tapping on your chest. She said that she had a disability of some kind that prevented her from following simple instructions. I understand that because I experience a similar thing. So I challenged her, which brought another emotional round of tears.

I explained to her that she thinks beyond linear thought, just like I do. So every time that she is giving instructions, she has to take time to translate it back into the tedious method of linear thought and it appears that she is slow. I reassured her that all of humanity is moving beyond linear thought and she is just ahead of the curve. Saying that she is disabled is the only way to explain to those who only know the linear thought of what is happening. I do that too. But I did not want her believing her own explanation when she really is so advanced. In fact, one of the first taps I led her through had to do with her first lifetime on earth and how lonely that was.

"I release feeling abandoned on earth; in all moments."

"I release rejecting earth; in all moments."

For many people, their first lifetime on earth is a sore disappointment. Living on earth compared to other planets is like being immersed in a sarcophagus. It is that stifling. Plus, on other planets, we have had a beautiful, long, powerful tail. So many people, when they get on earth, have trouble balancing with just the two legs instead of the powerful tripod of legs and tail. These people may have trouble with their lower back, tailbone or hips. She confirmed that she had chronic issues with her hip, which surprised her when she felt a release with the next tap.

"I release the trauma of losing my tail; in all moments."

"I reattach my tail; in all moments."

These taps, as strange as they were to her consciously, brought great relief to the whole hip area. She felt space in her hip area that was not there before and we both felt heat in her lower back, which I worked at moving through her whole spine by releasing the issues that were jamming her up energetically.

"I remove all the anger that I have stored in my beingness; in all moments."

"I release cursing earth; in all moments."

"I release hating earth; in all moments."

I was told by my Guides a while ago that people who defile the earth so easily have little affinity for it. They have been brought here begrudgingly and so treat the earth as if they are disgruntled children that resent their home situations. They need to awaken to gratitude for being here on earth and release old grudges of being brought to this planet unwittingly. They need to stop looking up at the stars to be saved and accept that all their old friends from their home planet have already incarnated here. In an indirect way, this will assist in relieving the pillaging of earth that is happening through the rape of all its fossil fuels.

"I release waiting to be rescued from earth; in all moments."

"I release looking to the stars for redemption; in all moments."

"I accept my earthly conditions; in all moments."

"I release the systemic rape of earth; in all moments."

Many people who pray to the heavens were initially waiting to be saved by their native planet from the fate of being on earth. But now, sending one's energy out into the ethers merely dissipates earth. People need to accept that they are here on earth and pour their love and energy back into the earth or it will eventually be depleted as it is run to the ground and all its energy is dissipated.

"I release dissipating the earth of its energy; in all moments."

"I release diluting my energy by pouring it into space; in all moments."

"I release diluting the earth's empowerment; in all moments."

The next issues that were revealed in my new client, who was amazed that she was having such profound shifts of energy so quickly, had to do with the experiences that were creating trauma during lifetimes on earth.

"I release being turned into a eunuch; in all moments."

"I release the trauma of having my legs cut off; in all moments."

Underneath that trauma, another past life revealed itself where she was lobotomized. That thing that she called a disability in herself, even though she was perfectly healthy, was a past life engram of the trauma of being lobotomized.

"I release the trauma of being lobotomized; in all moments."

As I led her through this tap, the energy in her head opened up and she felt light and expansive. I felt the issue in her right frontal lobe that was being addressed and repaired. She felt it too. She was not the same person that she was at the beginning of the session or who she had been for many lifetimes. She seemed to now be able to formulate the taps much more easily.

I asked her if she felt lighter and she did. I always describe this feeling as being like a mylar balloon. She described it as being expansive as coral. This was an issue. Coral is not contained. This told me that the natural casing on her energy field was compromised. This casing is the Wei chi. I led her through the taps to repair the Wei chi, not only on her physical body, but also her bodies on the astral, causal and mental realms as well.

"I repair and fortify the Wei chi of all my bodies; in all moments."

"I align all my bodies; in all moments."

"I am centered, empowered and immersed in divine love; in all moments."

After this, I addressed the theme that was running through her lifetimes. She was always having appendages cut off. It was creating a systemic cringing in her energy field. When I told her this and about the lobotomy, it was very validating to her. She suddenly realized why she felt flawed and incapacitated at the core. The taps and the understanding together worked to create a drastic shift in her. She also recalled how difficult it was for her to watch anyone get cut on a show. She was excited to note the reaction it caused in her and this validated what I was revealing about her.

Because it was a recurring theme, we addressed the first time that she ever got cut. This is called the initial cause or first cause. Since we work with all the lifetimes of a person at once, the way to remedy a reoccurring unwanted theme is to eliminate the first cause or the first time it ever happened in all the lifetimes of that person. It is like the events are a line of dominoes and we remove that first domino that knocks down all the other dominoes.

"I eliminate the first cause in regards to being cut into; in all moments."

"I eliminate the first cause in regards to having appendages cut off; in all moments."

This was the new client's very first introduction to my work. She thought she was contacting me for a superficial reason, but she innately knew that what we would address would work so much deeper. After working so deeply, I did address the more superficial issues that motivated her to desire to have a session with me. But her life is ever changed by this investment of an hour with me.

There was much more that we released. We released all the vows that she had taken in lifetimes of monastery living and issues with relationships. But the taps that I shared above are the ones that brought the deepest, most profound and drastic shifts to her energy. May you feel a shift as well by reading this and doing the taps.

Feeling Left Out

(Say each statement three times out loud while continuously tapping on the top of your head at the crown chakra and say it a fourth time while tapping on your chest.)

"I release feeling left out; in all moments."

"I release the belief that I am not included; in all moments."

"I release putting conditions on myself and others; in all moments."

"I release needing permission to participate; in all moments."

"I release the need for prerequisites; in all moments."

"I release the belief that I don't fit the bill; in all moments."

"I release missing a sense of belonging; in all moments."

"I release the belief that I don't belong; in all moments."

"I release resenting those who seem to belong; in all moments."

"I release the belief that others belong more than myself; in all moments."

"I release the fear of being called out; in all moments."

"I release the belief that I am an outsider; in all moments."

"I am comfortable in my position in life; in all moments."

"I am comfortable in my skin; in all moments."

"I belong where I am; in all moments."

"I am loved and of value right where I am; in all moments."

"I can join in if I choose to; in all moments."

"I am where I belong; in all moments."

Feeling Obligated

(Say each statement three times while tapping on your head and say it a fourth time while tapping on your chest.)

"I release being obligated; in all moments."

"I cut all tentacles to being obligated; in all moments."

"I release feeling obligated; in all moments."

"I release the belief that I am obligated; in all moments."

"I remove all vivaxes between myself and obligation; in all moments."

"I release confusing my purpose with obligation; in all moments."

"I remove all programming and conditioning that obligation has put on me; in all moments."

"I remove all engrams of obligation; in all moments."

"I nullify all contracts with obligation; in all moments."

"I collapse all portals of obligation; in all moments."

"I eliminate the first cause in regards to obligation; in all moments."

"I send all energy matrices into the light and sound that obligate me; in all moments."

"I command all complex energy matrices that obligate me to be escorted into the light and sound; in all moments."

"I recant all vows and agreements between myself and obligation; in all moments."

"I remove all curses between myself and obligation; in all moments."

"I remove all debt of obligation; in all moments."

"I remove all blessings between myself and obligation; in all moments."

"I sever all strings and cords between myself and obligation; in all moments."

"I dissolve all karmic ties between myself and obligation; in all moments."

"I remove all the pain, burden and limitations that obligation has put on me; in all moments."

"I remove all the fear, futility and unworthiness that obligation has put on me; in all moments."

"I remove all the illusion of separateness that obligation has put on me; in all moments."

"I remove all the rejection, abandonment and isolation that obligation has put on me; in all moments."

"I remove all that I have put on all others due to obligation; in all moments."

"I take back all that obligation has taken from me; in all moments."

"I give back to all others all that I have taken from them; in all moments."

"I release resonating with obligation; in all moments."

"I release emanating with obligation; in all moments."

"I dissolve all obligation from my sound frequency; in all moments."

"I dissolve all obligation from my light emanation; in all moments."

"I shift my paradigm from obligation to spiritual empowerment; in all moments."

"I dissolve all obligation from my whole beingness; in all moments."

"I transcend obligation; in all moments."

"I am centered and empowered in spiritual liberation; in all moments."

"I resonate, emanate and am interconnected with all life in spiritual liberation; in all moments."

Release the Misery

(Say each statement three times out loud while continuously tapping on the top of your head at the crown chakra and say it a fourth time while tapping on your chest.)

"I release making misery my lover; in all moments."

"I release taking misery to my bed; in all moments."

"I release romanticizing misery; in all moments."

"I release obsessing over misery; in all moments."

"I divorce misery; in all moments."

"I release giving misery form with my words; in all moments."

"I release giving misery form with my thoughts; in all moments."

"I release giving misery form with my beliefs; in all moments."

"I release feeding misery with emotion; in all moments."

"I remove all engrams of misery; in all moments."

"I remove all muscle memory of misery; in all moments."

"I filter out the misery; in all moments."

"I release playing the victim; in all moments."

"I dissipate the psychic energy of misery; in all moments."

"I extract all misery from all 32 layers of my auric field; in all moments."

"I extract all misery from my sound frequency; in all moments."

"I extract all misery from my light emanation; in all moments."

"I shift my paradigm from misery to joy; in all moments."

"I align all my bodies to joy; in all moments."

"I am centered and empowered in joy; in all moments."

"I resonate, emanate and am interconnected to all life in joy; in all moments."

Jealousy

There are two reasons to be jealous. The first reason is because on some level, one realizes that their present mate isn't their soul mate. They realize they will be leaving them at some point and they aren't ready to do that. They are taking themselves out of the moment and living in a perpetual state of breakup.

The other reason one is jealous is because they are reliving a past experience of losing a dear love. They are playing it over and over in their subliminal energy field. The love that they are enjoying shares close quarters with a painful memory of loss. Jealousy is a private excruciating hell of various degrees. Here are some taps to alleviate the angst:

(Say each statement three times while tapping on your head and say it a fourth time while tapping on your chest.)

"I release the anguish of being separated from my love; in all moments."

"I release the fear and trauma of my love leaving me; in all moments."

"I release being frozen in abandonment; in all moments."

"I release confusing love with competition; in all moments."

"I release competing for love; in all moments."

"I release seeing other women/men as the enemy; in all moments."

"I release feeling lonely and desperate in relationships; in all moments."

"I release pulling my love into a lonely and desperate place; in all moments."

"I release defining love as emptiness and need; in all moments."

"I release having relationships pull me into a void; in all moments."

"I redefine relationships as fullness and completion; in all moments."

"I shift the paradigm of my relationship from taking to giving; in all moments."

"I release being jealous; in all moments."

"I shift my paradigm from jealousy to peace; in all moments."

"My relationship is centered in joy, love, abundance, freedom, peace, contentment and wholeness; in all moments."

"I am totally centered in the moment; in all moments."

I have a dear friend whose soul mate crossed over. Every day a hawk flew over her house and called to her. She felt it was her husband reminding her of their love. It was very comforting to her and she had many dream experiences with them together.

One day, she called me very upset. There were two hawks together. In her grief, she thought that her husband had moved on and she was in excruciating pain. Because of jealousy, she failed to realize that she was the second hawk. She was being shown that she was still with her husband in the higher realms. It was only in the physical that she was experiencing separation. But on all other levels, they were still together.

Sadness

(Say each statement three times while tapping on your head and say it a fourth time while tapping on your chest.)

"I release feeling sad; in all moments."

"I release quantifying experiences as sad; in all moments."

"I remove all curses of sad; in all moments."

"I release the energetic quicksand of sad; in all moments."

"I release deeming random things as sad; in all moments."

"I dissipate all psychic streams of energy of sadness; in all moments."

"I release accepting any experience as sad; in all moments."

"I release drawing sadness to me; in all moments."

"I release processing life as sad; in all moments."

"I release being immersed in sadness; in all moments."

"I remove all sadness from all 32 layers of my auric field; in all moments."

"I send all energy matrices of sadness into the light and sound; in all moments."

"I command all complex energy matrices of sadness to be escorted into the light and sound; in all moments."

"I convert all sadness to joy; in all moments."

"I collapse and dissolve all portals to sadness; in all moments."

"I release accepting the sadness of others into my essence; in all moments."

"I release confusing sadness with compassion; in all moments."

"I extract all sadness from compassion; in all moments."

"I repair and fortify the Wei chi of all my bodies; in all moments."

"I eliminate the first cause in being sad; in all moments."

"I shift my paradigm from sadness to joy; in all moments."

"I transcend sadness; in all moments."

"I am centered and empowered in joy; in al moments."

Recharge the Energy in Your Feet

(Say each statement three times out loud while continuously tapping on the top of your head at the crown chakra and say it a fourth time while tapping on your chest.)

"I release neglecting my feet; in all moments."

"I release abusing my feet; in all moments."

"I release the pain, burden and trauma that my feet have endured; in all moments."

"I release the thankless horror of walking the shoals of life that my feet have had to bear; in all moments."

"I release the callous indifference shown to my feet; in all moments."

"I release relying on my feet as the last vestige for life; in all moments."

"I release relying on my feet as the last vestige for safety; in all moments."

"I release taking my feet for granted; in all moments."

"I release ignoring my feet; in all moments."

"I release treating my feet like inanimate objects; in all moments."

"I release torturing my feet by wearing heels; in all moments."

"I release suffocating my feet in synthetic layers; in all moments."

"I release denying energy to my feet; in all moments."

"I extract all the layers of emotional anguish built up in my feet; in all moments."

"I untwist the energy in my feet; in all moments."

"I release being cut off from my feet; in all moments."

"I untangle the energy in my feet; in all moments."

"I un-gnarl my feet and the bones within them; in all moments."

"I flush healing, loving energy perpetually through my feet; in all moments."

"I release cutting the communication of my feet off from the loving nature of earth; in all moments."

"I remove all vivaxes between my feet and pain; in all moments."

"I remove all tentacles between my feet and pain; in all moments."

"I remove all the mental anguish and abuse that my feet have had to endure; in all moments."

"I release wearing uncomfortable shoes to simulate my feet being bound; in all moments."

"I validate and appreciate my feet; in all moments."

"I empower my feet to reconnect to mother earth; in all moments."

"I am centered and empowered in happy, healthy, validated and fluid feet; in all moments."

Female Empowerment

These taps were implemented by dynamic healers at the same time the Million Women March was going on. We tapped into the synergy of that event and magnified the effectiveness of their intention. Please do these taps if you wish to be a part of the awakening of humanity.

(Say each statement three times while tapping on your head and say it a fourth time while tapping on your chest.)

"I declare myself a surrogate for female empowerment in doing these taps; in all moments."

"I gift all those who are indifferent to the plight of humanity, the sensitivities of an empath; in all moments."

"I strip all denial off of all those who are indifferent to the plight of humanity; in all moments."

"We release allowing male energy to run amok; in all moments."

"We remove all masks, walls and armor from all those who are indifferent to the plight of humanity; in all moments."

"We release the burden of being born female; in all moments."

"We release dreading our female incarnations; in all moments."

"We release enabling male superiority; in all moments."

"We release sinking into the background; in all moments."

"We release being complacent with male superiority; in all moments."

"We release diminishing ourselves to allow male superiority to shine; in all moments."

"I release hiding my gift to fly under the radar of male superiority; in all moments."

"I release creating the beast of male superiority; in all moments."

"I release being enamored with male superiority; in all moments."

"I release converting my empowerment to empty chatter; in all moments."

"We release being enslaved to male superiority; in all moments."

"We release diminishing ourselves to empower male superiority; in all moments."

"We remove all vivaxes between ourselves and male superiority; in all moments."

"We remove all tentacles between ourselves and male superiority; in all moments."

"We remove all our energy from male superiority; in all moments."

"I collapse and dissolve male superiority; in all moments."

"I remove all programming and conditioning of male superiority; in all moments."

"I remove all individual and universal engrams of male superiority; in all moments."

"I release indulging in male superiority; in all moments."

"I release using male superiority to diminish others; in all moments."

"I send all energy matrices into the light and sound that enable or propagate male superiority; in all moments."

"I command all complex energy matrices that enable or propagate male superiority to be escorted into the light and sound; in all moments."

"I crumble all constructs mandated by male superiority; in all moments."

"I nullify all contracts with male superiority; in all moments."

"I strip all illusion off of male superiority; in all moments."

"I eliminate the first cause in creating male superiority; in all moments."

"We hold an open portal for universal female empowerment; in all moments."

"We release being confused for androgynous humanoids; in all moments."

"We release the fear of human androgyny; in all moments."

"We release the fear of gay people; in all moments."

"We release confusing human gay people with androgynous humanoids; in all moments."

"I release being locked in the body; in all moments."

"I release the belief that I must be perfect to be empowered; in all moments."

"I release attacking imperfection; in all moments."

"I relinquish the ruthless pursuit of perfection; in all moments."

"I am centered and empowered in universal female empowerment; in all moments."

Female Issues

(Say three times while tapping on your head and say it a fourth time while tapping on your chest.)

"I release associating being female with being weak; in all moments."

"I release feeling at the mercy of male energy; in all moments."

"I release the trauma of being forced; in all moments."

"I release the guilt and shame of giving up my free will; in all moments."

"I release the trauma of having a baby; in all moments."

"I release the trauma of being raped; in all moments."

"I release the fear of motherhood; in all moments."

"I release the trauma of being a woman; in all moments."

"I release the trauma of child birth; in all moments."

"I release the trauma of losing my baby; in all moments."

"I release the trauma of being dominated; in all moments."

"I release the trauma of being pinned down; in all moments."

"I release the trauma of being fondled; in all moments."

"I release the trauma of being fingered; in all moments."

"I release the trauma of being passed around; in all moments."

"I release the fear of dying; in all moments."

"I release the trauma of being sent to my death; in all moments."

"I release the trauma of being sacrificed; in all moments."

"I release feeling alone; in all moments."

"I release being abandoned; in all moments."

"I release the trauma of being stabbed; in all moments."

"I remove all fatal wounds; in all moments."

"I release the trauma of bleeding out; in all moments."

"I release associating menstruation with dying; in all moments."

"I heal my pelvic bowl; in all moments."

Empowering Women

(Say each statement three times while tapping on your head and say it a fourth time while tapping on your chest.)

"I release the belief that women are evil; in all moments."

"I release the belief that women are whores; in all moments."

"I release the belief that women are weak; in all moments."

"I release hating women; in all moments."

"I release diminishing women; in all moments."

"I release raping women; in all moments."

"I release the trauma of being raped; in all moments."

"I release beating women; in all moments."

"I release killing women; in all moments."

"I release the trauma of childbirth; in all moments."

"I release robbing the womb; in all moments."

"I release the trauma of having my baby ripped from my womb; in all moments."

"I release the belief that women are inferior to men; in all moments."

"I release the belief that men are superior to women; in all moments."

"I release stealing women's gifts; in all moments."

"I release enslaving women; in all moments."

"I recant all vows and agreements between myself and female energy; in all moments."

"I remove all curses between myself and female energy; in all moments."

"I dissolve all diminishing views about women; in all moments."

"I remove all negative programming in regards to women; in all moments."

"I dissolve all karmic ties between myself and female energy; in all moments."

"I remove all the pain, burden and limitations that being female has put on me; in all moments."

"I remove all the pain burden and limitations that I have put on all women; in all moments."

"I take back all the joy, love, abundance, freedom, health, success, security, companionship, creativity, peace, life, wholeness and balance that being female has taken from me; in all moments."

"I give back all the joy, love, abundance, freedom, health, success, security, companionship, creativity, peace, life, wholeness and balance that I have taken from all women; in all moments."

"I release defining being female as inferior; in all moments."

"I empower female energy; in all moments."

"I release the power struggle between women and men; in all moments."

"I balance out the yin and yang in all moments."

"I am centered in equality between women and men; in all moments."

"I define women as joy, love, abundance, freedom, health, success, security, companionship, creativity, peace, life, wholeness and balance; in all moments."

"I make space in this world for empowered, valued female energy, equal to male energy; in all moments."

"I remove all blockages to having empowered, valued female energy equal to male in the world; in all moments."

"I stretch the world's capacity to accept empowered, valued female energy equal to male's in the world; in all moments."

Fibromyalgia

(Say each statement three times while tapping on your head and say it a fourth time while tapping on your chest.)

"I release storing emotional issues along the pathway of my nerves; in all moments."

"I release the inflammation in my nerves and nerve endings; in all moments."

"I remove all emotional issues that are stored along the pathway of my nerves; in all moments."

"I repair the myelin sheath on all my nerves and nerve endings; in all moments."

"I strengthen the myelin sheath on all my nerves and nerve endings; in all moments."

"I remove all issues that are pressing against my nerves and nerve endings; in all moments."

"I release using pain as a crutch; in all moments."

"I release needing to be validated; in all moments."

"I release attracting negative energy into my body through gossip or complaining; in all moments."

"I release allowing others to dump their issues into me; in all moments."

"I remove all the toxic energy that has been dumped in my essence; in all moments."

"I untangle all confusion between my sympathetic and parasympathetic nervous system; in all moments."

"I release poisoning myself; in all moments."

"I remove all toxins from my environment; in all moments."

"I release the belief that I need to allow people to dump on me; in all moments."

"I release being a caretaker; in all moments."

"I take care of myself; in all moments."

"I release being depleted by others; in all moments."

"I replenish my essence through the perpetual fountain of gratitude within; in all moments."

"I remove all engrams of being in pain; in all moments."

"I release punishing myself; in all moments."

"I collapse and dissolve all portals to pain; in all moments."

"I shift my paradigm from pain to optimal health; in all moments."

"I transcend all pain; in all moments."

"I mute all signals of pain; in all moments."

"I am centered and empowered in the gratitude of optimal health; in all moments."

Food Intolerances

(Say each statement three times while tapping on your head and say it a fourth time while tapping on your chest.)

"I release being poisoned; in all moments."

"I release finding it difficult to stomach life; in all moments."

"I release interpreting life as difficult; in all moments."

"I release the trauma of trying to survive; in all moments."

"I release eating rotting food; in all moments."

"I release being immersed in putrid living conditions; in all moments."

"I release processing sugar as poison; in all moments."

"I release confusing sugar as poison; in all moments."

"I remove all engrams of being poisoned; in all moments."

"I nullify all contracts with being poisoned; in all moments."

"I release eating garbage; in all moments."

"I release being subject to squalor; in all moments."

"I cleanse my body of all poisons; in all moments."

"I release associating natural sugars with poison to the body; in all moments."

"I fortify my body with trust and resilience; in all moments."

"I naturally flush out all that is not beneficial to the body; in all moments."

"I accept the blessing of healthy foods; in all moments."

"I release interpreting sugar as an enemy to the body; in all moments."

"I release rejecting the sweetness of life; in all moments."

"I trust the sweetness of life; in all moments."

"I am worthy and blessed to accept the sweetness of life; in all moments."

Food Issues Marathon

(Say each statement three times out loud while continuously tapping on the top of your head at the crown chakra and say it a fourth time while tapping on your chest.)

"I release the primal need to forage for food; in all moments."

"I release using foraging for food as a distraction from stress; in all moments."

"I release mourning my own innocence; in all moments."

"I release mourning a more innocent time; in all moments."

"I release the trauma of starving to death; in all moments."

"I release confusing hunger with starving to death; in all moments."

"I release the guilt of eating; in all moments."

"I release trying to feed the whole group through my body; in all moments."

"I dry up the void of depravity within; in all moments."

"I dry up the inner hunger; in all moments."

"I release defining being thin as unhealthy; in all moments."

"I release associating being thin with disease and poverty; in all moments."

"I release the trauma of being poor and diseased; in all moments."

"I release associating being thin as being invisible; in all moments."

"I release confusing being thin with being weak; in all moments."

"I release the fear of being weak; in all moments."

"I release protecting myself in a big body; in all moments."

"I release using weight to compensate for feeling weak; in all moments."

"I release confusing carrying extra weight with being strong and safe; in all moments."

"I release the fear of being attractive; in all moments."

"I release hiding my beauty; in all moments."

"I release using weight to hide; in all moments."

"I embrace my own beauty; in all moments."

"I release eating out of boredom; in all moments."

"I release eating as a coping mechanism; in all moments."

"I release eating because I am sad; in all moments."

"I release eating to fill a void; in all moments."

"I release eating to feel loved; in all moments."

"I release eating to feel comfort; in all moments."

"I release eating to feel safe; in all moments."

"I release eating to kill time; in all moments."

"I release eating to feel busy; in all moments."

"I release eating as a form of distraction; in all moments."

"I release eating for entertainment; in all moments."

"I release eating to be social; in all moments."

"I release eating to celebrate; in all moments."

"I release thinking of food as a friend; in all moments."

"I release the fear of being hungry; in all moments."

"I release eating to nurture myself; in all moments."

"I release being obsessed with food; in all moments."

"I release using food as a hobby; in all moments."

"I am centered and satiated in joy, love, abundance, freedom, health, life and wholeness; in all moments."

"I release feeding the pain; in all moments."

"I remove the pain; in all moments."

"I recant all vows and agreements between myself and the pain; in all moments."

"I remove all curses between myself and the pain; in all moments."

"I dissolve all karmic ties between myself and the pain; in all moments."

"I remove all the shame, burden and limitations that pain has put on me; in all moments."

"I withdraw all my energy from the pain; in all moments."

"I take back all the joy, love, abundance, freedom, health, success, security, companionship, peace, life and wholeness that the pain has taken from me; in all moments."

"I release resonating with the pain; in all moments."

"I release emanating with the pain; in all moments."

"I remove all the pain from my sound frequency; in all moments."

"I remove all the pain from my light body; in all moments."

"I shift my paradigm from pain to joy, love, abundance, freedom, health, success, security, companionship, peace, life and wholeness that the pain has taken from me; in all moments."

"I am centered and empowered in divine love; in all moments."

"I release the fear of being hungry; in all moments."

"I release confusing hunger for death; in all moments."

"I release going into survival mode when I am hungry; in all moments."

"I release defining a huge meal as security; in all moments."

"I release defining a huge meal as love; in all moments."

"I release confusing sugar for love; in all moments."

"I release confusing fatty foods with security; in all moments."

"I release the fear of not having enough; in all moments."

"I release perceiving mealtime as a competition; in all moments."

"I release all the pain and trauma of dying of starvation from my mealtime ritual; in all moments."

"I release confusing dieting with despair; in all moments."

"I release confusing dieting with suicide; in all moments."

"I release storing emotional issues in my physical body; in all moments."

"I release using my body for emotional storage; in all moments."

"I release declaring myself fat; in all moments."

"I release eating shame; in all moments."

"I release protecting myself in fat; in all moments."

"I release insulating myself from pain; in all moments."

"I recant all vows and agreements between myself and fat; in all moments."

"I remove all curses between myself and fat; in all moments."

"I dissolve all karmic ties between myself and fat; in all moments."

"I remove all the pain, burden and limitations that fat has put on me; in all moments."

Free All Souls

(Say each statement three times while tapping on your head and say it a fourth time while tapping on your chest.)

"We release being paralyzed in any one moment of time and space; in all moments."

"We free all souls trapped in any one moment of time and space; in all moments."

"We free all souls trapped in the past; in all moments."

"We free all souls trapped in anticipating the future; in all moments."

"We free all souls trapped in worshiping any one moment; in all moments."

"We free all souls trapped in waiting; in all moments."

"We free all souls trapped in fear; in all moments."

"We free all souls trapped in death; in all moments."

"We free all souls trapped in worship; in all moments."

"We free all souls trapped in delusion; in all moments."

"We free all souls trapped in illusion; in all moments."

"We free all souls trapped in the concept of one life; in all moments."

"We free all souls trapped in a limiting belief system; in all moments."

"We free all those paralyzed in the moment of Jesus' birth; in all moments."

"We free all souls trapped in time and space; in all moments.""

"We release the energy that is trapped in the telling of the moment of Jesus's birth; in all moments."

"We break free the energy that is encapsulated in the nativity scene story; in all moments."

"We rip open all moments that have been frozen in time and space; in all moments."

"We rip open and free all energy that has been encapsulated in nostalgia; in all moments."

"We rip open all encapsulated moments that have been used to paralyze souls; in all moments."

"We gush forth all the energy that has been trapped in any encapsulated moments; in all moments."

"We free all energy that has been frozen in encapsulation and return it to the collective; in all moments."

"We return the magic, wonder and sanctity of the moment to the fluid perpetual state of being; in all moments."

"All souls are immersed in the magic, wonder and sanctity of the moment in a perpetual state of being; in all moments."

"Joy, love and freedom abundantly flow in a perpetual state of providence for all; in all moments."

"All souls realize themselves as worthy, abundant and free; in all moments."

Freedom

(Say each statement three times out loud while continuously tapping on the top of your head at the crown chakra and say it a fourth time while tapping on your chest.)

"All vivaxes are removed; in all moments."

"All tentacles between myself and all others, are removed; in all moments."

"All engrams that I have put on all others are removed; in all moments."

"All engrams that all others have put on me are removed; in all moments."

"All curses or blessings between myself and all others are removed; in all moments."

"All intention between myself and all others are removed; in all moments."

"All programs and conditioning that I have put on all others is removed; in all moments."

"All programming and conditioning that all others have put on me is removed; in all moments."

"All glass ceilings that I have put on all others are removed; in all moments."

"All glass ceilings that all others have put on me are removed; in all moments."

"All the pain that I have put on all others is removed; in all moments."

"All the pain that all others have put on me is removed; in all moments."

"All the illusion of separateness is removed; in all moments."

"All energy matrices that I have put on all others or that all others have put on me are dissolved in the light and sound; in all moments."

"All the influence that I have put on all others or all the influence they have put on me are removed; in all moments."

"I am centered and empowered in gracing all with personal freedom; in all moments."

"I receive what I give; in all moments."

"I resonate, emanate and am interconnected with all life in freedom for all; in all moments."

Freedom from Oppression

Anybody who is tired of the status quo, wants to be wealthy, feels discouraged with the state of affairs, wants to make a difference, takes up causes, cares about the survival of other species, quietly subscribes to conspiracy theories, believes we can do better, wants to see change, or is just bored and indifferent, needs to do these taps.

(Say each statement three times out loud while continuously tapping on the top of your head at the crown chakra and say it a fourth time while tapping on your chest at the heart chakra.)

"I release being enslaved to the warlords of the wealthy; in all moments."

"I release humanity being enslaved to the warlords of the wealthy; in all moments."

"I release being shackled to the warlords of the wealthy; in all moments."

"I release humanity being shackled to the warlords of the wealthy; in all moments."

"I release engaging the warlords of the wealthy; in all moments."

"I release humanity engaging the warlords of the wealthy; in all moments."

"I recant all vows and agreements between myself and the warlords of the wealthy; in all moments."

"I recant all vows and agreements between humanity and the warlords of the wealthy; in all moments."

"I remove all curses between myself and the warlords of the wealthy; in all moments."

"I remove all curses between humanity and the warlords of the wealthy; in all moments."

"I remove all blessings between myself and the warlords of the wealthy; in all moments."

"I remove all blessings between humanity and the warlords of the wealthy; in all moments."

"I sever all strings and cords between myself and the warlords of the wealthy; in all moments."

"I sever all strings and cords between humanity and the warlords of the wealthy; in all moments."

"I dissolve all karmic ties between myself and the warlords of the wealthy; in all moments."

"I dissolve all karmic ties between humanity and the warlords of the wealthy; in all moments."

"I remove all shackles of the warlords of the wealthy from myself; in all moments."

"Humanity removes all shackles of the warlords from itself; in all moments."

"I remove all the implants that the warlords of the wealthy have embedded in me; in all moments."

"Humanity removes all the implants that the warlords of the wealthy have embedded within it; in all moments."

"I crumble all the archaic structures of the warlords of the wealthy; in all moments."

"Humanity crumbles all the archaic structures of the warlords of the wealthy; in all moments."

"I take back and restore my keystone from the warlords of the wealthy; in all moments."

"Humanity takes back and restores its keystone from the warlords of the wealthy; in all moments."

"The first rule of the warlords of the wealthy is eliminated; in all moments."

"The first rule of the warlords of the wealthy in regard to humanity is eliminated; in all moments."

"I remove all the pain, burden, limitations and engrams that the warlords of the wealthy have put on me; in all moments."

"Humanity removes all the pain, burden, limitations and engrams that the warlords of the wealthy have put on it; in all moments."

"I remove all the pain, burden, limitations and engrams that I have put on all others due to the warlords of the wealthy; in all moments."

"Humanity removes all the pain, burden, limitations and engrams that it has put on all others due to the warlords of the wealthy; in all moments."

"I take back all the joy, love, abundance, freedom, health, success, security, companionship, creativity, peace, life, wholeness, beauty, enthusiasm, contentment, spirituality, enlightenment, confidence, family, intellect and the ability to discern that the warlords of the wealthy have taken from me; in all moments."

"Humanity takes back all the joy, love, abundance, freedom, health, success, security, companionship, creativity, peace, life, wholeness, beauty, enthusiasm, contentment, spirituality, enlightenment, confidence, family, intellect and the ability to discern that the warlords of the wealthy have taken from it; in all moments."

"I give back to all others all the joy, love, abundance, freedom, health, success, security, companionship, creativity, peace, life, wholeness, beauty, enthusiasm, contentment, spirituality, enlightenment, confidence, family, intellect and the ability to discern that I have taken from them due to the warlords of the wealthy; in all moments."

"Humanity gives back to all others all the joy, love, abundance, freedom, health, success, security, companionship, creativity, peace, life, wholeness, beauty, enthusiasm, contentment, spirituality, enlightenment, confidence, family, intellect and the ability to discern that it has taken from all others due to the warlords of the wealthy; in all moments."

"I release resonating with the warlords of the wealthy; in all moments."

"Humanity releases resonating with the warlords of the wealthy; in all moments."

"I release emanating with the warlords of the wealthy; in all moments."

"Humanity releases emanating with the warlords of the wealthy; in all moments."

"I extract all of the warlords of the wealthy from my sound frequency; in all moments."

"I extract all of the warlords of the wealthy from humanity's sound frequency; in all moments."

"I extract all of the warlords of the wealthy from my light emanation; in all moments."

"I extract all of the warlords of the wealthy from humanity's light emanation; in all moments."

"I shift my paradigm from the warlords of the wealthy to joy, love, abundance, freedom, health, success, security, companionship, creativity, peace, life, wholeness, beauty, enthusiasm, contentment, spirituality, enlightenment, confidence, family, intellect and the ability to discern; in all moments."

"I shift humanity's paradigm from the warlords of the wealthy to joy, love, abundance, freedom, health, success, security, companionship, creativity, peace, life, wholeness, beauty, enthusiasm, contentment, spirituality, enlightenment, confidence, family, intellect and the ability to discern; in all moments."

"I transcend the warlords of the wealthy; in all moments."

"Humanity transcends the warlords of the wealthy; in all moments."

"I strip all the illusion off of the warlords of the wealthy; in all moments."

"Humanity strips all of the illusion off of the warlords of the wealthy; in all moments."

"I repair and fortify the Wei chi of all my bodies; in all moments."

"Humanity repairs and fortifies the Wei chi of all its layers; in all moments."

"I remove all masks, walls and armor off of the warlords of the wealthy; in all moments."

"Humanity removes all masks, walls and armor off of the warlords of the wealthy; in all moments."

"I am centered and empowered in divine love; in all moments."

"Humanity is centered and empowered in divine love; in all moments."

"I and humanity are aligned with truth; in all moments."

"I and humanity resonate and emanate joy, love, abundance, freedom, health, success, security, companionship, creativity, peace, life, wholeness, beauty, enthusiasm, contentment, spirituality, enlightenment, confidence, family, intellect and the ability to discern; in all moments."

Becoming a Star or Even a Galaxy

Recently, I facilitated a remote healing session for a dynamic healer. She has worked out so many of the issues of being in a human body that it is always a fascination that we find things to work on. As a person, she feels like strong, dynamic yet very kind, wise energy. Her sessions feel like we are doing research in ways to uplift all of humanity.

In a soul's journey, it starts out whole. Then souls start to have experiences that seem to diminish them and leave them fractured. They have to use all their strength and fortitude to gain wholeness again. They forget that they are infinite energy and believe they are a body and don't know how to believe in themselves again as an energetic being.

So what they do is identify with others that seem to have the qualities they seek. They may take on the qualities of bravery, justice and truth that they have borrowed from those who seem to have them. But along with the good qualities, they take on the energies of what it took to gain those experiences. In emotions, those could include fear and anger. In thoughts, they could be self-righteousness or superiority.

Since we are working in intangible realms, it is difficult to name what we are doing. We are working in energy using tangible means to create an upgrade. Of course, we are all pure love anyway, so this whole experience is useless as pure love. But from the human vantage point, it is priceless in recognizing one's self as pure love.

It is time to release fragmented energies. Fragmented energies are all concepts, feelings, emotions and behaviors and beliefs that do not add to one's wholeness. They are all the ghosts that we have allowed to live in our house and our body. They are all the things that siphon off out joy. They are things that we have agreed to out of ignorance. It is time to dissipate them and gain the wholeness of divinity.

(Say each statement three times out loud while tapping on the top of your head at the crown chakra and say it a fourth time while tapping on your chest at the heart chakra.)

"I release being attached to fragmented energies; in all moments."

"I release being disillusioned by fragmented energies; in all moments."

"I release being vested in fragmented energies; in all moments."

"I release giving over my power to fragmented energies; in all moments."

"I release invoking fragmented energies for empowerment; in all moments."

"I release gathering fragmented energies all around me; in all moments."

"I release identifying with fragmented energies; in all moments."

"I release getting tangled in fragmented energies; in all moments."

"I release being immersed in fragmented energies; in all moments."

"I recant all vows and agreements between myself and all fragmented energies; in all moments."

"I remove all curses between myself and all fragmented energies; in all moments."

"I sever all strings between myself and all fragmented energies; in all moments."

"I dissolve all karmic ties between myself and all fragmented energies; in all moments."

"I remove all the pain, burden, limitations, engrams and anger that all fragmented energies have put on me; in all moments."

"I remove all the pain, burden, limitations, engrams and anger that I have put on all others due to fragmented energies; in all moments."

"I take back all the joy, love, abundance, freedom, health, success, security, companionship, creativity, peace, life, wholeness, beauty, enthusiasm, contentment, spirituality, enlightenment and confidence that all fragmented energies have taken from me; in all moments."

"I give back all the joy, love, abundance, freedom, health, success, security, companionship, creativity, peace, life, wholeness, beauty, enthusiasm, contentment, spirituality, enlightenment and confidence that I have taken from all others due to fragmented energies; in all moments."

"I withdraw all my energy from all fragmented energies; in all moments."

"I collapse all fragmented energies and remove them from my beingness; in all moments."

"I release resonating with fragmented energies; in all moments."

"I release emanating with fragmented energies; in all moments."

"I remove all fragmented energies from my sound frequency; in all moments."

"I remove all fragmented energies from my light body; in all moments."

"I repair and fortify the Wei chi of both my sound frequency and my light emanation; in all moments."

"I shift society's paradigm from fragmented energies to joy, love, abundance, freedom, health, success, security, companionship, creativity, peace, life, wholeness, beauty, enthusiasm, contentment, spirituality, enlightenment and confidence; in all moments

"I transcend all fragmented energies; in all moments."

"I recalibrate the weave of my light emanation through and within my sound frequency; in all moments."

"I repair all compromise in my sound frequency's engagement of my light emanations; in all moments."

"I infuse recognition of my wholeness into the perfect engagement of my sound frequency with my light body; in all moments."

"I am centered and empowered in the wholeness of the perfect engagement of my sound frequency with my light body; in all moments."

"I infuse the wholeness of the perfect engagement of my sound frequency with my light body with infinite and perpetual joy, love abundance freedom, health, success, security, companionship, creativity, peace, life, wholeness, beauty, enthusiasm, contentment, spirituality, enlightenment and confidence; in all moments."

As we finished these taps, I saw my client as a beautiful, vibrant, pulsing silver cord of light and love. We were somewhere in a galaxy and I saw the brilliance of a star emerge. It was there before, but now it was emanating in all directions with a vibrancy that was palpable. This is no less than what I wish for you in doing these taps. May you see yourself shining in space as your own star or perhaps your own galaxy.

Free Yourself from Other Realities and Dimensions

(Say each statement three times out loud while continuously tapping on the top of your head at the crown chakra and say it a fourth time while tapping on your chest.)

"I remove all vivaxes between myself and all other realities and dimensions; in all moments."

"I remove all tentacles between myself and all other realities and dimensions; in all moments."

"I remove all programming and conditioning that all other realities and dimensions have put on me; in all moments."

"I remove all engrams that all other realities and dimensions have put on me; in all moments."

"I remove all the fear and isolation that all other realities and dimensions have put on me; in all moments."

"I release being manipulated by all realities and dimensions; in all moments."

"I release being a pawn for any realities or dimensions; in all moments."

"I release being at the mercy of any realities or dimensions; in all moments."

"I remove all the trauma that has been inflicted on me by any realities or dimensions; in all moments."

"I release being galvanized to complacency by any other realities or dimensions; in all moments."

"I release being drained of my life force by any other realities or dimensions; in all moments."

"I take back my life force from all realities and all dimensions; in all moments."

"I recant all vows and agreements between myself and all realities and all dimensions; in all moments."

"I am DONE diminishing myself; in all moments."

"I release being the amusement of other realities or dimensions; in all moments."

"I remove all curses between myself and all realities and all dimensions; in all moments."

"I remove all blessings between myself and all realities and all dimensions; in all moments."

"I sever all strings and cords and wires between myself and all realities and dimensions; in all moments."

"I dissolve all karmic ties between myself and all realities and dimensions; in all moments."

"I remove all the fear and isolation that I have put on all others in all realities and all dimensions; in all moments."

"I remove all the pain, burden and limitations that have been put on me by all realities and all dimensions; in all moments."

"I remove all the pain, burden and limitations that I have put on all others in all realities and all dimensions; in all moments."

"I give back all the good that I have taken from all others in all realities and all dimensions; in all moments."

"I take back all the good that has been taken from me in all realities and all dimensions; in all moments."

"I heal all those I have wounded in all realities and all dimensions; in all moments."

"I right all wrongs that I have committed in all realities and all dimensions; in all moments."

"I heal my body in all realities and in all dimensions; in all moments."

"I right all wrongs that have been done to me in all realities and in all dimensions; in all moments."

"I wipe my slate clean in all realities and in all dimensions; in all moments."

"I transcend all realities and dimensions; in all moments."

"I close up all portals between all realities and dimensions that don't mutually support both parties in being empowered in Divine Love; in all moments."

"I withdraw all my energy from all realities and all dimensions; in all moments."

"I strip all illusion off of all realities and all dimensions; in all moments."

"I withdraw my allegiance from any particular reality or dimension; in all moments."

"I release resonating with any realities or dimensions; in all moments."

"I release emanating with any realities or dimensions; in all moments."

"I extract all realities and dimensions from my beingness; in all moments."

"I extract all realities and dimensions from my sound frequency; in all moments."

"I extract all realities and dimensions from my light emanation; in all moments."

"I declare myself a pure particle of pure love; in all moments."

"I declare myself a pure channel for Divine Love in all realities and in all dimensions; in all moments."

"I align all my beingnesses in all realities, in all dimensions and in all moments."

"I am centered and empowered and imbued in Divine Love in all realities, in all dimensions and in all moments."

"Divine Love dissolves all reactionary states within my beingness in all realities, in all dimensions and in all moments."

Bad Ass Assistance

So many think that they are in it alone. They feel at the mercy of subtle energies. They think that anyone else would consider them insane if they knew the thoughts that were running through their head. Many feel like they are being controlled by outer influences. Let me assure you that you are not alone.

Do these taps with the understanding that there is a legion of assistance helping you regain your empowerment even if you don't know what that looks like or have never achieved it yet in this life. Please know that these taps are a powerful amulet to get yourself and your peace of mind back. I do understand. The group sessions that I facilitate have become a dynamic force of healing and empowerment in this world.

We are joined in our calls by the Ancient Ones who support all that I do. They support your freedom as well. We are all here to assist you in awakening from a hell or a glitch in your day, either one. Degrees don't matter. Empowerment does, in any degree. I see you. You are loved. You matter.

(Say each statement three times while tapping on your head and say it a fourth time while tapping on your chest.)

"We push all intruders out; in all moments."

"We push all controlling energy out; in all moments."

"We push all spying energy out; in all moments."

"We push all walk-ins out; in all moments."

"We send all energy matrices into the light and sound that are invading our space; in all moments."

"All complex energy matrices that are invading our space are escorted into the light and sound; in all moments."

"We are returned to wholeness; in all moments."

"Our Wei chi is repaired and fortified; in all moments."

"All that is sabotaging higher consciousness is dissolved in the light and sound; in all moments."

"All that is causing lethargy is dissolved into the light and sound; in all moments."

"We are joyful, abundant, empowered, whole and free; in all moments."

Frozen Shoulder

Recently, I facilitated a private remote session with someone who came to me for help with a frozen shoulder. Immediately, I got an impression of the issue. I saw her in a past life with a huge shield in the left hand, pulled and clenched to the body and in a very defensive stance. When we connected by phone for her session, she validated that it was indeed her left shoulder. She also validated that people in this lifetime seemed to attack her for no reason and it did make her defensive. I explained to her that the attacks were reminders or hints to the conscious mind of what she had suffered in the past without having to remember details. Her inner energy was not fluid but stuck in the position of the warrior.

I can tell that I am accurate in accessing an issue because the client will have difficulty hearing the taps I give them, retaining them enough to say them, and repeating them back to me. It was very difficult for this client to get through any of the taps. The energy was so stagnant and locked in her body that it was difficult to connect with her enough to help her release it by saying the taps.

The imagery of different lifetimes in war was layered within her. Besides the initial image, I saw her rotting in a dank dungeon chained to a wall, in many different battle scenarios and definitely spending many lifetimes living, fighting and dying in the Crusades. When someone has been in the Crusades, the Hallelujah song comes to me as a way to release the issues. She was so congested with these lifetimes that I sang the Hallelujah song to her. She cried profusely during it. This released the issues in her a bit. I then was able to lead her through some taps to free up her energy more.

Here are some taps that I lead her through: (Say each statement three times while tapping on your head and say it a fourth time while tapping on your chest.)

"I declare myself a surrogate for humanity." (Optional)

"I release fighting for my life; in all moments."

"I release the trauma of being attacked; in all moments."

"I release being in attack mode; in all moments."

"I release defending my life; in all moments."

"I release being defensive; in all moments."

"I release the guilt and trauma of killing others; in all moments."

"I release hating the Church; in all moments."

"I release fighting and dying for a cause I don't believe in; in all moments."

"I release the trauma of being at war; in all moments."

"I release infusing apathy into life; in all moments."

"I release the trauma of being tortured; in all moments."

"I release the trauma of being imprisoned; in all moments."

"I recant all vows and agreements between myself and all battles; in all moments."

"I remove all curses between myself and all battles; in all moments."

"I dissolve all karmic ties between myself and all battles; in all moments."

"I remove all the pain, burden and limitations that all battles have put on me; in all moments."

"I take back all the joy, love, abundance, freedom, health, peace, life and wholeness that all battles have taken from me; in all moments."

"I withdraw all my energy from all battles; in all moments."

"I release resonating with all battles; in all moments."

"I release emanating with all battles; in all moments."

"I remove all battles from my sound frequency; in all moments."

"I remove all battles from my light body; in all moments."

"I shift my paradigm from all battles to joy, love, abundance, freedom, health, life and wholeness; in all moments."

"I repair and fortify my Wei chi; in all moments."

"I am centered and empowered in Divine Love; in all moments."

At the end of the session, the client could feel the energy in her body as more fluid. She was happy and enthused with her session. She had been to many alternative and conventional healers. None were able to assist. I understood why. I had to really pin her down energetically to help her strip these issues off. It is similar to sitting on someone and stripping layers of tight clothing off of them. I went deep and was more relentless than they were able to be.

Maybe by doing the taps above, we all can shift the tide of current events. Maybe we can work as inside agents to free and uplift humanity. Maybe we can unhinge the unconscious allure for war and move humanity to peace! Who is willing to do this?

Gain Wisdom

(Say each statement three times out loud while continuously tapping on the top of your head and say it a fourth time while tapping on your chest.)

"I tap into the Wisdom of the Trees; in all moments."

"I tap into my tree embodiment; in all moments."

"I live, move and have my beingness within our tree essence; in all moments."

"I connect to the Universal Tree of Life; in all moments."

"I embrace our inner Tree; in all moments."

"I declare myself a surrogate for humanity in doing these taps; in all moments."

"I make space in this world to embrace truth; in all moments."

"I remove all blockages to embracing truth; in all moments."

"I stretch our capacity to embrace truth; in all moments."

"I remove all blinders off of seeing truth; in all moments."

"I release all resistance to truth; in all moments."

"I release resisting the healing energy; in all moments."

"I release all resistance to being physically healed; in all moments."

"I release all resistance to being emotionally healed; in all moments."

"I release all resistance to being mentally healed; in all moments."

"I release all resistance to being spiritually healed; in all moments."

"I embrace a total healing of my physical realm; in all moments."

"I accept a complete healing of my physical body; in all moments."

"I embrace a total healing of my astral realm; in all moments."

"I accept a complete healing of my emotional body; in all moments."

"I embrace a total healing of my causal realm; in all moments."

"I accept a complete healing of my causal body; in all moments."

"I embrace a total healing of my mental realm; in all moments."

"I accept a complete healing of my mental body; in all moments."

"I embrace a total healing of my spiritual realm; in all moments."

"I accept a complete healing of my spiritual body; in all moments."

"I untangle all my energies; in all moments."

"I wholeheartedly accept the love; in all moments."

"I drench myself in divine love; in all moments."

"I saturate myself in celestial sound; in all moments."

"I illuminate myself in illustrious light; in all moments."

"I connect with all other souls in the light and sound of love; in all moments."

"I lay down my sword and shield; in all moments."

Goals

When I facilitate private remote sessions, I learn so much about human nature. It is wonderful to share insights that are revealed to help people release deep core beliefs. By using taps to change core dynamics, lives are able to shift into more productivity and happiness relatively quickly.

What I have discovered recently is that people equivocate two concepts as one. If something doesn't involve both concepts, then they negate both gains. An example of this is someone who wants to be in a relationship, so they equivocate love with having a mate. They are so fixated on having a mate that they negate all the other forms of love that are bombarding them.

This is another clue to cracking the code why we are not all living in complete contentment. Here are a bunch of taps to strip down some of these belief systems so the "tappers" can be closer to achieving their goal of absolute bliss.

(Say each statement three times while tapping on your head and say it a fourth time while tapping on your chest.)

"I release confusing having possessions as joy; in all moments."

"I release confusing having money for joy; in all moments."

"I release defining joy as being in a relationship; in all moments."

"I release confusing sex for love; in all moments."

"I release defining love as being in a relationship; in all moments."

"I release confusing having money with having abundance; in all moments."

"I release trying to convert all my abundance into money; in all moments."

"I release confusing being vulnerable with freedom; in all moments."

"I release using illness as a form of validation; in all moments."

"I release defining success as a job; in all moments."

"I release confusing power for success; in all moments."

"I release defining security as being in a relationship; in all moments."

"I release confusing security as a job; in all moments."

"I release confusing being dominated as security; in all moments."

"I release confusing apathy for peace; in all moments."

"I release interpreting peace as boredom; in all moments."

"I release turning contentment into depression; in all moments."

"I release confusing an adrenaline rush as running for my life; in all moments."

"I release confusing exercising as looming death; in all moments."

"I release interpreting being busy as being fragmented; in all moments."

"I release confusing 'having it all' as losing myself; in all moments."

"I remove all conditions I have put on accepting joy; in all moments."

"I remove all conditions I have put on accepting love; in all moments."

"I remove all conditions I have put on accepting abundance; in all moments."

"I remove all conditions I have put on accepting freedom; in all moments."

"I remove all conditions I have put on accepting health; in all moments."

"I remove all conditions I have put on accepting success; in all moments."

"I remove all conditions I have put on accepting security; in all moments."

"I remove all conditions I have put on accepting companionship; in all moments."

"I remove all conditions I have put on accepting peace; in all moments."

"I remove all conditions I have put on accepting life; in all moments."

"I remove all conditions I have put on accepting wholeness; in all moments."

These may be hard to get through. They may get tangled in your mind. As you get through these, you may actually get a sense of more clarity with your goals.

Affirm Your Connection to God

(Say each statement three times out loud while tapping on the top of your head at the crown chakra, and say it a fourth time while tapping on your chest at the heart chakra.)

"I release being disillusioned with life; in all moments."

"I release being disconnected from source; in all moments."

"I release the belief that I am disconnected from source; in all moments."

"I release having the connection to source be diffused by the mind; in all moments."

"I release being stuck in the dead-end of the mind; in all moments."

"I release being short-circuited from source by the emotions; in all moments."

"I release believing that I am disconnected from source by my experiences; in all moments."

"I release believing that I am disconnected from source by my beliefs; in all moments."

"I release believing that I am disconnected from source by faith; in all moments."

"I release being hard-wired to believing that I am disconnected from source; in all moments."

"I release believing that I am disconnected from source by the mind; in all moments."

"I release believing that I am disconnected from source by the emotions; in all moments."

"I release believing that I am disconnected from source by peer pressure; in all moments."

"I release believing that I am disconnected from source by outer manipulation; in all moments."

"I remove all vivaxes between myself and being disconnected from source; in all moments."

"I remove all vivaxes between myself and the belief that I am disconnected from source; in all moments."

"I release rescinding my empowerment by the belief that I am disconnected from source; in all moments."

"I remove all tentacles between myself and the belief that I am disconnected from source; in all moments."

"I remove the claws of the belief that I am disconnected from source from my beingness; in all moments."

"I remove all programming and conditioning that the belief that I am disconnected from source has put on me; in all moments."

"I remove all engrams that the belief that I am disconnected from source has put on me; in all moments."

"I remove all the pain, burden, and limitations that the belief that I am disconnected from source has put on me; in all moments."

"I remove all the fear, futility, and unworthiness that the belief that I am disconnected from source has put on me; in all moments."

"I remove the illusion of separateness that the belief that I am disconnected from source has put on me; in all moments."

"I send all energy matrices into the light and sound that have me believing that I am separate from source; in all moments."

"I command all complex energy matrices that have me believing that I am separate from source to be escorted into the light and sound by my guides; in all moments."

"I release being used as a drone to convince others that they are separate from source; in all moments."

"I release the belief in my bones that I am disconnected from source; in all moments."

"I release creating a landmine out of life; in all moments."

"I nullify all contracts between myself and the belief that I am disconnected from source; in all moments."

"I release disconnecting myself from source; in all moments."

"I recant all vows and agreements between myself and the belief that I am disconnected from source; in all moments."

"I remove all curses between myself and the belief that I am disconnected from source; in all moments."

"I remove all blessings between myself and the belief that I am disconnected from source; in all moments."

"I sever all strings, cords, and wires between myself and the belief that I am disconnected from source; in all moments."

"I dissolve all karmic ties between myself and the belief that I am disconnected from source; in all moments."

"I withdraw all my energy from the belief that I am disconnected from source; in all moments."

"I strip all illusion off of the belief that I am disconnected from source; in all moments."

"I collapse and dissolve the belief that I am disconnected from source; in all moments."

"I take back all that the belief that I am disconnected from source has taken from me; in all moments."

"I release resonating with the belief that I am disconnected from source; in all moments."

"I release emanating with the belief that I am disconnected from source; in all moments."

"I extract all of the belief that I am disconnected from source from my sound frequency; in all moments."

"I extract all of the belief that I am disconnected from source from my light emanation; in all moments."

"I shift my paradigm from the belief that I am disconnected from source to the confidence and empowerment of Divine Love; in all moments."

"I transcend the belief that I am disconnected from source; in all moments."

"I am centered and empowered in the confidence and protection of Divine Love; in all moments."

Feeling Abandoned by God

By releasing all these limiting concepts of God that we had in the past, it will allow the true essence of God to imbue one's energy. So the Zen of it is by releasing God, one can actually be closer to God.

(Say each statement three times out loud while tapping on your head and say it a fourth time while tapping on your chest)

"I release personifying God; in all moments."

"I release diminishing God to attributes of man; in all moments."

"I release the belief that I disappointed God; in all moments."

"I release being abandoned by God; in all moments."

"I release the belief that I have failed God; in all moments."

"I release being rejected by God; in all moments."

"I release being afraid of God; in all moments."

"I release the belief that God is anything but love and loving; in all moments."

"I release diminishing myself for God; in all moments."

"I release harming others in the name of God; in all moments."

"I release using God as an excuse; in all moments."

"I release using God as a crutch; in all moments."

"I release the belief that God hates me; in all moments."

"I release associating God with self shame; in all moments."

"I release being persecuted for my beliefs; in all moments."

"I release the pain and trauma of being ostracized; in all moments."

"I release being disillusioned by God; in all moments."

"I release being pitted against others for the sake of God; in all moments."

"I release the belief that God wants me to feel unworthy; in all moments."

"I remove the false sense of humility; in all moments."

"I release cowering to God; in all moments."

"I release all outmoded concepts and beliefs about God; in all moments."

"I release enslaving others to my concept of God; in all moments."

"I release interfering with others' relationship with God; in all moments."

"I release using God to feel superior to others; in all moments."

"I release using God to abuse power; in all moments."

"I release being subjected to force in the name of God; in all moments."

"I release the trauma of being sacrificed to God; in all moments."

"I release hating God; in all moments."

"I release the belief that I am separate from God; in all moments."

"I release the need to prove myself to God; in all moments."

"I release defining God as slavery; in all moments."

"I release diminishing others to please God; in all moments."

"I release allowing concepts of God to interfere with my relationship to God; in all moments."

"I recant all vows and agreements between myself and God; in all moments."

"I remove all curses between myself and God; in all moments."

"I dissolve all karmic ties between myself and God; in all moments."

"I remove all the pain, burden, limitations and engrams that God has put on me; in all moments."

"I take back all the joy, love, abundance, freedom, health, life and wholeness that God has taken from me; in all moments."

"I remove all limiting concepts of God from my sound frequency; in all moments."

"I remove all limiting concepts of God from my light body; in all moments."

"I transcend all limiting concepts of God; in all moments."

"I redefine God as divine love; in all moments."

"I am centered and empowered in divine love; in all moments."

God Doesn't Hate You

In many of my sessions, clients come to me with deeply ingrained issues. My clients, in many lifetimes, have felt isolated and lonely and have been on the fringe of their respective societies. We have all been told in past lives that we are damned or sinners. In past times, God was vengeful and unforgiving. This may play out in their current lives as self-worth issues or self-punishment via health issues.

These might be especially helpful to atheists and agnostics as they may have suffered more with this issue. Here are some taps to assist with deep-seated feelings of unworthiness:

(Say each statement three times while tapping on your head, and say it a fourth time while tapping on your chest.)

"I release the belief that God hates me; in all moments."

"I release the belief that I am damned; in all moments."

"I release the belief that I am a sinner; in all moments."

"I release the belief that God is punishing me; in all moments."

"I release hating God; in all moments."

"I recant all vows and agreements between myself and God; in all moments."

"I remove all curses between myself and God; in all moments."

"I dissolve all karmic ties between myself and God; in all moments."

(Knowing that with God, there is no karma so this isn't God.)

"I remove all the pain, burden and limitations that God has put on me; in all moments."

"I take back all the joy, love, abundance, freedom, health, life and wholeness that God has taken from me; in all moments."

"I release the belief that God wants me to suffer; in all moments."

"I release the belief that I need to win God's favor; in all moments."

"I release the belief that I am separate from God; in all moments."

"I am centered in God's love; in all moments."

"I Am Love and Loved; in all moments."

Gratitude

(Say each statement three times out loud while continuously tapping on the top of your head at the crown chakra and say it a fourth time while tapping on your chest.)

"I repair and fortify the Wei chi of my heart chakra; in all moments."

"I breathe in the reverent and healing breath of gratitude into my heart chakra; in all moments."

"I heal my heart chakra with the reverence of gratitude; in all moments."

"Gratitude perpetually ebbs and flows through my heart chakra; in all moments."

"I expand the gratitude and reverence of my heart chakra to heal all aspects of my beingness; in all moments."

"Gratitude perpetually ebbs and flows through my beingness; in all moments."

"I expand the gratitude and reverence of my heart chakra to heal all aspects of my physical world; in all moments."

"Gratitude perpetually ebbs and flows through my physical world; in all moments."

"I expand the gratitude and reverence of my heart chakra to heal all aspects of all those I love; in all moments."

"Gratitude perpetually ebbs and flows through all those I love; in all moments."

"I expand the gratitude and reverence of my heart chakra to heal all aspects of the world of all those I love; in all moments."

"Gratitude perpetually ebbs and flows through the world of all those I love; in all moments."

"I expand the gratitude and reverence of my heart chakra to heal the whole world; in all moments."

"Gratitude perpetually ebbs and flows through the whole world; in all moments."

"The whole world is contained in the reverence and gratitude of my heart chakra; in all moments."

"I heal the whole world with the reverence of gratitude; in all moments."

"Gratitude perpetually ebbs and flows through the reverence and grace of my heart chakra to the world and back again; in all moments."

"I am centered and empowered in the healing reverence of gratitude; in all moments."

"All those I love are centered and empowered in the healing reverence of gratitude; in all moments."

"The whole world is centered and empowered in the healing reverence of gratitude; in all moments."

Nurture Gratitude and Sanctity for All Life

(Say each statement three times while tapping on your head and say it a fourth time while tapping on your chest.)

"I declare myself a surrogate for humanity in doing these taps; in all moments."

"I release being stuck in primal mode; in all moments."

"I release having my compassion turned off; in all moments."

"I shift my paradigm to being compassionate; in all moments."

"I release using outrage to hide my vulnerability; in all moments."

"I remove all self-righteousness; in all moments."

"I release desecrating life; in all moments."

"I send all energy matrices into the light and sound that cause me to desecrate life; in all moments."

"I command all complex energy matrices that cause me to desecrate life to be escorted into the light and sound; in all moments."

"I send all energy matrices into the light and sound that keep me immersed in primal mode; in all moments."

"I command all complex energy matrices that keep me immersed in primal mode to be escorted into the light and sound; in all moments."

"I convert all arrogance to compassion; in all moments."

"I remove all vivaxes between myself and primal mode; in all moments."

"I remove all tentacles between myself and primal mode; in all moments."

"I remove all programming and conditioning that primal mode has put on me; in all moments."

"I remove all engrams of primal mode from my beingness; in all moments."

"I withdraw all my energy from primal mode; in all moments."

"I strip all illusion off of primal mode; in all moments."

"I remove all masks, walls and armor that primal mode has put on me; in all moments."

"I relinquish my desire to kill; in all moments."

"I recant all vows and agreements between myself and primal mode; in all moments."

"I remove all curses between myself and primal mode; in all moments."

"I remove all blessings between myself and primal mode; in all moments."

"I sever all strings, cords and compulsions between myself and primal mode; in all moments."

"I dissolve all karmic ties between myself and primal mode; in all moments."

"I release the genetic propensity to be in primal mode; in all moments."

"I remove all the pain, burden and limitations that primal mode has put on me; in all moments."

"I remove all the pain, burden and limitations that I have put on all others due to primal mode; in all moments."

"I remove all the fear, futility and unworthiness that primal mode has put on me; in all moments."

"I remove all the fear, futility and unworthiness that I have put on all others due to primal mode; in all moments."

"I remove all the anger, ignorance and disconnection from my animal brethren that primal mode has put on me; in all moments."

"I remove all the anger, ignorance and disconnection from my animal brethren that I have put on all others due to primal mode; in all moments."

"I take back ALL that primal mode has taken from me; in all moments."

"I give back to all others ALL that I have taken from them due to primal mode; in all moments."

"I release resonating or emanating with primal mode; in all moments."

"I extract all of primal mode from my sound frequency and my light emanation; in all moments."

"I extract all of primal mode from the universal sound frequency and the universal light emanation; in all moments."

"I shift my paradigm from primal mode to gratitude and sanctity for all life; in all moments."

"I transcend primal mode; in all moments."

"I collapse and dissolve primal mode; in all moments."

"I am centered and empowered in gratitude and sanctity for all life; in all moments."

"I make space in this world for universal gratitude and sanctity for all life; in all moments."

"I remove all blockages to universal gratitude and sanctity for all life; in all moments."

"I stretch the world's capacity to embrace gratitude and sanctity for all life; in all moments."

"I resonate, emanate, and am interconnected with all life in gratitude and sanctity for all life; in all moments."

"The Universe resonates, emanates and is interconnected with all life in gratitude and sanctity for all life; in all moments."

Bow Out of Groups

(Say each statement three times while tapping on your head and say it a fourth time while tapping on your chest.)

"I declare myself a surrogate for humanity in doing these taps; in all moments."

"I release being enslaved to group mentality; in all moments."

"I release being at the mercy of a group mentality; in all moments."

"I release diminishing myself to stay part of a group; in all moments."

"I bow out of all groups that don't serve me; in all moments."

"I release being duped by groups; in all moments."

"I withdraw all my energy from all groups; in all moments."

Fifty Shades of Healing

From what I have found, one doesn't have to worry about the humility of a healer. It seems to be a prerequisite for true healing to take place, whether it is healing for one's self or for another. The healer doesn't have to worry much about the healed telling anyone about it. The human consciousness seems to forget such gifts as soon as they are accepted or soon after.

I think it is important in the current climate to document healing as a means to awaken those in complacency of what is possible. There are so many people who accept the diagnosis of terminal rather than fight for a new awareness that would make terminal not an absolute conclusion. Disease is a way of backing one into a corner, and healing is a way to paint one's self out of a corner.

Those of us who know the formula of healing could teach others our protocol. Healing is not as mystical as it was once thought. Healing is also not an absolute. It can be, but that depends on the facilitator and the subject. And there is not that much glory in healing others. As with anything else, there is a misconception of it. It is usually lonely and isolating to be so dedicated to one's craft. The only gain is the satisfaction of helping others, living one's purpose and sharing one's gifts.

Anyone has the potential to heal others, just like anyone can be an artist or a teacher. And anyone can heal themselves, just like anyone can pick up a writing utensil and create art. The passion, depth and ingenuity to do so are subjective things. But there is a protocol to it and some guidelines to follow. If you were an artist, you would always want to clean your brushes afterward so they stay pliable. The same is true with staying flexible as a healer.

There are outmoded belief systems around healers as with anything else. The fear of taking on karma is a big one. Karma is energy. Taking on karma can only happen if the facilitator is at the same vantage point as the subject. A trained healer wouldn't do this. A trained healer doesn't bring any component of themselves into the session unless it is to benefit the subject in some way. During a session, the subject learns nothing or little about the healer's personal realm. That would be gratuitous.

A way to pierce someone's energy is to use an issue that is near and dear to their hearts and find a soft spot in their energy to render them vulnerable. That is what many do when they inadvertently affront a healer. That is why it is important for a healer to stay detached and focused. It is balancing this vantage point with incredible love that is so empowering.

When I do energy work, my energy field is very soft and porous, and very expansive. It is a fine art for me to be so receptive and expansive in doing energy work and also ruthlessly defend my boundaries. When I do this, as I sometimes do when I am writing, people think I am harsh. They don't realize that I am protecting myself in a way and the harsh interaction is a boundary between those who have a subtle agenda and myself. They do not realize the offense and I don't have the articulation to explain it. But it happens.

On a very subtle level, there is a competition for power or one-upmanship. It is a side effect of living in a world where life itself is a competition. It is a subtle dynamic that plays out on more subtle realms than the conscious mind. As humanity advances in awareness, there is a great need to be aware of and to monitor very subtle impulses to diminish another. As we all learn to perceive in energy, we don't want to inadvertently do damage to others.

The perception of being kind and loving changes with how deep we choose to perceive life. It may seem kind to just stroke someone's ego and not upset their perception of the world. I believe it is more kind to help them learn the tools to accept a greater sense of empowerment of themselves outside the confines of a physical body. One of the best ways to prove one's empowerment to themselves is to know how to heal themselves. This removes some of the limiting perceptions that the world provided. Limiting beliefs and perceptions prevent people from being more dynamic and empowered than they presently are able to achieve as a group.

An Understanding of How Healing Works

One physical object can move another physical object that has a similar vibration. Solid matter can be moved by solid matter. Water can be moved by more water. Air can even be moved by more air. That is how the wind pushes around the clouds. They consist of a similar frequency.

Healing is possible because a healer's intention to move stagnant energy out of the body is a similar frequency of the stagnant energy itself. It is that simple. When an energy worker pours energy into the body, the intention is for it to push out the stagnant energy. We are at a time in our evolution where we can understand things that we cannot see. This is where technology has taken us.

There needs to be an upgrade in our understanding of energy as it pertains to us as humans. This awakening needs to match the upgrade in technology that is consistently happening. We can't be left behind in our understanding and awareness of the self. The empowering functioning of humanity depends on an upgrade in awareness. Otherwise we all just become slaves to technology.

Free Yourself! Cutting Edge Healing Taps

These taps were just discovered while facilitating a private session for another dynamic energy healer of a different modality. They immediately expanded and released so much instantly that we both felt a change in her. There was no shift. The results were an immediate calm expansiveness without movement.

You know how you want to be better in certain ways but feel limited? Even if you try and put in the effort, there seems to be something that interferes with you being the best you could possibly be? There is. They are energy matrices.

An energy matrix is a strong whirlpool of energy within your beingness that pulls everything into it. They can be so strong that they seem to take on a life and agenda of their own. They can have such pull that they interfere with your quality of life in so many ways.

If you want to be freer than you ever have been, try doing these taps. They are powerful, complete and extremely effective.

(Say each statement three times out loud while continuously tapping on the top of your head at the crown chakra and say it a fourth time while tapping on your chest.)

"I send all energy matrices to the Light and Sound that create resistance in me doing these taps; in all moments."

"I send all energy matrices to the Light and Sound that paralyze me in fear; in all moments."

"I send all energy matrices to the Light and Sound that sabotage my greatness; in all moments."

"I send all energy matrices to the Light and Sound that lead me to be a victim; in all moments."

"I send all energy matrices to the Light and Sound that create dis-ease; in all moments."

"I send all energy matrices to the Light and Sound that cause physical or emotional pain; in all moments."

"I send all energy matrices to the Light and Sound that cause mental anguish; in all moments."

"I send all energy matrices to the Light and Sound that harbor ignorance; in all moments."

"I send all energy matrices to the Light and Sound that diminish my effectiveness; in all moments."

"I send all energy matrices to the Light and Sound that interfere with my greatest Joy; in all moments."

"I send all energy matrices to the Light and Sound that cause feelings of unworthiness; in all moments."

"I send all energy matrices to the Light and Sound that separate me from giving and receiving love; in all moments."

"I send all energy matrices to the Light and Sound that interfere with me being love; in all moments."

"I send all energy matrices to the Light and Sound that interfere with my abundance; in all moments."

"I send all energy matrices to the Light and Sound that interfere with my freedom; in all moments."

"I send all energy matrices to the Light and Sound that interfere with my success; in all moments."

"I send all energy matrices to the Light and Sound that interfere with my optimal health; in all moments."

"I send all energy matrices to the Light and Sound that interfere with my creativity; in all moments."

"I send all energy matrices to the Light and Sound that interfere with peace; in all moments."

"I send all energy matrices to the Light and Sound that perpetuate dis-ease; in all moments."

"I send all energy matrices to the Light and Sound that feed hate; in all moments."

"I send all energy matrices to the Light and Sound that are of anger; in all moments."

"I send all energy matrices to the Light and Sound that feed want; in all moments."

"I send all energy matrices to the Light and Sound that create need; in all moments."

"I send all energy matrices to the Light and Sound that create isolation; in all moments."

"I send all energy matrices to the Light and Sound that take up physical mass in my body; in all moments."

"I send all energy matrices to the Light and Sound that drain my energy; in all moments."

"I send all energy matrices to the Light and Sound that rob me of nutrients; in all moments."

"I send all energy matrices to the Light and Sound that siphon off my body's oxygen; in all moments."

"I send all energy matrices to the Light and Sound that block communication within my body; in all moments."

"I send all energy matrices to the Light and Sound that stifle my truth; in all moments."

"I send all energy matrices in the world that induce war into the Light and Sound; in all moments."

"I send all energy matrices in the world that promote poverty into the Light and Sound; in all moments."

"I send all energy matrices in the world that promote power and greed into the Light and Sound; in all moments."

"I send all energy matrices to the Light and Sound that interfere with world peace; in all moments."

"I send all energy matrices to the Light and Sound that interfere with my highest quality of life; in all moments."

"I send all energy matrices to the Light and Sound that have fractured me; in all moments."

"I send all energy matrices to the Light and Sound that work against my wholeness; in all moments."

"I send all energy matrices to the Light and Sound that prevent me from being in utter and complete love; in all moments."

"I send all energy matrices to the Light and Sound that keep me immersed in drama; in all moments."

"I send all energy matrices to the Light and Sound that trap me in matter; in all moments."

"I send all energy matrices to the Light and Sound that trap me in energy; in all moments."

"I send all energy matrices to the Light and Sound that trap me in space; in all moments."

"I send all energy matrices to the Light and Sound that trap me in time; in all moments."

"I send all energy matrices to the Light and Sound that create addictions; in all moments."

"I send all energy matrices to the Light and Sound that interfere with me seeing my beauty; in all moments."

"I send all energy matrices to the Light and Sound that steal my enthusiasm; in all moments."

"I send all energy matrices to the Light and Sound that prevent my contentment; in all moments."

"I send all energy matrices to the Light and Sound that impersonate God; in all moments."

"I send all energy matrices to the Light and Sound that show up as evil; in all moments."

"I send all energy matrices to the Light and Sound that interfere with my spirituality; in all moments."

"I send all energy matrices to the Light and Sound that prevent my enlightenment; in all moments."

"I send all energy matrices to the Light and Sound that zap my confidence; in all moments."

"I send all energy matrices to the Light and Sound that limit my intellect; in all moments."

"I send all energy matrices to the Light and Sound that interfere with my ability to discern; in all moments."

"I send all energy matrices to the Light and Sound that affect my family in any of these ways; in all moments."

"I send all energy matrices to the Light and Sound that separate me from being with all others in love; in all moments."

"I send all energy matrices to the Light and Sound that interfere with world peace; in all moments."

"I send all energy matrices to the Light and Sound that hinder the upliftment of humanity; in all moments."

"I send all energy matrices in the world that are stuck in old consciousness to the Light and Sound; in all moments."

"I send all energy matrices in the world to the Light and Sound that don't support the fifth dimension level of consciousness; in all moments."

"I send all energy matrices to the Light and Sound that limit the vibration of my sound frequency; in all moments."

"I send all energy matrices to the Light and Sound that limit the brilliancy of my Light and Sound emanation; in all moments."

"I flush out all residual energy matrices that don't serve my highest good and send them to the Light and Sound; in all moments."

Eliminating Dis-ease

When a friend is fighting a life changing illness, here are some of the things I suggest to them. They realize that I am not a medical doctor and all suggestions are meant to enhance their medical professional's assistance.

- Remove all scented items from the environment, from perfume, to candles to scented personal items. They are all chemicals that add stress to the body.
- Stop using antiperspirant. Switch to a deodorant. Sweat is a means to release toxins. To prevent the sweating is to prevent the release of the poisons.
- Wear only natural fibers. Wearing synthetic fibers is like wearing a plastic tarp. It cuts off the breathing process of the skin.
- Remove all toxic people and situations from your environment. Physical dis-ease is merely emotional issues that have become so laden in the body that they bleed through to affect the physical body as well.
- Take Ossage Orange tincture. It is known to starve cancer cells.
- Stop eating dairy. Many older people are concerned with bone density so they over compensate by loading up on dairy. This is not helpful.
- Kill the parasites in your body. Parasite cleanses can be tedious and difficult. The easier way to kill the parasites is to get a tens unit and run a low electrical current through the body. This will kill the parasites and is more effective than the walnut tincture and wormwood because they are not deterred by the blood-brain barrier so can cleanse the brain of parasites too.
- Don't tell people about your health issues. Everyone has opinions about illness. Their thoughts, emotions and experiences can have a negative affect on your situation.
- Take time to center each day. Visualize infinite light and love coming into the top of your head and saturating your whole body and dissolving everything that is not love and light.
- Send yourself love. The cells of your body have a consciousness, and as such, they want to be appreciated.
- Get plenty of hugs and love from a good pet.

- Say only kind things about yourself. Monitor your thoughts to only speaking and thinking uplifting ones. Be consciously grateful.
- Don't own a diagnosis. It is not yours. If something is yours, you are going to get attached to it and have more trouble getting rid of it. Think of it more as an experience that is passing through.

These are just a very few things to help one's self. They are a good practice for all.

Healing Blueprint: Chicken Soup for the Whole Energy System

I just finished a private remote session for someone who was really stuffed up. She could hardly breathe. I didn't follow any of the protocol for taps that I have created. I just led her through what came through in the moment.

In many eras of humanity, the only way to escape was to get sick and die. That is what the slave song, "Sweet Low, Sweet Chariot" is expressing. It is saying how death will come and bring relief. We bring this mentality in when we get overwhelmed. Also, when we fear getting a disease, sometimes it is conjuring a memory of being sick with that disease in a past life. We can let go of the fear and memory. It is helpful to dismantle this mindset.

The session ended up being a powerful blueprint for optimal health. I encourage everyone to do these taps and to keep them handy when they are starting to feel run down. These are a gift to anyone who recognizes them as that.

By the end of the hour, her energy was strong and she sounded clear.

(Say each statement three times while tapping on your head and say it a fourth time while tapping on your chest.)

"I release long-standing ideas; in all moments."

"I release invalidating my soul; in all moments."

"I release being invalidated; in all moments."

"I release invalidating female energy; in all moments."

"I release forgoing my truth; in all moments."

"I release betraying myself; in all moments."

"I release betraying my truth; in all moments."

"I release using illness as an escape; in all moments."

"I recant my vow of silence; in all moments."

"I release punishing myself; in all moments."

"I release the trauma of being bashed in the head; in all moments."

"I release breathing in poison; in all moments."

"I recant my vow of servitude; in all moments."

"I recant my vow of self-deprecation; in all moments."

"I recant my vow of self-deprivation; in all moments."

"I recant my vow of martyrdom; in all moments."

"I release poisoning myself; in all moments."

"I release eating putrid food; in all moments."

"I release taking myself out of the game; in all moments."

"I release removing myself from the herd in a negative way; in all moments."

"I release losing my voice; in all moments."

"I release using illness as an excuse; in all moments."

"I release making myself sick; in all moments."

"I pass all toxins through; in all moments."

"I release punishing myself; in all moments."

"I release being derogatory to myself; in all moments."

"I release manifesting self-deprecation through illness; in all moments."

"I release plugging up my essence with toxins; in all moments."

"I release the fear of responsibility; in all moments."

"I release the fear of failure; in all moments."

"I release the fear of being in over my head; in all moments."

"I release stockpiling stagnant energy; in all moments."

"I release the trauma of failing; in all moments."

"I release alleviating stress through illness; in all moments."

"I release using illness to nurture myself; in all moments."

"I release defining illness as nurturing; in all moments."

"I infuse chicken soup into my soul; in all moments."

"I infuse optimal health into my sound frequency; in all moments."

"I imbue optimal health into my light body; in all moments."

"I recalibrate my life source to optimal health; in all moments."

"I infuse encouragement and energy into every one of my red blood cells; in all moments."

"I infuse empowerment and encouragement into every one of my white blood cells; in all moments."

"I instantaneously extract all toxins from my beingness; in all moments

"I pour love as the strongest vitamin into my whole beingness; in all moments."

"I infuse vitamin love into my sound frequency; in all moments."

"I imbue vitamin love into my light body; in all moments."

"I resonate and emanate with vitamin love; in all moments."

"I remove all residual sadness from my beingness; in all moments."

"I am a poster child for optimal health; in all moments."

"I declare my specialness through optimal health; in all moments."

"I repair and fortify the Wei chi of all my bodies; in all moments."

"I remove all the toxins from all my bodies; in all moments."

"I heal all my bodies; in all moments."

"I repair and fortify the Wei chi of all my systems; in all moments."

"I remove all the toxins from all my systems; in all moments."

"I heal all my systems; in all moments."

"I repair and fortify the Wei chi of all my organs; in all moments."

"I remove all the toxins from all my organs; in all moments."

"I heal all my organs; in all moments."

"I repair and fortify the Wei chi of all the cells of my beingness; in all moments."

"I remove all the toxins from all the cells of my beingness; in all moments."

"I heal all the cells of my beingness; in all moments."

"I am a powerhouse for optimal health; in all moments."

"Optimal health flows from an infinite source into me; in all moments."

"Optimal health flows through me back into an infinite source; in all moments."

"I am a perpetual conduit of optimal health; in all moments."

"Optimal health is divine love; in all moments."

"I am a conduit of divine love; in all moments."

"I am divine love; in all moments."

"I perpetually flow to and from Source; in all moments."

"I am a breath of love; in all moments."

"I breathe love; in all moments."

"I let go of 'the story'; in all moments."

"I stay in the love; in all moments."

"I am a love story; in all moments."

During the dark ages, ignorance and disease were rampant. They go hand in hand. If so many people are ill, it tells us that ignorance is rampant as well. Disease and enlightenment do not resonate together. To stamp out disease, one must also stamp out ignorance. This is what enlightenment entails.

Please share this with all those who are receptive. It is a way to create a healthier world and to bring about enlightenment.

Removing All Genetic Dis-eases

There is a belief that genetic diseases are caused by one of our relatives that came before us and had difficult issues. They stored the issues in their DNA and passed them down to many who came after them. Why that makes sense is because some genetic diseases haven't always been a part of our lineage. They are a newer phenomenon.

In a healing session, I was told one of my issues was passed down by my father's grandmother who was really unhappy. In my session, it was released from affecting me. But what about my siblings who could be affected by this relative? What if I released the pain and anguish of this relative as a means to release it from all who came after? What if all genetic diseases could be released by healing or disconnecting from all the relatives who came before us? Why not try? What if it isn't just diseases but genetic propensity to have undesirable traits that we can release? Maybe our lives and the lives of many others can be improved by sending our ancestors love and easing their pain. What a concept? Maybe it has never been tried on a mass scale. Here is to trying something outside the box.

Here are the taps to assist in disconnecting from all our past relatives. May it bring relief to many. (Say each statement three times out loud while tapping on your head and say it a fourth time while tapping on your chest.)

"I release carrying the pain and dis-ease of all my ancestors; in all moments."

"I release identifying with the angst of all my ancestors; in all moments."

"I release being enslaved to the angst of all my ancestors; in all moments."

"I release the genetic propensity for pain and dis-ease; in all moments."

"I release storing pain and angst in my DNA; in all moments."

"I release being a victim of my ancestor's angst; in all moments."

"I recant all vows and agreements between myself and all my ancestors; in all moments."

"I remove all curses between myself and all my ancestors; in all moments."

"I dissolve all karmic ties between myself and all my ancestors; in all moments."

"I remove all the pain, burden, limitations and engrams that all my ancestors have put on me; in all moments."

"I remove all the pain, burden, limitations and engrams that I have put on all my ancestors; in all moments."

"I give back all the joy, love, abundance, freedom, health, success, security, companionship, creativity, peace, life and wholeness that I have taken from all my ancestors; in all moments."

"I take back all the joy, love, abundance, freedom, health, success, security, companionship, creativity, peace, life and wholeness that all my ancestors have taken from me; in all moments."

"I withdraw all my energy from all my ancestors; in all moments."

"I release resonating with all my ancestors; in all moments."

"I release emanating with all my ancestors; in all moments."

"I remove all my ancestors from my sound frequency; in all moments."

"I remove all my ancestors from my light body; in all moments."

"I shift my paradigm from any or all my ancestors to the purity and stillness of now; in all moments."

"I am centered and empowered in joy, love, abundance, freedom, health, success, security, companionship, creativity, peace, life and wholeness; in all moments."

Science has discovered that DNA can be changed. So here is using an organic tool with a focused intention to shift one back into health.

The Energy Healers of All Professions

Whenever there is an issue that arises of any nature, there are two ways to deal with it. The first way is to NOT address it and hope that it goes away on its own. The second way is to address it proactively. I have been born and raised on the former. It works out some of the times but may create systemic issues that can usually be buried with alcohol, other addictive behavior or pure denial.

The second way is to address an issue as soon as it varies from the norm. In doing this, once it is addressed, there is no more concern about the issue and one's own mind doesn't wander into the realms of acerbating the condition. I see this play out with issues with my furry family. They have taught me this valuable insight. With them, I address the issue immediately. There have been times when I was convinced that a situation was insurmountable but a conversation with the vet showed me otherwise.

I have watched situations that seemed insurmountable to me smoothly melt away when addressing them with the right professional. To be a control freak is to not realize that the Universe works directly through those of integrity who agree to assist you. The key is to finding them and then trusting. If anyone controls any situation, it should be to bring as many of these individuals into your realm of influence as possible and then treat them justly and with respect. This is what successful people do.

What I have come to realize is that every person who serves with their passion is a healer. So many issues have become so much easier by giving the issue over to the right professional. This system has been contaminated by the arrogance of position and the trust that has been lost in giving credence to the wrong person or group. To find those people who serve in any capacity in their vocation out of love for what they do is vital. These people are the energy healers of their chosen profession and keep the system running.

Use research, your gut, serendipity of the Universe and common sense combined to find the best professionals to trust. Weed out the ones that offend, belittle, demand, insist and decree. They are not the ones for you. Find the people who see your value, speak to you kindly, care about your concerns, reassure you in a considerate way and go above and beyond. These are the people that resonate as your personal healers of your life situations.

Once you know how this empowerment feels, it will be easy to trust again. Life is not about conceding your power. The adventure of life is about navigating through it without having to concede your true nature.

Healing Energy

(Say each statement three times while tapping on your head and say it a fourth time while tapping on your chest.)

"I tap into the Wisdom of the Trees; in all moments."

"I tap into my tree embodiment; in all moments."

"I live, move and have my beingness within our tree essence; in all moments."

"I connect to the Universal Tree of Life; in all moments."

"I embrace our inner tree; in all moments."

"I declare myself a surrogate for humanity in doing these taps; in all moments."

"I make space in this world to embrace healing; in all moments."

"I remove all blockages to embrace healing; in all moments."

"I stretch our capacity to embrace healing; in all moments."

"I remove all blinders off of seeing healing; in all moments."

"I release all resistance to healing; in all moments."

"I release resisting the healing energy; in all moments."

"I release all resistance to being physically healed; in all moments."

"I release all resistance to being emotionally healed; in all moments."

"I release all resistance to being mentally healed; in all moments."

"I release all resistance to being spiritually healed; in all moments."

"I embrace a total healing of my physical realm; in all moments."

"I accept a complete healing of my physical body; in all moments."

"I embrace a total healing of my astral realm; in all moments."

"I accept a complete healing of my emotional body; in all moments."

"I embrace a total healing of my causal realm; in all moments."

"I accept a complete healing of my causal body; in all moments."

"I embrace a total healing of my mental realm; in all moments."

"I accept a complete healing of my mental body; in all moments."

"I embrace a total healing of my spiritual realm; in all moments."

"I accept a complete healing of my spiritual body; in all moments."

"I untangle all my energies; in all moments."

"I wholeheartedly accept the love; in all moments."

"I drench myself in divine love; in all moments."

"I saturate myself in Celestial Sound; in all moments."

"I illuminate myself in Illustrious Light; in all moments."

"I connect with all other Souls in the Light and Sound of Love; in all moments."

"I lay down my sword and shield; in all moments."

Healing Worksheet for Any Body Part

Your _____ is doing everything it can to help you. It is protecting you, it is stretching for you, it's being used as a storage tank, and it's releasing toxins. Please don't expect it to be perfect. Please don't reject it or blame it. Show some respect to your personal boundary and sentry in this world.

Every cell of your body has consciousness. Think of them all as a group of little whole people doing the best they can to help you. How would you feel it someone ignored you, invalidated you, blamed you when you were only trying to do your best? This is what you do the cells of your body. Then when they are sick, you simply poison or burn them or simply cut them out of your body with no thank you or gratitude. No wonder there are whole parts of your body that are stressed. No wonder going to the doctors is so stressful.

Why not try this technique of loving and forgiving all aspects of yourself? Use this technique on any body part or the whole body. You can use this technique every day on a different aspect of the body. It will help you release the intangible element of disease. It is also a way to help you not feel powerless at the hands of disease. You are in control. This worksheet will give you your empowerment back.

Give it to anyone who is in pain, suffering, harboring a diagnosis, in treatment, feels powerless, likes to talk about their issues or is in a position to share it with others. Sit with them and do the first set with them. In doing this, you are a dynamic healer and a very empowered soul.

Here is teaching all how to be their own healers.

(Say each statement three times while tapping on your head and say it a fourth time while tapping on your chest.)

"I release melting into the background; in all moments."

"I release the fear of being persecuted; in all moments."

"I release the trauma of hearing my own _____suffer; in all moments."

"I release the trauma of watching my _____suffer; in all moments."

"I release the trauma of being covered in pain; in all moments."

"I release the trauma of being covered disease; in all moments."

"I release the trauma of having my _____violated; in all moments."

"I release the trauma of being tortured or killed; in all moments."

"I release the trauma of having my _____pierced; in all moments."

"I remove all vivaxes between my _____and pain; in all moments."

"I remove all tentacles between my _____and pain; in all moments."

"I remove the claws of pain from my skin's beingness; in all moments."

"I release the trauma of being scalded; in all moments."

"I release the trauma of having my _____singed; in all moments."

"I release reliving torture; in all moments."

"I release holding back a wall of sadness; in all moments."

"I release confusing love and pain; in all moments."

"I untangle all the pain from the love; in all moments."

"I strip away all the pain; in all moments."

"I dissolve all the pain into the light and sound; in all moments."

"I remove all programming and conditioning of pain from my _____; in all moments."

"I remove all engrams of pain from my _____; in all moments."

"I remove all engrams of humiliation from my _____; in all moments."

"I remove all engrams of shame from my _____; in all moments."

"I remove all engrams of unworthiness from my _____; in all moments."

"I remove all engrams of persecution from my _____; in all moments."

"I remove all engrams of torture from my _____; in all moments."

"I remove all engrams of rejection from my _____; in all moments."

"I remove all engrams of ugliness from my _____; in all moments."

"I remove all engrams of depravity from _____; in all moments."

"I remove all engrams of futility from my _____; in all moments."

"I remove all engrams of anguish from my _____; in all moments."

"I release the trauma and helplessness of watching my _____ rot; in all moments." .

"I remove all engrams of putrid from my _____; in all moments."

"I release cursing my _____; in all moments."

"I release faulting my _____ for doing its job; in all moments."

"I release rejecting my _____; in all moments."

"I release blaming my _____; in all moments."

"I release scapegoating my _____; in all moments."

"I nullify all contracts between my _____ and pain; in all moments."

"I remove all engrams of martyrdom from my _____; in all moments."

"I send all energy matrices of pain into the light and sound; in all moments."

"I command all complex energy matrices of pain to be escorted into the light and sound; in all moments."

"I heal my _____; in all moments."

"I infuse joy, love, health, and forgiveness into my _____; in all moments."

"I infuse security into my _____; in all moments."

"I appreciate my _____; in all moments."

"I infuse gratitude and resiliency into my _____; in all moments."

"I regenerate my _____; in all moments."

Heal Yourself of Being a Sinner

You may not feel like a sinner in this life, but perhaps it was ingrained in a past life. If you feel unworthy, defeated or uncomfortable in your skin, these may help.

(Say each statement three times out loud while continuously tapping on the top of your head at the crown chakra and say it a fourth time while tapping on your chest.)

"I release being deemed a sinner; in all moments."

"I release believing that I am a sinner; in all moments."

"I release agreeing to be a sinner; in all moments."

"I release allowing the fear of being a sinner to wear down my constitution; in all moments."

"I release the belief that I am damned; in all moments."

"I remove the curse of being a sinner from my beingness; in all moments."

"I cleanse the depth of my soul of all sin; in all moments."

"I remove all sin from my beingness; in all moments."

"I absolve myself of all sin; in all moments."

"I release squelching my own greatness to avoid sin; in all moments."

"I release the belief that I am damned; in all moments."

"I release the belief that I am going to hell; in all moments."

"I release immersing myself in hell to honor an agreement with sin; in all moments."

"I remove all matrices between myself and being deemed a sinner; in all moments."

"I remove all tentacles between myself and being deemed a sinner; in all moments."

"I remove all engrams that being deemed a sinner has put on me; in all moments."

"I recant all vows and agreements between myself and being deemed a sinner; in all moments."

"I remove all curses and blessings between myself and being deemed a sinner; in all moments."

"I sever all strings and cords between myself and being deemed a sinner; in all moments."

"I dissolve all karmic ties between myself and being deemed a sinner; in all moments."

"I remove all the pain, burden, limitations and illusion of separateness that being deemed a sinner has put on me; in all moments."

"I take back all that being deemed a sinner has taken from me; in all moments."

"I send all energy matrices into the light and sound that deem me a sinner; in all moments."

"I extract all of being a sinner from my sound frequency and light emanation; in all moments."

"I shift my paradigm from being a sinner to being pure love; in all moments."

"I transcend being a sinner; in all moments."

"I am centered and empowered in being pure love; in all moments."

"Being pure love is my reality and my expression; in all moments."

Stop Being Rigid or Head Strong

(Say each statement three times while tapping on your head and say it a fourth time while tapping on your chest.)

"I relinquish my defensiveness; in all moments."

"I release the fear of being vulnerable; in all moments."

"I release confusing vulnerability with being unsafe; in all moments."

"I untangle the rigid dregs; in all moments."

"I dissolve the rigid dregs; in all moments."

"I release being headstrong; in all moments."

"I shift my paradigm from headstrong to heart strong; in all moments."

"I release going forward in male energy; in all moments."

"I embrace and balance my female energy; in all moments."

Headaches

(Say each statement three times while tapping on your head and say it a fourth time while tapping on your chest.)

"I hydrate myself; in all moments."

"I restore fluidity to my head and neck muscles; in all moments."

"I replenish every cell of my essence; in all moments."

"I release being bashed in the skull; in all moments."

"I remove all congestion from all nasal cavities; in all moments."

"I release firming up my skull with emotional congestion; in all moments."

"I release grinding my energy; in all moments."

"I release being a control freak; in all moments."

"I relax my atoms; in all moments."

"I awaken to optimal health; in all moments."

"I stretch my capacity to relax; in all moments."

"I release all tension; in all moments."

"I release overthinking; in all moments."

"I am calm and present; in all moments."

Address Hearing of Voices

Voices are psychic energies that exist in sound. They are void of light. Since physical form is made of sound frequencies woven with light emanations, they are not capable of having form. Because they only operate in one single mode, they seem to be powerful but are not. Just think of them as a hiccup in your sound frequency and deal with them in that way.

Any power they seem to have is coming from you. You are the powerful one. With this understanding, you can easily repair the chink in your energetic armor and get back to balance, probably better than you ever have been able to. Sure you can ignore the voices. That will dry them up too. They are being psychically blasted out of existence with divine love by me and everyone who reads this message and sees in energy. It is a simple matter.

Too many have lost their calm over such things. But that is merely the result of living in a society that has been blind to perceiving in energy and has kept itself in denial. Society's coping mechanism of labeling everything as crazy or normal no longer works. An empowered world means understanding dynamics that we, until recently, have left unexplored.

(Say each statement three times while tapping on your head and say it a fourth time while tapping on your chest.)

"I declare myself a surrogate for humanity and all those who hear voices; in all moments."

"I dry up all the psychic energy that causes one to hear voices; in all moments."

"I release invalidating or dismissing anyone who hears voices; in all moments."

"I release giving energy to the energy that causes one to hear voices; in all moments."

"I release ignoring those who hear voices; in all moments."

"I release trusting the voices; in all moments."

"I release using hearing voices to 'opt out'; in all moments."

"I release being manipulated by the voices; in all moments."

"I repair all auditory or mental functions that make me susceptible to hearing voices; in all moments."

"I release allowing the energy that causes one to hear voices to have an audience; in all moments."

"I dry up all portals to hearing voices; in all moments."

"I release believing the voices; in all moments."

"I release labeling anyone for hearing voices; in all moments."

"I release the genetic propensity to hear voices; in all moments."

"I strip all illusion off of hearing voices; in all moments."

"I collapse and dissolve all portals to hearing voices; in all moments."

"I remove all masks, walls and armor that the voices have put on me; in all moments."

"I eliminate the first cause in regards to hearing voices; in all moments."

"I release all muscle memory of hearing voices; in all moments."

"I release being susceptible to substances that cause me to hear voices; in all moments."

"I remove all conditions and substances from my environment that cause me to hear voices; in all moments."

"I release being conditioned to hear voices; in all moments."

"I release confusing the voices for God; in all moments."

"I release confusing the voices for spiritual guidance; in all moments."

"I release feeding the voices by being afraid; in all moments."

"I release being held hostage by the voices; in all moments."

"I release all emotional attachment to the voices; in all moments."

"I release giving my power to the voices; in all moments."

"I release defending the voices; in all moments."

"I release being trapped in trying to figure out the voices; in all moments."

"I release using the voices to feel empowered; in all moments."

"I release using the voices as an excuse; in all moments."

"I release giving up ownership of my life; in all moments."

"I release giving up my free will; in all moments."

"I release trying to make reason of the voices; in all moments."

"I remove all trauma that causes me to hear voices; in all moments."

"I release using the voices to feel special; in all moments."

"I release giving the voices form or an identity; in all moments."

"I remove all engrams that contribute to me hearing voices; in all moments."

"I untangle the voices from my free will; in all moments."

"I convert all the energy that causes me to hear voices into divine love; in all moments."

"I nullify all contracts with the voices; in all moments."

"I remove all vortexes with any energy that causes me to hear voices; in all moments."

"I remove all tentacles between myself and the voices; in all moments."

"I repair the erosion of my free will that hearing voices has caused; in all moments."

"I release feeling special for hearing voices; in all moments."

"I release using hearing voices to feel special; in all moments."

"I remove all programming and conditioning that hearing voices has put on me; in all moments."

"I send all energy matrices into the light and sound that cause me to hear voices; in all moments."

"I command all complex energy matrices that cause me to hear voices to be escorted into the light and sound; in all moments."

"I recant all vows and agreements between myself and the voices; in all moments."

"I remove all curses that the voices have put on me; in all moments."

"I remove all blessings that the voices have put on me; in all moments."

"I sever all strings and cords between myself and the voices; in all moments."

"I dissolve all karmic ties between myself and the voices; in all moments."

"I remove all the pain, burden and limitations that the voices have put on me; in all moments."

"I remove all the fear, futility and unworthiness that the voices have put on me; in all moments."

"I remove all the lies, distortions and illusion of separateness that the voices have taken from me; in all moments."

"I take back all the joy, love, abundance, freedom, health, success, security, companionship, creativity, peace, life, wholeness, beauty, enthusiasm, contentment, spirituality, enlightenment, confidence, family, intellect, the ability to discern, integrity and empowerment that the voices have taken from me; in all moments."

"I release giving the voices my resonance; in all moments."

"I release resonating with the voices; in all moments."

"I release emanating with the voices; in all moments."

"I extract all of the voices from my sound frequency; in all moments."

"I extract all of the voices from my light emanation; in all moments."

"I extract all the voices from all 32 layers of my auric field; in all moments."

"I extract all the voices from my whole beingness; in all moments."

"I shift my paradigm from the voices to the empowerment of my own calm; in all moments."

"I transcend hearing voices; in all moments."

"I am centered and empowered in the calm of Divine Love; in all moments."

"I resonate, emanate and am interconnected with all life in the calm of Divine Love; in all moments."

Hearing

(Say each statement three times while tapping on your head and say it a fourth time while tapping on your chest.)

"I release drowning out the horror; in all moments."

"I release the deafening sounds of war; in all moments."

"I release the indifference of not being heard; in all moments."

"I release the pain and anguish of being ignored; in all moments."

"I release selective hearing; in all moments."

"I release muffling out the world; in all moments."

"I open up my atoms to the music of life; in all moments."

"I remove all engrams of war; in all moments."

"I release the buildup of hearing ugliness; in all moments."

"I release shutting out the world; in all moments."

"I release needing an excuse to remove myself from others; in all moments."

"I release the deafening cries of anguish; in all moments."

"I release needing to isolate; in all moments."

"I release building inner walls; in all moments."

"I release making excuses; in all moments."

"I develop healthy boundaries and protection; in all moments."

"I am safe without shutting down my faculties; in all moments."

"I allow myself to be present; in all moments."

"I release the shame of being criticized; in all moments."

"I release admonishing myself; in all moments."

"I awaken to the sweet music of life; in all moments."

Being Heart Centered

(Say each statement three times while tapping on your head and say it a fourth time while tapping on your chest.)

"I release micro-managing the universe; in all moments."

"I release dictating to the universe from the microcosm; in all moments."

"I release refusing what the universe gifts me; in all moments."

"I release arguing with the universe; in all moments."

"I release second-guessing the universe; in all moments."

"I release being invalidated; in all moments."

"I release feeling alone in the universe; in all moments."

"I release fighting male energy to be empowered; in all moments."

"I release reverting to male energy to empower myself; in all moments."

"I release confusing power for empowerment; in all moments."

"I release using power to empower myself; in all moments."

"I release the belief that power is the way to empowerment; in all moments."

"I release the primal need to be saved; in all moments."

"I save myself; in all moments."

"I release giving away my power for short-term gain; in all moments."

"I am comfortable beyond the mind; in all moments."

"I release the need to solidly truth into thought; in all moments."

"I embrace the mindless state; in all moments."

"I am centered, empowered, and exist beyond the mind; in all moments."

"I resonate, emanate, and am interconnected with all life beyond the mind; in all moments."

"I am conscious of my empowerment beyond the mind; in all moments."

"I resonate, emanate and am interconnected with all life in conscious empowerment; in all moments."

Heal Your Heart

(Say each statement three times while tapping on the top of your head and say it a fourth time while tapping on your chest.)

"I release telling my heart it is broken; in all moments."

"I release calling my heart heavy; in all moments."

"I remove all energetic obstructions in my heart; in all moments."

"I release storing hate and fear in my heart; in all moments."

"I release neglecting my heart; in all moments."

"I release overtaxing my heart; in all moments."

"I release betraying my heart; in all moments."

"I release ignoring my heart; in all moments."

"I remove all vivaxes between my heart and pain; in all moments."

"I remove all vivaxes between my heart and loss; in all moments."

"I send all energy matrices into the light and sound that diminish the function of my heart; in all moments."

"I release the genetic propensity to hold dis-ease in my heart; in all moments."

"I lower my LDLs; in all moments."

"I release wearing dis-ease in my heart as a badge of honor; in all moments."

"I release using pain in my heart to maintain a sense of belonging; in all moments."

"I release using pain in my heart as an excuse; in all moments."

"I release using pain in my heart to feel connected to a loved one; in all moments."

"I recant all vows and agreements between myself and my heart; in all moments."

"I remove all curses between myself and my heart; in all moments."

"I remove all the pain, burden and limitations my heart has put on me; in all moments."

"I remove all the pain, burden and limitations that I have put on my heart; in all moments."

"I take back all the joy, love, abundance, freedom, health, life and wholeness that my heart has taken from me; in all moments."

"I give back all the joy, love, abundance, freedom, health, life and wholeness that I have taken from my heart; in all moments."

"I transcend heart issues; in all moments."

"I make peace with my heart; in all moments."

"I shift my paradigm from dis-ease to health; in all moments."

"I am centered in joy, love, abundance, freedom, health, life and wholeness; in all moments."

"I release pouring pain, frustration and helplessness into my heart; in all moments."

"I remove all the pain, frustration and helplessness from my heart; in all moments."

"I pour joy, love, gratitude and resiliency into my heart; in all moments."

"I repair and fortify the integrity, resiliency and function of my heart; in all moments."

"I am centered and empowered in a joyful, loving, abundant, healthy and resilient heart; in all moments."

Heart and Back

(Say each statement three times while tapping on the top of your head and say it a fourth time while tapping on your chest.)

"I release pouring pain, frustration and helplessness into my heart; in all moments."

"I remove all the pain, frustration and helplessness from my heart; in all moments."

"I pour joy, love, gratitude and resiliency into my heart; in all moments."

"I repair and fortify the integrity, resiliency and function of my heart; in all moments."

"I am centered and empowered in a joyful, loving, abundant, healthy and resilient heart; in all moments."

"I release pouring pain, frustration and helplessness into my back; in all moments."

"I remove all the pain, frustration and helplessness from my back; in all moments."

"I pour joy, love, gratitude and resiliency into my back; in all moments."

"I repair and fortify the integrity, resiliency and function of my back; in all moments."

"I am centered and empowered in a joyful, loving, abundant, healthy and resilient back; in all moments."

"I release pouring pain, frustration and helplessness into my nervous system; in all moments."

"I remove all the pain, frustration and helplessness from my nervous system; in all moments."

"I pour joy, love, gratitude and resiliency into my nervous system; in all moments."

"I repair and fortify the integrity, resiliency and function of my nervous system; in all moments."

"I am centered and empowered in a joyful, loving, abundant, healthy and resilient nervous system; in all moments."

Hell

I just finished facilitating a remote phone session. The person was a dynamic healer and had done most of the work on her own, but there was a dynamic that had reappeared in her life. It seemed that when she was feeling totally complete in her relationship, another negative relationship reemerged. It was obvious that this dynamic was meant to prevent her from being completely happy.

Inwardly, I saw this person from her past representing her relationship with Shiva, a Goddess of another religion I am not equipped to talk about. All I got from her session was that Shiva was a means to break up energy. This relationship that came back into her life was reflective of her dedication to the Goddess Shiva. It had reappeared to break up her happiness.

I led her in recanting her vow to Shiva. As she did this, I saw her swimming in the river Styx, which is the river of the dead. I have facilitated other sessions where the client was trapped in hell. This was a version of this. When we hold strong belief systems, we trap our energy into the parameters of that belief for as long as our energy holds to those beliefs. We can move into a new incarnation but part of our energy can be trapped in the old belief system.

As I used a tap to assist her in pulling herself out of the river Styx, I noticed how many other souls were also trapped in the river Styx. In fact, the whole river consisted of the fear of souls who believed that they were trapped in this experience. They were all flowing in a perpetual state of fear into the depth of Hades (hell).

(Say each statement three times while tapping on your head and say it a fourth time while tapping on your chest.)

"I recant all vows and agreements with Shiva; in all moments."

"I remove all vivaxes between myself and Shiva; in all moments."

"I recant all vows and agreements with the Angel of Death; in all moments."

"I remove all vivaxes between myself and the Angel of Death; in all moments."

"I pull all souls out of the river Styx; in all moments."

"I pull all souls out of fear; in all moments."

"I dry up the river Styx; in all moments."

"I pull all souls out of the Cave of Adullam; in all moments."

"I pull all souls out of hell; in all moments."

"I pull all souls out of the shadow of the valley of death; in all moments."

"I pull all souls out of the ground; in all moments."

"I pull all souls out of purgatory; in all moments."

"I pull all souls out of all pseudo heavens; in all moments."

"I pull all souls out of mind loops; in all moments."

"I pull all souls out of drama; in all moments."

"I pull all souls out of war; in all moments."

"I dry up the Crusades; in all moments."

"I pull all souls out of limiting belief systems; in all moments."

"I pull all souls out of the lower worlds; in all moments."

"I pull all souls out of the 'them versus us' mode; in all moments."

"I pull all souls out of the victim consciousness; in all moments."

"I pull all souls out of matter, energy, space and time; in all moments."

"I free all souls; in all moments."

Hiatal Hernia

(Say each statement three times while tapping on your head and say it a fourth time while tapping on your chest.)

"I release trying to stomach life; in all moments."

"I release needing to hold it together; in all moments."

"I heal all causal wounds; in all moments."

"I repair the muscles of my torso; in all moments."

"I release the trauma of being gutted; in all moments."

"I release the trauma of having my entrails eaten; in all moments."

"I release being stalked like prey; in all moments."

"I release being hunted down; in all moments."

"I release being taken down; in all moments."

"I remove all the trauma stored in my entrails; in all moments."

"I release being torn apart; in all moments."

"I remove all engrams of being gutted; in all moments."

"I release the trauma of being gutted; in all moments."

"I repair my organs and intestines; in all moments."

"I release reliving horror; in all moments."

"I release being torn apart; in all moments."

"I calm all my energies; in all moments."

"I put myself together; in all moment"

"I wipe the slate clean; in all moments."

"I proceed in calm; in all moments."

High Blood Pressure

When you can "hear" your blood pressure or feel your heart pumping fast, take a deep breath and sink into yourself. Take another breath and sink some more. With each breath, feel yourself sink as much as possible. When you have sunk as much as possible, visualize your energy spreading out. You may notice that the energy in your heart is thick. Visualize sticking a straw into it and siphoning out the thick gunky energy. Siphon it into a bubble of light and send it away. See it dissolve into the light.

Then put all your attention on your heart. See it in a deflated sack. Visualize blowing love into the sack until your heart is saturated in light and is freestanding in a clear strong globe of light. Hear the Bee Gees song, "Staying Alive," playing in the background and calm the heart down so it is beating in rhythm with the song. If you want to be silly, (humor is relaxing), see your heart dancing on a disco dance floor with a strobe light. See the whole heart sack (pericardium) filled up with incredible light.

Visualize the purity and the magnitude of that light flowing through the valves leading out of the heart and into the body. Visualize it so strong and pure that it dissolves all the stagnant energy that is in the arteries until they are all clear passages. See the purity continue all the way to the veins and clean out the veins as well. Sense the energy loop around the body in a fluid, cohesive, calm rhythm. Feel the love literally coursing through your veins.

Visualize changing your vantage point so that you see your body as the globe of light with the loops of lights coming and going from it. See it as a pure, flowing structure. Practice doing this technique many times until you can conjure it up and give good energy to your heart and whole cardiovascular system at will.

(Say each statement three times while tapping on your head and say it a fourth time while tapping on your chest.)

"I release putting pressure on myself; in all moments."

"I release feeling pressured; in all moments."

"I relieve my internal pressure; in all moments."

"I ease up on myself; in all moments."

"I lower my systolic pressure; in all moments."

"I lower my diastolic pressure; in all moments."

"I ease the stress of life; in all moments."

"I release the belief that I don't have an out; in all moments."

"I release worrying; in all moments."

"I release feeling like a cornered animal; in all moments."

"I release painting myself in a corner; in all moments."

"I convert all worry to peace; in all moments."

"I remove all engrams of being trapped; in all moments."

"I relinquish all obsessive thoughts; in all moments."

"I release running for my life; in all moments."

"I relax all my atoms; in all moments."

Hoarding

(Say each statement three times out loud while continuously tapping on the top of your head at the crown chakra and say it a fourth time while tapping on your chest at the heart chakra.)

"I release hoarding possessions to feel secure; in all moments."

"I release the trauma of losing everything; in all moments."

"I release being trapped in the experience of losing everything; in all moments."

"I remove all engrams of losing everything; in all moments."

"I release using possessions, feelings, experiences or thoughts to fill up an emptiness; in all moments."

"I release hoarding emotions to feel alive; in all moments."

"I release hoarding memories to feel connected; in all moments."

"I release hoarding opinions to seem intelligent; in all moments."

"I release hoarding anything to feel important; in all moments."

"I release the belief that quantity equals substance; in all moments."

"I release being lost in a sea of possessions; in all moments."

"I release being lost in a sea of emotions; in all moments."

"I release being lost in a sea of memories; in all moments."

"I release being lost in a sea of opinions; in all moments."

"I release being lost in an entanglement of possessions, emotions, memories and thoughts; in all moments."

"I remove all possessions that have outlasted their purpose; in all moments."

"I remove all emotions that have outlasted their purpose; in all moments."

"I remove all memories that have outlasted their purpose; in all moments."

"I remove all experiences that have outlasted their purpose; in all moments."

"I remove all thoughts and opinions that have outlasted their purpose; in all moments."

"I free my whole soul; in all moments."

"I fill myself with empowerment and divine love; in all moments."

"I am centered in the empowerment of feeling full and complete; in all moments."

Holiday Over Indulgence

(Say each statement three times out loud while continuously tapping on the top of your head at the crown chakra and say it a fourth time while tapping on your chest.)

"I release placating my spiritual craving with candy; in all moments."

"I release placating my spiritual craving with over indulgence; in all moments."

"I release using over indulgence to mock up a spiritual connection; in all moments."

"I release confusing social obligation with spirituality; in all moments."

"I release being coerced into over indulgence; in all moments."

"I release feeling left out if I don't over indulge; in all moments."

"I release confusing spirituality with a sugar fix; in all moments."

"I release confusing spirituality with family ritual; in all moments."

"I release the belief that I need to be socially savvy to be spiritual; in all moments."

"I release being sent mixed messages by society; in all moments."

"I release being sent mixed messages by religion; in all moments."

"I release being sent wrong messages by family; in all moments."

"I release poisoning my inner connection with 'Source' with outer conditioning; in all moments."

"I release switching out my inner connection with 'Source' for outer conditioning; in all moments."

"I release believing that pagans are heathens; in all moments."

"I untangle all the outer misnomers and my inner connection to 'Source'; in all moments."

"I strip off an dissolve all the outer misnomers from my inner connection to 'Source'; in all moments."

"I release confusing my sacred stillness with the need to prove my devotion; in all moments."

"I release the belief that I need to or possibly can prove my inner connection to 'Source' ; in all moments."

"I honor 'Source' through my kindness to all beings; in all moments."

"I honor 'Source' by appreciating and valuing myself; in all moments."

"I shift my paradigm from demonstrative outer acts of devotion to honoring 'Source' with kindness; in all moments."

"I am centered and empowered in my reverence and appreciation to 'Source'; in all moments."

Home and Family

(Say each statement three times while tapping on your head and say it a fourth time while tapping on your chest; in all moments.")

"I release being taken from my home; in all moments."

"I release having my home taken from me; in all moments."

"I release being separated from my family; in all moments."

"I release being sold into slavery; in all moments."

"I release having my village overtaken by the enemy; in all moments."

"I release being forced to serve the enemy; in all moments."

"I release being deduced to a slave in my own home; in all moments."

"I release the trauma of having my family sold into slavery; in all moments."

"I release letting my family down; in all moments."

"I release being helpless in protecting my family; in all moments."

"I release being rendered helpless on my own turf; in all moments."

"I release being disheartened; in all moments."

"I release having my home deduced to a prison; in all moments."

"I release being trapped in my own home; in all moments."

"I release associating my home and family with being a failure; in all moments."

"I release mourning my home; in all moments."

"I release being deduced to a nomad; in all moments."

"I release dying in my search for a home; in all moments."

"I remove all engrams of being usurped from my home; in all moments."

"I remove all remorse in regards to my home; in all moments."

"I remove all guilt in regards to my home and family; in all moments."

"I release being born to the enemy; in all moments."

"I forgive my enemy; in all moments."

"I make space in this world to reunite with my home; in all moments."

"I forgive all transgressions with my home; in all moments."

"I remove all blockages to reuniting with my home; in all moments."

"I reunite with my home; in all moments."

"I am safe, loved, centered and empowered in my ideal home; in all moments."

Homesickness

(Say each statement three times out loud while continuously tapping on the top of your head at the crown chakra and say it a fourth time while tapping on your chest.)

"I release the trauma of migrating; in all moments."

"I release migrating for death; in all moments."

"I release the fear of letting down my family; in all moments."

"I release the heaviness of needing to provide for others; in all moments."

"I release the fear of disaster; in all moments."

"I release the fear of failing when being met with disaster; in all moments."

"I release running from disaster; in all moment"

"I release feeling responsible for life and death; in all moments."

"I release the fear of losing by forging on; in all moments."

"I accept my abundance as mainstay; in all moments."

"I release all the mind eddies that I've been stuck in; in all moments."

"I release being transfixed on a tapestry; in all moments."

"I release relinquishing my stance for others; in all moments."

"I release diminishing myself compared to my spirit guides; in all moments."

"I accept my stance as a spirit guide to others; in all moments."

"I release separating from spirit guides through matter, energy, space and time; in all moments."

"I break through to my greatest empowerment through the heart; in all moments."

"I manifest my greatest aspiration with my love; in all moments."

"I strengthen the manifestation of my aspiration with pure intention; in all moments."

"I release taking my heart-mind connection off kilter; in all moments."

"I strengthen and empower my heart-mind connection; in all moments."

Release Being Homophobic

Recently, I facilitated a session for a mother of many children. She was longing for and lamenting a past opportunity to be with someone that was very dear to her. But she rejected the relationship and the woman crossed before they could formulate a committed relationship.

People are surprised at how deep my sessions delve within their own psyche. This woman was very progressive in this lifetime and assumed that she was in all her lifetimes. But in past lifetimes, she was very much a bigot and against same sex relationships. She thought she was very open with her love for this other woman. But energies from her past lifetime were surfacing enough to sabotage a very loving relationship that she could have enjoyed with this woman.

She and I were both surprised at the harsh taps that were used to release this schism within herself. The harsh vibrations of the words used here are not meant to offend but to break through the facade of denial that was preventing this woman from enjoying a same sex relationship that would have fulfilled her. May no offense be taken by this post. The verbiage of the taps is meant to free people who have kept themselves from understanding why they are not attracting a life partner.

What was revealed in her session seemed like a breakthrough in understanding why so many gay people are unhappy in their love life. Not that this is different for heterosexual relationships. But the taps would be different. I would love to see these taps shared among the gay community to alleviate any peripheral self-admonishment. I would love to see them shared openly within society to alleviate any discrimination to gay people of any kind.

(Say each statement three times while tapping on your head and say it a fourth time while tapping on your chest.)

"I do these taps for myself and as a surrogate for society; in all moments."

"I release being homophobic; in all moments."

"I release hating fags; in all moments."

"I release hating dykes; in all moments."

"I release hating myself; in all moments."

"I release denying myself a loving partner; in all moments."

"I release hating those that I am attracted to; in all moments."

"I release denying my natural tendencies; in all moments."

"I release being ashamed of myself; in all moments."

"I release being ashamed of whom I love; in all moments."

"I remove all programing and conditioning in regards to choosing a mate; in all moments."

"I remove all engrams that inhibit my ability to choose the mate of my choice; in all moments."

"I release the fear of loving whom I love; in all moments."

"I dissipate all hate, prejudice, judgment and fear in regards to being with whom I love; in all moments."

"I remove all control that prevents me from being with whom I love; in all moments."

"I release the belief that God hates me for being gay; in all moments."

"I release the belief that God cares about anyone's sexual orientation; in all moments."

"I render ineffective and dissipate any group mentality that diminishes people who love those of the same sex; in all moments."

"I render ineffective the religious and governmental diminishing of those who are attracted to the same sex; in all moments."

"I release all the demonizing that is done to those who love a same sex partner; in all moments."

"I unequivocally accept those who are attracted to the same sex; in all moments."

"I am centered and empowered in Universal acceptance of same sex relationships; in all moments."

Again apologies if anyone is offended with the words used here to release an ugly form of bigotry.

Attachment to the Shackles

The reason more people aren't free is because they are emotionally attached to their shackles. We are no different from an abused animal that is fearful of coming out of its cage. Yet we are not apt to understand the nature of what the cage is because we have forgotten the freedom beyond the cage. If we lived in another time, how peculiar would it be to think of people sitting around and staring at a box on the wall all day? To them, that would seem like a shackle. They would be right.

Here is to releasing humanity from shackles of all kinds. We don't need to realize what they are to release from them. Perhaps it is better if we don't. Because shackles have held us imprisoned in many ways: physically, emotionally, habitually and mentally. Here is to leveling the playing field by removing all shackles so that free will has a chance.

(Say each statement three times out loud while tapping on your head and say it a fourth time while tapping on your chest.)

"I declare myself a surrogate for humanity in doing these taps; in all moments."

"I release being enslaved to any and all shackles; in all moments."

"I release being dependent on any or all shackles; in all moments."

"I remove the glass ceiling of any and all shackles from my beingness; in all moments."

"I release using any and all shackles to diminish myself; in all moments."

"I release the genetic propensity to subscribe to any and all shackles; in all moments."

"I remove all propensity to accept or wear shackles from my DNA; in all moments."

"I remove the muscle memory of accepting shackles; in all moments."

"I release using shackles as an excuse to not transcend; in all moments."

"I release using shackles as a security blanket; in all moments."

"I release confusing shackles for love or nurturing; in all moments."

"I release being at the mercy of any or all shackles; in all moments."

"I release using any and all shackles to feel safe; in all moments."

"I release using any shackles to define myself; in all moments."

"I dry up all psychic streams that keep me connected to any shackles; in all moments."

"I withdraw all my energy from any and all shackles; in all moments."

"I release being manipulated, coerced, duped, corrupted or enslaved by any and all shackles; in all moments."

"I remove all vivaxes between myself and any and all shackles; in all moments."

"I remove all tentacles between myself and any and all shackles; in all moments."

"I remove the grip of any and all shackles from my beingness; in all moments."

"I collapse and dissolve all portals to any source that dispenses shackles; in all moments."

"I release perpetuating the limitations of any and all shackles; in all moments."

"I strip all illusion off of any and all shackles; in all moments."

"I remove all masks, walls and armor from the perpetuation of any and all shackles in any form; in all moments."

"I remove all masks, walls and armor that any and all shackles have put on me; in all moments."

"I eliminate the first cause in regards to being held by any and all shackles; in all moments."

"I remove all programming and conditioning that any and all shackles have put on me; in all moments."

"I remove all engrams of any and all shackles; in all moments."

"I remove all muscle memory of wearing any and all shackles; in all moments."

"I send all energy matrices into the light and sound that use any and all shackles to limit humanity; in all moments."

"I command all complex energy matrices that use any and all shackles to limit humanity to be escorted into the light and sound; in all moments."

"I send all energy matrices into the light and sound that perpetuate the use of any and all shackles; in all moments."

"I command all complex energy matrices that perpetuate the use of any and all shackles to be escorted into the light and sound; in all moments."

"I nullify all contracts with any and all shackles; in all moments."

"I nullify all contracts with everyone and everything that perpetuates any and all shackles; in all moments."

"I recant all vows and agreements between myself and any and all shackles; in all moments."

"I collapse and dissolve all the limitations of any and all shackles; in all moments."

"I remove all curses between myself and any and all shackles; in all moments."

"I remove all blessings between myself and any and all shackles; in all moments."

"I dissolve all karmic ties between myself and any and all shackles; in all moments."

"I cut all the cords and ties to any and all shackles; in all moments."

"I remove all the pain, burden, limitations and control that any and all shackles have put on me; in all moments."

"I remove all the pain, burden, limitations, and control that I have put on all others due to any and all shackles; in all moments."

"I take back all the joy, love, abundance, freedom, health, success, security, companionship, creativity, peace, life, wholeness, beauty, enthusiasm, contentment, spirituality, enlightenment, confidence, intellect, the ability to discern and empowerment that any and all shackles have taken from me; in all moments."

"I give back to all others all the joy, love, abundance, freedom, health, success, security, companionship, creativity, peace, life, wholeness, beauty, enthusiasm, contentment, spirituality, enlightenment, confidence, intellect, the ability to discern and empowerment that I have taken from them due to any and all shackles; in all moments."

"I convert all the dependency on shackles into exponential freedom; in all moments."

"I release resonating with any and all shackles; in all moments."

"I release emanating with any and all shackles; in all moments."

"I extract all shackles from my sound frequency and the Universal sound frequency; in all moments."

"I extract all shackles from my light emanation and the Universal light emanation; in all moments."

"I shift my paradigm and the Universal paradigm from any and all shackles to exponential freedom; in all moments."

"I transcend any and all shackles individually and universally; in all moments."

"I am individually and universally centered and empowered in exponential freedom; in all moments."

"I resonate, emanate and am interconnected with all life in individual and Universal exponential freedom; in all moments."

Bigotry

(Say each statement three times while tapping on your head and say it a fourth time while tapping on your chest.)

"We declare ourselves surrogates for humanity in doing these taps; in all moments."

"We also declare ourselves surrogates for society in doing these taps; in all moments."

"We release being poisoned with bigotry; in all moments."

"We release being entrenched in bigotry; in all moments."

"We release perpetuating bigotry; in all moments."

"We release the genetic propensity towards bigotry; in all moments."

"We release being entangled in bigotry; in all moments."

"We release being blind, deaf and mute to our subtle senses; in all moments."

"We awaken all our subtle senses; in all moments."

"We release needing labels to feel safe; in all moments."

"We release being stuck in the primal mode of fear; in all moments."

"We release being shackled to bigotry; in all moments."

"We release allowing bigotry to be our common denominator; in all moments."

"We release being subjugated by bigotry; in all moments."

"We release being poisoned with bigotry; in all moments."

"We release being enslaved to bigotry; in all moments."

"We nullify all contracts between ourselves and bigotry; in all moments."

"We release systemic bigotry; in all moments."

"We remove all vivaxes between ourselves and bigotry; in all moments."

"We remove all tentacles between ourselves and bigotry; in all moments."

"We remove the claws of bigotry from our beingness; in all moments."

"We release being ruled by bigotry; in all moments."

"We remove all programming and conditioning that bigotry has put on us; in all moments."

"We remove all engrams of all bigotry; in all moments."

"We send all energy matrices of bigotry into the light and sound; in all moments."

"We command all complex energy matrices of bigotry to be escorted into the light and sound; in all moments."

"We send all energy matrices into the light and sound that perpetuate bigotry; in all moments."

"We command all complex energy matrices that perpetuate bigotry to be escorted into the light and sound; in all moments."

"We recant all vows and agreements between ourselves and bigotry; in all moments."

"We strip all illusion off of bigotry; in all moments."

"We remove all masks, walls and armor from bigotry; in all moments."

"We shatter all glass ceilings that bigotry has put on us; in all moments."

"We eliminate the first cause in regards to bigotry; in all moments."

"We remove all curses between ourselves and bigotry; in all moments."

"We remove all blessings between ourselves and bigotry; in all moments."

"We strip all entitlement off of bigotry; in all moments."

"We remove all the pain, burden and limitations that bigotry has put on us; in all moments."

"We remove all the fear, futility and unworthiness that bigotry has put on us; in all moments."

"We remove all the apathy, indifference and devastation that bigotry has put on us; in all moments."

"We remove all the rejection, abandonment and illusion of separateness that bigotry has put on us; in all moments."

"We remove all that we have put on all others due to bigotry; in all moments."

"We take back all that bigotry has taken from us; in all moments."

"We give back all that we have taken from others due to bigotry; in all moments."

"We collapse and dissolve all bigotry; in all moments."

"We release resonating or emanating with bigotry; in all moments."

"We extract all bigotry from our sound frequency; in all moments."

"We extract all bigotry from our light emanation; in all moments."

"We extract all bigotry from all 32 layers of our auric field; in all moments."

"We extract all bigotry from our whole beingness; in all moments."

"We abolish bigotry as a construct; in all moments."

"We shift our paradigm from bigotry to love and acceptance; in all moments."

"We transcend bigotry; in all moments."

"We are centered and empowered in universal love and acceptance; in all moments."

"We resonate, emanate, and are interconnected with all life in universal love and acceptance; in all moments."

Calling All Light Workers

(Say each statement three times out loud while continuously tapping on the top of your head at the crown chakra and say it a fourth time while tapping on your chest.)

"We are the voice of light workers everywhere in doing these taps; in all moments."

"We channel the pure intention of light workers everywhere in doing these taps; in all moments."

"We pierce through the fear and apathy in this world with our love; in all moments."

"We crush the facade of indifference that ensconces the earth; in all moments."

"We awaken all the sleeping souls with our loving intention; in all moments."

"We calm and nurture all the terrified souls with our loving presence; in all moments."

"We feed all the starving souls with the abundance of divine love; in all moments."

"We quench the thirst of all souls with the nectar of divine love; in all moments."

"We close the gaping wounds of all suffering souls with the balm of divine love; in all moments."

"We heal the dis-ease of humanity with a pure intention of divine love; in all moments."

"We remove all anger and hidden agendas in the blueprint of humanity; in all moments."

"We remove all impingement from all souls in believing their true worth; in all moments."

"We remove the acquiescence of humanity to being poisoned; in all moments."

"We remove the acquiescence of humanity to be controlled; in all moments."

"We remove the acquiescence of humanity to be manipulated; in all moments."

"We remove the acquiescence of humanity to be brainwashed; in all moments."

"We release humanity being held hostage by terror; in all moments."

"We release terror being mass produced to ensconce humanity; in all moments."

"We release humanity being entertained by the plight of others; in all moments."

"We shift humanity's paradigm from war cries to love songs; in all moments."

"We shift humanity's paradigm from sadness to joy; in all moments."

"We shift humanity's paradigm from fear to love; in all moments."

"We shift humanity's paradigm from darkness to light; in all moments."

"We shift humanity's paradigm from lack to abundance; in all moments."

"We gather up and return all energy that has been stolen from all souls; in all moments."

"We shift all souls' paradigm from fragmentation to wholeness; in all moments."

"We repair and fortify the Wei chi of all the bodies of all souls; in all moments."

"We align all the bodies of all souls; in all moments."

"We center and empower all souls in divine love; in all moments."

"We strip all illusion off of all those who abuse souls; in all moments."

"We withdraw and return to all souls all the energy that they have given to all those who abuse them; in all moments."

"We remove all masks, walls and armor from all those who abuse others; in all moments."

"We shift humanity's paradigm from slavery to freedom; in all moments."

"We remove all physical, emotional and mental shackles from all souls; in all moments."

"We shift humanity's paradigm from dis-ease to health; in all moments."

"We shift all souls' paradigm from failure to success; in all moments."

"We shift all souls' paradigm from abandonment to belonging; in all moments."

"We shift humanity's paradigm from isolation to interconnectedness; in all moments."

"We shift humanity's paradigm from fragmentation to wholeness; in all moments."

"We shift humanity's paradigm from ignorance to enlightenment; in all moments."

"We shatter all glass ceilings on humanity; in all moments."

"Humanity is centered, empowered and imbued in divine love; in all moments."

"Humanity resonates and emanates enlightenment; in all moments."

"We infuse divine love and enlightenment into humanity's sound frequency and light emanation; in all moments."

Change It!

If you don't like the state of the world, do these taps. See if you feel a shift, lightness or a sense that everything will be okay after doing them.

(Say each statement three times out loud while continuously tapping on the top of your head at the crown chakra and say it a fourth time while tapping on your chest.)

"I declare myself a surrogate for humanity in doing these taps; in all moments."

"I release being seduced by mass manipulation; in all moments."

"I release the fear of being left out; in all moments."

"I release primal fears being tapped by mass manipulation; in all moments."

"I release being a mouthpiece for mass manipulation; in all moments."

"I release vehemently defending mass manipulation; in all moments."

"I release being given purpose by mass manipulation; in all moments."

"I release confusing mass manipulation for truth; in all moments."

"I release truth being switched out by and for mass manipulation; in all moments."

"I strip all illusion off of mass manipulation; in all moments."

"I release the fear of being nothing without mass manipulation; in all moments."

"I release partaking in mass manipulation; in all moments."

"I remove all masks, walls and armor from mass manipulation; in all moments."

"I strip off all the illusion that mass manipulation has put on me; in all moments."

"I remove all masks, walls and armor that mass manipulation has put on me; in all moments."

"I remove all vivaxes between myself and mass manipulation; in all moments."

"I release being enslaved to mass manipulation; in all moments."

"I remove all tentacles between myself and mass manipulation; in all moments."

"I release defining myself by mass manipulation; in all moments."

"I untangle myself from mass manipulation; in all moments."

"I remove the claws of mass manipulation from my beingness; in all moments."

"I close all portals and wormholes between myself and mass manipulation; in all moments."

"I remove all programming and conditioning that mass manipulation has put on me; in all moments."

"I remove all engrams that mass manipulation has put on me; in all moments."

"I send all energy matrices into the light and sound that connect me with mass manipulation; in all moments."

"I send all energy matrices into the light and sound that empower mass manipulation; in all moments."

"I command all complex energy matrices to be escorted into the light and sound that are vested in mass manipulation; in all moments."

"I recant all vows and agreements between myself and mass manipulation; in all moments."

"I remove all curses between myself and mass manipulation; in all moments."

"I remove all blessings between myself and mass manipulation; in all moments."

"I release my individuality being shot down by mass manipulation; in all moments."

"I sever all strings, cords and wires between myself and mass manipulation; in all moments."

"I dissolve all karmic ties between myself and mass manipulation; in all moments."

"I remove all the pain, burden and limitations that mass manipulation has put on me; in all moments."

"I remove all the pain, burden and limitations that I have put on all others due to mass manipulation; in all moments."

"I remove all the fear, futility and unworthiness that mass manipulation has put on me; in all moments."

"I remove all the fear, futility and unworthiness that I have put on all others due to mass manipulation; in all moments."

"I remove all the illusion of separateness that mass manipulation has put on me; in all moments."

"I remove all the illusion of separateness that I have put on all others due to mass manipulation; in all moments."

"I take back all the good that mass manipulation has taken from me; in all moments."

"I give back to all others all that I have taken from them due to mass manipulation; in all moments."

"I repair and fortify the Wei chi of all my bodies; in all moments."

"I make whole all those I have compromised; in all moments."

"I remove all controlling devices that mass manipulation has put in me; in all moments."

"I remove all controlling devices that I have put in all others due to mass manipulation; in all moments."

"I release resonating with mass manipulation; in all moments."

"I release emanating with mass manipulation; in all moments."

"I extract all of mass manipulation from my sound frequency; in all moments."

"I extract all of mass manipulation from my light emanation; in all moments."

"I extract mass manipulation from my whole beingness; in all moments."

"I release being bombarded by mass manipulation; in all moments."

"I release bombarding others with mass manipulation; in all moments."

"I shift my paradigm from mass manipulation to exponential freedom; in all moments."

"I transcend mass manipulation; in all moments."

"I collapse and dissolve mass manipulation; in all moments."

"I am centered and empowered in exponential freedom; in all moments."

"I resonate, emanate and reflect exponential freedom to all; in all moments."

Conformity

(Say each statement three times out loud while tapping on the top of your head and say it a fourth time while tapping on your chest.)

"I declare myself a surrogate for humanity in doing these taps; in all moments."

"We unfurl the billow of our true essence; in all moments."

"We un-hatch the safety catch on our heart chakra; in all moments."

"We infuse unbridled bliss and gratitude into every fiber of our essence; in all moments."

"We release partitioning off love; in all moments."

"We release denying love to some; in all moments."

"We melt all aversion to love with our kindness; in all moments."

"We singe through all apathy with our sincerity; in all moments."

"We de-compartmentalize love; in all moments."

"We melt away the ego with Divine Love; in all moments."

"We blur the line between self and others; in all moments."

"We shift our paradigm from working for a wage to living our purpose; in all moments."

"We shift our paradigm from being told what to do, to knowing our own truth; in all moments."

"We shift our paradigm from slavery to freedom; in all moments."

"We shift our paradigm from dis-ease to self-healing; in all moments."

"We break through to the dawn of systemic awakening of the true self; in all moments."

"We crack through the shell of the orb of indifference; in all moments."

"We perpetually imbue our love into the heartbeat of humanity; in all moments."

"We feel the awakening of humanity through our own circadian rhythms; in all moments."

"We perpetuate our life force within the fluid nectar of each sapling tree; in all moments."

"We are grounded in our wisdom to the sentience of each majestic tree; in all moments."

"We are as fluid and flexible as each blade of grass in an organic field; in all moments."

"We are vested in each soul as deeply as every atom of our own essence; in all moments."

"We pour perpetual love into every atom of our essence; in all moments."

"We pour perpetual love into every soul in existence; in all moments."

"We infuse Divine Love into every atom of our essence; in all moments."

"We infuse Divine Love into the sound frequency of every soul in existence; in all moments."

"We imbue Divine Love into the light emanation of every atom of our essence; in all moments."

"We imbue Divine Love into the light emanation of every soul in existence; in all moments."

"We release refusing any soul the honor and respect any child of light deserves; in all moments."

"We show every soul honor and respect through their own accountability; in all moments."

"We make power and manipulation obsolete; in all moments."

"We render fear and ignorance obsolete; in all moments."

"We render ego supremacy obsolete; in all moments."

"We render male dominance obsolete; in all moments."

"We render the practice of enslaving individuals obsolete; in all moments."

"We shift our paradigm to the empowerment of tapping into source; in all moments."

"We align the microcosm with the macrocosm and center them both in Divine Love; in all moments."

"Both the microcosm and macrocosm resonate, emanate and perpetuate Divine Love; in all moments."

Cut the Rhetoric

(Say each statement three times while tapping on your head and say it a fourth time while tapping on your chest.)

"I declare myself a surrogate for humanity in doing these taps; in all moments."

"All vestment in rhetoric is released; in all moments."

"All enslavement to rhetoric is released; in all moments."

"All illusion is stripped off of all rhetoric; in all moments."

"I release the belief that rhetoric is inevitable; in all moments."

"I release giving energy to rhetoric; in all moments."

"I release converting energy into rhetoric; in all moments."

"All vivaxes between myself and rhetoric are removed; in all moments."

"All primal urge to attack due to rhetoric is removed; in all moments."

"All primal urge to withdraw due to rhetoric is removed; in all moments."

"All primal urge to disengage due to rhetoric is removed; in all moments."

"All masks, walls, and armor on rhetoric are removed; in all moments."

"All demonizing of others using rhetoric is removed; in all moments."

"All psychic attacks of rhetoric are dissipated; in all moments."

"All psychic streams of energy of rhetoric are dissipated; in all moments."

"Rhetoric is untangled from truth; in all moments."

"Rhetoric is stripped away from truth; in all moments."

"All paralysis due to rhetoric is released; in all moments."

"All tentacles between myself and rhetoric are severed; in all moments."

"All programming and conditioning due to rhetoric are removed; in all moments."

"All engrams of rhetoric are removed; in all moments."

"All energy and support of all rhetoric are withdrawn; in all moments."

"All energy matrices of rhetoric are sent into the Light and Sound; in all moments."

"All complex energy matrices of rhetoric are escorted into the Light and Sound; in all moments."

"All contracts with rhetoric are nullified; in all moments."

"All vows and agreements with rhetoric are recanted; in all moments."

"All curses between myself and rhetoric are removed; in all moments."

"All curses of rhetoric are removed; in all moments."

"All blessings of rhetoric are removed; in all moments."

"All strings, cords and ties of rhetoric are severed; in all moments."

"All karmic ties with rhetoric are dissolved; in all moments."

"All pain, burden and limitations of rhetoric are removed; in all moments."

"All fear, futility and unworthiness due to rhetoric are removed; in all moments."

"All loyalty to rhetoric is removed; in all moments."

"All anger, entitlement and illusion of separateness due to rhetoric are removed; in all moments."

"All resonating and emanating with rhetoric are released; in all moments."

"The first cause in the initiation of all rhetoric is eliminated; in all moments."

"I withdraw all my energy from all rhetoric; in all moments."

"I extract all rhetoric from all 32 layers of my auric field; in all moments."

"I extract all rhetoric from my whole beingness; in all moments."

"I shift my paradigm from all rhetoric to universal joy, love, abundance and freedom; in all moments."

"I transcend all rhetoric; in all moments."

"All that was deprived due to rhetoric is returned; in all moments."

"All wounds inflicted due to rhetoric are healed; in all moments."

"All rhetoric is extracted from all individual and universal sound frequencies; in all moments."

"All rhetoric is extracted from all individual and universal light emanations; in all moments."

"All rhetoric is collapsed and dissolved; in all moments."

"All energy systems that have been compromised by rhetoric are repaired; in all moments."

"All energy systems resonate, emanate and are interconnected in divine love; in all moments."

"I am centered and empowered in universal joy, love, abundance and freedom; in all moments."

"I resonate, emanate and am interconnected to all life in universal joy, love, abundance and freedom; in all moments."

Devastation

(Say each statement three times out loud while continuously tapping on the top of your head at the crown chakra and say it a fourth time while tapping on your chest at the heart chakra.)

"I declare myself a surrogate for the world in doing these taps; in all moments."

"I release being energetically raped; in all moments."

"I release burning out of control; in all moments."

"I release being stripped of all resources; in all moments."

"I release being devoid of love; in all moments."

"I release struggling to maintain my balance; in all moments."

"I release letting all my inhabitants down; in all moments."

"I release being poisoned; in all moments."

"I release being plagued by power and dis-ease; in all moments."

"I release breaking out in rashes of war; in all moments."

"I release being drained of my life force; in all moments."

"I release being humiliated and abused; in all moments."

"I release being a scapegoat; in all moments."

"I release allowing my energy to be pissed away; in all moments."

"I take back all the energy that has been taken from me; in all moments."

"I repair all the layers of my auric field; in all moments."

"I release being enslaved, in all moments."

"I remove all curses and blessings that have been put on me; in all moments."

"I recant all vows and agreements between myself and being diminished; in all moments."

"I remove all vivaxes between myself and being diminished; in all moments."

"I remove all tentacles between myself and being diminished; in all moments."

"I remove the claws of control from my beingness; in all moments."

"I send all energy matrices into the light that diminish me; in all moments."

"I sever all strings and cords between myself and being diminished; in all moments."

"I align all my bodies; in all moments."

"I dissolve all karmic ties between myself and being diminished; in all moments."

"I withdraw all my energy from being diminished; in all moments."

"I remove all the pain, burden, limitations and illusion of separateness that being diminished has put on me; in all moments."

"I transcend being diminished; in all moments."

"I extract all of being diminished from both my sound frequency and light emanation; in all moments."

"I infuse joy, love, abundance in both my sound frequency and light emanation; in all moments."

"I infuse freedom, peace, and wholeness into my sound frequency and light emanation; in all moments."

"I strip all illusion off of being diminished; in all moments."

"I remove all masks, walls and armor from all those who diminish; in all moments."

"I put out all fires with divine love; in all moments."

"I drench myself with divine love; in all moments."

"I am centered, empowered and saturated in divine love; in all moments."

"I hold my stance in divine love; in all moments."

"I repair and fortify my Wei chi; in all moments."

"I release hiding my empowerment; in all moments."

"I perpetuate my empowerment; in all moments."

"I maintain the charge of empowerment and divine love through my beingness; in all moments."

Disarming Negative Intentions

A longtime client woke me up first thing in the morning to tell me about an important dream. She knows of my focus on energetically disarming all power plays so that humanity can heal itself and she does every set of taps that I post to assist in the process just like I encourage everyone else to do as well.

In the dream, this abusive man that she knows was being held hostage in a circle. He was unable to do any damage to anyone anymore except that there was a machete that he had wielded that he was unable to call back. It was out there. She was upset because in the dream, she was unable to call back the machete.

The dream was pretty self-explanatory. Male energy has been disabled from sending out any more destructive forces in the world. All new ways of diminishing others, power mongering and hoarding are being prevented from happening. But the machete represents all the negative intentions that have already been activated. Those things must all play out unless they are deactivated. I wonder if it was missed on the client that the machete is the new weapon of choice.

She called me to ask me to deactivate the machete. She asked me to create a set of taps specifically for this purpose. Here they are. We are speeding up the process of uplifting consciousness and creating peace by doing these.

(Say each statement three times out loud while continuously tapping on the top of your head at the crown chakra and say it a fourth time while tapping on your chest at the heart chakra. Say each word deliberately. They are not just words but a vibration that you are initiating to shift energy. Pause after each word. Say it in a commanding but even tone, not as a question.)

"I declare myself a surrogate for humanity in doing these taps; in all moments."

"I deactivate all negative intentions; in all moments."

"I call back the machete; in all moments."

"I ground all killing machines; in all moments."

"I castrate power; in all moments."

"I strip all power plays of their momentum; in all moments."

"I ground all power plays; in all moments."

"I ground all negative intentions; in all moments."

"I extract all power plays from the universal sound frequency; in all moments."

"I extract all power plays from the universal light frequency; in all moments."

"I extract all negative intentions from the universal sound frequency; in all moments."

"I extract all negative intentions from the universal light emanation; in all moments."

"I send all energy matrices into the light that perpetuate negative intentions; in all moments."

"I send all energy matrices into the light that perpetuate power plays; in all moments."

"I command all complex energy matrices that perpetuate negative intentions to be escorted into the light and sound; in all moments."

"I command all complex energy matrices that perpetuate power plays to be escorted into the light by my guides; in all moments."

"I deactivate all ignoble intentions; in all moments."

"I shift the Universal paradigm from ignoble intentions to perpetual peace and empowerment of all; in all moments."

"I shift the Universal paradigm from power plays to perpetual peace and empowerment of all; in all moments."

"I am universally centered and empowered in perpetual peace and empowerment of all; in all moments."

Dissolving All the Hypocrisy in the World

(Say each statement three times out loud while tapping on the top of your head at the crown chakra and say it a fourth time while tapping on your chest at the heart chakra.)

"We declare ourselves surrogates for humanity in doing these taps; in all moments."

"We release being encased in hypocrisy; in all moments."

"We release being a hypocrite; in all moments."

"We release being bonded together in hypocrisy; in all moments."

"We release diluting our energy with hypocrisy; in all moments."

"We release minimizing our effectiveness with hypocrisy; in all moments."

"We release being swayed from right action by hypocrisy; in all moments."

"We release being swayed from balanced emotions by hypocrisy; in all moments."

"We release being swayed from clear thought by hypocrisy; in all moments."

"We release being swayed from our internal discernment by hypocrisy; in all moments."

"We release being pawns for hypocrisy; in all moments."

"We release being manipulated by hypocrisy; in all moments."

"We release being a mouthpiece for hypocrisy; in all moments."

"We release being inbred into hypocrisy; in all moments."

"We remove all vivaxes between ourselves and hypocrisy; in all moments."

"We remove all tentacles between ourselves and hypocrisy; in all moments."

"We remove the claws of hypocrisy from our beingness; in all moments."

"We remove all programming and conditioning that hypocrisy has put on us; in all moments."

"We remove all engrams of hypocrisy; in all moments."

"We remove all the pain, burden, and limitations that hypocrisy has put on us; in all moments."

"We remove all the pain, burden, and limitations that we have put on all others due to hypocrisy; in all moments."

"We remove all the fear, futility, and unworthiness that hypocrisy has put on us; in all moments."

"We remove all the fear, futility, and unworthiness that we have put on all others due to hypocrisy; in all moments."

"We remove all the entitlement, self-righteousness, and illusion of separateness that hypocrisy has put on us; in all moments."

"We remove all the entitlement, self-righteousness, and illusion of separateness that we have put on all others due to hypocrisy; in all moments."

"We take back all that hypocrisy has taken from us; in all moments."

"We give back to all others all that we have taken from them due to hypocrisy; in all moments."

"We strip all illusion off of hypocrisy; in all moments."

"We withdraw all our energy and support from hypocrisy; in all moments."

"We collapse and dissolve all portals and passageways to hypocrisy; in all moments."

"We remove all masks, walls, and armor from hypocrisy; in all moments."

"We recant all vows and agreements between ourselves and hypocrisy; in all moments."

"We remove all curses between ourselves and hypocrisy; in all moments."

"We remove all blessings between ourselves and hypocrisy; in all moments."

"We sever all strings and cords between ourselves and hypocrisy; in all moments."

"We dissolve all karmic ties between ourselves and hypocrisy; in all moments."

"We collapse and dissolve all hypocrisy; in all moments."

"We release resonating with hypocrisy; in all moments."

"We release emanating with hypocrisy; in all moments."

"We extract all hypocrisy from our beingness; in all moments."

"We extract all hypocrisy from our sound frequency; in all moments."

"We extract all hypocrisy from our light emanation; in all moments."

"We shift our paradigm from hypocrisy to the purity and spontaneity of Divine Truth; in all moments."

"We transcend all hypocrisy; in all moments."

"We are centered and empowered in the purity and spontaneity of Divine Truth; in all moments."

"We resonate, emanate, and are interconnected with all life in the purity and spontaneity of Divine Truth; in all moments."

Dissolving the Deepest Divide

We originate from a place of purity and love. It is so pristine that it only exists in light and sound. All the dross that we identify with here on earth does not exist. We only get the rarest hint of our true nature through kind, selfless acts and communing with nature and what is untainted by the human mind.

It isn't until we incarnate into this world of harsh vibrations that we identify with the things we come into contact with. They imprint on us and formulate the things that define us here, our likes and dislikes. As light and sound beings, we have no preference for anything of a base nature. But as humans, who are terrified to be freed of the worlds of illusion, we become accustomed to certain vantage points. These are liken to wearing a comfortable robe. We do not want give them up.

As a species in this physical world, we are in the process of transcending. We have actually already transcended but we are merely awakening to this fact. Many of us have had enough heartache and loss to surrender easily to the love. But many are so attached to the experience of this coarse reality, as bloody and as cruel as it is, that they wish to continue the process of living in the harsh illusion of this environment.

The best way to do this is to hold on dearly to the identifications that we have made in this world. One of the first distinctions we have made from other individuals was adopting our skin color. There has always been a core root race that was dominant. The root races of black, white, yellow and red skin have been a way to differentiate ourselves from other individuals so we could gain the perspective in our education as soul of "them versus us". We would not learn love, compassion and freedom if we were not privy to the opposites as a contrast. These were afforded us by having different skin colors from others.

It stands to reason that this was the first primal issue that differentiated us from others in our first incarnation as a human. It makes sense for those who are hell-bent in NOT transcending, they would take umbrage with those of different skin colors as a means to stay entrenched in the human consciousness. It reflects their primal fear of transcending. We may help them by assisting them in stripping off some of that fear.

We do that with this exercise of taps that removes that identification with a particular root race. This will have the added benefit of erasing the prejudice that shows up in this world. By doing these taps as a surrogate for all of humanity, we are demonstrating the presence of our God force and our own benevolent make up that strip us of ignoble intentions, blind spots and false identifications. At the core, we are all pure love. This is what we need to return to.

(Say each statement three times while tapping on your head and say each statement a fourth time while tapping on your chest.)

"I declare myself a surrogate for humanity in doing these taps; in all moments."

"We strip all denial off of the world in identifying with a particular root race; in all moments."

"We release allowing root races to divide us; in all moments."

"We release allowing any root race to be segregated or diminished by anyone or any group; in all moments."

"We dissipate the systemic indifference that allows any root race to be deemed superior; in all moments."

"We remove all masks, walls and armor from allegiance to any root race; in all moments."

"We release allowing the superiority of any root race to be condoned by the elite; in all moments."

"We release allowing root races to poison the earth with hate; in all moments."

"We release allowing root races to be validated as superior to another; in all moments."

"We release allowing root races to gain power over another; in all moments."

"We release allowing root races to threaten our personal freedoms; in all moments."

"We release sitting by and watching root races be unloving to each other; in all moments."

"We strip all illusion off of allegiance to root races; in all moments."

"We release allowing root races to segregate us; in all moments."

"We release being indifferent or apathetic to any root race; in all moments."

"We release allowing any root races to erode our civil liberties; in all moments."

"We release being separated from our humanity by a particular root race; in all moments."

"We release being terrorized by root races; in all moments."

"We break up the power mongers of any particular root race; in all moments."

"We release being immersed in ignorance by any particular root race; in all moments."

"We prevent root races from instilling fear in the masses; in all moments."

"We release denying our responsibilities in dealing with the segregation of root races; in all moments."

"We release enabling the segregation of root races; in all moments."

"We release being stripped of our progressiveness by any particular root race; in all moments."

"We release being complacent with the segregation of root races; in all moments."

"We release allowing root races to mandate mainstream segregation; in all moments."

"We eliminate the first cause in the segregation of root races; in all moments."

"We strip all illusion and defenses off of the segregation of root races; in all moments."

"We release converting our empowerment to loyalty to one particular root race; in all moments."

"We release being enslaved to any particular root race; in all moments."

"We remove all vivaxes between ourselves and the segregation of root races; in all moments."

"We remove all tentacles between ourselves and the segregation of root races; in all moments."

"We withdraw all our energy from the segregation of root races; in all moments."

"We collapse and dissolve all of the segregation of root races; in all moments."

"We remove all programming and conditioning the segregation of root races has put on us; in all moments."

"We remove all individual and universal engrams of the segregation of root races; in all moments."

"We release allowing any particular root race to rob us of our empowerment; in all moments."

"We release allowing any root races to diminish others; in all moments."

"We send all energy matrices into the light and sound that empower the segregation of root races; in all moments."

"We command all complex energy matrices that enable the segregation of root races to be escorted into the light and sound; in all moments."

"We send all energy matrices into the light and sound that allow any particular root race to wield power; in all moments."

"We command all complex energy matrices that allow any root race to wield power to be escorted into the light and sound; in all moments."

"We send all energy matrices into the light and sound that allow any root race to diminish another; in all moments."

"We command all complex energy matrices that allow any root race to diminish another to be escorted into the light and sound; in all moments."

"We recant all vows and agreements between ourselves and all root races; in all moments."

"We remove all curses between ourselves and all root races; in all moments."

"We remove all blessings between ourselves and all root races; in all moments."

"We sever all strings, cords and wires between ourselves and all root races; in all moments."

"We dissolve all karmic ties between ourselves and all root races; in all moments."

"We remove all the pain, burden, limitations, fear, futility, unworthiness and illusion of separateness that all root races have put on each other; in all moments."

"We give back to all root races all the joy, love, abundance, freedom, health, success, security, companionship, creativity, peace, life, wholeness, beauty, enthusiasm, contentment, spirituality, enlightenment, confidence, the ability to discern and empowerment that all root races have taken from them; in all moments."

"We strip all root races of all their ignoble intentions; in all moments."

"We strip root races of their illusions of grandeur; in all moments."

"We crumble all constructs created by any particular root race; in all moments."

"We nullify all contracts between ourselves and all root races; in all moments."

"We eliminate the first cause in all ignoble intentions between all root races; in all moments."

"We release being locked in the sites of any particular root race; in all moments."

"We release humanity from engaging in a race war; in all moments."

"We release being targeted by any particular race; in all moments."

"We relinquish the ruthless pursuit of any root race; in all moments."

"We release resonating or emanating with any particular root race; in all moments."

"We extract all of root races from our individual and universal sound frequency; in all moments."

"We extract all of root races from our individual and universal light emanation; in all moments."

"We extract all of root races from all 32 layers of our individual and universal aura; in all moments."

"We extract all of root races from our whole beingness; in all moments."

"We shift our paradigm from root races to universal, individual empowerment and peace; in all moments."

"We transcend allegiance to any root race; in all moments."

"We are centered and empowered in universal and individual freedom and peace; in all moments."

"We infuse universal and individual freedom and peace into our sound frequency; in all moments."

"We imbue universal and individual freedom and peace into our light emanation; in all moments."

"We resonate, emanate and are interconnected to all life in universal and individual freedom and peace; in all moments."

Please share these with others and ask them to personally do them. Please know you are empowering goodness and kindness in doing these. It is necessary. We don't have to answer hate with hate. We just need to stand in our empowerment and allow hate to empty its tank. This exercise will assist just that in happening.

Dogma

If you are frustrated by current affairs, doing these taps will loosen the grip that human dogma has on the psyche of society.

(Say each statement three times while tapping on your head and say it a fourth time while tapping on your chest.)

"I declare myself a surrogate for humanity in doing these taps; in all moments."

"I release being enslaved by human dogma; in all moments."

"I release being lied to by human dogma; in all moments."

"I release being dependent on human dogma; in all moments."

"I release being in denial about human dogma; in all moments."

"I are impervious to all subtle manipulation and ploys of human dogma; in all moments."

"I extract all human dogma out of our consciousness; in all moments."

"I release using human dogma as a security blanket; in all moments."

"I release using human dogma as a crutch; in all moments."

"I release using human dogma as a means NOT to transcend; in all moments."

"I nullify all contracts with all human dogma; in all moments."

"I release the belief that human dogma is fair and unbiased; in all moments."

"I release the primal fear that entrenched us in human dogma; in all moments."

"I release being corralled in by human dogma; in all moments."

"I dissipate the inner conflict that human dogma uses to enslave us; in all moments."

"I shift our paradigm from human dogma to self-empowerment; in all moments."

"I eliminate the first cause in the creation of human dogma; in all moments."

"I strip all illusion off of all human dogma; in all moments."

"I remove all masks, walls and armor that human dogma has put on us; in all moments."

"I untangle human dogma from humanity; in all moments."

"I strip away the human dogma from humanity; in all moments."

"I dissipate all the psychic energy of human dogma; in all moments."

"I remove all engrams of human dogma; in all moments."

"I recant all vows and agreements between ourselves and human dogma; in all moments."

"I remove all curses between ourselves and human dogma; in all moments."

"I remove all blessings between ourselves and human dogma; in all moments."

"I dissolve all karmic ties between ourselves and human dogma; in all moments."

"I sever all strings and cords between ourselves and human dogma; in all moments."

"I remove all the pain, burden, limitations and engrams that human dogma has put on us; in all moments."

"I remove all the pain, burden, limitations and engrams that we have put on others due to human dogma; in all moments."

"I take back all the joy, love, abundance, freedom, health, success, security, companionship, peace, life, wholeness, beauty, enthusiasm, confidence and enlightenment that human dogma has taken from us; in all moments."

"I extract all human dogma from our sound frequency and our light emanation; in all moments."

"I release resonating with human dogma; in all moments."

"I release emanating with human dogma; in all moments."

"I shift our paradigm from human dogma to joy, love, abundance, freedom, health, success, security, companionship, peace, life, wholeness, beauty, enthusiasm, confidence and enlightenment; in all moments."

"I transcend all human dogma; in all moments."

"I am centered and empowered in the divinity of our own individuality; in all moments."

"I make space in this world for Universal truth and freedom; in all moments."

"I remove all blockages to Universal truth and freedom; in all moments."

"I stretch our capacity to manifest and accept Universal truth and freedom; in all moments."

"I am centered and empowered in Universal truth and freedom; in all moments."

"I resonate, emanate and am interconnected with Universal truth and freedom; in all moments."

Don't Allow Hope to Die

We can no longer watch from a distance as the misinformed wield power and whittle away liberties that generations have dedicated their life to enacting. The beast is at the door. If you are feeling sick inside as you watch him erode our quality of life with a single swoop of a pen then you OWE it to your peace of mind to do these taps. We owe it to future generations. Have you ever thought of what you would do if you lived when Hitler was coming up the ranks?

You are empowered by the intention here. These taps are addressing a real threat at a deep energetic level. I was awakened from a deep slumber to write and share these. It is not too late. This is a way of finally stepping up to the plate in the comfort of your own home and making your intentions count for something. It doesn't matter if you don't believe they work, feel silly, are overwhelmed by the length or get confused. DO THESE TAPS.

Do just one or two if that is all you can do. But then come back to them. Play a game with yourself. Do one on each commercial of your favorite show. It is time you realize that you don't have the luxury of complacency. Beauty, trust, security, nature and hope will perhaps die unless you do these. You can't afford to be complacent or wait for someone else to do something about him. IT IS UP TO YOU. This is your world.

Say the taps out loud if you can and say them slowly. Don't run through them. Pause before the phrase, "in all moments."

Say each statement a total of four times. The first three times tap the top of your head and the fourth time tap the middle of your chest.

"I declare myself a surrogate for the world inhabitants in doing these taps; in all moments."

"We gift the misinformed with the sensitivities of an empath; in all moments."

"We gift the misinformed with the intelligence and awareness of the awakened; in all moments."

"We strip all denial off of the uninformed in dealing with the world; in all moments."

"We release allowing the misinformed to run scared and amok; in all moments."

"We release the misinformed being used as pawns by those with an agenda; in all moments."

"We dissipate the systemic indifference that allows the misinformed to go unchecked; in all moments."

"We release being outnumbered by the misinformed; in all moments."

"We remove all masks, walls, and armor from the misinformed; in all moments."

"We release the burden of being saddled with the misinformed; in all moments."

"We release allowing the misinformed to be duped by the elite; in all moments."

"We release allowing the misinformed to poison the earth; in all moments."

"We release allowing the misinformed to limit our freedoms; in all moments."

"We release allowing the misinformed to segregate us into the haves and have-nots; in all moments."

"We release allowing the misinformed to segregate us into the ignorant and the aware; in all moments."

"We release allowing the misinformed to decide humanity's fate; in all moments."

"We release allowing the misinformed to be used by power mongers; in all moments."

"We release allowing the misinformed to play God with our personal freedoms; in all moments."

"We release passively watching while the misinformed hold the world hostage; in all moments."

"We release sitting by and watching the misinformed dismantle inalienable rights; in all moments."

"We strip all illusion off of the misinformed; in all moments."

"We give back to the misinformed all that worry has inflicted upon them; in all moments."

"We release allowing the misinformed to desecrate humanity; in all moments."

"We release allowing the misinformed to pull us into war; in all moments."

"We release the misinformed being indifferent or apathetic to the plight of others; in all moments."

"We release allowing the misinformed to concede to erosion of our civil liberties; in all moments."

"We release being separated from our humanity by the misinformed; in all moments."

"We release allowing the misinformed to be used to perpetuate mass slavery; in all moments."

"We release being manipulated by those that manipulate the misinformed; in all moments."

"We break up the cluster of power mongers that use the misinformed to control us; in all moments."

"We release being plummeted into ignorance by the misinformed; in all moments."

"We release the fear that the misinformed instill in the masses; in all moments."

"We release denying our responsibilities in dealing with the misinformed; in all moments."

"We release enabling the misinformed; in all moments."

"We release being stripped of our progressiveness by the misinformed; in all moments."

"We release being complacent with the misinformed; in all moments."

"We release allowing the misinformed the benefit of the doubt by withholding truth; in all moments."

"We release allowing the misinformed to fly under the radar; in all moments."

"We release creating the beast of the misinformed; in all moments."

"We release ever empowering the misinformed in any way; in all moments."

"We eliminate the first cause in empowering the misinformed; in all moments."

"We release being passive in regards to the misinformed; in all moments."

"We release being tolerant of the musings of the misinformed; in all moments."

"We stop the onslaught of power mucking done by perpetuating the misinformed; in all moments."

"We strip all illusion and defenses off those who use the misinformed to control the world; in all moments."

"We release converting our empowerment to passivity towards the misinformed; in all moments."

"We release being enslaved to the misinformed; in all moments."

"We release being enslaved by those who perpetuate the misinformed; in all moments."

"We release diminishing ourselves to humor the misinformed; in all moments."

"We remove all vivaxes between ourselves and the misinformed; in all moments."

"We remove all tentacles between ourselves and the misinformed; in all moments."

"We remove all our energy and support from humoring the misinformed; in all moments."

"We collapse and dissolve the ability of the misinformed to minimize or diminish the integrity of humanity; in all moments."

"We remove all programming and conditioning that allow the misinformed to diminish our voice; in all moments."

"We remove all individual and universal engrams of the misinformed; in all moments."

"We release indulging the misinformed; in all moments."

"We release allowing the misinformed to rob the awakened of their voice; in all moments."

"We release allowing the misinformed to diminish others; in all moments."

"We send all energy matrices into the light and sound that enable the misinformed; in all moments."

"We command all complex energy matrices that enable the misinformed to be escorted into the light and sound; in all moments."

"We send all energy matrices into the light and sound that allow the misinformed to perpetuate power; in all moments."

"We command all complex energy matrices that allow the misinformed to perpetuate power to be escorted into the light and sound; in all moments."

"We send all energy matrices into the light and sound that prevent us from reasoning with the misinformed; in all moments."

"We command all complex energy matrices that prevent us from reasoning with the misinformed to be escorted into the light and sound; in all moments."

"We release allowing the misinformed to showcase humanity's shortcomings; in all moments."

"We recant all vows and agreements between ourselves and the misinformed; in all moments."

"We remove all curses between ourselves and the misinformed; in all moments."

"We remove all blessings between ourselves and the misinformed; in all moments."

"We sever all strings, cords and wires between ourselves and the misinformed; in all moments."

"We dissolve all karmic ties between ourselves and the misinformed; in all moments."

"We remove all the pain, burden, limitations, fear, futility, unworthiness and illusion of separateness that the misinformed has put on us; in all moments."

"We give back to the misinformed all that we have taken from them; in all moments."

"We take back all the joy, love, abundance, freedom, health, success, security, companionship, creativity , peace, life, wholeness, beauty, enthusiasm, contentment, spirituality, enlightenment, confidence, ability to discern and empowerment that the misinformed have taken from us; in all moments."

"We strip the misinformed of all their self-righteousness; in all moments."

"We strip the misinformed of all their ignorance; in all moments."

"We strip the misinformed of their ignorance; in all moments."

"We limit the misinformed to the confines of controlling their own life; in all moments."

"We crumble all constructs created by the misinformed; in all moments."

"We nullify all contracts with the misinformed; in all moments."

"We strip all illusion off of the dangerous musings of the misinformed; in all moments."

"We eliminate the first cause in all dangerous musings of the misinformed; in all moments."

"We hold an open portal for universal awakening of the misinformed; in all moments."

"We hold an open portal for the crumbling of all the lies that paralyze the misinformed; in all moments."

"We hold an open portal for Universal awakening and higher awareness; in all moments."

"We release being locked in agreement with the musings of the misinformed; in all moments."

"We release being governed by the misinformed; in all moments."

"We release the belief that the misinformed must be allowed to go unchecked; in all moments."

"We release being targeted by the misinformed; in all moments."

"We relinquish the ruthless hold of the misinformed on humanity; in all moments."

"We release resonating or emanating with the misinformed; in all moments."

"We extract all of the misinformed from our individual and Universal sound frequency; in all moments."

"We extract all of the misinformed from our individual and Universal light emanation; in all moments."

"We extract all of the misinformed from all 32 layers of our individual and Universal aura; in all moments."

"We extract all of the misinformed from our whole beingness; in all moments."

"We shift our paradigm from the misinformed to Universal individual awakening and awareness; in all moments."

"We transcend the misinformed; in all moments."

"We are centered and empowered in universal individual awakening and awareness; in all moments."

"We infuse Universal individual awakening and awareness into our sound frequency; in all moments."

"We imbue Universal individual awakening and awareness into our light emanation; in all moments."

"We resonate, emanate and are interconnected to all life in Universal individual awakening and awareness; in all moments."

Do You Have a Minute to Free Humanity?

(Say each statement three times while tapping on your head and say it a fourth time while tapping on your chest.)

"I declare myself a surrogate for all the inhabitants of the world in doing these taps; in all moments."

"I break all energy grids between myself and war; in all moments."

"I free humanity of all power grids of war; in all moments."

"I break all energy grids between myself and poverty; in all moments."

"I free humanity of all power grids of poverty; in all moments."

"I break all energy grids between myself and slavery; in all moments."

"I free humanity of all power grids of slavery; in all moments."

"I break all energy grids between myself and lack; in all moments."

"I free humanity of all power grids of lack; in all moments."

"I break all energy grids between myself and fossil fuels; in all moments."

"I free humanity of all power grids of fossil fuels; in all moments."

"I break all energy grids between myself and ignorance; in all moments."

"I free humanity of all power grids of ignorance; in all moments."

"I break all energy grids between myself and power; in all moments."

"I free humanity of all power grids of power; in all moments."

"I break all energy grids between myself and power mongers; in all moments."

"I free humanity of all power grids of power mongers; in all moments."

"I break all energy grids between myself and pollution; in all moments."

"I free humanity of all power grids of pollution; in all moments."

"I break all energy grids between myself and cultural clash; in all moments."

"I free humanity of all power grids of cultural clash; in all moments."

"I break all energy grids between myself and unworthiness; in all moments."

"I free humanity of all power grids of unworthiness; in all moments."

"I break all energy grids between myself and worship of monetary wealth; in all moments."

"I free humanity of all power grids of worship of monetary wealth; in all moments."

"I break all energy grids between myself and apathy; in all moments."

"I free humanity of all power grids of apathy; in all moments."

"I break all energy grids between myself and linear existence; in all moments."

"I free humanity of all power grids of linear existence; in all moments."

"I break all energy grids between myself and third dimensional limitations; in all moments."

"I free humanity of all power grids of third dimensional limitations; in all moments."

"I break all energy grids between myself and inequality; in all moments."

"I free humanity of all power grids of inequality; in all moments."

"I break all energy grids between myself and arrogance; in all moments."

"I free humanity of all power grids of arrogance; in all moments."

"I break all energy grids between myself and illusion; in all moments."

"I free humanity of all power grids of illusion; in all moments."

"I break all energy grids between myself and limitations; in all moments."

"I free humanity of all power grids of limitations; in all moments."

"I break all energy grids between myself and illness; in all moments."

"I free humanity of all power grids of illness; in all moments."

"I break all energy grids between myself and degeneration; in all moments."

"I free humanity of all power grids of degeneration; in all moments."

"I break all energy grids between myself and crime; in all moments."

"I free humanity of all power grids of crime; in all moments."

"I break all energy grids between myself and addiction; in all moments."

"I free humanity of all power grids of addiction; in all moments."

"I break all energy grids between myself and primal mode; in all moments."

"I free humanity of all power grids of primal mode; in all moments."

Eradicating War

We are enjoying a ceasefire. I would like to think it is more than a time for Israel to reload supplies that we are giving them. So much of the hardware that kills has been initiated by the U.S. But so many are uncomfortable speaking about war because it sets a target site on them. I don't want to be a target but since I feel so much of the conflict in the world within my own body, I feel compelled to try and resolve it.

It is a great opportunity for the world to see war from a distant vantage point. If one stays detached, they will see that both sides are good people and innocence everywhere is suffering. People who get mad at this statement are being drawn into war. It really is as simple as seeing the good in people. If individuals don't fuel the conflict, it will naturally dry up like a limited supply of arsenals. Opinions, passion, finger pointing and great intellectual debate actually generate the interest and support that fuels the conflict. That is why representatives of both are on news channels now.

We could all study up, take sides, argue points and use our wits and talents to make one side right and one side wrong. Some people reading this right now want to let me have it for my naive approach. But has it been tried? That is, withdrawing all support for either side being vindicated and just pour love and healing peaceful intentions in the whole region?

I am fortunate enough to NOT know the details. I choose not to know. Yes, both sides want their position known and are rallying support for their side on the news shows. To me, this is similar to two fighting children wanting to tell mom what the other did. Mom, in her infinite wisdom, takes no side and loves both children equally. She knows there are issues but trusts that there is enough love to work things out. Why can't we do the same?

Please don't try to educate me on the merits of either side. I will just see that as a justification for killing. With all our evolution of knowledge, to still be destroying what others hold sacred destroys an aspect of ourselves. We are all connected. When a child on the other side of the world loses their teddy bear, it matters to me. When terror is inflicted on others, it affects us all. When mass murder over ideas is still sanctioned as a solution, we all show up as barbarians. Nothing is worth taking life. No God worthy of being worshiped condones murder.

(Say each statement three times out loud while tapping on your head. Say it a fourth time while tapping on your chest.)

"I declare myself as a surrogate for the macrocosm; in all moments."

"We release condoning war; in all moments."

"We release supplying energy to war; in all moments."

"We withdraw all our energy from war; in all moments."

"We release killing innocence; in all moments."

"We release choosing power over love; in all moments."

"We release defining God in petty terms; in all moments."

"We release choosing ideals over people; in all moments."

"We release the arrogance of man; in all moments."

"We think for ourselves; in all moments."

"We release being victims of war; in all moments."

"We release being an advocate of war; in all moments."

"We release the belief that God is vindictive; in all moments."

"We release enjoying the excitement of war; in all moments."

"We release being bored with peace; in all moments."

"We release having a disregard for the reverence of life; in all moments."

"We recant all vows and agreements between ourselves and war; in all moments."

"We remove all curses between ourselves and war; in all moments."

"We dissolve all karmic ties between ourselves and war; in all moments."

"We remove all the pain, burden, limitations and engrams that war has put on us; in all moments."

"We remove all the pain, burden, limitations and engrams that we have put on everyone due to war; in all moments."

"We take back all the joy, love, abundance, freedom, health, success, security, companionship, peace, life, wholeness, beauty, enthusiasm, confidence, spirituality and enlightenment that war has taken from us; in all moments."

"We give back all the joy, love, abundance, freedom, health, success, security, companionship, peace, life, wholeness, beauty, enthusiasm, confidence, spirituality and enlightenment that war has taken from everyone; in all moments."

"We release resonating with war; in all moments."

"We release emanating with war; in all moments."

"We remove all war from our sound frequency; in all moments."

"We remove all war from our light body; in all moments."

"We shift our paradigm from war to joy, love, abundance, freedom, health, success, security, companionship, peace, life, wholeness, beauty, enthusiasm, confidence, spirituality and enlightenment; in all moments."

"We eradicate war as an option and a concept; in all moments."

"We transcend war; in all moments."

"We are centered and empowered in divine love for everyone; in all moments."

We all feel so helpless. But what if it was the EXACT OPPOSITE? What if just one of us could harness an intention so loving that it could end world fighting? What if just one of us could draw in such a surging vast, amount of divine love that, like a tidal wave, it could singe out all the embers of war? What if we have been enslaving ourselves to a complacency that is an illusion? What if we are all the proverbial elephant that has not realized yet that the chain that holds him tied to the post is his belief and not the actual chain?

Some believe that peace will never happen on earth. They believe this is a warring world and have accepted that. I have been taught to challenge every belief, no matter the source. Truth itself is always evolving. Challenging everything that we have been told is a way to continue to evolve ourselves.

Free the World of Judeo-Christian Principles

Unfortunately, what was once held sacred has been bastardized for those who wish to control the masses. It is time for all souls to take up their own counsel and to refute the hysteria and rhetoric of mass manipulation.

(Say each statement three times while tapping on your head and say it a fourth time while tapping on your chest.)

"All vivaxes between Judeo-Christian principles and the world are removed; in all moments."

"All tentacles between Judeo-Christian principles and the world are severed; in all moments."

"The claws of Judeo-Christian principles are removed from the world; in all moments."

"All contracts between Judeo-Christian principles and the world are nullified; in all moments."

"All vows and agreements between Judeo-Christian principles and the world are recanted; in all moments."

"All curses between Judeo-Christian principles and the world are removed; in all moments."

"All blessings between Judeo-Christian principles and the world are removed; in all moments."

"Judeo-Christian principles are released from being a mascot for God; in all moments."

"All strings and cords between Judeo-Christian principles and the world are severed; in all moments."

"All karmic ties between Judeo-Christian principles and the world are dissolved; in all moments."

"All manipulation that has been induced by using Judeo-Christian principles is removed; in all moments."

"All engrams of Judeo-Christian principles are removed from the world; in all moments."

"All programming and conditioning done in Judeo-Christian principles' name are removed; in all moments."

"All control done in Judeo-Christian principles' name is removed; in all moments."

"The desecration of humanity by Judeo-Christian principles is released; in all moments."

"All illusion is stripped off of using Judeo-Christian principles for control; in all moments."

"All masks, walls and armor are removed from all those who use Judeo-Christian principles for control; in all moments."

"All of Judeo-Christian principles' energy is removed from the world and returned to individuals; in all moments."

"All fighting done in Judeo-Christian principles' name is nullified and dissipated; in all moments."

"All energy matrices that use Judeo-Christian principles for control are sent into the light and sound to dissolve; in all moments."

"All complex energy matrices that use Judeo-Christian principles for control are escorted into the light and sound to dissolve; in all moments."

"All energy matrices that use Judeo-Christian principles as a crutch are sent into the light and sound to dissolve; in all moments."

"All complex energy matrices that use Judeo-Christian principles as a crutch are escorted into the light and sound to dissolve; in all moments."

"All energy matrices that trap individuals in time and space using Judeo-Christian principles are escorted into the light and sound to dissolve; in all moments."

"All complex energy matrices that trap individuals in time and space using Judeo-Christian principles are escorted into the light and sound to dissolve; in all moments."

"All energy matrices that recreate the crucifixion are sent into the light and sound to dissolve; in all moments."

"All complex energy matrices that recreate the crucifixion are escorted into the light and sound to dissolve; in all moments."

"All energy matrices that use Judeo-Christian principles for ill-gotten gains are sent into the light and sound to dissolve; in all moments."

"All complex energy matrices that use Judeo-Christian principles for ill-gotten gains are escorted into the light and sound to dissolve; in all moments."

"All energy matrices that use Judeo-Christian principles to enslave the world are sent into the light and sound to dissolve; in all moments."

"All complex energy matrices that use Judeo-Christian principles to enslave the world are escorted into the light and sound to dissolve; in all moments."

"All energy matrices that use Judeo-Christian principles to diminish others are sent into the light and sound to dissolve; in all moments."

"All complex energy matrices that use Judeo-Christian principles to diminish others are escorted into the light and sound to dissolve; in all moments."

"All the pain, burden and limitations that Judeo-Christian values have put on individuals are removed; in all moments."

"All the pain, burden and limitations put on the world using Judeo-Christian principles are removed; in all moments."

"All that is put on the world by Judeo-Christian principles is removed; in all moments."

"All that has been put on the world in the name of Judeo-Christian principles is removed; in all moments."

"All the illusion of separateness that has been put on individuals in the name of Judeo-Christian principles is removed; in all moments."

"All the bounty of higher consciousness is returned to all those who were trapped in Judeo-Christian principles; in all moments."

"All bounty of higher consciousness is given to the world; in all moments."

"The world resonates and emanates with higher consciousness; in all moments."

"Higher consciousness is infused in the world's sound frequency; in all moments."

"Higher consciousness is imbued in the world's light emanation; in all moments."

"All individuals of the world resonate, emanate and are interconnected with all life in higher consciousness; in all moments."

You can easily do these taps again and switch out the phrase Judeo-Christian principles for Patriotism.

Goodness Prevails

(Say each statement three times while tapping on your head and say it a fourth time while tapping on your chest.)

"I declare myself a surrogate for the world in doing these taps; in all moments."

"Truth overtakes and dissipates lies; in all moments."

"Compassion overtakes and dissipates judgment; in all moments."

"Integrity overtakes and dissipates deceit; in all moments."

"Kindness overtakes and dissipates cruelty; in all moments."

"Heroes overtake and dissipate victims; in all moments."

"Enthusiasm overtakes and dissipates depression; in all moments."

"Individuality overtakes and dissipates belonging; in all moments."

"Peace overtakes and dissipates war; in all moments."

"Giving overtakes and dissipates taking; in all moments."

"Organic overtakes and dissipates synthetic; in all moments."

"Sustainable energy overtakes and dissipates fossil fuel; in all moments."

"Sincerity overtakes and dissipates arrogance; in all moments."

"Joy overtakes and dissipates sadness; in all moments."

"Creativity overtakes and dissipates conformity; in all moments."

"Freedom overtakes and dissipates control; in all moments."

"Health overtakes and dissipates dis-ease; in all moments."

"Empowerment overtakes and dissipates mass consensus; in all moments."

"Love overtakes and dissipates All; in all moments."

Hate

(Say each statement three times while tapping on your head and say it a fourth time while tapping on your chest.)

"We declare ourselves surrogates for the haters; in all moments."

"We release feeling displaced; in all moments."

"We release feeling invalidated; in all moments."

"We dissipate the psychic streams of energy that induce us to violence; in all moments."

"We dissipate all psychic streams of energy of hate; in all moments."

"We snap out of the primal mode of hate; in all moments."

"We release being easily influenced; in all moments."

"We send all energy matrices into the light and sound that induce hate; in all moments."

"We command all complex energy matrices that induce hate to be escorted into the light and sound; in all moments."

"We release being motivated by hate; in all moments."

"We release using hate to define us; in all moments."

"We remove all masks, walls and armor that hate has put on us; in all moments."

"We strip all illusion off of the lies that induce us to hate; in all moments."

"We nullify all contracts with hate; in all moments."

"We awaken from the stupor of hate; in all moments."

"We collapse and dissolve all portals of hate; in all moments."

"We eliminate the first cause that induced us to hate; in all moments."

"We dry up the well of hate; in all moments."

"We free our atoms from the tension of hate; in all moments."

"We convert all the anger to love; in all moments."

"We make space in ourselves to being in love; in all moments."

"We remove all blockages to being in love; in all moments."

"We are centered and satiated in divine love; in all moments."

"We stretch our capacity to love; in all moments."

"We resonate, emanate and are interconnected with all life in love; in all moments."

How to Get Back to Truth

The beauty of these taps is that you don't consciously have to discern truth to do these. Truth knows itself. Truth will reveal itself. It tries to all the time. But humans have been so conditioned to lies that they lack the ability to discern truth. Sure, they can see how silly some other faiths' practices seem. But they have blind spots to their own.

(Say each statement three times while tapping on your head and say it a fourth time while tapping on your chest.)

"I declare myself a surrogate for society in doing these taps; in all moments."

"I declare myself a surrogate for practitioners of all faiths in doing these taps; in all moments."

"I release being led astray of truth; in all moments."

"I remove all blind spots to truth; in all moments."

"I nullify all contracts that lead us astray of truth; in all moments."

"I remove all vivaxes between ourselves and being led astray of truth; in all moments."

"I remove all tentacles between ourselves and being led astray of truth; in all moments."

Jen Ward

"I strip all illusion off of all that has led us astray of truth; in all moments."

"I remove all masks, walls and armor from all those who have led us astray of truth; in all moments."

"I remove all programming and conditioning of all that has led us astray of truth; in all moments."

"I remove all engrams of all that separates us from truth; in all moments."

"I withdraw all our energy from all that separates us from truth; in all moments."

"I crumble the facade of all that separates us from truth; in all moments."

"I crumble the facade of all that has led us away from truth; in all moments."

"I send all energy matrices into the light and sound that separate us from truth; in all moments."

"I send all energy matrices into the light and sound that lead us astray of truth; in all moments."

"I command all complex energy matrices that separate us from truth to be escorted into the light and sound; in all moments."

"I command all complex energy matrices that lead us astray of truth to be escorted into the light and sound; in all moments."

"I release being used to demonize truth; in all moments."

"I send all energy matrices into the light that demonize truth; in all moments."

"I command all complex energy matrices that demonize truth to be escorted into the light and sound; in all moments."

"I send all energy matrices into the light and sound that thwart truth; in all moments."

"I command all complex energy matrices that thwart truth to be escorted into the light and sound; in all moments."

"I recant all vows and agreements between ourselves and all that leads us astray of truth; in all moments."

"I remove all curses between ourselves and all that leads us astray of truth; in all moments."

"I remove all blessings between ourselves and all that leads us astray of truth; in all moments."

"I sever all strings, cords, wires and communication between ourselves and all that leads us astray of truth; in all moments."

"I dissolve all karmic ties between ourselves and all that leads us astray of truth; in all moments."

"I remove from ourselves and all others all that those who lead us astray of truth have put on us; in all moments."

"I take back for ourselves and all others all that those who lead us astray of truth have taken from us; in all moments."

"I collapse and dissolve all portals to all those who lead others astray of truth; in all moments."

"I release resonating or emanating with those who lead others astray of truth; in all moments."

"I extract all that leads others astray of truth from our sound frequency; in all moments."

246

"I extract all that leads others astray of truth from our light emanation; in all moments."

"I extract all that leads others astray of truth from the universal sound frequency; in all moments."

"I extract all the leads others astray of truth from the universal light emanation; in all moments."

"I extract all that leads others astray of truth from our whole beingness; in all moments."

"I extract all that leads others astray of truth from all worlds, realities and dimensions; in all moments."

"I shift our paradigm from all those who lead others astray of truth to the enlightenment of truth; in all moments."

"I transcend all those who lead others astray of truth; in all moments."

"I collapse and dissolve all untruth; in all moments."

"I collapse and dissolve all vehicles of untruth; in all moments."

"I am centered and empowered in the enlightenment of universal truth; in all moments."

"I resonate, emanate, and am interconnected with all life in the enlightenment of universal truth; in all moments."

Humanity's Indifference

(Say each statement three times while tapping on your head and say it a fourth time while tapping on your chest.)

"Humanity is released from the grip of indifference; in all moments."

"Humanity is released from being enslaved to indifference; in all moments."

"Humanity is released from worshiping indifference; in all moments."

"All illusion is stripped off all indifference; in all moments."

"All layers of indifference are stripped off of humanity; in all moments."

"All vivaxes between humanity and indifference are removed; in all moments."

"All ignorance due to indifference is dissipated from humanity; in all moments."

"All primal urge to play it small due to indifference is removed from humanity; in all moments."

"All primal urge to disengage due to indifference is removed from humanity; in all moments."

"All masks, walls, and armor of indifference are removed from humanity; in all moments."

"All demonizing of others induced by indifference is removed from all of humanity; in all moments."

"All psychic streams of indifference are dissipated from humanity; in all moments."

"Indifference is untangled from humanity; in all moments."

"Indifference is stripped away from humanity; in all moments."

"All paralysis due to indifference is released from humanity; in all moments."

"All tentacles between humanity and indifference are severed; in all moments."

"All programming and conditioning due to indifference is removed from humanity; in all moments."

"All engrams of indifference are removed from humanity; in all moments."

"All of humanity's energy is withdrawn from indifference; in all moments."

"All energy matrices that hold humanity in indifference are sent into the Light and Sound; in all moments."

"All complex energy matrices that hold humanity in indifference are escorted into the Light and Sound; in all moments."

"All contracts between humanity and indifference are nullified; in all moments."

"The first cause that holds humanity in indifference is eliminated; in all moments."

"All vows and agreements between humanity and indifference are recanted; in all moments."

"All curses between humanity and indifference are removed; in all moments."

"All blessings between humanity and indifference are removed; in all moments."

"All strings, cords and ties between humanity and indifference are severed; in all moments."

"All karmic ties between humanity and indifference are dissolved; in all moments."

"All pain, burden and limitations that indifference has put on humanity are removed; in all moments."

"All fear, futility and unworthiness that indifference has put on humanity are removed; in all moments."

"All loyalty to indifference is removed from humanity; in all moments."

"All anger, entitlement and illusion of separateness induced onto humanity by indifference are removed; in all moments."

"Humanity releases resonating and emanating with indifference; in all moments."

"All lack caused by indifference is removed; in all moments."

"All that the indifference has taken is returned to humanity; in all moments."

"All wounds inflicted by indifference are healed from humanity; in all moments."

"All engrams of indifference that were imprinted on humanity are removed; in all moments."

"All programming and conditioning that indifference has put on humanity are removed; in all moments."

"All indifference is extracted from humanity; in all moments."

"All indifference is extracted from humanity's sound frequency and light emanation; in all moments."

"The indifference is collapsed and dissolved; in all moments."

"All energy systems of humanity that have been compromised by indifference are repaired; in all moments."

"All energy systems resonate, emanate and are interconnected in divine love; in all moments."

"Humanity shifts its paradigm from indifference to compassion; in all moments."

"Humanity transcends indifference; in all moments."

"Humanity is centered and empowered in Universal compassion and divine love; in all moments."

"Humanity resonates, emanates and is interconnected with all life in Universal compassion and divine love; in all moments."

Ignorance or Want

(Say each statement three times while tapping on your head and say it a fourth time while tapping on your chest.)

"I declare myself a surrogate for humanity in doing these taps; in all moments."

"We release indulging in ignorance or want; in all moments."

"We release being inundated with ignorance or want; in all moments."

"We release being defined by ignorance or want; in all moments."

"We dissipate all psychic energy of ignorance and want; in all moments."

"We remove all vivaxes between ourselves and ignorance or want; in all moments."

"We remove all tentacles between ourselves and both ignorance and want; in all moments."

"We remove all engrams of ignorance and want; in all moments."

"We remove all engrams that both ignorance or want have put on us; in all moments."

"We release personifying ignorance or want; in all moments."

"We collapse and dissolve all portals to both ignorance and want; in all moments."

"We nullify all contracts with both ignorance and want; in all moments."

"We send all energy matrices of ignorance and want into the Light and Sound; in all moments."

"We command all complex energy matrices of ignorance and want to be escorted into the Light and Sound; in all moments."

"We release harboring ignorance or want; in all moments."

"We recant all vows and agreements between ourselves and both ignorance or want; in all moments."

"We remove all curses between ourselves and both ignorance and want; in all moments."

"We remove all blessings between ourselves and both ignorance and want; in all moments."

"We sever all strings and cords between ourselves and both ignorance and want; in all moments."

"We dissolve all karmic ties between ourselves and both ignorance and want; in all moments."

"We remove all the pain, burden, and limitations that ignorance and want have put on us; in all moments."

"We take back ALL that ignorance and want have taken from us; in all moments."

"We release resonating with ignorance or want; in all moments."

"We release emanating with ignorance or want; in all moments."

"We extract all ignorance and want from our Sound frequency; in all moments."

"We extract all ignorance and want from our Light emanation; in all moments."

"We transcend both ignorance and want; in all moments."

"We shift our paradigm from ignorance and want to Universal Love and Peace; in all moments."

"We align all our bodies to Universal Love and Peace; in all moments."

"We are centered and empowered in Universal Love and Peace; in all moments."

"We resonate, emanate, and are interconnected with all life in Universal Love and Peace; in all moments."

New Consciousness

There is residual energy that is a byproduct of transcending. It is like the ash in the furnace that needs to be emptied out every once in a while. These taps slough off the residual energy that is a by-product of awakening.

(Say each statement three times while continuously tapping on your head and say it a fourth time while tapping on your chest.)

"I declare myself a surrogate for humanity in doing these taps; in all moments."

"I release being buried under energetic ash; in all moments."

"I sweep my world clean of energetic ash with the wind of divine love; in all moments."

"I release searching through energetic ash for meaning; in all moments."

"I release looking for purpose in energetic ash; in all moments."

"I release searching for baubles in the energetic ash; in all moments."

"I release the restlessness with new consciousness; in all moments."

"I release mourning old consciousness; in all moments."

"I release the ego let-down of new consciousness; in all moments."

"I remove all vivaxes between myself and all residual energy; in all moments."

"I release being enslaved to residual energy; in all moments."

"I release forging my sense of self out of residual energy; in all moments."

"I remove all tentacles between myself and all residual energy; in all moments."

"I remove the dust of all residual energy from my beingness; in all moments."

"I remove all programming and conditioning that all residual energy has on me; in all moments."

"I remove all engrams that all residual energy has in me; in all moments."

"I withdraw all my essence from all residual energy; in all moments."

"I strip all illusion off of all residual energy; in all moments."

"I send all energy matrices of all residual energy into the light; in all moments."

"I command all complex energy matrices of residual energy to be escorted into the light and sound; in all moments."

"I send all energy matrices into the light and sound that depend on residual energy; in all moments."

"I command all complex energy matrices that depend on residual energy to be escorted into the light and sound; in all moments."

"I send all energy matrices into the light and sound that breed in residual energy; in all moments."

"I command all complex energy matrices that breed in residual energy to be escorted into the light and sound; in all moments."

"I send all energy matrices into the light and sound that feed on residual energy; in all moments."

"I command all complex energy matrices that feed on residual energy to be escorted into the light and sound; in all moments."

"I remove all calcification of residual energy from my beingness; in all moments."

"I release confusing residual energy for purpose; in all moments."

"I release romanticizing residual energy; in all moments."

"I recant all vows and agreements between myself and all residual energy; in all moments."

"I remove all curses between myself and all residual energy; in all moments."

"I remove all blessings between myself and all residual energy; in all moments."

"I sever all strings and cords between myself and all residual energy; in all moments."

"I dissolve all karmic ties between myself and all residual energy; in all moments."

"I release weighing myself down with residual energy; in all moments."

"I release breathing life into residual energy; in all moments."

"I release diluting my effectiveness with residual energy; in all moments."

"I remove all the pain, burden and limitations that I have put on myself and all others due to residual energy; in all moments."

"I remove all the fear, futility and unworthiness that I have put on myself and all others due to residual energy; in all moments."

"I remove all regret, remorse and illusion of separateness that I have put on myself and all others due to residual energy; in all moments."

"I take back all that I have deprived myself due to residual energy; in all moments."

"I give back to all others all that I have deprived them of due to residual energy; in all moments."

"I remove all residual energy from my physical form; in all moments."

"I remove all residual energy from the astral world; in all moments."

"I remove all residual energy from the causal realm; in all moments."

"I remove all residual energy from the mental realm; in all moments."

"I remove all residual energy from the etheric realm; in all moments."

"I extract all residual energy from my sound frequency; in all moments."

"I extract all residual energy from my light emanation; in all moments."

"I extract all residual energy from all 32 layers of my auric field; in all moments."

"I extract all residual energy from my whole essence; in all moments."

"I turn my attention and interest from residual energy; in all moments."

"I transcend all residual energy; in all moments."

"I shift my paradigm from all residual energy to awakening new consciousness; in all moments."

"I am centered and empowered in the awakening of new consciousness; in all moments."

"I am centered and empowered and vested in all life in the awakening of new consciousness; in all moments."

Peace

(Say each statement three times while tapping on your head and say it a fourth time while tapping on your chest.)

"I declare myself a surrogate for Peace; in all moments."

"I infuse a loving, pure intention for Peace into the heart of humanity; in all moments."

"I recant all vows and agreements between myself and war; in all moments."

"I remove all curses between myself and war; in all moments."

"I dissolve all karmic ties between myself and war; in all moments."

"I remove all the pain, burden and limitations that war has put on me; in all moments."

"I take back all the joy, love, abundance, freedom, health, success, security, companions, peace, life and wholeness that war has taken from me; in all moments."

"I withdraw all the all my energy from war; in all moments."

"I release resonating with war; in all moments."

"I release emanating with war; in all moments."

"I remove all of war from my sound frequency; in all moments."

"I remove all of war from my light emanation; in all moments."

"I shift my paradigm from war to Peace; in all moments."

"I shift my paradigm from war to joy, love, abundance, freedom, health, success, security, companionship, peace, life and wholeness; in all moments."

"I awaken my enthusiasm for and acceptance of Peace; in all moments."

"I make space in this world for Universal Peace; in all moments."

"I remove all blockages to Universal Peace; in all moments."

"I stretch my capacity to accept Universal Peace; in all moments."

"I add my loving intention to the cause of Universal Peace; in all moments."

"I am centered and empowered in divine love; in all moments."

"I am a conduit for divine love; in all moments."

"I uplift all of humanity with my love; in all moments."

Prejudice

Whatever demographic you have an aversion or reaction to, you can put in place of the word Muslim.

(Say each statement three times while tapping on your head and say it a fourth time while tapping on your chest.)

"I declare myself a surrogate for humanity in doing these taps; in all moments."

"I release hating Muslims; in all moments."

"I release demonizing Muslims; in all moments."

"I release being the enemy of Muslims; in all moments."

"I release the belief that I am superior to Muslims; in all moments."

"I nullify all contracts with Muslims; in all moments."

"I withdraw all my energy from hating Muslims; in all moments."

"I extract all the hate that I have projected onto Muslims; in all moments."

"I dry up all psychic streams that mandate the diminishing of Muslims; in all moments."

"I send all energy matrices into the light and sound that compel me to hate Muslims; in all moments."

"I command all complex energy matrices that compel me to hate Muslims to be escorted into the light and sound; in all moments."

"I remove all engrams of hating Muslims; in all moments."

"I remove all programming and conditioning to hate Muslims; in all moments."

"I strip all illusion off of hating Muslims; in all moments."

"I remove all masks, walls and armor that hating Muslims has put on me; in all moments."

"I eliminate the first cause in regards to hating Muslims; in all moments."

"I release being immersed in hating Muslims; in all moments."

"I untangle all my energy from hating Muslims; in all moments."

"I release the genetic propensity to hate Muslims; in all moments."

"I dissolve all of the hating of Muslims with the purity of divine love; in all moments."

"I view all Muslims from the vantage point of love; in all moments."

"I remove all vortexes between myself and hating Muslims; in all moments."

"I dry up all instincts to hate Muslims; in all moments."

"I recant all vows and agreements to hate Muslims; in all moments."

"I remove all curses that I put on Muslims; in all moments."

"I remove all blessings I put on hating Muslims; in a moments."

"I sever all strings and cords between myself and hating Muslims; in all moments."

"I dissolve all karmic ties between myself and hating Muslims; in all moments."

"I remove all the pain, burden and limitations that I have put on all Muslims; in all moments."

"I remove all the fear, futility and unworthiness I have put on all Muslims; in all moments."

"I release ostracizing Muslims; in all moments."

"I give back all that I have taken from Muslims; in all moments."

"I extract all hate of Muslims from my sound frequency and the universal sound frequency; in all moments."

"I extract all hate of Muslims from my light emanation and the universal light emanation; in all moments."

"I release individually or universally resonating or emanating with hating Muslims; in all moments."

"I transcend hating Muslims; in all moments."

"I shift my paradigm from hating Muslims to seeing all souls as pure love; in all moments."

"I am centered and empowered in seeing all souls as pure love; in all moments."

"I resonate, emanate and am interconnected with all life in seeing all souls as pure love; in all moments."

Protesting Energetically

(Say each statement three times while tapping on your head and say it a fourth time while tapping on your chest.)

"We declare ourselves surrogates for humanity in doing these taps; in all moments."

"We dissipate the hate; in all moments."

"We release using hate to validate ourselves; in all moments."

"We release using hate as a controlling factor; in all moments."

"We release being bound together with hate; in all moments."

"We release justifying the hate; in all moments."

"We release being hate generators; in all moments."

"We release being conduits of hate; in all moments."

"We release being blinded by hate; in all moments."

"We release blurting hate; in all moments."

"We release being defined by hate; in all moments."

"We release being used by hate; in all moments."

"We release personifying hate; in all moments."

"We release justifying hate; in all moments."

"We release choosing hate over love; in all moments."

"We strip all illusion off of hate; in all moments."

"We collapse and dissolve all portals to hate; in all moments."

"We release the white-washing of hate; in all moments."

"We remove all masks, walls, and armor that hate has put on us; in all moments."

"We deactivate all vortexes of hate; in all moments."

"We remove all primal hate; in all moments."

"We release the genetic propensity to hate; in all moments."

"We flush all hate out of our DNA; in all moments."

"We eliminate the first cause in regards to hate; in all moments."

"We remove all segregation that hate has put on us; in all moments."

"We release being deduced to ignorance by hate; in all moments."

"We release the arrogance of hate; in all moments."

"We release complying with the hate; in all moments."

"We release being subjugated by hate; in all moments."

"We send all energy matrices of hate into the light and sound to dissolve; in all moments."

"We command all complex energy matrices of hate to be escorted into the light and sound to be dissolved; in all moments."

"We nullify all contracts between ourselves and hate; in all moments."

"We recant all vows and agreements between ourselves and hate; in all moments."

"We remove all curses between ourselves and hate; in all moments."

"We release confusing hate for love; in all moments."

"We release using hate as a crutch to not transcend; in all moments."

"We release using hate as an anchor to the third dimension; in all moments."

"We release using hate as a security blanket; in all moments."

"We release the fear of being separated from our consciousness; in all moments."

"We release using hate to preserve our sense of identity; in all moments."

"We release using hate to compensate for feeling unworthy to be loved; in all moments."

"We remove all blessings between ourselves and hate; in all moments."

"We dissipate all idealism that justifies hate; in all moments."

"We dissipate all psychic streams of hate; in all moments."

"We sever all strings and cords between ourselves and hate; in all moments."

"We dissolve all karmic ties between ourselves and hate; in all moments."

"We remove all the pain, burden, and limitations that hate has put on us; in all moments."

"We remove all the fear, futility, and illusion of separateness that hate has put on us; in all moments."

"We remove all the abandonment, rejection, and anger that hate has put on us; in all moments."

"We remove all that we have put on others due to hate; in all moments."

"We take back all the joy, love and abundance that hate has taken from us; in all moments."

"We take back all the freedom, health and success that hate has taken from us; in all moments."

"We take back all the security, companionship and creativity that hate has taken from us; in all moments."

"We take back all the peace, life and wholeness that hate has taken from us; in all moments."

"We take back all the spiritually, enlightenment and confidence that hate has taken from us; in all moments."

"We take back all the family, intellect and ability to discern that hate has taken from us; in all moments."

"We take back all the individuality, empowerment and expansiveness that hate has taken from us; in all moments."

"We give back all that we have taken from others due to hate; in all moments."

"We heal our beingness; in all moments.

"We shift our paradigm from hate to love; in all moments."

"We transcend hate; in all moments."

"We transcend all idealism that perpetuates hate; in all moments."

"We are centered and empowered in divine love; in all moments."

"We extract all hate from our sound frequency; in all moments."

"We extract all hate from our light emanation; in all moments."

"We resonate, emanate and are interconnected with all life in divine love; in all moments."

Reinstate Integrity

(Say each statement three times while tapping on your head and say it a fourth time while tapping on your chest.)

"All negative portals are collapsed and dissolved; in all moments."

"All negative energy in the world is dissipated; in all moments."

"I think, speak, observe and love in energy; in all moments."

"The world thinks, speaks, observes and loves in energy; in all moments."

"All imbalances in the world are dissipated; in all moments."

"All self-righteous taking in the world is alleviated; in all moments."

"All portals of self-righteous taking are collapsed and dissolved; in all moments."

"All portals of apathy and ignorance are collapsed and dissolved; in all moments."

"All engrams of repetitious behavior are washed away; in all moments."

"All engrams of programming and conditioning are washed away; in all moments."

"All engrams of enslavement are washed away; in all moments."

"All engrams of imprisonment are washed away; in all moments."

"All portals to female defilement are collapsed and dissolved; in all moments."

"All engrams of female defilement are washed away; in all moments."

"All portals to male domination are collapsed and dissolved; in all moments."

"All engrams of male domination are washed away; in all moments."

"Space is made in the world for goodness to prevail; in all moments."

"All blockages to goodness prevailing in the world are removed; in all moments."

"Propensity for goodness to prevail in the world is expanded; in all moments."

"The world is centered and empowered in goodness prevailing; in all moments."

"The world resonates, emanates, and is interconnected with all life in goodness prevailing; in all moments."

Release the Anguish of 9/11

These are the powerful taps. Humanity is empowered to transcend every difficulty. To do these taps is a great form of service to honor all who have been affected in the events of September 11. This is a means to dissipate the psychic energy around the day.

(Say each statement three times out loud while continuously tapping on the top of your head at the crown chakra and say it a fourth time while tapping on your chest.)

"I declare myself a surrogate for humanity in doing these taps; in all moments."

"We close all portals to anguish; in all moments."

"We extract all negative charge vibration out of the date 9-11; in all moments."

"We heal all wounds from 9-11; in all moments."

"We free all souls trapped in 9-11; in all moments."

"We remove all vivaxes between 9-11 and anguish; in all moments."

"We remove all tentacles between 9-11 and anguish; in all moments."

"We send all energy matrices into the light and sound that keep 9-11 trapped in anguish; in all moments."

"We send all energy matrices into the light and sound that prevent us from moving on after 9-11; in all moments."

"We remove all programming and conditioning that 9-11 has put on us; in all moments."

"We remove all engrams that 9-11 has put on us; in all moments."

"We remove all engrams that the anguish of 9-11 has put on us; in all moments."

"We send all energy matrices into the light and sound that trap us in the anguish of 9-11; in all moments."

"We close the portal to the anguish of 9-11 at ground zero; in all moments."

"We cleanse and sanctify ground zero; in all moments."

"We recant all vows and agreements between humanity and the anguish of 9-11; in all moments."

"We remove all curses between humanity and the anguish of 9-11; in all moments."

"We remove all blessings between humanity and the anguish of 9-11; in all moments."

"We sever all strings and cords between humanity and the anguish of 9-11; in all moments."

"We dissolve all karmic ties between humanity and the anguish of 9-11; in all moments."

"We remove all the pain, burden, and limitations that the anguish of 9-11 has put on humanity; in all moments."

"We remove from all of humanity all the helplessness and illusion of separateness that the anguish of 9-11 has put on us; in all moments."

"We take back for humanity all the joy, love, abundance and freedom that the anguish of 9-11 has taken from us; in all moments."

"We take back for humanity all the health, success, security and wholeness that the anguish of 9-11 has taken from us; in all moments."

"We take back for all of humanity all the beauty, enthusiasm, contentment and peace that the anguish of 9-11 has taken from us; in all moments."

"We withdraw all our energy from the anguish of 9-11; in all moments."

"We strip all illusion off the anguish of 9-11; in all moments."

"We remove all masks, walls and armor from the anguish of 9-11; in all moments."

"We collapse and dissolve the anguish of 9-11; in all moments."

"We release resonating with the anguish of 9-11; in all moments."

"We release emanating with the anguish of 9-11; in all moments."

"We extract all of the anguish of 9-11 from humanity's sound frequency; in all moments."

"We extract all of the anguish of 9-11 from humanity's light emanation; in all moments."

"Humanity transcends the anguish of 9-11; in all moments."

"Humanity is centered and empowered in divine love; in all moments."

"We repair and fortify the Wei chi of humanity; in all moments."

"We re-institute the integrity of humanity; in all moments."

"Humanity resonates and emanates divine love; in all moments."

Release Being in Primal Mode

Primal mode gets in the way of humanity transcending. People are stuck in primal mode and create a ritual and rationale around it. It is to the extent that whole demographics are entrenched in primal mode. Perhaps all of society is paralyzed by it.

When people follow a way of doing something just because it has always been done that way, that is evidence of being stuck in primal mode. More evidence is when people are no longer able to discern for themselves. In some ways, it has never been acceptable to think for ourselves. But higher awareness is necessary for transcendence.

That is what enlightenment is--higher awareness. One can't be enlightened and still be in primal mode.

(Say each statement three times while tapping on your head and say it a fourth time while tapping on your head.)

"We declare ourselves surrogates for humanity in doing these taps; in all moments."

"We release being in primal mode; in all moments."

"We strip all illusion off of primal mode; in all moments."

"We release preferring primal mode; in all moments."

"We release advocating for primal mode; in all moments."

"We release using primal mode to enslave others; in all moments."

"We release using primal mode to push an agenda; in all moments."

"We remove all vivaxes between ourselves and primal mode; in all moments."

"We release the genetic propensity to stay in primal mode; in all moments."

"We remove all tentacles between ourselves and primal mode; in all moments."

"We remove the claws of primal mode from our beingness; in all moments."

"We remove all engrams of primal mode from our beingness; in all moments."

"We remove all programing and conditioning that primal mode has put on us; in all moments."

"We remove all masks, walls and armor from primal mode; in all moments."

"We withdraw all our energy from primal mode; in all moments."

"We send all energy matrices into the light and sound that keep us stuck in primal mode; in all moments."

"We command all complex energy matrices that keep us stuck in primal mode to be escorted into the light and sound; in all moments."

"We release reverting to primal mode; in all moments."

"We deactivate the muscle memory of primal mode; in all moments."

"We nullify all contracts with primal mode; in all moments."

"We recant all vows and agreements between ourselves and primal mode; in all moments."

"We remove all curses between ourselves and primal mode; in all moments."

"We remove all blessings between ourselves and primal mode; in all moments."

"We sever all strings and cords between ourselves and primal mode; in all moments."

"We dissolve all karmic ties between ourselves and primal mode; in all moments."

"We release allowing primal mode from preventing us from transcending; in all moments."

"We release the primal anguish that anchors us to lower consciousness; in all moments."

"We remove all that primal mode has put on us; in all moments."

"We take back all that primal mode has taken from us; in all moments."

"We release all identification with primal mode; in all moments."

"We release resonating or emanating with primal mode; in all moments."

"We extract all of primal mode from our sound frequency; in all moments."

"We extract all of primal mode from our light emanation; in all moments."

"We extract all of primal mode from our whole beingness; in all moments."

"We shift our paradigm from primal mode to transcendence; in all moments."

"We transcend primal mode; in all moments."

"We are centered and empowered in transcendence; in all moments."

"We resonate, emanate and are interconnected with all life in transcendence; in all moments."

Releasing All Ignoble Intentions

Here are some powerful taps from a group session. It is releasing all ignoble intentions. ISIL, dictators and all power plays are all ignoble intentions. Do these taps to do some good for humanity.

(Say each statement three times out loud while continuously tapping on the top of your head at the crown chakra and say it a fourth time while tapping on your chest at the heart chakra.)

"I declare myself a surrogate for humanity in doing these taps; in all moments."

"I access the macrocosm through my microcosm; in all moments."

"I dip into my own well of enlightenment; in all moments."

"I release bowing out of the fabric of life; in all moments."

"I release being the dropped stitch in the fabric of life; in all moments."

"I remove all vivaxes between myself and being the dropped stitch; in all moments."

"I remove all tentacles between myself and being the dropped stitch; in all moments."

"I release dropping the stitch by compartmentalizing myself; in all moments."

"I remove all engrams that being the dropped stitch has put on me; in all moments."

"I remove all programming and conditioning that being the dropped stitch has put on me; in all moments."

"I pull out the stitching of all my ignoble intentions; in all moments."

"I send all energy matrices into the light and sound that immerse me in ignoble intentions; in all moments."

"I send all energy matrices into the light and sound that cause me to drive ignoble intentions; in all moments."

"I remove all vivaxes between myself and all ignoble intentions; in all moments."

"I remove all tentacles between myself and all ignoble intentions; in all moments."

"I remove all engrams that all ignoble intentions have put on me; in all moments."

"I remove all programming and conditioning that all ignoble intentions have put on me; in all moments."

"I release being the driving force behind all ignoble intentions; in all moments."

"I release allowing my love to be converted to fear to fuel ignoble intentions; in all moments."

"I recant all vows and agreements between myself and all ignoble intentions; in all moments."

"I remove all curses between myself and all ignoble intentions; in all moments."

"I remove all blessings between myself and all ignoble intentions; in all moments."

"I send all energy matrices into the light and sound that support ignoble intentions; in all moments."

"I sever all strings and cords and wires between myself and all ignoble intentions; in all moments."

"I dissolve all karmic ties between myself and all ignoble intentions; in all moments."

"I remove all the pain, burden and limitations that all ignoble intentions have put on me; in all moments."

"I remove all the pain, burden and limitations that all ignoble intentions have caused me to put on others; in all moments."

"I remove all the suffering and illusion of separateness that all ignoble intentions have put on me; in all moments."

"I remove all the suffering and illusion of separateness that all ignoble intentions have caused me to put on others; in all moments."

"I take back all the good that all ignoble intentions have taken from me; in all moments."

"I give back to all others all the good that all ignoble intentions have caused me to take from them; in all moments."

"I release resonating with any or all ignoble intentions; in all moments."

"I release emanating with any or all ignoble intentions; in all moments."

"I extract all ignoble intentions from my sound frequency and the universal sound frequency; in all moments."

"I extract all ignoble intentions from my light emanation and the universal light emanation; in all moments."

"I shift my paradigm from all ignoble intentions to universal goodwill; in all moments."

"I shift the world's paradigm from all ignoble intentions to goodwill for all; in all moments."

"I transcend all ignoble intentions; in all moments."

"I empower the world to universally transcend all ignoble intentions; in all moments."

"I and the world are centered and empowered in divine love; in all moments."

"I and the world take our rightful place in the universal tapestry; in all moments."

Stop Us from Revisiting the Fate of Atlantis or Lemuria

Many people romanticize the times of Atlantis and Lemuria. They think they were so wonderful, but they were a time of incredible abuse and manipulation. They used psychic arts and tactics to control the masses. We are seeing hints of it in our current society. We see it in the lying and distortion in cultural differences and rhetoric.

These engrams (energetic memories) of Atlantis and Lemuria are seen today in the schisms in social structures. Our beliefs and understandings are twisted and skewed to benefit the most ruthless power mongers. This is what happened in Atlantis and Lemuria. These old practices have been revisited in us.

This powerful series of taps is a way to free humanity from mimicking the same trajectory course as Atlantis and Lemuria.

(Say each statement three times while tapping on your head and say it a fourth time while tapping on your chest.)

"We declare ourselves surrogates for humanity in doing these taps; in all moments."

"We release romanticizing Atlantis or Lemuria; in all moments."

"We remove all nostalgia for Atlantis or Lemuria; in all moments."

"We release reliving Atlantis or Lemuria; in all moments."

"We remove all power grids between ourselves and Atlantis or Lemuria; in all moments."

"We remove all power grids between ourselves and both Atlantis and Lemuria; in all moments."

"We release being affected by the power mongers of Atlantis and Lamuria; in all moments."

"We release the trajectory course of following the fate of Atlantis and Lemuria; in all moments."

"We withdraw all our energy from Atlantis and Lemuria; in all moments."

"We release emulating Atlantis and Lemuria; in all moments."

"We remove all programming and conditioning that Atlantis and Lemuria have put on us; in all moments."

"We release being shackled to Atlantis and Lamuria; in all moments."

"We release being a breeding ground for the power plays of Atlantis and Lemuria; in all moments."

"We release the psychic grip of Atlantis and Lemuria on our beingness; in all moments."

"We release our awareness being thwarted by the power mongers of Atlantis and Lemuria; in all moments."

"We nullify all contracts with both Atlantis and Lemuria; in all moments."

"We release being imprisoned in matter, energy, space, and time with Atlantis and Lemuria; in all moments."

"We release being victims of Atlantis and Lemuria; in all moments."

"We remove all vivaxes between ourselves and Atlantis and Lemuria; in all moments."

"We remove all tentacles between ourselves and Atlantis and Lemuria; in all moments."

"We remove all schisms created by Atlantis and Lemuria; in all moments."

"We remove all engrams of Atlantis and Lemuria; in all moments."

"We remove all controlling devices implanted in our beingness by Atlantis and Lemuria; in all moments."

"We release reliving the fate of Atlantis and Lemuria; in all moments."

"We send all energy matrices into the Light and Sound that infuse humanity with the power mongers of Atlantis and Lemuria; in all moments."

"We command all complex energy matrices that infuse the power mongers of Atlantis and Lemuria into humanity to be escorted into the Light and Sound; in all moments."

"We send all energy matrices of the power mongers of Atlantis and Lemuria into the Light and Sound; in all moments."

"We command all complex energy matrices of the power mongers of Atlantis and Lemuria to be escorted into the Light and Sound; in all moments."

"We clear the ethers of the power mongers and their control; in all moments."

"We recant all vows and agreements between ourselves and Atlantis and Lemuria; in all moments."

"We remove all curses between ourselves and Atlantis and Lemuria; in all moments."

"We remove all cultural bias between ourselves and Atlantis and Lemuria; in all moments."

"We remove all blessings between ourselves and Atlantis and Lemuria; in all moments."

"We sever all strings, cords, and energy grids between ourselves and Atlantis and Lemuria; in all moments."

"We dissolve all karmic ties between ourselves and Atlantis and Lemuria; in all moments."

"We remove all the pain, burden and limitations that Atlantis and Lemuria have put on us; in all moments."

"We remove all the fear, futility and slavery that Atlantis and Lemuria have put on us; in all moments."

"We strip all illusion off of Atlantis and Lemuria; in all moments."

"We strip off all illusion that Atlantis and Lemuria have put on us; in all moments."

"We remove all anger, apathy and indifference that Atlantis and Lemuria have put on us; in all moments."

"We remove all ignorance, confusion and chaos that Atlantis and Lemuria have put on us; in all moments."

"We remove all abandonment, rejection and illusion of separateness that Atlantis and Lemuria have put on us; in all moments."

"We remove all aberrations that Atlantis and Lemuria have put on us; in all moments."

We remove all muscle memory of Atlantis and Lemuria; in all moments."

We remove all psychic energy streams of control that Atlantis and Lemuria have put on us; in all moments."

We take back ALL that Atlantis and Lemuria have taken from us; in all moments."

We take back our Sound frequency and Light emanation that Atlantis and Lemuria have taken from us; in all moments."

We take back all the energy that Atlantis and Lemuria have siphoned off of us; in all moments."

We release resonating and emanating with Atlantis and Lemuria; in all moments."

We extract all of Atlantis and Lemuria from our Sound frequency; in all moments."

We extract all of Atlantis and Lemuria from our Light emanation; in all moments."

We shift our paradigm from Atlantis and Lemuria to transcendence and spiritual empowerment; in all moments."

We transcend Atlantis and Lemuria; in all moments."

We are centered and empowered in the transcendence and spiritual awareness of Divine Love; in all moments."

We collapse and dissolve all portals to Atlantis and Lemuria; in all moments."

We remove all masks, walls and armor that Atlantis and Lemuria have put on us; in all moments."

We remove all masks, walls and armor from all power mongers of Atlantis and Lemuria; in all moments."

We eliminate the first cause of being controlled by Atlantis and Lemuria; in all moments."

We resonate, emanate and are interconnected with all life in the transcendence of Divine Love; in all moments."

The Struggle Between Good and Evil

If you are paying attention, we are living out the Book of Revelation right now. If you are frustrated by current affairs, doing these taps will loosen the grip that the struggle between good and evil has on the psyche of society.

(Say each statement three times while tapping on your head and say it a fourth time while tapping on your chest.)

"I declare myself a surrogate for humanity in doing these taps; in all moments."

"I release being enslaved by the struggle between good and evil; in all moments."

"I release being deceived by the struggle between good and evil; in all moments."

"I release being dependent on the struggle between good and evil; in all moments."

"I release being in denial about the struggle between good and evil; in all moments."

"I am impervious to all subtle manipulation and ploys of the struggle between good and evil; in all moments."

"I extract all of the struggle between good and evil out of my consciousness; in all moments."

"I release using the struggle between good and evil as a limitation; in all moments."

"I release using the struggle between good and evil as a crutch; in all moments."

"I release using the struggle between good and evil as a means NOT to transcend; in all moments."

"I nullify all contracts with all the struggle between good and evil; in all moments."

"I release the belief that the struggle between good and evil is fair and unbiased; in all moments."

"I release the primal fear that entrenched me in the struggle between good and evil; in all moments."

"I release being pulled down by the struggle between good and evil; in all moments."

"I dissipate the inner conflict that the struggle between good and evil uses to enslave me; in all moments."

"I shift my paradigm from the struggle between good and evil to self-empowerment; in all moments."

"I eliminate the first cause in the struggle between good and evil; in all moments."

"I strip all illusion off of all the struggle between good and evil; in all moments."

"I remove all masks, walls and armor that the struggle between good and evil has put on me; in all moments."

"I untangle the struggle between good and evil from Humanity; in all moments."

"I strip away the struggle between good and evil from humanity; in all moments."

"I dissipate all the psychic energy of the struggle between good and evil; in all moments."

"I remove all engrams of the struggle between good and evil; in all moments."

"I release the fear of the struggle between good and evil; in all moments."

"I release being paralyzed in the struggle between good and evil; in all moments."

"I release being duped by choosing sides in the struggle between good and evil; in all moments."

"I recant all vows and agreements between myself and the struggle between good and evil; in all moments."

"I remove all curses between myself and the struggle between good and evil; in all moments."

"I remove all blessings between myself and the struggle between good and evil; in all moments."

"I dissolve all karmic ties between myself and the struggle between good and evil; in all moments."

"I sever all strings and cords between myself and the struggle between good and evil; in all moments."

"I remove all the pain, burden, limitations and engrams that the struggle between good and evil has put on me; in all moments."

"I remove all the pain, burden, limitations and engrams that I have put on others due to the struggle between good and evil; in all moments."

"I take back all the joy, love, abundance, freedom, health, success, security, companionship, peace, life, wholeness, beauty, enthusiasm, confidence and enlightenment that the struggle between good and evil has taken from us; in all moments."

"I extract all the struggle between good and evil from my sound frequency; in all moments."

"I extract all the struggle between good and evil from my light emanation; in all moments."

"I release resonating with the struggle between good and evil; in all moments."

"I release emanating with the struggle between good and evil; in all moments."

"I shift my paradigm from the struggle between good and evil to joy, love, abundance, freedom, health, success, security, companionship, peace, life, wholeness, beauty, enthusiasm, confidence and enlightenment; in all moments."

"I transcend all of the struggle between good and evil; in all moments."

"I am centered and empowered in the divinity of my own individuality; in all moments."

"I make space in this world for my truth and freedom; in all moments."

"I remove all blockages to my truth and freedom; in all moments."

"I stretch my capacity to manifest and accept my truth and freedom; in all moments."

"I am centered and empowered in my truth and freedom; in all moments."

"I resonate, emanate and am interconnected with all life in my truth and freedom; in all moments."

Taps to Repair Human Consciousness

(Say each statement three times while tapping on your head and say it a fourth time while tapping on your chest.)

"I declare myself a surrogate for humanity in doing these taps; in all moments."

"We release holding such a low bar in the expectations of humanity; in all moments."

"We shatter the glass ceiling on humanity; in all moments."

"We make silt of the resistance; in all moments."

"We rub out all the indoctrination of the human consciousness; in all moments."

"We remove all the ingrained conditioning; in all moments."

"We release the disconnect between the human consciousness and truth; in all moments."

"We repair the schism between the human consciousness and joy; in all moments."

"We repair the schism between the human consciousness and divinity; in all moments."

"We repair the schism between human consciousness and love; in all moments."

"We repair the schism between human consciousness and abundance; in all moments."

"We repair the schism between human consciousness and freedom; in all moments."

"We repair the schism between human consciousness and wholeness; in all moments."

"We infuse joy love abundance into the human consciousness' sound frequency; in all moments."

"We imbue joy, love and abundance into the human consciousness' light emanation; in all moments."

"We infuse freedom, health and wholeness into the human consciousness' sound frequency; in all moments."

"We imbue freedom, health and wholeness in the human consciousness' light emanation; in all moments."

"Human consciousness resonates, emanates and is interconnected with all life in empowerment; in all moments."

"We shift the whole flow of the Universe from introversion to expansion; in all moments."

The Third Dimension

(Say each statement three times out loud while continuously tapping on the top of your head at the crown chakra and say it a fourth time while tapping on your chest.)

"I declare myself a surrogate for humanity in doing these taps; in all moments."

"We release backsliding; in all moments."

"We release letting power slide; in all moments."

"We release the burden of the masses; in all moments."

"We remove all vivaxes between ourselves and the third dimension; in all moments."

"We remove all tentacles between ourselves and the third dimension; in all moments."

"We send all energy matrices into the light that keep us trapped in the third dimension; in all moments."

"We remove all programming and conditioning from the third dimension; in all moments."

"We remove all engrams that the third dimension has put on us; in all moments."

"We recant all vows and agreements between ourselves and the third dimension; in all moments."

"We remove all curses between ourselves and the third dimension; in all moments."

"We remove all blessings between ourselves and the third dimension; in all moments."

"We sever all strings and cords between ourselves and the third dimension; in all moments."

"We dissolve all karmic ties between ourselves and the third dimension; in all moments."

"We strip all illusion off the third dimension; in all moments."

"We remove all masks, walls, and armor from the third dimension; in all moments."

"We withdraw all our energy from the third dimension; in all moments."

"We distance ourselves from the third dimension; in all moments."

"We remove all the pain, burden, limitations, and illusion of separateness that the third dimension has put on us; in all moments."

"We take back all that the third dimension has taken from us; in all moments."

"We release overlaying the third dimension; in all moments."

"We separate all the places that are overlaying the third dimension; in all moments."

"We separate all the ways consciousness overlays the third dimension; in all moments."

"We release resonating with the third dimension; in all moments."

"We release emanating with the third dimension; in all moments."

"We extract all of the third dimension from our sound frequency; in all moments."

"We extract all of the third dimension from our light emanation; in all moments."

"We release being titillated by the doings of the third dimension; in all moments."

"We shift our paradigm from the third dimension to the fifth and above; in all moments."

"We transcend the third dimension; in all moments."

"We leave war behind at the third dimension; in all moments."

"We leave sexual debauchee behind at the third dimension; in all moments."

"We leave mail dominance behind at the third dimension; in all moments."

"We leave sadness and depression behind at the third dimension; in all moments."

"We leave hatred and fear behind at the third dimension; in all moments."

"We leave lack and depravity behind at the third dimension; in all moments."

"We leave slavery and manipulation behind at the third dimension; in all moments."

"We leave sickness and disease behind at the third dimension; in all moments."

"We leave failure and unworthiness behind at the third dimension; in all moments."

"We leave insecurity and uncertainty behind at the third dimension; in all moments."

"We leave abandonment and rejection behind at the third dimension; in all moments."

"We leave apathy and conformity behind at the third dimension; in all moments."

"We leave death and decay behind at the third dimension; in all moments."

"We leave feeling fractured and fragmentation behind at the third dimension; in all moments."

"We leave ugliness and judgment behind at the third dimension; in all moments."

"We leave all false Gods and sheep mentality behind at the third dimension; in all moments."

"We leave all programming and conditioning behind at the third dimension; in all moments."

"We separate ourselves from all attributes of the third dimension; in all moments."

"We distance ourselves from all attributes of the third dimension; in all moments."

"We are centered and empowered in the fifth dimension and above; in all moments."

"We resonate and emanate the fifth dimension and above; in all moments."

Ignoble Intentions

(Say each statement three times out loud while tapping on the top of your head at the crown chakra and say it a fourth time while tapping on your chest at the heart chakra.)

"I release giving form to unworthy imagery; in all moments."

"I release giving energy to unworthy intentions; in all moments."

"I release manifesting unworthy dreams; in all moments."

"I release preoccupying my attention with ignoble thoughts; in all moments."

"I release giving life to ignoble intentions; in all moments."

"I breathe life form into my highest potential; in all moments."

"I pour energy into the greatest intentions for myself and the world; in all moments."

"I manifest dreams beyond my greatest possible wonderment; in all moments."

"I focus my intention and breathe life into the highest manifestation of the greatest good; in all moments."

"I coordinate my heart and mind in synergy with miraculous results; in all moments."

"I stretch my capacity manifest miraculous results; in all moments."

"I remove all blockages to manifesting miraculous results; in all moments."

"I stretch my capacity to accept my own empowerment; in all moments."

"I am centered and empowered in manifesting miracles for myself and humanity; in all moments."

Illusion

(Say each statement three times while tapping on your head and say it a fourth time while tapping on your chest.)

"I declare myself a surrogate for humanity in doing these taps; in all moments."

"I release being invested in illusion; in all moments."

"I release being weighed down by illusion; in all moments."

"I release being enslaved to illusion; in all moments."

"I release being duped by illusion; in all moments."

"I release perpetuating illusion; in all moments."

"I dissipate the psychic energy of illusion; in all moments."

"I nullify all contracts with illusion; in all moments."

"I strip all illusion off of illusion; in all moments."

"I remove all masks, walls and armor from illusion; in all moments."

"I collapse and dissolve all portals of illusion; in all moments."

"I remove all vivaxes between ourselves and illusion; in all moments."

"I remove all tentacles between ourselves and illusion; in all moments."

"I remove all engrams of illusion from our world; in all moments."

"I remove all programming and conditioning that illusion has put on us; in all moments."

"I shatter all glass ceilings of illusion; in all moments."

"I eliminate the first cause in regards to illusion; in all moments."

"I send all energy matrices of illusion into the light and sound; in all moments."

"I command all complex energy matrices of illusion to be escorted into the light and sound; in all moments."

"I release using illusion as a crutch; in all moments."

"I recant all vows and agreements between ourselves and illusion; in all moments."

"I remove all curses between ourselves and illusion; in all moments."

"I remove all blessings between ourselves and illusion; in all moments."

"I sever all strings and cords between ourselves and illusion; in all moments."

"I dissolve all karmic ties between ourselves and illusion; in all moments."

"I remove all the pain, burden and limitations that illusion has put on us; in all moments."

"I release enjoying the illusion; in all moments."

"I release converting our empowerment to illusion; in all moments."

"I remove all the pain, burden and limitations I have put on others due to illusion; in all moments."

"I take back ALL that illusion has taken from us; in all moments."

"I give back to all others all that I have taken from them due to illusion; in all moments."

"I shift our paradigm to universal clarity; in all moments."

"I am centered and empowered in universal clarity; in all moments."

"I transcend illusion; in all moments."

"I release resonating with illusion; in all moments."

"I release emanating with illusion; in all moments."

"I extract all illusion from our sound frequency; in all moments."

"I extract all illusion from our light emanation; in all moments."

"I infuse universal joy, love, peace and truth into our sound frequency; in all moments."

"I infuse universal joy, love, peace, and truth into our light emanation; in all moments."

"I am centered and empowered in universal joy, love, peace, and truth; in all moments."

"I resonate, emanate, and am interconnected with all life in universal joy, love, peace, and truth; in all moments."

Impatience

(Say each statement three times while tapping on your head and say it a fourth time while tapping on your chest.)

"I release being disappointed; in all moments."

"I release being lied to; in all moments."

"I take back all the energy wasted in anticipation; in all moments."

"I remove all engrams of being disappointed; in all moments."

"I release the belief that good things are fleeting to me; in all moments."

"I release the need to snatch up good things before the opportunity is lost; in all moments."

"I release the disappointment of missed opportunity; in all moments."

"I remove all engrams of missing opportunities; in all moments."

"I remove all muscle memory of missing opportunities; in all moments."

"I release the trauma of being born; in all moments."

"I remove all aversion to waiting; in all moments."

"I remove all vivaxes between waiting and being disappointed; in all moments."

"I release confusing waiting for disappointment; in all moments."

"I release being left out; in all moments."

"I release having to compete for all that I attain; in all moments."

"I release feeling inconsequential; in all moments."

"I release all need; in all moments."

"I release all want; in all moments."

"I infuse waiting with contentment; in all moments."

"I replace need with contentment; in all moments."

"I replace want with contentment; in all moments."

"I shift my paradigm from impatience to contentment; in all moments."

"I convert all impatience to contentment; in all moments."

"I infuse contentment into my essence; in all moments."

"I am centered and empowered in contentment; in all moments."

"I resonate, emanate and am interconnected with all life in contentment; in all moments."

Impotence/Heal Your Manhood

(Say three times while tapping on your head and say it a fourth time while tapping on your chest.)

"I release the trauma of being circumcised; in all moments."

"I release the pain and humiliation of being circumcised; in all moments."

"I remove all judgment to my penis; in all moments."

"I remove all shame from my penis; in all moments."

"I release the fear of not measuring up; in all moments."

"I release the trauma of expectations; in all moments."

"I release the fear of disappointing; in all moments."

"I remove all hesitation from my penis; in all moments."

"I release being disconnected from my penis; in all moments."

"I re-attach my penis; in all moments."

"I heal my penis; in all moments."

"I release the fear of underperforming; in all moments."

"I release the embarrassment of erecting; in all moments."

"I release aging; in all moments."

"I regenerate my penis; in all moments."

"I optimize my performance; in all moments."

"I release holding guilt, shame and fear of procreating in my penis; in all moments."

"I infuse joy, love, abundance and freedom into my penis; in all moments."

"I release the trauma of having my scrotum cut off; in all moments."

"I release the trauma of being a eunuch; in all moments."

"I reattach my scrotum; in all moments."

"I heal my scrotum; in all moments."

Indifference

(Say each statement three times out loud while tapping on the top of your head at the crown chakra and say it a fourth time while tapping on your chest at the heart chakra.)

"I release being indifferent to life; in all moments."

"I release living outside of my passion; in all moments."

"I release being complacent; in all moments."

"I release being numb to my own joy; in all moments."

"I release giving up hope of something better; in all moments."

"I release lowering my expectations; in all moments."

"I release being depressed; in all moments."

"I release sabotaging my own joy; in all moments."

"I release giving up on myself; in all moments."

"I release waiting to be rescued; in all moments."

"I am my own hero; in all moments."

"I rescue myself by empowering myself; in all moments."

"I take back my joy; in all moments."

"I am centered, empowered and enlivened in joy; in all moments."

Be an Individual

It is funny that someone becomes famous for standing apart from others in some unique way. Yet as soon as they become known, that individuality is stripped away from them in so many ways. They have to be afraid of public opinion or what their sponsors think. In a way, it strips them of a lot of the originality that was so appealing. Perhaps we do this to ourselves in so many ways.

(Say each statement three times while tapping on your head and say it a fourth time while tapping on you chest.)

"I release losing my individualism; in all moments."

"I release energetically melding into the pot; in all moments."

"I release being a diluted version of myself; in all moments."

"I release the fear of standing out; in all moments."

"I release trying to blend; in all moments."

"I convert all the energy of trying to blend into being an original; in all moments."

"I release demonizing originals; in all moments."

"I release wearing originals down to a nub; in all moments."

"I release resenting originals; in all moments."

"I release copying originals at the expense of my own wonder; in all moments."

"I extract myself from all conformity; in all moments."

"I shatter all illusion of conformity; in all moments."

"I remove all that conformity has put on me; in all moments."

"I take back all that conformity has taken from me; in all moments."

"I transcend conformity; in all moments."

Individuality

The issue isn't that we aren't powerful. The issue is that we don't understand the incredible potential energy that we have when we connect the wires between our heart and mind. Why do you think so many of us have gotten beaten down to such an extent? It is because when enough of us figure out the blueprint, we will all be as effective as Gandhi, as insightful as Einstein, as loving as Mother Theresa and as motivating as Mandela.

We, as individuals, are all world changers. We are made to be that. But when we throw our energy into a group and allow that group to manage our sails, we lose the breeze. We are only as great as the greatest member of our group and we are hindered by the least of them. Why not decide that humanity itself is the only thing we give our lifeblood to. We can support all the groups we want but from the vantage point of our own individuality. It is not about dropping out; it is about plugging more in.

This means thinking for ourselves: seeing the hidden agenda in every statement, feeling the energy pull of every intention, and giving only to those intentions that truly benefit humanity. Once one pulls one's self free of the fibers of others agendas, it is clearer to see the subtle form of control with which the individuals have given their power to. They can break the spell. That is the importance of claiming one's individuality.

(Say each statement three times out loud while tapping on your head and say it a fourth time while tapping on your chest.)

"I release the primal fear of being separated from the herd; in all moments."

"I release hiding in groups for security; in all moments."

"I release being enslaved to group dynamics; in all moments."

"I release being dependent on groups; in all moments."

"I release losing my identity in groups; in all moments."

"I shatter the glass ceiling of all groups; in all moments."

"I recant all vows and agreements between myself and all groups; in all moments."

"I remove all curses between myself and all groups; in all moments."

"I dissolve all karmic ties between myself and all groups; in all moments."

"I sever all strings and cords between myself and all groups; in all moments."

"I remove all the pain, burden, limitations and engrams that all groups have put on me; in all moments."

"I remove all the pain, burden, limitations and engrams that I have put on all others for the sake of a group; in all moments."

"I take back all the joy, love, abundance, freedom, health, success, security, companionship, peace, life, wholeness, beauty, enthusiasm, confidence and enlightenment that all groups have taken from me; in all moments."

"I withdraw all my energy from all groups; in all moments."

"I release resonating with all groups; in all moments."

"I release emanating with all groups; in all moments."

"I remove all groups from my sound frequency; in all moments."

"I remove all groups from my light body; in all moments."

I shift my paradigm from all groups to joy, love, abundance, freedom, health, success, security, companionship, peace, life, wholeness, beauty, enthusiasm, confidence and enlightenment; in all moments."

"I transcend all groups; in all moments."

"I am centered and empowered in the divinity of my own individuality; in all moments."

"I make space in this world for the realization of the empowerment of my own individuality; in all moments."

"I remove all blockages to the realization of the empowerment of my own individuality; in all moments."

"I stretch my capacity to manifest and accept the empowerment of my own individuality; in all moments."

"I am centered and empowered in divine love; in all moments."

Think about it. Have you ever really been honored to your full potential in any group? Have you ever soared to your greatest heights? Have the groups on earth honored all its members? Have they disparaged nonmembers? The only group that is going to honor all life is the one where all are included equally. That is the group of humanity where all are important.

Inflammation

(Say each statement three times while tapping on your head and say it a fourth time while tapping on your chest.)

"I release being surrounded by incompetence; in all moments."

"I release the need to do everything; in all moments."

"I release seething in anger and frustration; in all moments."

"I release distributing frustration through my essence to control it; in all moments."

"I release seething on a cellular level; in all moments."

"I release the systemic need to manage the world; in all moments."

"I release the systemic seething; in all moments."

"I release the need to control; in all moments."

"I release storing frustration and anger in my parasympathetic nervous system; in all moments."

"I remove all anger stored in my parasympathetic nervous system; in all moments."

"I release the internal struggle between the sympathetic and parasympathetic nervous system; in all moments."

"I release the internal fight; in all moments."

"I remove all anger and frustration stored at a cellular level; in all moments."

"I release the internal exhaustion; in all moments."

"I give my body permission to rest; in all moments."

"I rest from the internal struggle; in all moments."

"I surrender the inner fight; in all moments."

"I surrender the outer struggle; in all moments."

"I release the need to feign disaster; in all moments."

"I remove the weight of the burden from my shoulders; in all moments."

"I relinquish control; in all moments."

"I release overriding the commands of my internal functions; in all moments."

"All is fine without my control; in all moments."

"My body runs smoothly without my conscious input; in all moments."

"I release the fear of losing the calm without my conscious input; in all moments."

"I release confusing my efficient body functions with incompetent people and social systems; in all moments."

"I convert all incompetency to competency; in all moments."

"My body functions are a reflection of my competence; in all moments."

"All is safe without my assistance; in all moments."

"My body functions are competent; in all moments."

Inner Child

Let's face it. Not everyone has had a happy childhood. Some of us have come into a lonely, loveless life where nurturing and kindness was something we watched happen to others from afar. Some of us are still numb from the experience. Some of us have not been able to gain the momentum in life that those who have been treasured have to their advantage.

There are great techniques to change the script of what we endured at the mercy of the world. A good technique is to visualize yourself as an angel of light and go to the baby you once were. Pour incredible love into yourself in baby form. Give yourself all the encouragement and nurturing that was withheld from you. Return often to the child the baby grows into and comfort yourself in those lonely, scary moments that you have endured.

You can also tap into earlier lifetimes when you were loved. Realize that this lifetime is only one experience and it does not define the totality of who you are.

(Say each statement three times while tapping on your head and say it a fourth time while tapping on your chest.)

"I release the trauma of being born; in all moments."

"I release the trauma of being molested; in all moments."

"I release the trauma of losing my innocence; in all moments."

"I release mourning my innocence; in all moments."

"I release being a scapegoat; in all moments."

"I release being the black sheep; in all moments."

"I release the belief that my parents hate me; in all moments."

"I release the belief that I am unlovable; in all moments."

"I release being numb; in all moments."

"I immerse every aspect of my essence in kindness and understanding; in all moments."

"I regain my wonder; in all moments."

"I reawaken my imagination and creativity; in all moments."

"I release the belief that I am damaged; in all moments."

"I release defining my childhood as unhappy; in all moments."

"I release being shattered; in all moments."

"I make myself whole; in all moments."

"I nurture every aspect of myself; in all moments."

"I heal all my wounds; in all moments."

"I shift the paradigm of my childhood to joy, love, abundance, security, peace and wholeness; in all moments.

"I am loved, nurtured and valued; in all moments."

Insomnia

So many people suffer with insomnia. It can be freeing to get an understanding of it. I had a friend years ago and she would not be able to sleep. She would lay paralyzed in the bed. It was dark and scary to her. What she was not receptive to was the understanding that she was asleep when this happened. She was not awake.

When we go to sleep, we slip out of our physical body and are free to "roam" around the universe in our astral body. The astral body is very similar to the physical body. Sometimes when we are very tired or have had trauma, we slip into our astral body. We don't realize this because it feels so similar to the physical body, but the rooms are more angular and there are experiences that happen there that we are protected from experiencing in the physical. Children are so much in their astral body that those who see monsters and imaginary friends are spending some of their time in their astral body. When we are overtired, we slip in the astral body without realizing it and can't move the physical body. That gives some the sensation of being paralyzed.

I have had the experience of being killed and not being aware that I am dead. I have lain in a pile of dead soldiers and did not realize why the soldiers walking around were not helping me. I am not certain how long I stayed in that situation. I have seen the trauma of staying with the dead body happen with some of my clients in their past lives. Sometimes they were put in the ground and buried but did not realize they were dead. This manifests as a terror of being buried alive, buried in the ground or being put in a coffin. Sometimes, when people think they are awake but really in their astral body, they go back to that experience without consciously realizing it. That is why they put so much credence on being asleep. The trauma of dying but not crossing properly is horrific. That is what insomnia represents to those who suffer from it.

I recently had a client who had been suffering from extreme insomnia. She had very strong past lives that were interfering with the process. In a past life, she was on watch for the safety of the village. "He" fell asleep and did not warn of incoming danger. Because he fell asleep, the town was rampaged and his people were killed. It created incredible guilt around falling to sleep.

I had another client who got really agitated at the same time every night. It was an hour before dawn. Tuning in, it was revealed that they were executed at sunrise. When they woke up, they were going right back in the trauma of waiting to be executed. It was their private hell, which is what insomnia is to many.

If any of this resonates as a possibility, here are some taps that have helped: (Say each statement three times while tapping on your head and say it a fourth time while tapping on your chest.)

"I release the trauma of not crossing over; in all moments."

"I release confusing sleep with being dead; in all moments."

"I release the trauma of waiting to be executed; in all moments."

"I release confusing not sleeping with looming death; in all moments."

"I release confusing insomnia with being dead; in all moments."

"I release the trauma of being buried alive; in all moments."

"I release the guilt and trauma of falling asleep; in all moments."

"I recalibrate the separation between the physical and astral experience; in all moments."

"I release confusing sleep with death; in all moments."

"I release the trauma of being murdered in my sleep; in all moments."

"I recant all vows and agreements between myself and sleep; in all moments."

"I release resisting sleep; in all moments."

"I remove all curses between myself and sleep; in all moments."

"I dissolve all karmic ties between myself and sleep; in all moments."

"I remove all the guilt, fear, limitations and trauma that sleep has put on me; in all moments."

"I take back all the joy, love, abundance, freedom, health, peace, life and wholeness that sleeping has taken from me; in all moments."

"I resonate with sleep; in all moments."

"I emanate with sleep; in all moments."

"I infuse peaceful sleep into my sound frequency; in all moments."

"I imbue peaceful sleep into my light body; in all moments."

"I shift my paradigm from insomnia to peaceful sleep; in all moments."

"I am centered and empowered in peaceful, loving sleep experiences; in all moments."

"I make space in this world for eight hours of REM sleep; in all moments."

"I remove all blockages to having eight hours of REM sleep; in all moments."

"I stretch my capacity to stay in eight hours of REM sleep; in all moments."

The most recent client did these taps with me and yawned through the whole session. They reported the next morning that their sleep was 85% percent better but then after they told me, they fell back to sleep and had great dreams. So here you go! Sweet dreams.

Integrity

(Say each statement three times out loud while continuously tapping on the top of your head at the crown chakra and say it a fourth time while tapping on your chest at the heart chakra.)

"I release the belief that integrity is lost; in all moments."

"I release agreeing to a lack of integrity; in all moments."

"I release partaking in the desecration of integrity; in all moments."

"I release deducing integrity to a pipe dream; in all moments."

"I release negating the existence of integrity; in all moments."

"I release dismissing the presence of integrity; in all moments."

"I release diminishing the innate presence of integrity; in all moments."

"I make space in my awareness to accept the presence of integrity; in all moments."

"I remove all blockages to accepting the presence of integrity; in all moments."

"I stretch my capacity to accept the presence of integrity; in all moments."

"I make space in this world to live in integrity; in all moments."

"I remove all blockages to living in integrity; in all moments."

"I stretch my capacity to live in integrity; in all moments."

"I accept the guidance of my spirit guides including integrity; in all moments."

"I allow integrity to reconnect me to the receptiveness of sincerity and truth; in all moments."

"I am centered and empowered in the receptivity of sincerity and truth; in all moments."

"I bring integrity back to my life; in all moments."

"I bring integrity back to the world; in all moments."

Invalidation

(Say each statement three times out loud while continuously tapping on the top of your head at the crown chakra and say it a fourth time while tapping on your chest at the heart chakra. Say each word deliberately. They are not just words but a vibration that you are initiating to shift energy. Pause after each word. Say them all.)

"I release invalidating my own joy; in all moments."

"I release deflecting the joy; in all moments."

"I release harboring the opposite of joy; in all moments."

"I inhale pure joy through every orifice of my being; in all moments."

"I release invalidating my own gratitude; in all moments."

"I release deflecting gratitude; in all moments."

"I release harboring the opposite of gratitude; in all moments."

"I inhale pure gratitude through every orifice of my being; in all moments."

"I release invalidating my own abundance; in all moments."

"I release deflecting abundance; in all moments."

"I release harboring the opposite of abundance; in all moments."

"I inhale pure abundance through every orifice of my being; in all moments."

"I release invalidating my own freedom; in all moments."

"I release deflecting freedom; in all moments."

"I release harboring the opposite of freedom; in all moments."

"I inhale pure freedom through every orifice of my being; in all moments."

"I release invalidating my own health; in all moments."

"I release deflecting health; in all moments."

"I release harboring the opposite of health; in all moments."

"I inhale pure health through every orifice of my being; in all moments."

"I release invalidating my own success; in all moments."

"I release deflecting success; in all moments."

"I release harboring the opposite of success; in all moments."

"I inhale pure success through every orifice of my being; in all moments."

"I release invalidating my own love; in all moments."

"I release deflecting love; in all moments."

"I release harboring the opposite of love; in all moments."

"I inhale pure love through every orifice of my being; in all moments."

"I release invalidating my own wholeness; in all moments."

"I release deflecting wholeness; in all moments."

"I release harboring the opposite of wholeness; in all moments."

"I inhale pure wholeness in every orifice of my being; in all moments."

Template to Release Any Issue

(Say this statement three times out loud while continuously tapping on the top of your head at the crown chakra and say it a fourth time while tapping on your chest at the heart chakra.)

Fill in each blank with the same name for each statement.

"I declare myself a surrogate for humanity in doing these taps; in all moments."

"I release forfeiting my happiness for _____ ; in all moments."

"I release putting _____ before my happiness; in all moments."

"I release being sabotaged by _____; in all moments."

"I release being hated by _____; in all moments."

"I release hating _____; in all moments."

"I release being affected by _____; in all moments."

"I release being targeted by _____; in all moments."

"I release being _____'s enemy; in all moments."

"I release being enslaved by _____; in all moments."

"I release enslaving others due to _____; in all moments."

"I withdraw all my energy from _____; in all moments."

"I extract all of_____ from my auric field; in all moments."

"I extract all of_____ from my body; in all moments."

"I extract all of_____ from my home; in all moments."

"I extract all of_____ from my career; in all moments."

"I extract all of_____ from all my relationships; in all moments."

"I extract all of_____ from all those I love; in all moments."

"I extract all of_____ from my projects; in all moments."

"I extract all of_____ from my abundance; in all moments."

"I extract all of_____ from my joy; in all moments."

"I extract all of_____ from my freedom; in all moments."

"I extract all of_____ from my health; in all moments."

"I extract all of_____ from all my success; in all moments."

"I extract all of_____ from my security; in all moments."

"I extract all of_____ from my peace; in all moments."

"I extract all of_____ from my wholeness; in all moments."

"I extract all of_____ from my confidence; in all moments."

"I extract all of_____ from my whole beingness; in all moments."

"I take back my career from _____; in all moments."

"I take back my confidence from _____; in all moments."

"I take back my abundance from _____; in all moments."

"I take back my joy from _____; in all moments."

"I take back my freedom from _____; in all moments."

"I take back my abundance from _____; in all moments."

"I take back my health from _____; in all moments."

"I take back my success from _____; in all moments."

"I take back my creativity from _____; in all moments."

"I take back my peace from _____; in all moments."

"I take back my life from _____; in all moments."

"I take back my wholeness from _____; in all moments."

"I take back my beauty from _____; in all moments."

"I take back my success from _____; in all moments."

"I take back my enthusiasm from _____; in all moments."

"I take back my potential from _____; in all moments."

"I take back all those I love from _____; in all moments."

"I remove all vivaxes between myself and _____; in all moments."

"I remove all tentacles between myself and _____; in all moments."

"I remove all engrams that _____ has put on me; in all moments."

"I remove all programing and conditioning that _____ has done to me; in all moments."

"I send all energy matrixes into the light and sound that support or perpetuate _____; in all moments."

"I remove all the claws of _____from my beingness; in all moments."

"I remove all forms of control and all control devices that _____inserted in me; in all moments."

"I recant all vows and agreements between myself and _____; in all moments."

"I remove all curses between myself and _____; in all moments."

"I remove all blessings between myself and _____; in all moments."

I sever all strings, cords and wires between myself and _____; in all moments."

"I dissolve all karmic ties between myself and _____; in all moments."

"I remove all the pain, burden, limitations and illusion of separateness that _____ has put on me; in all moments."

"I remove all the pain, burden, limitations and illusion of separateness that I have put on all others due to _____ in all moments."

"I take back all the joy, love, abundance, freedom, health, success, security, companionship, creativity, peace, life, wholeness, beauty, enthusiasm, contentment, spirituality, enlightenment, confidence, family, intellect, the ability to discern, and truth that _____ has taken from me; in all moments."

"I give back to all others all the joy, love, abundance, freedom, health, success, security, companionship, creativity, peace, life, wholeness, beauty, enthusiasm, contentment, spirituality, enlightenment, confidence, family, intellect, the ability to discern and truth that I have taken from them due to _____ ; in all moments."

"I release resonating with _____ ; in all moments."

"I release emanating with _____ ; in all moments."

"I withdraw all my energy from _____ ; in all moments."

"I strip all illusion off of _____ ; in all moments."

"I remove all masks, walls and armor from _____ ; in all moments."

"I collapse and dissolve _____ ; in all moments." (Only for ideas NOT PEOPLE)

"I release resonating with _____ ; in all moments."

"I release emanating with _____; in all moments."

"I extract all of _____ from my sound frequency; in all moments."

"I extract all of _____ from my light emanation; in all moments."

"I shift my paradigm from _____ to joy, love, abundance, freedom, health, success, security, companionship, creativity, peace, life, wholeness, beauty, enthusiasm, contentment, spirituality, enlightenment, confidence, family, intellect, the ability to discern and truth; in all moments."

"I am centered and empowered in joy, love, abundance, freedom, health, success, security, companionship, creativity, peace, life, wholeness, beauty, enthusiasm, contentment, spirituality, enlightenment, confidence, family, intellect, the ability to discern and truth; in all moments."

"I repair and fortify the Wei Chi of all my bodies; in all moments."

"I resonate and emanate joy, love, abundance, freedom, health, success, security, companionship, creativity, peace, life, wholeness, beauty, enthusiasm, contentment, spirituality, enlightenment, confidence, family, intellect, the ability to discern, and truth; in all moments."

In Sympathy with Jesus

Recently, I facilitated a private remote session with a new client. She was feeling like she was in hell. She indeed was. In a past life, she was fed the fear of fire and brimstone and believed that hell was what she deserved. We did a bunch of taps to literally and figuratively remove her from hell.

But we also released all her dynamics with God. She wondered if she wanted to really do that. I explained how anything that we release about her dynamics with God was not with the true God but the God that man had made in his image. We were releasing all the concepts and beliefs of revenge, judgment and petty ego that man was prone to needing, not God.

After we did all these taps, she realized her voice changed. It had a richer tone and was more confident. She was thrilled. But we weren't done yet. In past lives, she was devoted to Jesus. When she read the parts of him being tortured and scorned, she resonated with such sympathy with him that she took on some of the pain that he had endured.

In her energy field, she saw Jesus as an enlightened soul who would have been devastated by how man has used him to wield power and to destroy innocence. She was appalled at how Jesus was dishonored by all the wars and genocide that were committed in his name. It had made her personal hell more expansive as she was in sympathy with him.

So we did some taps to free Jesus, if this is possible. What if Jesus is trapped somehow in the thought forms and all the devastation that man has done in his name? What if our intention to free him could do some good in some subjective way? Here are some of the taps that may be helpful to him.

"I release betraying Jesus; in all moments."

"I release being indifferent to Jesus; in all moments."

"I release letting Jesus down; in all moments."

"I release burdening Jesus; in all moments."

"I remove all the burden that I have put on Jesus; in all moments."

"I remove all the burden that I have taken on in sympathy with Jesus; in all moments."

"I sever all strings and cords between Jesus and all the thought forms that have been put on him; in all moments."

"I free Jesus from the emotional bondage he has been tangled in; in all moments."

"I release envisioning Jesus drowning in sorrow; in all moments."

"I release Jesus being frozen in a state of torture; in all moments."

"I separate the truth of Jesus from the ignorance of Jesus; in all moments."

"I free Jesus from the ignorance that has been encapsulated around him; in all moments."

"I empower, honor and love Jesus in the depth and freedom of his truth; in all moments."

"I release all the arrogance and presumptuousness pervading Jesus; in all moments."

"I release Jesus being used by power; in all moments."

"I heal all those who have suffered in Jesus' name; in all moments."

"I remove all curses on Jesus; in all moments."

"I remove all blessings that have turned to curses on Jesus; in all moments."

"I free Jesus from his private hell; in all moments."

"I recant all vows and agreements between Jesus and ignorance; in all moments."

"I remove all curses between Jesus and ignorance; in all moments."

"I remove all blessings between Jesus and ignorance; in all moments."

"I remove all vivaxes between Jesus and ignorance; in all moments."

"I remove all tentacles between Jesus and ignorance; in all moments."

"I send all energy matrices into the light and sound that immerse Jesus or his name and image in ignorance; in all moments."

"I strip all illusion off of ignorance; in all moments."

"I dissolve all karmic ties between Jesus and ignorance; in all moments."

"I sever all strings and cords between Jesus and ignorance; in all moments."

"I remove all the pain, burden, limitations and engrams that ignorance has put on Jesus; in all moments."

"I take back and give to Jesus all the joy, love, abundance, freedom, health and wholeness that ignorance has taken from him; in all moments."

"I release Jesus resonating with ignorance; in all moments."

"I release Jesus emanating with ignorance; in all moments."

"I release Jesus attracting ignorance; in all moments."

"I remove all ignorance from Jesus' sound frequency; in all moments."

"I remove all ignorance from Jesus' light body; in all moments."

"Jesus transcends ignorance; in all moments."

"Jesus is centered and empowered in truth and divine love; in all moments."

"I resonate and emanate divine love and truth; in all moments."

These taps really seemed to lighten my client. They are not meant to offend anyone's belief system but to help each person cleanse their own relationship with their beliefs and sense of responsibility. They may benefit some in feeling free and enlightened. This is their purpose. If they offend, please just walk away and recognize this is the way for someone else to honor Jesus.

Release Shutting Down One's Own Joy

I have a friend who hasn't been very much fun to be around. She has only wanted to do things that she enjoys doing, and when someone else wants to do something or go somewhere different, she refuses. She gets anxious to get home. She has never enjoyed going to events and she treats every occasion as something to dread. As kind as she is, the relationship has been one-sided and devoid of spontaneity and joy. We recently got to the root of the matter.

I wanted her to spend the afternoon with me. I just blurted out, "You don't have to be afraid to die; we are just going shopping." She started crying at that statement and continued until I picked her up.

When I arrived at her house, I saw images of one of her past lives that was affecting her joy in this life. There was more than one image that overlaid the one I was seeing vividly. This showed that the trauma was ingrained and reinforced in many lifetimes. What happens is there is a small transgression to a part of the body or psyche and that part becomes vulnerable to similar transgressions in different scenarios. For example, if I see someone was decapitated in a causal (past life) image, I may also see hangings, chokings or other injuries to the same area of the body.

The trauma of being surprised by an attack was so ingrained that my friend was shutting down her own hormones as a response. It was as if her excitement became a trigger for trauma and so she preferred to stay in a slightly depressed state instead of risk having the attack be relived in any way. Her own enthusiasm conjured up a state of distress. This happens more than people realize and can be addressed with the taps.

(Say each statement three times while tapping your head and say it a fourth time while tapping on your chest.)

"I release the fear and trauma of being Shanghai'd; in all moments."

"I release associating spontaneity with being Shanghai'd; in all moments."

"I release forgoing spontaneity for security; in all moments."

"I release being imprisoned in a routine; in all moments."

"I release converting my life into a fortress; in all moments."

"I release confusing excitement for danger; in all moments."

"I release using fear to squelch my enthusiasm; in all moments."

"I release diminishing my life to a monotonous state; in all moments."

"I release squelching my own enthusiasm; in all moments."

"I release shutting down my own happiness; in all moments."

"I release the pain and trauma of the 'attack'; in all moments."

"I release allowing small issues to trigger the 'attack'; in all moments."

"I release holding myself hostage; in all moments."

"I release the fear that loved ones will hurt me; in all moments."

"I release seeing enemies in loved ones; in all moments."

"I release turning my sacred space into a prison; in all moments."

After the taps, the sun broke through from behind the clouds (this happens more than sounds credible to mention). My friend saw everyday things in her neighborhood that she had never noticed before. She enjoyed a presence and an enthusiasm that I have never experienced from her before. It was pleasant all the way around.

Converging into Joy

Someone said that I have such a beautiful soul. I told her that she is seeing her own beautiful soul because we converge into one. This was the exchange that is the seed for these taps.

(Say each statement three times out loud while continuously tapping on the top of your head at the crown chakra and say it a fourth time while tapping on your chest.)

"I converge with complete joy; in all moments."

"I converge with complete love; in all moments."

"I converge with complete abundance; in all moments."

"I converge with complete freedom; in all moments."

"I converge with complete health; in all moments."

"I converge with complete success; in all moments."

"I converge with complete companionship; in all moments."

"I converge with complete creativity; in all moments."

"I converge with complete peace; in all moments."

"I converge with complete life; in all moments."

"I converge with complete wholeness; in all moments."

"I converge with nature; in all moments."

"I converge with complete awareness; in all moments."

"I converge with complete beauty; in all moments."

"I converge with complete enthusiasm; in all moments."

"I converge with complete contentment; in all moments."

"I converge with complete spirituality; in all moments."

"I converge with complete enlightenment; in all moments."

"I converge with complete transcendence; in all moments."

"I converge with complete illumination; in all moments."

"I converge with complete bliss; in all moments."

Remove All Labels

(Say each statement three times out loud while continuously tapping on the top of your head at the crown chakra and say it a fourth time while tapping on your chest.)

"I release being labeled; in all moments."

"All labels are rejected; in all moments."

"I release using labels to define myself; in all moments."

"I shatter the glass ceiling of all labels used to define me; in all moments."

"I release using labels as a crutch; in all moments."

"I release using labels to diminish others; in all moments."

"I release using labels to validate myself; in all moments."

"I recant all vows and agreements between myself and all labels; in all moments."

"I remove all blessings and curses between myself and all labels; in all moments."

"I sever all strings and cords between myself and all labels; in all moments."

"I dissolve all karmic ties between myself and all labels; in all moments."

"I remove all the pain, burden, limitations, expectations and engrams that labels have put on me; in all moments."

"I remove all the pain, burden, limitations, expectations and engrams that labels have caused me to put on others; in all moments."

"I take back all the joy, love, abundance, freedom, health, success, confidence and wholeness that labels have taken from me; in all moments."

"I give back all the joy, love, abundance, freedom, health, success, confidence and wholeness that labels have caused me to take from all others; in all moments."

"I shift my paradigm from all labels to the expansiveness, individuality and freedom of Soul; in all moments."

"I transcend all labels; in all moments."

"I am centered and empowered in the expansiveness, individuality and freedom of Soul; in all moments."

Stop the Judgment

(Say each statement three times out loud while continuously tapping on the top of your head at the crown chakra and say it a fourth time while tapping on your heart chakra.)

"I release being categorized or judged because of my gender; in all moments."

"I release being categorized or judged because of my physical attributes; in all moments."

"I release being categorized or judged because of my beliefs; in all moments."

"I release being categorized or judged because of my religious affiliations; in all moments."

"I release being categorized or judged because of my political views; in all moments."

"I release being categorized or judged because of my social status; in all moments."

"I release being categorized or judged because of my demeanor; in all moments."

"I release being categorized or judged because of my sexual orientation; in all moments."

"I release being categorized or judged because of my size; in all moments."

"I release being categorized or judged because of my family; in all moments."

"I release being categorized or judged because of my opinions; in all moments."

"I release being categorized or judged because of my race; in all moments."

"I release being categorized or judged because of my choices; in all moments."

"I release being categorized or judged because of my impediments; in all moments."

"I release being categorized or judged because of my occupation; in all moments."

"I release being categorized or judged because of my mental capacity; in all moments."

"I shift my paradigm to fluid, free existence; in all moments."

"I make space in this world for a fluid free existence for all; in all moments."

"I remove all blockages to a fluid free existence for all; in all moments."

"I stretch the world's capacity to manifest a fluid, free existence for all; in all moments."

Lead with Kindness

(Say each statement three times out loud while continuously tapping on the top of your head at the crown chakra and say it a fourth time while tapping on your chest.)

"I release the belief that showing kindness is displaying weakness; in all moments."

"I release the belief that I am weak; in all moments."

"I release the fear of being bullied for being kind; in all moments."

"I release coming out of my center to be kind; in all moments."

"I stand in my center to reinforce kindness; in all moments."

"I release confusing kindness with vulnerability; in all moments."

"I am both kind and strong; in all moments."

"I exude strength from kindness; in all moments."

"I release forgoing kindness to fit in; in all moments."

"I shift my paradigm from being ashamed of kindness to being proud of kindness; in all moments."

"I release mingling unworthiness into kindness; in all moments."

"I release mistrusting genuine kindness; in all moments."

"I release judging kindness as weak; in all moments."

"I empower kindness everywhere; in all moments."

"I connect to all others in kindness; in all moments."

"I am imbued in kindness; in all moments."

"I am centered and empowered in kindness; in all moments."

"I encourage all others to center and be empowered in kindness; in all moments."

"I resonate and emanate kindness; in all moments."

Releasing "Bad" Knees

I facilitated a private remote session with a regular client. She was feeling great except for her knees. I tuned into her knees. They were under so much pressure literally and figuratively. There were so many lifetimes when they had endured trauma and a lack of consideration. They are a keystone of support for the body, yet they continuously get met with indifference and a lack of consideration.

I saw all these past lives reverberating from her knees. I saw so much trauma in that one little area. It was like they could not endure one more fraction of dis-ease. It made me think of all the people who are replacing their knees. Maybe it would be healthier to the whole body just to appreciate the knees that they have and release all the trauma that they have endured.

Just because we can remove the problem for one lifetime, that does not remove the disease. It would be better to address the issues head on (or knee on), so the knees are not an issue in the next incarnation.

Here are the taps I led her through. The whole body was relieved. So many energy channels go down the legs to ground us out. All those channels were opened up with these taps.

(Say each statement three times out loud while tapping on the head and say it a fourth time while tapping on your chest.)

"I release the trauma of having my kneecaps shattered; in all moments."

"I release the trauma of having my legs cut off at the knees; in all moments."

"I release shoving my knees into the ground; in all moments."

"I release the trauma of having my extremities pulled off; in all moments."

"I release betraying my knees; in all moments."

"I release sacrificing my knees to God; in all moments."

"I release being speared in my knees; in all moments."

"I release having my legs crushed; in all moments."

"I release storing unworthiness in my knees; in all moments."

"I release storing torture in my knees; in all moments."

"I release storing depravity in my knees; in all moments."

"I release punishing my knees; in all moments."

"I remove all vivaxes between my knees and pain; in all moments."

"I remove all tentacles between my knees and pain; in all moments."

"I nullify all agreements between my knees and pain; in all moments."

"I release my knees being blessed or cursed with pain; in all moments."

"I remove all engrams of pain from my knees; in all moments."

"I send all energy matrices into the light and sound that immerse my knees in pain; in all moments."

"I sever all strings and cords between my knees and pain; in all moments."

"I dissolve all karmic ties between myself and pain; in all moments."

"I remove all pain from my knees; in all moments."

"I release telling my knees that they are worthless; in all moments."

"I release being indifferent to my knees; in all moments."

"I heal the knees of my etheric body; in all moments."

"I heal the knees of my mental body; in all moments."

"I heal the knees of my causal body; in all moments."

"I heal the knees of my astral body; in all moments."

"I heal the knees of my physical body; in all moments."

"I recant all vows and agreements between myself and my knees; in all moments."

"I remove all curses between myself and my knees; in all moments."

"I sever all strings and cords between myself and my knees; in all moments."

"I dissolve all karmic ties between myself and my knees; in all moments."

"I remove all the pain, burden, limitations and engrams that my knees have put on me; in all moments."

"I remove all the pain, burden, limitations and engrams that I have put on my knees; in all moments."

"I take back all the joy, love, abundance, freedom, health, life and wholeness that my knees have taken from me; in all moments."

"I give back all the joy, love, abundance, freedom, health, life and wholeness that I have taken from my knees; in all moments."

"I infuse infinite joy, love, abundance, freedom, health, life and wholeness into the sound frequency of my knees; in all moments."

"I imbue infinite joy, love, abundance, freedom, health, life and wholeness into the light body of my knees; in all moments."

"I repair and fortify the Wei chi of my knees in all my bodies; in all moments."

"The sound frequency of my knees resonates with joy, love, abundance, freedom, health, life and wholeness; in all moments."

"The light body of my knees emanates with joy, love, abundance, freedom, health, life and wholeness; in all moments."

"I align the knees in all my bodies; in all moments."

"The knees in all my bodies is centered and empowered with joy, love, abundance, freedom, health, life and wholeness; in all moments."

Call Back Your Kundalini Energy

Kundalini energy is the furnace of the whole energy system. The furnace serves its own function. It is not meant to be used as a tool for folly intentions. It is meant to fire up one's whole beingness. Those who are depressed and depleted in this life may have depleted their kundalini energy in a past life. This is done by using it to wield power. If you want to gain your fire back, try these taps.

(Say each statement three times while tapping on your head and say it a fourth time while tapping on your chest.)

"I release abusing my kundalini energy; in all moments."

"I release abusing energy; in all moments."

"I release confusing my kundalini energy with hell; in all moments."

"I call back my kundalini energy; in all moments."

"I purify my kundalini energy; in all moments."

"I re-seat my kundalini energy; in all moments."

"I align my kundalini energy with all my energy systems; in all moments."

"I clear all passageways between my kundalini energy and all my energy systems; in all moments."

"I seal my kundalini energy; in all moments."

"I ignite my kundalini energy; in all moments."

"I regain my function and purpose as a spiritual being; in all moments."

"I am centered and empowered in my function and purpose; in all moments."

Letting Go

They say that there are 20 things you should let go of to be happy. So here are 20 taps to help you let go. Maybe doing these before the holidays will help you enjoy the season a little bit better. Maybe they can prevent a bout or two of depression. Maybe you know someone who would benefit from them as well. It could be the best gift they ever receive.

(Say each statement three times while tapping on your head and say it a fourth time while tapping on your chest.)

"I release needing the approval of others; in all moments."

"I release all anger and resentment; in all moments."

"I release the negative image of myself; in all moments."

"I release holding out for the perfect partner; in all moments."

"I release pining for the perfect life; in all moments."

"I release expecting an overnight fortune; in all moments."

"I release making excuses; in all moments."

"I release thinking about my ex; in all moments."

"I release being stubborn; in all moments."

"I release procrastinating; in all moments."

"I release all my baggage; in all moments."

"I remove all negativity; in all moments."

"I release all judgment; in all moments."

"I remove all jealousy; in all moments."

"I release all insecurity; in all moments."

"I release depending on others for my happiness; in all moments."

"I release all of the past; in all moments."

"I release the belief that being rich will make me happy; in all moments."

"I release the need for control; in all moments."

"I release all expectations; in all moments."

Light and Sound of God

(Say each statement three times while tapping on your head and say it a fourth time while tapping on your chest.)

"I dissolve all pain into the light and sound of God; in all moments."

"I dissolve all disease into the light and sound of God; in all moments."

"I dissolve all conflict into the light and sound of God; in all moments."

"I dissolve all deceit into the light and sound of God; in all moments."

"I dissolve all ignorance into the light and sound of God; in all moments."

"I dissolve all male dominance into the light and sound of God; in all moments."

"I dissolve all transgressions into the light and sound of God; in all moments."

"I dissolve all matter into the light and sound of God; in all moments."

"I dissolve all stagnant energy into the light and sound of God; in all moments."

"I dissolve all space into the light and sound of God; in all moments."

"I dissolve all time into the light and sound of God; in all moments."

"I dissolve all vivaxes into the light and sound of God; in all moments."

"I dissolve all tentacles into the light and sound of God; in all moments."

"I dissolve all engrams into the light and sound of God; in all moments."

"I dissolve all pain, programing and conditioning into the light and sound of God; in all moments."

"I dissolve all energy matrices into the light and sound of God; in all moments."

"I dissolve all complex energy matrices into the light and sound of God; in all moments."

"I dissolve all contracts into the light and sound of God; in all moments."

"I dissolve all vows and agreements into the light and sound of God; in all moments."

"I dissolve all curses into the light and sound of God; in all moments."

"I dissolve all blessings into the light and sound of God; in all moments."

"I dissolve all karma into the light and sound of God; in all moments."

"I dissolve all illusion into the light and sound of God; in all moments."

"I dissolve all linear limitations into the light and sound of God; in all moments."

Limitations

Think of someone, something or some group that has limited you in some way. Put that name in each line.

(Say each statement three times while tapping on your head and say it a fourth time while tapping on your chest.)

"I release being limited by my role as a daughter/son; in all moments."

"I release being limited by my role as a mother/father; in all moments."

"I release being limited by my role as a sister/brother; in all moments."

"I release being limited by my role as a ___(insert occupation)___; in all moments."

"I release being limited by my role as a female/male; in all moments."

"I release being limited by my role as a human; in all moments."

"I release being limited by the role of a physical being; in all moments."

"I release being limited by the role of an emotional being; in all moments."

"I release being limited by the role of a thinking being; in all moments."

"I release being limited by the role of all my experiences; in all moments."

"I embrace myself as an expanded expression of universal love in form; in all moments."

"I am centered and empowered as an expanded expression of Universal love in form; in all moments."

"I release being limited by _____; in all moments."

"I release being lied to by _____; in all moments."

"I remove all blind loyalty to _____; in all moments."

"I release being enslaved by _____; in all moments."

"I release being enslaved to _____; in all moments."

"I release being cursed by _____; in all moments."

"I release the fear of repercussions of leaving _____; in all moments."

"I release confusing _____ for the highest truth; in all moments."

"I remove all vivaxes between myself and _____; in all moments."

"I release giving our proxy to _____; in all moments."

"I release pinning all our hopes on _____; in all moments."

"I untangle all our energy from _____; in all moments."

"I extract all of _____ from our beingness; in all moments."

"I remove all tentacles between myself and _____; in all moments."

"I remove the claws of _____ from our beingness; in all moments."

"I strip all illusion off of _____; in all moments."

"I remove all masks, walls and armor from _____; in all moments."

"I remove all masks, walls and armor of _____ from our beingness; in all moments."

"I shatter all glass ceilings that _____ has put on me; in all moments."

"I shatter all illusion of superiority that _____ has put on me; in all moments."

"I withdraw all our energy from _____; in all moments."

"I release being deceived by _____; in all moments."

"I eliminate the first cause in regards to _____; in all moments."

"I eliminate the first cause in moving off the path of love; in all moments."

"I eliminate the first cause in moving away from truth; in all moments."

"I eliminate the first cause in being programmed and conditioned; in all moments."

"I eliminate the first cause in ignoring the Ancient Ones; in all moments."

"I exonerate myself; in all moments."

"I remove all programming and conditioning that _____ has put on me; in all moments."

"I remove all engrams of _____ from our beingness; in all moments."

"I nullify all contracts with _____; in all moments."

"I send all energy matrices of _____ into the light; in all moments."

"I send all energy matrices of _____ into the sound; in all moments."

"I command all complex energy matrices of _____ to be escorted into the light and sound; in all moments."

"I recant all vows and agreements between myself and _____; in all moments."

"I release romanticizing _____; in all moments."

"I release using _____ to hide from truth; in all moments."

"I remove all curses between myself and _____; in all moments."

"I remove all curses that we have put on all others due to _____; in all moments."

"I release influencing others for _____; in all moments."

"I remove all blessings between myself and _____; in all moments."

"I remove all blessings that we have put on all others for the sake of _____; in all moments."

"I sever all strings, cords and wires between myself and _____; in all moments."

"I sever all strings, cords and wires between myself and all others due to _____; in all moments."

"I dissolve all karmic ties between myself and _____; in all moments."

"I dissolve all karmic ties between myself and all others due to _____; in all moments."

"I remove all the pain, burden and limitations that _____ has put on me; in all moments."

"I remove all the pain, burden and limitations that we have put on all others due to _____; in all moments."

"I remove all the fear, futility and unworthiness that _____ has put on me; in all moments."

"I remove all indoctrination, slavery and illusion of separateness that _____ has put on me; in all moments."

"I remove all the fear, futility and unworthiness that I have put on all others due to _____; in all moments."

"I remove all indoctrination, slavery and illusion of separateness that we have put on all others due to _____; in all moments."

"I take back ALL that _____ has taken from me; in all moments."

"I give back to all others ALL that we have taken from them due to, or on behalf of, _____; in all moments."

"I extract all of _____ from our beingness; in all moments."

"I extract all of _____ from the universal embodiment of humanity; in all moments."

"I extract all of _____ from the 32 layers of our auric field and all 32 layers of the universal auric field; in all moments."

"I extract all of _____ from our sound frequency and the universal sound frequency; in all moments."

"I extract all of _____ from our light emanation and the universal light emanation; in all moments."

"I shift our paradigm from _____to exponential love and truth; in all moments."

"I shift the universal paradigm from _____ to exponential love and truth; in all moments."

"I individually and universally transcend _____; in all moments."

"I am individually and universally centered and empowered in exponential love and truth; in all moments."

"I individually and universally resonate, emanate and am interconnected with all life in exponential love and truth; in all moments."

Dismantle Limiting Algorithms

(Say each statement three times while tapping on your head and say it a fourth time while tapping on your chest.)

"All lower world algorithms are dismantled; in all moments."

"All power algorithms are dismantled; in all moments."

"All manipulating algorithms are dismantled; in all moments."

"All dis-ease algorithms are dismantled; in all moments."

"All failure algorithms are dismantled; in all moments."

"All top one percent algorithms are dismantled; in all moments."

"All political algorithms are dismantled; in all moments."

"All religious algorithms are dismantled; in all moments."

"All male dominated algorithms are dismantled; in all moments."

"All psychically influenced algorithms are dismantled; in all moments."

"All fear perpetuating algorithms are dismantled; in all moments."

"All illusionary algorithms are dismantled; in all moments."

"All media-biased algorithms are dismantled; in all moments."

"All deceitful algorithms are dismantled; in all moments."

"All terrorist algorithms are dismantled; in all moments."

"All pollution algorithms are dismantled; in all moments."

"All discrimination algorithms are dismantled; in all moments."

"All war algorithms are dismantled; in all moments."

"All dictator algorithms are dismantled; in all moments."

"All oligarchy algorithms are dismantled; in all moments."

"All desecration of earth algorithms are dismantled; in all moments."

"All fracking algorithms are dismantled; in all moments."

"All poisoning algorithms are dismantled; in all moments."

"All algorithms of poverty are dismantled; in all moments."

"All algorithms of unworthiness are dismantled; in all moments."

"All algorithms of abandonment, rejection, and despair are dismantled; in all moments."

"All algorithms of isolation are dismantled; in all moments."

"All algorithms of greed are dismantled; in all moments."

"All algorithms of control are dismantled; in all moments."

"All algorithms of false Gods are dismantled; in all moments."

"All algorithms of desecration of trees and nature are dismantled; in all moments."

"All algorithms of slavery are dismantled; in all moments."

"All algorithms of lies are dismantled; in all moments."

"All algorithms of matter, energy, space and time are dismantled; in all moments."

"All algorithms of archaic structures are dismantled; in all moments."

"All algorithms of rigidity are dismantled; in all moments."

"All algorithms of mental aberrations are dismantled; in all moments."

"All algorithms of mental illness are dismantled; in all moments."

"All algorithms of mental limitations are dismantled; in all moments."

"All algorithms of mind eddies are dismantled; in all moments."

"All algorithms of debauchery are dismantled; in all moments."

"All algorithms of sin and hell are dismantled; in all moments."

"All algorithms of anger and pain are dismantled; in all moments."

"All algorithms of apathy and indifference are dismantled; in all moments."

"All algorithms of dishonoring integrity and innocence are dismantled; in all moments."

"All algorithms of crime and abuse are dismantled; in all moments."

"All algorithms of self-loathing are dismantled; in all moments."

"All algorithms of hunger are dismantled; in all moments."

"All negative algorithms are dismantled; in all moments."

"All algorithms that do not support universal transcendence are dismantled; in all moments."

"All algorithms of spiritual blindness are dismantled; in all moments."

"All of existence is centered and empowered in joy, love, abundance, freedom, and truth; in all moments."

"All of existence resonates, emanates, and is interconnected in joy, love, abundance, freedom and truth; in all moments."

Limitations of the Gods

(Say each statement three times out loud while continuously tapping on the top of your head at the crown chakra and say it a fourth time while tapping on your chest at the heart chakra.)

"We declare ourselves surrogates for humanity in doing these taps; in all moments."

"We release worshiping the gods; in all moments."

"We release serving the gods; in all moments."

"We release being enslaved to the gods; in all moments."

"We release sending our energy to the gods; in all moments."

"We release having our DNA thwarted by the gods; in all moments."

"We remove all the dis-ease we have carried in our DNA; in all moments."

"We remove all of the negative characteristics we have carried in our DNA; in all moments."

"We remove all limitations that have been programmed into our DNA; in all moments."

"We release the genetic propensity to worship the gods; in all moments."

"We remove all controlling devices that the gods have implanted in us; in all moments."

"We release confusing the gods for source; in all moments."

"We remove all vivaxes between ourselves and the gods; in all moments."

"We cut all tentacles between ourselves and the gods; in all moments."

"We remove all engrams of the gods; in all moments."

"We eliminate the first cause in being conditioned by the gods; in all moments."

"We dry up all psychic energy of the gods; in all moments."

"We remove all programming and conditioning that the gods have put on us; in all moments."

"We withdraw all our energy from the gods; in all moments."

"We strip all illusion off the gods; in all moments."

"We remove all masks, walls and armor from the gods; in all moments."

"We collapse and dissolve all portals to the gods; in all moments."

"We send all energy matrices into the light and sound that enslave us to the gods; in all moments."

"We command all complex energy matrices that enslave us to the gods to be escorted into the light and sound; in all moments."

"We send all energy matrices into the light and sound that deceive us in regards to the gods; in all moments."

"We command all complex energy matrices that deceive us in regards to the gods to be escorted into the light and sound; in all moments."

"We send all energy matrices into the light and sound that romanticize the gods; in all moments."

"We command all complex energy matrices that romanticize the gods to be escorted into the light and sound; in all moments."

"We shatter all glass ceilings that the gods have put on us; in all moments."

"We dismantle all energy sources that the gods have planted on earth; in all moments."

"We nullify all contracts between ourselves and the gods; in all moments."

"We recant all vows and agreements between ourselves and the gods; in all moments."

"We remove all curses that the gods have put on us; in all moments."

"We remove all blessings between ourselves and the gods; in all moments."

"We release being kept in primal mode by the gods; in all moments."

"We release the fear of existing beyond the gods; in all moments."

"We sever all strings, cords and psychic connections between ourselves and the gods; in all moments."

"We dissolve all karmic ties between ourselves and the gods; in all moments."

"We remove all the pain, burden and limitations that the gods have put on us; in all moments."

"We remove all the fear, futility and ignorance that the gods have put on us; in all moments."

"We remove all the anger, abandonment and unworthiness that the gods have put on us; in all moments."

"We remove all the thirst for war and illusion of separateness that the gods have put on us; in all moments."

"We remove all the horror that the gods have put on us; in all moments."

"We take back all the joy, love abundance, freedom, health, success, security, companionship, creativity, peace, life, wholeness, beauty, enthusiasm, contentment, spirituality, enlightenment and confidence, individualism and empowerment that the gods have taken from us; in all moments."

"We break all energy grids between ourselves and the gods; in all moments."

"We release resonating with the gods; in all moments."

"We release emanating with the gods; in all moments."

"We regenerate our 12-stranded DNA; in all moments."

"We take back our sensitivities; in all moments."

"We reclaim our subtle perceptions; in all moments."

"We awaken our ability to perceive in energy; in all moments."

"We extract all of the gods from our sound frequency; in all moments."

"We extract all of the gods from our light emanation; in all moments."

"We extract all of the gods from all 32 layers of our auric field; in all moments."

"We extract all of the gods from our whole beingness; in all moments."

"We shift our paradigm from the gods to universal individuality and freedom; in all moments."

"We transcend the gods; in all moments."

"We banish all of the gods from earth; in all moments."

"We are centered and empowered in universal individuality and freedom; in all moments."

"We resonate, emanate and are interconnected with all life in universal individuality and freedom; in all moments."

"We infuse universal empowerment and freedom into our sound frequency; in all moments."

"We imbue universal empowerment and freedom into our light emanation; in all moments."

"We abolish all prisons of all kinds; in all moments."

Coping with Loneliness

Loneliness is so misunderstood. It feels like a punishment from God. There were times in our history when we were an outcast and those who loved us abandoned us. These experiences are tangled up in our own ability to comfort ourselves.

If we are able to sit with ourselves, we begin to realize that we use other people and activities to prevent us from being alone with ourselves. When we are alone with ourselves, it is our time to sort out all the experiences that we have ever had and process them into wisdom.

Having an aversion to loneliness is in a sense spiritual procrastination. Because at some point, all that we have experienced, all that we have learned, all the wisdom that we have accrued, need to be separated from the pain that helped etch it into our inner bodies and assimilated as our truth. Loneliness is not a punishment; it is a privilege to have time to glean from the depth of our own wisdom. It is God extracting all the chaos away from us so we can partake of the splendor of the joy, love, abundance, and freedom, which are our core essence.

Say these taps to assist: (Say each statement three times while tapping on your head and say it a fourth time while tapping on your chest.)

"I release the aversion to being alone; in all moments."

"I recant my vow of solitude; in all moments."

"I release confusing being alone with being abandoned; in all moments."

"I release confusing being alone with being unlovable; in all moments."

"I release confusing being alone with unworthiness; in all moments."

"I release using solitude to feel safe; in all moments."

"I release using solitude as a coping mechanism; in all moments."

"I release using solitude as avoidance; in all moments."

"I release the belief that God is punishing me; in all moments."

"I release the belief that I am damned; in all moments."

"I release the belief that God hates me; in all moments."

"I release confusing being alone with being nothing; in all moments."

"I partake of the fullness of my own emptiness; in all moments."

"I release the aversion to my own inner sanctum; in all moments."

"I shift my attention from outward to inward; in all moments."

"I release hating myself; in all moments."

"I forgive myself; in all moments."

"I make space within to love and nurture myself; in all moments."

"I remove all blockages to loving and nurturing myself; in all moments."

"I stretch my capacity to love and nurture myself; in all moments."

"I am centered, abundant and complete in my own loving nature; in all moments."

"I shift my paradigm from being the watcher to the knower; in all moments."

"I am a powerhouse of Divine Light, Love, Sound, Healing, Health, Joy, Abundance, Beauty, Wholeness and Peace; in all moments."

We are so taught to forsake our own wonderful essence and to look for sustenance in the crass noise and confusion of the outer world. It is when we turn this around in ourselves by being comfortable with the loneliness that we uncover our true nature. By using loneliness as precipice, we can dive into the sanctity of our own omniscience, omnipresence and omnipotence.

Heal an Unimaginable Loss

(Say each statement three times out loud while continuously tapping on the top of your head at the crown chakra and say it a fourth time while tapping on your chest.)

"I release the guilt and trauma of miscarrying; in all moments."

"I release the belief that I let my baby down; in all moments."

"I release blaming myself; in all moments."

"I release blaming others; in all moments."

"I remove all engrams of losing my baby; in all moments."

"I release letting my baby's father down; in all moments."

"I release the belief that I won't be able to have a baby; in all moments."

"I release being immersed in guilt, fear and regret; in all moments."

"I release the fear of getting pregnant again; in all moments."

"I release getting lost in trying to figure out why it happened; in all moments."

"I release allowing a miscarriage to define me; in all moments."

"I release fixating on the loss; in all moments."

"I shift my paradigm from sorrow to gratitude; in all moments."

"I send all energy matrices into the light that prevent me from getting pregnant in total joy; in all moments."

"I trust there was a reason that benefits my growth; in all moments."

"I am centered and empowered in love and gratitude for the ability to conceive and carry my baby to term; in all moments."

"I release rejecting my connection with my baby; in all moments."

"I am sustained in the confidence and security of loving my baby unconditionally; in all moments."

Losing Faith

(Say each statement three times out loud while continuously tapping on the top of your head at the crown chakra and say it a fourth time while tapping on your heart chakra.)

"I release being led astray by false prophets; in all moments."

"I release betraying Jesus; in all moments."

"I release losing faith; in all moments."

"I release losing heart; in all moments."

"I release living outside of truth; in all moments."

"I release being a hypocrite; in all moments."

"I release disappointing Jesus; in all moments."

"I release believing lies about Jesus; in all moments."

"I release being weak; in all moments."

"I release desecrating my spirit; in all moments."

"I release desecrating my body; in all moments."

"I live in the true love and light of Jesus; in all moments."

"I dedicate myself as a vessel for love and light; in all moments."

"I grace this world as a vessel for the love and light of Jesus; in all moments."

"I am centered and empowered in being a vessel of the love and light of Jesus; in all moments."

"I resonate and emanate the love and light of Jesus; in all moments."

Missing One's Home Planet

In private sessions, many people secretly admit that they don't feel like they are in their natural habitat. Some feel like they come from a different land and feel isolated from their true home. Many don't want to admit this because they are afraid of seeming strange. Some of them have imagery of being on another planet. They never share this because they are very sane and don't want to appear otherwise.

I have also had clients have vivid recall of being in a situation where the waters were rising quickly and there was no hope for escape. The waves were very high and they were flooding the land at the highest point. They have watched their whole civilization drown. In the present, they live with that dread within them. Some have identified it as Atlantis. Some have felt a kinship to Lemuria. Some of them have vivid recall of dynamic civilizations that still live somewhere within their memories.

May these taps assist in releasing the inner stress for those who have nothing in this world to validate an inner turmoil that they have difficulty even admitting to themselves.

(Say each statement three times while tapping on your head and say it a fourth time while tapping on your chest.)

"I release being homesick; in all moments."

"I release hating earth; in all moments."

"I release associating life on earth with dread; in all moments."

"I release living in anticipation of a cataclysm; in all moments."

"I release the fear of remembering; in all moments."

"I release the trauma of being usurped from my homeland; in all moments."

"I release the grief and devastation of the cataclysm; in all moments."

"I release the fear of cataclysm; in all moments."

"I release the trauma of losing my tail; in all moments."

"I release the trauma of losing my wings; in all moments."

"I reattach and heal my tail; in all moments."

"I reattach and heal my wings; in all moments."

"I release associating being human with being in a sarcophagus; in all moments."

"I release the devastation of mass translation; in all moments."

"I release the fear of mass translation; in all moments."

"I remove all the pain, trauma and limitations that the cataclysm has put on me; in all moments.

"I take back all the joy, love, abundance, freedom, peace, life and wholeness that the cataclysm has taken from me; in all moments.

"I shift my paradigm from cataclysm to joy, love, abundance, freedom, peace, life and wholeness; in all moments."

Some things don't need to make sense to the conscious mind to be effective. In fact, sometimes dealing with things in the abstract is a way to bypass the mind's sometimes menacing control. If this exercise brings any relief in any small way, then it is worth doing. Sometimes the more the conscious mind objects, the more one would benefit from them. The energy that is freed up can be better put to use in having a happy life.

Release the Anguish of Losing a Child

Whether you have physically or emotionally lost a child, these taps will assist in releasing the anguish and guilt so that healing can occur. These will be a helpful way to heal the pain of giving up a child for adoption. It is a way to send your love to the child wherever they may be.

(Insert the child's name in the blank. Say each statement three times while tapping on your head and say it a fourth time while tapping on your chest.)

"I release giving up on _____; in all moments."

"I release rejecting _____; in all moments."

"I release blaming _____; in all moments."

"I release being disconnected from _____; in all moments."

"I release associating _____ with anguish; in all moments."

"I release defining _____ as anguish; in all moments."

"I release the trauma of losing _____; in all moments."

"I extract all anguish out of _____; in all moments."

"I heal _____; in all moments."

"I release the fear of being vulnerable to _____; in all moments."

"I bare my Soul to _____; in all moments."

"I pour incredible love into _____; in all moments."

"I earnestly give _____ my milk; in all moments."

"I let go of the story; in all moments."

"I release being stuck in _____ versus me; in all moments."

"I release competing with _____; in all moments."

"I forgive myself; in all moments."

"I heal myself; in all moments."

"I forgive all others; in all moments."

"I repair the Wei chi of our family; in all moments."

"Our family is centered and empowered in divine love; in all moments."

"I repair and fortify the Wei chi of all my bodies; in all moments."

"I am centered and empowered in divine love; in all moments."

Heal Everyone's Ability to Love

(Say each statement three times while tapping on your head and say it a fourth time while tapping on your chest.)

"We make space in this world for everyone to experience love; in all moments."

"We release everyone from tangling suffering with love; in all moments."

"We release everyone from confusing suffering for love; in all moments."

"We release everyone from rejecting love to avoid suffering; in all moments."

"We release the symbiotic relationship between love and suffering; in all moments."

"We release everyone from partaking in suffering to have love; in all moments."

"We remove all blockages to everyone experiencing love; in all moments."

"We release everyone's belief that love leads to suffering; in all moments."

"We stretch everyone's capacity to experience love; in all moments."

"We make space in this world for everyone to register love; in all moments."

"We remove all blockages to everyone registering love; in all moments."

"We stretch everyone's capacity to register love; in all moments."

"We take the brake off everyone's ability to accept love; in all moments."

"We make whole all those who have an aversion to the sharing of truth; in all moments."

"We heal all those who have an aversion to the sharing of truth; in all moments."

"We release everyone from punishing themselves; in all moments."

"We release everyone from admonishing themselves; in all moments."

"We release everyone from isolating themselves; in all moments."

"We release everyone from their self-inflicted prison; in all moments."

"We remove all schisms from everyone's beingness; in all moments."

"We remove all dis-ease from everyone's beingness; in all moments."

"We infuse joy, love, and abundance into everyone's microcosm; in all moments."

"We infuse freedom, health, and success into everyone's microcosm; in all moments."

"We infuse security, companionship, and creativity into everyone's microcosm; in all moments."

"We infuse peace, life and wholeness into everyone's microcosm; in all moments."

Love!

The more we all accept love as individuals, the more that it will get saturated into the group consciousness of humanity and uplift every form of life everywhere. If we are not motivated to do it for ourselves, we can be motivated by our desire to raise the quality of love for all.

People are still feeling separate from the love! It is such a waste of our goodness. Here are some taps to help: (Say each statement three times while tapping on your head and say it a fourth time while tapping on your chest.)

"I release rejecting love; in all moments."

"I release closing the door to love; in all moments."

"I release that I am unworthy of love; in all moments."

"I release the belief that love hates me; in all moments."

"I release making love a stranger; in all moments."

"I release micromanaging love; in all moments."

"I release confusing sex for love; in all moments."

"I release confusing love for imprisonment; in all moments."

"I release using treating love as a commodity; in all moments."

"I release limiting love to emotional expressions; in all moments."

"I release entwining love with disillusionment; in all moments."

"I release the belief that I am separate from love; in all moments."

"I shift my paradigm to embrace love; in all moments."

"I accept love in all forms and expressions; in all moments."

"I am a conduit of love; in all moments."

"I am a magnet of love; in all moments."

"I am centered, empowered and imbued in love; in all moments."

"I am a powerhouse of Divine Love; in all moments."

Lucid Dreaming

When you fall to sleep, you slip out of your physical body and have experiences in worlds of higher vibrations. If you don't remember your dreams, it is not because you are not experiencing anything when you fall asleep. It is because what you are experiencing while asleep is so far removed from your physical experience that there is no reference point to bring the experience back with you when you awake. If you make the commitment to write down your dreams when you awake, it tells your higher self that you are interested in knowing more truth. Otherwise, your higher self assumes you prefer to be blissfully ignorant.

(Say each statement three times while tapping on your head and say it a fourth time while tapping on your chest.)

"I release dismissing my dreams; in all moments."

"I release forgetting my dreams upon awakening; in all moments."

"I release filtering out the truth of my dreams; in all moments."

"I release filtering out the truth that my higher self is conveying to me; in all moments."

"I release allowing conventional conditioning to interfere with me receiving higher truth; in all moments."

"I free up all the energy that interferes with my higher understanding; in all moments."

"I convert all energy that interferes with my higher understanding to lucid clarity of awareness; in all moments."

"I remove all filters that scramble information intended for my waking consciousness; in all moments."

"I remove all programming and conditioning that prevent me from accepting higher understanding; in all moments."

"I decipher all dream symbols into clear understanding for the waking consciousness; in all moments."

"I make space in my consciousness for lucid clarity of higher awareness; in all moments."

"I remove all blockages to lucid clarity of higher awareness; in all moments."

"I stretch my capacity to receive and accept lucid clarity of higher awareness; in all moments."

"I am centered and empowered in lucid clarity of higher awareness; in all moments."

"I resonate, emanate and am interconnected with all life in lucid clarity of higher awareness; in all moments."

Cleanse Your Lungs

(Say each statement three times while tapping on your head and say it a fourth time while tapping on your chest.)

"I release storing sadness in my lungs; in all moments."

"I dissipate all the sadness stored in my lungs; in all moments."

"I release the trauma of drowning; in all moments."

"I release the trauma of gasping for air; in all moments."

"I release the trauma of trying to catch my breath; in all moments."

"I heal all puncture wounds; in all moments."

"I repair my lungs; in all moments."

"I return elasticity to my lungs; in all moments."

"I clear all passages in my lungs; in all moments."

"I flush out all my alveoli; in all moments."

"I remove all excess eosinophils from my lungs; in all moments."

"I remove all fluid from my passageways; in all moments."

"I release being deprived air; in all moments."

"I release ingesting toxins; in all moments."

"I release reliving trauma; in all moments."

"I release the trauma of taking my last breath; in all moments."

"I release reliving taking my last breath; in all moments."

"I repair my ribs; in all moments."

"I exhale and inhale with ease; in all moments."

"I expand my lungs; in all moments."

"I am flexible and resilient; in all moments."

Lying

(Say each statement three times out loud while continuously tapping on the top of your head at the crown chakra and say it a fourth time while tapping on your heart chakra.)

"I declare myself a surrogate for humanity in doing these taps; in all moments."

"I release being lied to; in all moments."

"I release confusing a lie for the truth; in all moments."

"I release quantifying lying; in all moments."

"I release sanctioning small lies; in all moments."

"I release the belief that any lie is small; in all moments."

"I release condoning lying; in all moments."

"I release lying to be nice; in all moments."

"I release the belief that it is kind to lie; in all moments."

"I release the fear of the truth; in all moments."

"I release being unkind to others in the name of the truth; in all moments."

"I release the belief that the truth hurts; in all moments."

"I release being attached to the lies; in all moments."

"I recant all vows and agreements between myself and all lies; in all moments."

"I sever all strings and cords between myself and all lies; in all moments."

"I dissolve all karmic ties between myself and all lies; in all moments."

"I remove all the pain, burden, limitations and engrams that all lies have put on me; in all moments."

"I take back all the joy, love, abundance, freedom, life and wholeness that all lies have taken from me; in all moments."

"I withdraw all my energy from all lies; in all moments."

"I strip all illusion off of all lies; in all moments."

"I extract all lies from my sound frequency; in all moments."

"I extract all lies from my light body; in all moments."

"I release resonating and emanating with lies; in all moments."

"I shift my paradigm from lies to truth; in all moments."

"I transcend all lies; in all moments."

"I am centered and empowered in the divinity and kindness of absolute truth; in all moments."

"I resonate and emanate the divinity and kindness of the absolute truth; in all moments."

Lymph

(Say each statement three times while tapping on my head and say it a fourth time while tapping on your chest.)

"I release storing stagnant energy in my lymph nodes; in all moments."

"I remove the feeling of isolation, rejection and abandonment from all my lymph nodes; in all moments."

"I release the feeling of being disconnected from my lymphatic system; in all moments."

"I release feeling disconnected; in all moments."

"I return fluidity to my lymphatic system; in all moments.'"

"I return all single nodes to the collective; in all moments."

"I return worthiness and empowerment to all of my lymph nodes; in all moments."

"I empower all lymph nodes with optimal health; in all moments."

"All lymph nodes are worthy and important; in all moments."

"All lymph nodes are connected to all others in empowerment and optimal ability to function; in all moments."

"I flush out all lymph nodes with divine health; in all moments."

"All lymph nodes are cleansed, repaired, strengthened and healed; in all moments."

Release Male Slanted Truth

(Say each statement three times out loud while continuously tapping on the top of your head at the crown chakra and say it a fourth time while tapping on your chest.)

"I release giving my power to male slanted truth; in all moments."

"I release being at the mercy of male slanted truth; in all moments."

"I release being enslaved to male slanted truth; in all moments."

"I release using male slanted truth as a crutch; in all moments."

"I release subscribing to male slanted truth out of habit; in all moments."

"I release feeling dependent on male slanted truth; in all moments."

"I release feeling beholden to male slanted truth; in all moments."

"I release being brainwashed by male slanted truth; in all moments."

"I recant all vows and agreements between myself and male slanted truth; in all moments."

"I remove all curses between myself and male slanted truth; in all moments."

"I remove all blessings between myself and male slanted truth; in all moments."

"I sever all strings and cords between myself and male slanted truth; in all moments."

"I dissolve all karmic ties between myself and male slanted truth; in all moments."

"I remove all the pain, burden, limitations and engrams that male slanted truth has put on me; in all moments."

"I remove all the pain, burden, limitations and engrams that I have put on all others due to male slanted truth; in all moments."

"I take back all the joy, love, abundance, freedom, health, success, security, companionship, creativity, peace, life, wholeness, beauty, enthusiasm, contentment, spirituality, enlightenment and confidence that male slanted truth has taken from me; in all moments."

"I give back all that I have taken from all others due to male slanted truth; in all moments."

"I withdraw all my energy from male slanted truth; in all moments."

"I release resonating with male slanted truth; in all moments."

"I release emanating with male slanted truth; in all moments."

"I remove all of male slanted truth from my sound frequency; in all moments."

"I remove all of male slanted truth from my light body; in all moments."

"I shift my paradigm from male slanted truth to absolute truth; in all moments."

"I strip all illusion off of male slanted truth; in all moments."

"I transcend male slanted truth; in all moments."

"I repair and fortify the psyche of all my bodies; in all moments."

"I am centered and empowered in absolute truth; in all moments."

"I make space in this world for all to know absolute truth; in all moments."

"I remove all blockages to the world knowing absolute truth; in all moments."

"I stretch my capacity to recognize absolute truth; in all moments."

"I stretch my capacity to embrace absolute truth; in all moments."

"I resonate and emanate absolute truth; in all moments."

"I empower the world to resonate and emanate absolute truth; in all moments."

Jen Ward

Releasing Deeply Engrained Masochism

I just finished a session with a really spiritual woman who sabotages herself. As I am facilitating the session, I am also receiving a download of information from my Spirit Guides on the pandemic of masochism that plagues the world.

Here is the definition of masochism. The condition in which gratification depends on one's suffering physical pain or humiliation.

At first, I was shown addictions as a form of masochism. How when you "use" you are shamed even as you do it and still continue to do it. But then I was shown all these different addictions, preferences and scenarios that seemed masochistic in nature:

- Choosing a 9 to 5 job over a life's passion
- All through history, women being submissive to men
- Declaring ourselves unworthy in the eyes of our God
- Sending our heartiest people to war and deeming it noble
- Poisoning our own bodies with sugar and toxins
- Allowing our children to be killed in their schools and accepting it as the norm
- Decorating and even mutilating the body to meet an unreachable standard of beauty
- Poisoning our own environment and choosing ill health over addressing the issue
- Giving our power over to governing factions that insult our intelligence
- Allow ourselves to be manipulated by companies so we can be mildly entertained
- Worship manufactured celebrities that make us feel inferior in comparison

If these issues aren't masochistic, they hedge eerily close to it. Here are the taps I led my client through: (Say each statement three times out loud while tapping on your head and say it a fourth time while tapping on your chest.)

"I release distracting myself with masochism; in all moments."

"I release society being distracted by masochism; in all moments."

"I release sabotaging myself with masochism; in all moments."

"I release society being sabotaged by masochism; in all moments."

"I strip off all the illusion and intrigue of mass masochism; in all moments."

"I release being enslaved to masochism; in all moments."

"I release society being enslaved to masochism; in all moments."

"I recant all vows and agreements between myself and masochism; in all moments."

"I recant all vows and agreements between society and masochism; in all moments."

"I remove all curses between myself and masochism; in all moments."

"I remove all curses between society and masochism; in all moments."

"I sever all ties cords between myself and masochism; in all moments."

"I sever all ties and cords between masochism and society; in all moments."

"I dissolve all karmic ties between myself and masochism; in all moments."

"I dissolve all karmic ties between society and masochism; in all moments."

"I shatter all mystique of masochism; in all moments."

"I remove all the pain, burden, limitations and engrams that masochism has put on me; in all moments."

"I remove all the pain, burden, limitations and engrams that masochism has put on society; in all moments."

"I take back all the joy, love, abundance, freedom, health, success, security, companionship, creativity, peace, life, wholeness, beauty, enthusiasm, contentment, spirituality, empowerment, enlightenment, dance and ingenuity that masochism has taken from me; in all moments."

"I retrieve for society all the joy, love, abundance, freedom, health, success, security, companionship, creativity, peace, life, wholeness, beauty, enthusiasm, contentment, spirituality, empowerment, enlightenment, dance and ingenuity that masochism has taken from it; in all moments."

"I release resonating with masochism; in all moments."

"I release society resonating with masochism; in all moments."

"I release emanating with masochism; in all moments."

"I release society emanating with masochism; in all moments."

"I remove all masochism from my sound frequency; in all moments."

"I remove all masochism from society's sound frequency; in all moments."

"I remove all masochism from my light body; in all moments."

"I remove all masochism from society's light body; in all moments."

"I shift my paradigm from masochism to joy, love, abundance, freedom, health, success, security, companionship, creativity, peace, life, wholeness, beauty, enthusiasm, contentment, spirituality, empowerment, enlightenment, dance and ingenuity; in all moments."

"I shift society's paradigm from masochism to joy, love, abundance, freedom, health, success, security, companionship, creativity, peace, life, wholeness, beauty, enthusiasm, contentment, spirituality, empowerment, enlightenment, dance and ingenuity; in all moments."

"I am centered and empowered in divine love; in all moments."

"Society is centered and imbued in divine love; in all moments."

"I shift the world's paradigm from society to humanity; in all moments."

I was trying to make this a shorter set of taps to accommodate some people's preference. But when I was writing these, I heard a huge crack in my home as if the building was settling. I opted to listen and typed out the long version. It is too important of an issue to glaze over. We have been glazed over to long.

Living Beyond the Mayan Calendar

These taps could have been done after 2012. We have outgrown the limitations of the Mayan calendar but just haven't consciously caught up to this realization. Much of what we are doing is merely reliving old engrams of an outmoded consciousness. That is why dynamic healing is so possible. Because the rules have changed. We are now waiting for old engrams to slough off so new freedom can be realized. These taps will speed up the process of our conscious awareness accepting the upgrade to humanity.

(Say each statement three times out loud while tapping on your head and say it a fourth time while tapping on your chest.)

"I release being enslaved to the Mayan Calendar; in all moments."

"I remove the glass ceiling of the Mayan Calendar from my beingness; in all moments."

"I release using the Mayan Calendar to validate limited beliefs; in all moments."

"I release the genetic propensity to subscribe to the Mayan Calendar; in all moments."

"I release using Mayan Calendar as an excuse to not transcend; in all moments."

"I release using Mayan Calendar as a crutch; in all moments."

"I release being at the mercy of the Mayan Calendar; in all moments."

"I release using the Mayan Calendar to edify an agenda; in all moments."

"I release using the Mayan Calendar to define myself; in all moments."

"I dry up all psychic streams that keep us trapped in the Mayan Calendar; in all moments."

"I withdraw all my energy from the Mayan Calendar; in all moments."

"I release being manipulated, coerced, duped, corrupted or enslaved by the Mayan Calendar; in all moments."

"I remove all vivaxes between myself and the Mayan Calendar; in all moments."

"I remove all tentacles between myself and the Mayan Calendar; in all moments."

"I remove the claws of the Mayan Calendar from my beingness; in all moments."

"I collapse and dissolve all portals to the Mayan Calendar; in all moments."

"I release perpetuating the limitations of the Mayan Calendar; in all moments."

"I strip all illusion off of the Mayan Calendar; in all moments."

"I remove all masks, walls and armor from the perpetuation of the Mayan Calendar; in any form; in all moments."

"I eliminate the first cause in regards to the limitations of the Mayan Calendar; in all moments."

"I remove all programming and conditioning that the Mayan Calendar has put on me; in all moments."

"I remove all engrams of the Mayan Calendar; in all moments."

"I remove all muscle memory of the Mayan Calendar; in all moments."

"I send all energy matrices into the light and sound that use the Mayan Calendar to limit humanity; in all moments."

"I command all complex energy matrices that use the Mayan Calendar to limit humanity to be escorted into the light and sound; in all moments."

"I send all energy matrices into the light and sound that perpetuate the Mayan Calendar; in all moments."

"I command all complex energy matrices that perpetuate the Mayan Calendar to be escorted into the light and sound; in all moments."

"I nullify all contracts with the Mayan Calendar; in all moments."

"I nullify all contracts with everyone and everything that perpetuate the Mayan Calendar; in all moments."

"I recant all vows and agreements between myself and the Mayan Calendar; in all moments."

"I collapse and dissolve all the limitations of the Mayan Calendar; in all moments."

"I remove all curses between myself and the Mayan Calendar; in all moments."

"I remove all blessings between myself and the Mayan Calendar; in all moments."

"I dissolve all karmic ties between myself and the Mayan Calendar; in all moments."

"I cut all the cords and ties to the Mayan Calendar; in all moments."

"I remove all the pain, burden, limitations and controlling devices that the Mayan Calendar has put on me; in all moments."

"I remove all the pain, burden, limitations, and controlling devices that I have put on all others due to the Mayan Calendar; in all moments."

"I take back all the joy, love, abundance, freedom, health, success, security, companionship, creativity, peace, life, wholeness, beauty, enthusiasm, contentment, spirituality, enlightenment, confidence, intellect, the ability to discern and empowerment that the Mayan Calendar has taken from me; in all moments."

"I give back to all others all the joy, love, abundance, freedom, health, success, security, companionship, creativity, peace, life, wholeness, beauty, enthusiasm, contentment, spirituality, enlightenment, confidence, intellect, the ability to discern and empowerment that I have taken from them due to the Mayan Calendar; in all moments."

"I convert all the devotion to the limitations of Mayan Calendar into exponential freedom; in all moments."

"I release resonating with the limitations of the Mayan Calendar; in all moments."

"I release emanating with the limitations of the Mayan Calendar; in all moments."

"I extract all the limitations of the Mayan Calendar from my sound frequency and the Universal sound frequency; in all moments."

"I extract all the limitations of the Mayan Calendar from my light emanation and the Universal light emanation; in all moments."

"I shift my paradigm and the Universal paradigm from the limitations of the Mayan Calendar to exponential freedom; in all moments."

"I transcend the Mayan Calendar individually and universally; in all moments."

"I am individually and universally centered and empowered in exponential freedom; in all moments."

"I resonate, emanate and am interconnected with all life in individual and Universal exponential freedom; in all moments."

Change Your Mind

(Say each statement three times while tapping on your head and say it a fourth time while tapping on your chest.)

"All algorithms of want are dismantled; in all moments."

"All algorithms of need are dismantled; in all moments."

"All algorithms of unworthiness are dismantled; in all moments."

"All algorithms of hating my job are dismantled; in all moments."

"All algorithms of feeling unattractive are dismantled; in all moments."

"All algorithms of aging are dismantled; in all moments."

"All algorithms of degeneration are dismantled; in all moments."

"All algorithms of worry are dismantled; in all moments."

"All algorithms of overeating are dismantled; in all moments."

"All algorithms of deprivation are dismantled; in all moments."

"All algorithms of deprecation are dismantled; in all moments."

"All algorithms of being in our perfect home are implemented; in all moments."

"All algorithms of systemic pain are dismantled; in all moments."

"All algorithms of fibromyalgia are dismantled; in all moments."

"All algorithms of loss and regret are dismantled; in all moments."

"All algorithms of stubbornness are dismantled; in all moments."

"All algorithms of neediness are dismantled; in all moments."

"All algorithms of genetic propensities are dismantled; in all moments."

"All algorithms of fragmentation are dismantled; in all moments."

"All algorithms of over-mentalizing are dismantled; in all moments."

"All algorithms of distracting issues are dismantled; in all moments."

"All algorithms of energy blocks are dismantled; in all moments."

"All algorithms of physical blocks are dismantled; in all moments."

"All algorithms of financial blocks are dismantled; in all moments."

"All algorithms of emotional blocks are dismantled; in all moments."

"All algorithms of causal blocks are dismantled; in all moments."

"All algorithms of mental blocks are dismantled; in all moments."

"All algorithms of etheric blocks are dismantled; in all moments."

"All algorithms of spiritual blocks are dismantled; in all moments."

"Algorithms of Omniscience are implemented; in all moments."

"Algorithms of Omnipresence are implemented; in all moments."

"Algorithms of Omnipotence are implemented; in all moments."

"Algorithms of Abundance are implemented; in all moments."

"Algorithms of Compatibility are implemented; in all moments."

"Algorithms of Companionship are implemented; in all moments."

"Algorithms of Joy are implemented; in all moments."

"Algorithms of Love are implemented; in all moments."

"Algorithms of Freedom are implemented; in all moments."

"Algorithms of Health are implemented; in all moments."

"Algorithms of Success are implemented; in all moments."

"Algorithms of Creativity are implemented; in all moments."

"Algorithms of Wholeness are implemented; in all moments."

"Algorithms of Beauty are implemented; in all moments."

"Algorithms of Enthusiasm are implemented; in all moments."

"Algorithms of Gratitude are implemented; in all moments."

"Algorithms of Peace are implemented; in all moments."

"Algorithms of Multi-dimensional Travel are implemented; in all moments."

"Algorithms of Spirituality are implemented; in all moments."

"Algorithms of Enlightenment are implemented; in all moments."

"Algorithms of Empowerment are implemented; in all moments."

Changing the Filter/Brain Filter

The brain filters out almost 90% of the information that it is bombarded with. It pulls in only that which is relevant to its daily life. Without this filter, the psyche would be overwhelmed and would not be able to function. We choose what we bring into the world by what we give our attention to. That is a huge reason to focus on seeing the positive in all situations so that the brain will know that the positive is relevant in our daily life.

Today, I facilitated a session with a client who has done much spiritual work on herself and much of it with me. At the beginning of the session, she wanted to ask why she was not manifesting abundance. We worked on this extensively and yet energetically I could see her stuck in the problem. Instead of being receptive to the session, she was stuck in the mental realms and tried to pull me down into the mind instead of allowing me to pull her up.

Release negatively programming yourself.

(Say each statement three times out loud while continuously tapping on the top of your head at the crown chakra and say it a fourth time while tapping on your chest.)

"I release programming problems into myself; in all moments."

"I release telling myself that I am flawed; in all moments."

"I release telling the world that I am flawed; in all moments."

"I release programming sadness or depression into myself; in all moments."

"I release telling myself that I am depressed; in all moments."

"I release telling the world that I am depressed; in all moments."

"I release programming isolation into myself; in all moments."

"I release telling myself that I am unlovable; in all moments."

"I release telling the world that I am unlovable; in all moments."

"I release programming poverty into myself; in all moments."

"I release telling myself that I am poor or broke; in all moments."

"I release telling the world that I am poor; in all moments."

"I release programming slavery into myself; in all moments."

"I release telling myself that I am trapped; in all moments."

"I release telling the world that I am trapped; in all moments."

"I release programming disease into myself; in all moments."

"I release telling myself that I am sick; in all moments."

"I release telling the world that I am sick; in all moments."

"I release programming obesity into myself; in all moments."

"I release telling myself that I am fat; in all moments."

"I release telling the world that I am flawed; in all moments."

"I release programming failure into myself; in all moments."

"I release telling myself that I am a failure; in all moments."

"I release telling the world that I am flawed; in all moments."

"I release programming myself to be broken; in all moments."

"I release telling myself that I am broken; in all moments."

"I release telling the world that I am broken; in all moments."

As I was experiencing this exchange between myself and my client, I was given another key as to why some people manifest wonderful things in their life and why some do not. The answer I was given was a huge key to help her release during the session and also a huge key to assist so many people. It seemed to be an answer that was given to me straight from the heart of truth.

"I filter out sadness; in all moments."

"I filter out fear; in all moments."

"I filter out hate; in all moments."

"I filter out poverty; in all moments."

"I filter out failure; in all moments."

"I filter out dis-ease; in all moments."

"I filter out insecurity; in all moments."

"I filter out loneliness; in all moments."

"I filter out chaos; in all moments."

"I filter out loss; in all moments."

"I filter out need; in all moments."

"I filter out want; in all moments."

"I filter out jealously; in all moments."

"I filter out gossip; in all moments."

"I filter out dissent; in all moments."

"I filter out fragmentation; in all moments."

"I filter out weakness; in all moments."

"I filter out illusion; in all moments!

"I release filtering out Joy; in all moments."

"I release filtering out Love; in all moments."

"I release filtering out Abundance; in all moments."

"I release filtering out Freedom; in all moments."

"I release filtering out Success; in all moments."

"I release filtering out Health; in all moments."

"I release filtering out Security; in all moments."

"I release filtering out Companionship; in all moments."

"I release filtering out Peace; in all moments."

"I release filtering out creativity; in all moments."

"I release filtering out Wholeness; in all moments."

Whenever a negative concept, person or situation presents itself in your life, name it and then say this tap, "I filter out _____; in all moments." Then name its positive opposite and then insert it in this tap: "I release filtering out _____; in all moments." This may be the missing piece for many. This may be the component that finally gets the mind on board with positive change.

Core Beliefs

There are many inconsistencies between what the concept of a word is and what it means to an individual. There are a few of them that show up in private sessions. Here are some taps to untangle the core beliefs around positive words.

(Say each statement three times while tapping on your head and say it a fourth time while tapping on your chest.)

"I release the belief that being free will leave me helpless; in all moments'

"I release defining freedom as helplessness; in all moments."

"I release the fear of abusing power; in all moments."

"I release relinquishing my power in the fear of abusing power; in all moments."

"I release the belief that being rich entails overwhelming responsibility; in all moments."

"I release the aversion to being rich; in all moments."

"I release using dis-ease to escape responsibility; in all moments."

"I release using illness as an excuse; in all moments."

"I release using illness as a call to be nurtured; in all moments."

" I release the fear of being attractive; in all moments."

"I release defining being attractive as unsafe; in all moments."

"I release defining relationships as a form of enslavement; in all moments."

"I release confusing love for power; in all moments."

"I release the belief that security is boring; in all moments."

"I release buying security with my freedom; in all moments."

"I release the belief that creativity is frivolous; in all moments."

"I release defining Peace as complacency; in all moments."

"I shift my paradigm to Joy, Love, Abundance, Freedom and Wholeness; in all moments."

Negative Programming

Your brain is a 3 D printer ready to manifest anything that you tell it. You tell it things and it manifests them. It is that simple. The reason we don't see more evidence of this is because we give it a statement to program it but then we give it another one and another one. People are so fickle that they vacillate in their commands and so change the programming. Every statement is a form of programming the mind. So at first we say, "Life is Good", and it is. But then we say things like "they are breaking my heart" or "It's killing me" These are ways that we program the mind to create these experiences for ourselves. We are breaking our own hearts in that way.

(Say each statement three times out loud while tapping on the top of your head at the crown chakra and say it a fourth time while tapping on your chest at the heart chakra)

"I release programming myself for negative outcomes; in all moments."

"I release manifesting negative outcomes with my words and my thoughts; in all moments."

"I release lowering the bar to what I allow for myself; in all moments."

"I release refuting my own empowerment; in all moments."

"I release the effects of telling myself that "someone is killing me"; in all moments."

"I release the effects of telling myself that someone is breaking my heart; in all moment "

"I release "killing myself" with my words and thoughts; in all moments."

"I release breaking my own back; in all moments."

"I release breaking my own heart; in all moments."

"I release making myself sick to death over anything; in all moments."

"I release diminishing my wellbeing with the drama of my words; in all moments."

"I release being irresponsible with my words and thoughts; in all moments."

"I gear all words and thoughts to the highest manifestation of joy, love, abundance, freedom and wholeness; in all moments."

"I am centered and empowered in manifesting the highest good; in all moments."

Millionaire Marathon

(Say each statement three times while tapping on your head and say it a fourth time while tapping on your chest.)

"I recant my vow of poverty; in all moments."

"I recant my vow of self deprivation; in all moments."

"I recant my vow of humility; in all moments."

"I am agreeable to wealth; in all moments."

"I resonate with wealth; in all moments."

"I release the fear of being wealthy; in all moments."

"I release the belief that being wealthy is overwhelming; in all moments."

"I release the belief that being wealthy means sacrificing my happiness; in all moments."

"I release the belief that being wealthy is too much work; in all moments."

"I release the belief that being wealthy is being spiritually bankrupt; in all moments."

"I release the belief that being wealthy is stressful; in all moments."

"I release the belief that being wealthy means selling out; in all moments."

"I release defining being wealthy as being selfish; in all moments."

"I release defining being wealthy as being spiritually unaware; in all moments."

"I release defining being wealthy as being evil; in all moments."

"I release defining being wealthy as sacrificing happiness; in all moments."

"I release defining being wealthy as being spiritually bankrupt; in all moments."

"I release the resistance to wealth; in all moments."

"I release the aversion to wealth; in all moments."

"I release the fear of wealth; in all moments."

"I release all limited beliefs about wealth; in all moments."

"I remove all negative programming regarding wealth; in all moments."

"I remove and dissolve all negative engrams regarding wealth; in all moments."

"I release being programmed to financially fail; in all moments."

"I remove all conscious and unconscious negative programming regarding wealth; in all moments."

"I infuse the sound frequency of my consciousness and subconscious to resonate with being a millionaire; in all moments."

"I imbue the light body of my consciousness and subconscious to emanate with being a millionaire; in all moments."

"Both my consciousness and subconscious resonate and emanate with being a millionaire; in all moments."

"I remove all negative correlations between my spiritual well being and wealth; in all moments."

"I remove all negative correlations between my mental well being and wealth; in all moments."

"I remove all negative correlations between my emotional well being and wealth; in all moments."

"I remove all negative correlations between my physical well being and wealth; in all moments."

"I reject all negative associations between my spiritual well being and wealth; in all moments."

"I reject all negative associations between my mental well being and wealth; in all moments."

"I reject all negative associations between my emotional well being and wealth; in all moments."

"I reject all negative associations between my physical well being and wealth; in all moments."

"I release all non supportive beliefs about money; in all moments."

"I release all non supportive opinions about money; in all moments."

"I release all non supportive feelings about money; in all moments."

"I release all non supportive experiences regarding money; in all moments."

"I shift my paradigm from believing negatively about money to believing that money is positive and uplifting; in all moments."

"I shift my paradigm from thinking negatively about money to thinking that money is positive and uplifting; in all moments."

"I shift my paradigm from feeling negatively about money to feeling that money is positive and uplifting; in all moments."

"I shift my paradigm from experiencing negativity about money to experiencing money as positive and uplifting; in all moments."

"I create a spiritual space to hold wealth; in all moments."

"I create a mental space to hold wealth; in all moments."

"I create an emotional space to hold wealth; in all moments."

"I create a physical space to hold wealth; in all moments."

"I remove all blockages to holding a spiritual space for wealth; in all moments."

"I remove all blockages to holding a mental space for wealth; in all moments."

"I remove all blockages to holding a emotional space for wealth; in all moments."

"I remove all blockages to holding a physical space for wealth; in all moments."

"I stretch my capacity to hold a spiritual space for wealth; in all moments."

"I stretch my capacity to hold a mental space for wealth; in all moments."

"I stretch my capacity to hold a emotional space for wealth; in all moments."

"I stretch my capacity to hold a physical space for wealth; in all moments."

"I align myself spiritually, mentally, emotionally and physically for wealth; in all moments."

"I resonate with a millionaire soul; in all moments."

"I resonate with a millionaire mind; in all moments."

"I resonate with a millionaire heart; in all moments."

"I resonate with a millionaire body; in all moments."

"My higher self creates a millionaire spiritual experience; in all moments."

"My higher self creates a millionaire mental experience; in all moments."

"My higher self creates a millionaire emotional experience; in all moments."

"My higher self creates a millionaire physical experience; in all moments."

"I am centered and empowered in spiritual wealth; in all moments."

"I am centered and empowered in mental wealth; in all moments."

"I am centered, and empowered in emotional wealth; in all moments."

"I am centered, and empowered in physical wealth; in all moments."

"I am centered, aligned and empowered in spiritual, mental, emotional and physical wealth; in all moments."

"I am spiritually, mentally, emotionally and physically centered and empowered in being rich; in all moments."

"I empower all the world with my wealth; in all moments."

"I uplift humanity with my wealth; in all moments."

"I passionately and enthusiastically empower wealth in all others; in all moments."

"I graciously and enthusiastically receive wealth into my life; in all moments."

"I spiritually, mentally, emotionally and physically choose to get paid; in all moments."

"I spiritually, mentally, emotionally and physically graciously and enthusiastically accept payment; in all moments."

"My attention and awareness embraces wealth for all; in all moments."

"I release diminishing my self worth and net worth; in all moments."

"I perpetuate an exponential self worth and net worth; in all moments."

"My net worth is worth millions and my self worth is priceless; in all moments."

"I am excellent at managing money; in all moments."

"I shift my paradigm from micromanaging the Universe to managing my own wealth; in all moments."

"I release hating money; in all moments."

"I release being the enemy of money; in all moments."

"I release treating money like a stranger; in all moments."

"I release treating wealth as a foreign object; in all moments."

"I spiritually, mentally, emotionally and physically love money; in all moments."

"I am spiritually, mentally, emotionally and physically friends with money; in all moments."

"Money is spiritually, mentally, emotionally and physically devoted to me; in all moments."

"I am centered and empowered in my friendship of money; in all moments."

"My money perpetuates more money; in all moments."

"My money perpetuates my wealth; in all moments."

"Money is a seedbed for my millions; in all moments."

"My millions perpetuate the upliftment of humanity; in all moments."

"My millions are the seedbed for the wealth of humanity; in all moments."

"I am gracious and enthusiastic in continuously learning and gaining awareness; in all moments."

"I am wealthy in all ways; in all moments."

"I believe in being generous; in all moments."

"I have a generous mentality; in all moments."

"I have a generous heart; in all moments."

"I personify generosity; in all moments."

"I have a receptive soul; in all moments."

"I have a receptive mind; in all moments."

"I have a receptive heart; in all moments."

"I personify receptivity; in all moments."

"I have the essence of a millionaire; in all moments."

"I have a millionaire mind; in all moments."

"I have a millionaire heart; in all moments."

"I am the embodiment of being a millionaire; in all moments."

"I repair and fortify the financial Wei chi of all my bodies; in all moments."

"I align all the spiritual, mental, emotional and physical financial aspects of myself; in all moments."

"I release and dissolve anything that does not support the divinity of my wealth; in all moments."

"I equivocate my wealth with joy, love, abundance, freedom and wholeness; in all moments."

"I am centered and empowered in being a millionaire; in all moments."

Release Crying Poor

(Say each statement three times out loud while continuously tapping on the top of your head at the crown chakra and say it a fourth time while tapping on your chest.)

"I release the belief that it is noble to be poor; in all moments."

"I release subscribing to only one kind of wealth; in all moments."

"I release converting my other forms of wealth into monetary gain; in all moments."

"I release have such a high conversion rate for monetary rate; in all moments."

"I release crying poor to get special treatment; in all moments."

"I release being a martyr in money issues; in all moments."

"I release being uncomfortable with wealth; in all moments."

"I release thinking of money as evil; in all moments."

"I release confusing monetary wealth with responsibility; in all moments."

"I release believing that I must be poor; in all moments."

"I release telling people that I am poor; in all moments."

"I release an aversion to wealth; in all moments."

"I recant all vows of poverty and unworthiness; in all moments."

"I release the belief that spirituality is the polarized opposite of wealth; in all moments."

"I remove all limiting engrams including all those of lack; in all moments."

"I claim both my goodness and my wealth; in all moments."

"I shift my paradigm from 'have not' to 'have' in all moments."

"I claim my birthright of joy, love, abundance and freedom; in all moments."

"I am centered and abundant in my own empowerment of wealth; in all moments."

"I resonate and emanate wealth; in all moments."

Stop Chasing Money

I recently facilitated a session with someone who was very concerned about having money. There was no financial struggle, but sill the issue of money was always in the forefront. She sabotaged relationships if the suitor wasn't affluent. She deferred to her parents way into her adulthood because they were rich. Happiness was elusive.

In her session, it became clear that there was no separation made between happiness and money. She thought of them as one and the same. She did not think it was possible to have happiness without money. But I made her look at the situation a lot closer. She did know rich people who weren't happy, so the words did NOT mean the same thing. She had chosen money over relationships, yet that did not make her happy either.

Happiness and money may be on parallel paths sometimes, but that doesn't mean they are synonymous. I brought up the analogy of owning a dog. If your dog doesn't come to you and you chase after it, it will keep running away. This was similar to her relationship with money. She was chasing it and it was running away.

If you want to get your dog back, you walk in the other direction so that it happily follows you. She needed to walk away from money towards happiness and trust that the comfortable finances would follow. The same thing could be true of happiness. If one chases it, it may be elusive. But if one just walks the path, it will walk right by their side.

Here are some taps to assist if this issue resonates as an issue for you: (Say each statement three times while tapping on your head and say it a fourth time while tapping on your chest.)

"I release the belief that money is happiness; in all moments."

"I release chasing money; in all moments."

"I release choosing money over happiness; in all moments."

"I release being enslaved by money; in all moments."

"I release the belief that being poor equals happiness; in all moments."

"I release the belief that money and happiness are at cross purposes; in all moments."

"I release the belief that money is the only form of wealth; in all moments."

"I release negating my own abundance; in all moments."

"I shift my paradigm to happiness and abundance; in all moments."

"I am centered in happiness and abundance; in all moments."

Tapping into Money Marathon

(Say each statement three times out loud while continuously tapping on the top of your head at the crown chakra and say it a fourth time while tapping on your chest.)

"I release basing my worth on making money; in all moments."

"I release using making money to validate my existence; in all moments."

"I release the belief that making money is the answer to all problems; in all moments."

"I release obsessing over making money; in all moments."

"I release equivocating making money with self love; in all moments."

"I release using making money as a contingency to loving myself; in all moments."

"I release using making money to prove my importance; in all moments."

"I release pushing money away through desire; in all moments."

"I release pushing money away by trying to make it; in all moments."

"I release the belief that I am incapable of making money; in all moments."

"I release being beaten down by the process of making money; in all moments."

"I release confusing the ability to make money with having abundance; in all moments."

"I release the belief that making money is a natural process; in all moments."

"I release coming out of my center to make money; in all moments."

"I release dissipating my energy trying to make money; in all moments."

"I release pushing money away by trying to generate it; in all moments."

"I release the belief that money is the answer to all my problems; in all moments."

"I release sabotaging monetary abundance with making money; in all moments."

"I release sabotaging monetary abundance with NOT making money; in all moments."

"I released being enslaved to the process of making money; in all moments."

"I released being enslaved to NOT making money; in all moments."

"I recant all vows and agreements between myself and making money; in all moments."

"I recant all vows and agreements between myself and NOT making money; in all moments."

"I remove all curses between myself and making money; in all moments."

"I remove all curses between myself and NOT making money; in all moments."

"I remove all blessings between myself and making money; in all moments."

"I remove all blessings between myself and NOT making money; in all moments."

"I sever all strings and cords between myself and making money; in all moments."

"I sever all strings and cords between myself and NOT making money; in all moments."

"I dissolve all karmic ties between myself and making money; in all moments."

"I dissolve all karmic ties between myself and NOT making money; in all moments."

"I release punishing myself by not making money; in all moments."

"I release using NOT making money as a scapegoat; in all moments."

"I withdraw all my energy from making money; in all moments."

"I withdraw all my energy from NOT making money; in all moments."

"I release resonating with making money; in all moments."

"I release resonating with NOT making money; in all moments."

"I release emanating with making money; in all moments."

"I release emanating with NOT making money; in all moments."

"I extract all of making money from my sound frequency; in all moments."

"I extract all of NOT making money from my sound frequency; in all moments."

"I extract all of making money from my light emanation; in all moments."

"I extract all of NOT making money from my light emanation; in all moments."

"I shift my paradigm from making money to joy, love, abundance, freedom, health, success, security, companionship, creativity, peace, life, wholeness, beauty, enthusiasm, contentment, spirituality, enlightenment, confidence, family, intelligence and the ability to discern; in all moments."

"I shift my paradigm from NOT making money to joy, love, abundance, freedom, health, success, security, companionship, creativity, peace, life, wholeness, beauty, enthusiasm, contentment, spirituality, enlightenment, confidence, family, intelligence and the ability to discern; in all moments."

"I transcend making money; in all moments."

"I transcend NOT making money; in all moments."

"I release allowing an outside source to dictate my monetary abundance; in all moments."

"I release allowing the past to dictate my monetary abundance; in all moments."

"I release sabotaging my monetary abundance; in all moments."

"I release allowing any aspect of my internal dialogue to diminish my monetary abundance; in all moments."

"I shift my paradigm from making money to monetary abundance; in all moments."

"I shift my paradigm from NOT making money to monetary abundance; in all moments."

"I release micromanaging the process of monetary abundance; in all moments."

"I am centered and empowered in monetary abundance; in all moments."

"I resonate and emanate monetary abundance; in all moments."

Move Forward

(Say each statement three times out loud while continuously tapping on the top of your head at the crown chakra and say it a fourth time while tapping on your chest.)

"I release being stuck in the same old state of consciousness; in all moments."

"I release being paralyzed to move forward; in all moments."

"I release depending on someone else to move me forward; in all moments."

"I release denying my own ability to move me forward; in all moments."

"I release overthinking the process of moving forward; in all moments."

"I release the belief that God is punishing me; in all moments."

"I release working against the natural process; in all moments."

"I release micromanaging the universe; in all moments."

"I release converting my competency into drama; in all moments."

"I remove all vivaxes between myself and all thought eddies; in all moments."

"I remove all vivaxes between myself and all emotion eddies; in all moments."

"I dry up all thought eddies; in all moments."

"I dry up all emotion eddies; in all moments."

"I pull myself out, out of all mental quicksand; in all moments."

"I pull myself out, out of all causal quicksand; in all moments."

"I pull myself out, out of all emotional quicksand; in all moments."

"I pull myself out of all physical quicksand; in all moments."

"I remove all vivaxes between myself and all old states of consciousness; in all moments."

"I remove all tentacles between myself and all old states of consciousness; in all moments."

"I remove the claws of all old states of consciousness from my beingness; in all moments."

"I remove all programming and conditioning that all old states of consciousness have put on me; in all moments."

"I remove all engrams that all old states of consciousness have put on me; in all moments."

"I declare myself a surrogate for humanity in doing these taps; in all moments."

"I send all energy matrices into the light and sound that trap me in old states of consciousness; in all moments."

"I send all energy matrices into the light and sound that cause me to prefer old states of consciousness; in all moments."

"I strip all illusion off of all old states of consciousness; in all moments."

"I withdraw all my energy from all old states of consciousness; in all moments."

"I remove all masks, walls and armor from all old states of consciousness; in all moments."

"I recant all vows and agreements between myself and all old states of consciousness; in all moments."

"I remove all curses between myself and all old states of consciousness; in all moments."

"I remove all blessings between myself and all old states of consciousness; in all moments."

"I sever all strings and cords between myself and all old states of consciousness; in all moments."

"I dissolve all karmic ties between myself and all old states of consciousness; in all moments."

"I remove all the pain, burden, and limitations that all old states of consciousness have put on me; in all moments."

"I remove all the disconnectedness and illusion of separateness that all old states of consciousness have put on me; in all moments."

"I release contributing to building or perpetuating all old states of consciousness; in all moments."

"I release indulging in old states of consciousness; in all moments."

"I release resurrecting old states of consciousness; in all moments."

"I release breathing my empowerment into old states of consciousness; in all moments."

"I take back the good that all old states of consciousness have taken from me; in all moments."

"I collapse and dissolve all old states of consciousness; in all moments."

"I release resonating with old states of consciousness; in all moments."

"I release emanating with old states of consciousness; in all moments."

"I extract all old states of consciousness from my beingness; in all moments."

"I extract all old states of consciousness from my sound frequency; in all moments."

"I extract all old states of consciousness from my light emanation; in all moments."

"I shift my paradigm from old states of consciousness to the dawn of spiritual empowerment; in all moments."

"I transcend all old states of consciousness; in all moments."

"I am centered and empowered in the dawn of spiritual empowerment; in all moments."

"I seed society with the dawn of spiritual empowerment; in all moments."

Multiple Personalities

(Say each statement three times while tapping on your head and say it a fourth time while tapping on your chest.)

"I remove fractioning off my energy; in all moments."

"I release feeling unsafe in my wholeness; in all moments."

"I remove all schisms from my energy; in all moments."

"I release drawing in foreign energies to protect myself; in all moments."

"I release taking on different personalities to cope; in all moments."

"I reassure all energies of my capability to be whole; in all moments."

"I pour gratitude into all energies that have protected me; in all moments."

"I bless all energies that have protected me and send them into the light and sound; in all moments."

"I purify all energies that have impersonated me and convert them into love; in all moments."

"I am safe and empowered; in all moments."

"I send all energy matrices that impersonate me into the light and sound; in all moments."

"I command all complex energy matrices that impersonate me to be escorted into the light and sound; in all moments."

"I heel all schisms in my energy; in all moments."

"I release drawing in personalities from other realities and dimensions to fortify me; in all moments."

"I purify the experience of linear existence in this world; in all moments."

"I limit the parameters of my own persona to those in this linear existence; in all moments."

"I secure the parameters of my own persona; in all moments."

"I release feeling vulnerable in linear reality; in all moments."

"I release feeling squelched; in all moments."

"I release feeling diminished in linear existence; in all moments."

"I maintain my awareness and freedom as I comply with linear parameters; in all moments.'"

"I release needing appendage personalities; in all moments."

"I release allowing appendage personalities to dominate; in all moments."

"I release the fear of losing my edge; in all moments."

"I release the fear of losing my uniqueness; in all moments."

"I merge appendage personalities into my wholeness; in all moments."

"I align all my bodies in wholeness; in all moments."

"I repair and fortify the Wei chi of all my bodies; in all moments."

"I am centered an empowered in wholeness; in all moments."

"I resonate, emanate and am interconnected with all life in wholeness; in all moments."

Activating Your Muscle Memory

After Peyton Manning's injury that was a possible end to his career, he was training with a long, beloved coach that he respected. He had been out of commission for a while and the speculation was that his career was over. But the coach was very wise. What he said is the seed for this powerful exercise.

He told Peyton that no one was going to be able to tell him how to get to the top of his game again but himself. He held the blueprint of how to be the greatest quarterback in his muscle memory. The coach pushed him to throw the ball repeatedly. He told him by going through the motions, he would activate the muscle memory of how to be great again. Peyton went on to win another super bowl ring.

You hold muscle memory of being happy, loved, healthy, nurtured, safe, etc. Here is an exercise to activate the achievement of your highest potential. Do these taps and then just go about your life. As with Peyton learning to throw again, you need to move to activate the muscle memory. Try picking up old hobbies, reactivating passions you left by the wayside, digging into the earth and life and being present as much as possible with your surroundings and the people that you love. Your highest success lies in the awakening of your own presence in each moment. Yes. It is that simple.

(Say each statement three times while tapping on your head and say it a fourth time while tapping on your chest.)

"I release micro-managing the universe; in all moments."

"I declare myself a surrogate for humanity in doing these taps; in all moments."

"I activate the muscle memory of my greatest joy; in all moments."

"I activate the muscle memory of being in love; in all moments."

"I activate the muscle memory of being abundant; in all moments."

"I activate the muscle memory of being free; in all moments."

"I activate the muscle memory of being healthy; in all moments."

"I activate the muscle memory of being young; in all moments."

"I activate the muscle memory of being successful; in all moments."

"I activate the muscle memory of being safe; in all moments."

"I activate the muscle memory of knowing companionship; in all moments."

"I activate the muscle memory of being connected; in all moments."

"I activate the muscle memory of being nurtured; in all moments."

"I activate the muscle memory of being creative; in all moments."

"I activate the muscle memory of being at peace; in all moments."

"I activate the muscle memory of surging with life; in all moments."

"I activate the muscle memory of being adventurous; in all moments."

"I activate the muscle memory of being fearless; in all moments."

"I activate the muscle memory of being complete; in all moments."

"I activate the muscle memory of being beautiful; in all moments."

"I activate the muscle memory of being enlightened; in all moments."

"I activate the muscle memory of being empowered; in all moments."

"I activate the muscle memory of achieving my highest potential; in all moments."

"I am centered, empowered and immersed in the fluidity of life; in all moments."

Transcending Neck and Throat Issues

(Say each statement three times out loud while continuously tapping on the top of your head at the crown chakra and say it a fourth time while tapping on your chest.)

"I release the trauma of being decapitated; in all moments."

"I release the trauma of being choked to death; in all moments."

"I release the trauma of being hanged; in all moments."

"I release the trauma of having my neck broken; in all moments."

"I release the trauma of having my throat slit; in all moments."

"I release drowning on my own blood; in all moments."

"I release being whiplashed; in all moments."

"I remove all the chains and shackles from my neck; in all moments."

"I mend my neck bones; in all moments."

"I heal all my neck wounds; in all moments."

"The pain and trauma of being hung is released; in all moments."

"The pain and trauma of being decapitated is released; in all moments."

"The pain and trauma of falling to my death is released; in all moments."

"The pain and trauma of breaking my neck is released; in all moments."

"The pain and trauma of having my neck snapped is released; in all moments."

"The pain and trauma of being choked is released; in all moments."

"The pain and trauma of being shackled at the throat is released; in all moments."

"The humiliation and degradation of being pulled along by the neck is released; in all moments."

"The paralyzing trauma of being captured and enslaved is released; in all moments."

"Living like a slave is released; in all moments."

"The fear of being grabbed from behind is released; in all moments."

"The pain and trauma of being killed for a minor transgression is released; in all moments."

"The devastating lingering effects of being captured is released; in all moments."

"The pain and trauma of being burned alive is released; in all moments."

"The effects of sucking down thick smoke is released; in all moments."

"The pain and trauma of being orally violated and made to swallow is released; in all moments."

"Associating oral sex with being violated, raped or injured is released; in all moments."

"The pain and trauma of being forced to swallow caustic items is released; in all moments."

"The memory of sucking down thick smoke from my throat is released; in all moments."

"All the trauma stored in the neck and throat is released; in all moments."

"The belief that my neck is too weak is released; in all moments."

"The neck is untwisted; in all moments."

"Overcompensating by bulking up my neck muscles is released; in all moments."

"Blaming the neck or throat is released; in all moments."

"The paradigm to trust my neck is shifted; in all moments."

"The paradigm to relax my neck is realized; in all moments."

"I am centered and empowered in a relaxed, confident neck; in all moments."

Address Nervous System Disorders

(Say each statement three times out loud while continuously tapping on the top of your head at the crown chakra and say it a fourth time while tapping on your chest.)

"I re-empower my sympathetic nervous system; in all moments."

"I release my body begging for love through tremors; in all moments."

"I release drying up my nervous system like a sponge; in all moments."

"I pour infinite and perpetual love into my body through my nervous system; in all moments."

"I quench my body's thirst for love through my nervous system; in all moments."

"I recharge and regenerate all the energy systems of my beingness; in all moments."

"I plug my entire nervous system into all their proper energy systems; in all moments."

"I awaken all the communication centers in both my nervous system and my entire energy system; in all moments."

"I align and open up all the communication centers between my entire energy system and my nervous system; in all moments."

"I repair the myelin sheath on my entire nervous system; in all moments."

"I remove any and all blockages in my brain that prevent it from functioning at optimal capacity; in all moments."

"I repair all disconnects between my nervous system and my brain; in all moments."

"I remove all schisms between my brain and my nervous system; in all moments."

"I awaken and align all communication centers between my brain and my nervous system; in all moments."

"I am centered and empowered in an optimal working brain communicating efficiently with an optimal working nervous system; in all moments."

Opinions

"In my humble opinion" is an oxymoron. Opinions are anything but humble.

(Say each statement three times tapping on the top of your head and say it a fourth time while tapping on your chest.)

"I release using opinions to hide my lack of awareness; in all moments."

"I release hoarding opinions as facts; in all moments."

"I release gorging on opinions; in all moments."

"I release using opinions to validate myself; in all moments."

"I release being laden in heavy layers of opinions; in all moments."

"I release sharing opinions to feel important; in all moments."

"I release confusing opinions for truth; in all moments."

"I release adopting others' opinions as my own; in all moments."

"I release confusing opinions for power; in all moments."

"I release using opinions to diminish truth; in all moments."

"I release using opinions to railroad others; in all moments."

"I release using opinions to seem superior to others; in all moments."

"I release clinging strongly to opinions; in all moments."

"I release confusing opinions with virtue; in all moments."

"I release inundating the world with opinions; in all moments."

"I release controlling others with opinions; in all moments."

"I release using opinions to feel worthy; in all moments."

"I drop all opinions to embrace truth; in all moments."

"I shift my paradigm from opinions to awareness; in all moments."

"I am centered and empowered in the stillness of universal love and truth; in all moments."

Optimism

(Say each statement three times out loud while continuously tapping on the top of your head at the crown chakra and say it a fourth time while tapping on your chest.)

"I release obsessing over my weight; in all moments."

"I release complaining about the weather; in all moments."

"I release the fear of the next incoming bill; in all moments."

"I release living in dread and disdain; in all moments."

"I release waking up in dread; in all moments."

"I release treating each day like the day before; in all moments."

"I release limiting my options with limiting thoughts and beliefs; in all moments."

"I release telling myself that I am getting old; in all moments."

"I release focusing on aches and pains; in all moments."

"I release the belief that disease is inevitable; in all moments."

"I release professing gloom and doom; in all moments."

"I release giving up all hope; in all moments."

"I release throwing in the towel; in all moments."

"I release the belief that I am a powerless grunt; in all moments."

"I release spinning my wheels; in all moments."

"I awaken to a positive outlook; in all moments."

"I shift my whole paradigm to positive potential; in all moments."

"I am centered and empowered in joy, love, abundance, freedom and wholeness; in all moments."

Eliminating the Initial Cause of Pain

In the game of dominoes, that first tile is so important. If the first domino were not there, the whole chain reaction would not occur. It is this way in life as well. Have you ever done something that set off a whole chain of reactions? It was so devastating that the results were life changing and not in a good way? You so wish you could take that one course of events back?

This is how it goes in the way of life as well. At one point, we were so full of joy, love, beauty, health, abundance. We were also all free and whole. But then that one instance happened in our repertoire of experiences that caused us to veer a little bit from absolute best. It was the first thing that caused us pain. It was the first cause in a long lineage of causes and effects.

That first cause is like the grain of sand that was introduced into the clam's shell to eventually create the pearl. It is the small center of the snowball that was sent down the hill out of control. We wish we could pull those things back. We wish we could stop the avalanche of events. We wish we knew how or what they even were.

In the worlds of energy, there is no time and space. In energy, you are happy and whole. The goal is to get back to that reality in the present. The way to do that is to reach through time and space with your intention and remove that first domino. You want to eliminate that first cause in the chain of reactions so none of the pain that ensues is ever initiated.

(Say each statement three times out loud while continuously tapping on the top of your head at the crown chakra and say it a fourth time while tapping on your chest.)

"I eliminate the first cause that initiated weight gain; in all moments."

"I eliminate the first cause that initiated lack; in all moments."

"I eliminate the first cause that initiated disease; in all moments."

"I eliminate the first cause that initiated weakness; in all moments."

"I eliminate the first cause that initiated fear; in all moments."

"I eliminate the first cause that initiated want; in all moments."

"I eliminate the first cause that initiated greed; in all moments."

"I eliminate the first cause that initiated unworthiness; in all moments."

"I eliminate the first cause that initiated depression; in all moments."

"I eliminate the first cause that initiated sadness; in all moments."

"I eliminate the first cause that initiated imbalance; in all moments."

"I eliminate the first cause that initiated physical pain; in all moments."

"I eliminate the first cause that initiated emotional pain; in all moments."

"I eliminate the first cause that initiated mental torment; in all moments."

"I eliminate the first cause that initiated a sense of separation; in all moments."

"I eliminate the first cause that initiated hate; in all moments."

"I eliminate the first cause that initiated slavery; in all moments."

"I eliminate the first cause that initiated failure; in all moments."

"I eliminate the first cause that initiated insecurity; in all moments."

"I eliminate the first cause that initiated rejection; in all moments."

"I eliminate the first cause that initiated abandonment; in all moments."

"I eliminate the first cause that initiated pollution; in all moments."

"I eliminate the first cause that initiated apathy; in all moments."

"I eliminate the first cause that initiated denial; in all moments."

"I eliminate the first cause that initiated wearing masks; in all moments."

"I eliminate the first cause that initiated having walls; in all moments."

"I eliminate the first cause that initiated wearing armor; in all moments."

"I eliminate the first cause that initiated coming out of my center; in all moments."

"I eliminate the first cause that initiated war; in all moments."

"I eliminate the first cause that initiated manipulation; in all moments."

"I eliminate the first cause that initiated death; in all moments."

"I eliminate the first cause that initiated suffering; in all moments."

"I eliminate the first cause that initiated any schisms; in all moments."

"I eliminate the first cause that initiated fragmentation; in all moments."

"I eliminate the first cause that initiated ugliness; in all moments."

"I eliminate the first cause that initiated discontent; in all moments."

"I eliminate the first cause that initiated ignorance; in all moments."

"I eliminate the first cause that initiated indifference; in all moments."

"I eliminate the first cause that initiated giving away my power; in all moments."

"I eliminate the first cause that initiated lack of discernment; in all moments."

"I am centered and empowered in the divinity of wholeness; in all moments."

Doing this exercise may be the best thing you do for yourself.

Releasing Pain Marathon

Recently, I facilitated a remote session on a wonderful healer. She has been working on herself for many years. She has been dealing with pain and thought she had done all she could to address the issues. After her session, she was surprised at the oversight. There was much revealed.

When I tuned in for her session, I saw her in a past life groveling on her knees in excruciating pain to God. There was a flood of memories of times when she was subservient to God. She said she had done extensive work in releasing these issues. But they were showing up in her session.

We went through the whole protocol on her relationship with God. We then went through the whole protocol with her relationship with all of God's minions. It brought great relief. Under that layer there were some interesting findings. She had done a lot of work on her issues with God, but her God issues were hiding in her body under the auspices of pain. She had converted her God issues to physical pain. She was thinking of pain in God terms, that it was omniscient and omnipotent.

Here are some of the taps we did and I have done with others specifically around pain.

(Say each statement three times out loud while continuously tapping on the top of your head at the crown chakra and say it a fourth time while tapping on your chest.)

"I release being at the mercy of pain; in all moments."

"I release giving pain my power; in all moments."

"I release using pain to validate myself; in all moments."

"I release using pain as a crutch; in all moments."

"I release being enslaved to pain; in all moments."

"I release using pain as an excuse; in all moments."

"I release using pain to feel important; in all moments."

"I release using pain to punish myself; in all moments'

"I release using pain to declare myself unworthy; in all moments."

"I release the belief that pain is omniscient; in all moments."

"I release the belief that pain is omnipresent; in all moments."

"I release the belief that pain is omnipotent; in all moments."

"I release worshiping pain; in all moments."

"I release being trapped in hell; in all moments."

"I release converting hell into pain; in all moments."

"I release using pain to express being in hell; in all moments."

"I release making a God out of pain; in all moments."

"I release storing hell in my nerve endings; in all moments."

"I remove all vivaxes between myself and pain; in all moments."

"I remove all tentacles between myself and pain; in all moments."

"I release trying to validate myself through pain; in all moments."

"I remove the claws of pain from my beingness; in all moments."

"I release being disconnected from the cause of the source of pain; in all moments."

"I remove all engrams that remind me or immerse me in pain; in all moments."

"I release echoing others' anguish in pain; in all moments."

"I remove all programming and conditioning that pain has put on me; in all moments."

"I remove all engrams that cause me to relive past torture; in all moments."

"I send all energy matrices into the light and sound that immerse me in pain; in all moments."

"I send all energy matrices into the light and sound that thrive on me being in pain; in all moments."

"I send all energy matrices into the light and sound that inflict pain on me; in all moments."

"I send all energy matrices into the light and sound that take glee out of seeing me in pain; in all moments."

"I command all complex energy matrices that ensconce me in pain to be escorted into the light and sound; in all moments."

"I recant all vows and agreements between myself and pain; in all moments."

"I remove all curses between myself and pain; in all moments."

"I sever all strings and cords between myself and all pain; in all moments."

"I dissolve all karmic ties between myself and pain; in all moments."

"I sever all strings and cords between myself and my pain body; in all moments."

"I step out of my pain body and disintegrate it; in all moments."

"I remove all the pain, burden, limitations and engrams that pain has put on me; in all moments."

"I take back all the joy, love, abundance, freedom, health, success, security, companionship, creativity, peace, life, wholeness, beauty, enthusiasm, contentment, spirituality, enlightenment and confidence that pain has taken from me; in all moments."

"I strip all illusion off of pain; in all moments."

"I remove all masks, walls and armor from pain; in all moments."

"I release being permeated in pain; in all moments."

"I withdraw all my energy from pain; in all moments."

"I annihilate all concepts of pain; in all moments."

"I annihilate all memories of pain; in all moments."

"I annihilate all feelings of pain; in all moments."

"I annihilate all physical components of pain; in all moments."

"I convert all pain to a joyous expression of gratitude; in all moments."

"I collapse and dissolve all pain; in all moments."

"I release resonating with pain; in all moments."

"I release emanating with pain; in all moments."

"I extract all pain from my sound frequency; in all moments."

"I extract all pain from my light body; in all moments."

"I extract all pain from my whole beingness; in all moments."

"I shift my paradigm from pain to joy, love, abundance, freedom, health, success, security, companionship, creativity, peace, life, wholeness, beauty, enthusiasm, contentment, spirituality, enlightenment and confidence; in all moments."

"I transcend pain; in all moments."

"I am centered and empowered in the divinity of optimal health; in all moments."

"I resonate and emanate divinity of optimal health; in all moments."

Pain/God Association

In past lifetimes, God was associated with painful practices and suffering. Today, as more people become spiritually enlightened, their bodies are still carrying the belief that enlightenment comes through pain. So the more aware they are, the more pain they put themselves in. These taps address that core issue.

Please realize that God NEVER wanted or wants us to suffer. Pain is something that man has inflicted on the world, not God. Man in his arrogance thought he could be the mouthpiece of God. But if you think about it, God is not even God. God is a word that has been used to symbolize the formless, nameless love. Even uttering Its name is limiting Its sacred stretch to the mental realms. God exists beyond the mind. And so do you.

(Say each statement three times out loud while continuously tapping on the top of your head at the crown chakra and say it a fourth time while tapping on your chest.)

"I release the belief that I need to suffer to gain spiritual awareness; in all moments."

"I remove all vivaxes between God and pain; in all moments."

"I remove all vivaxes between myself and pain; in all moments."

"I release associating God with pain; in all moments."

"I release associating pain with God; in all moments."

"I remove all tentacles between God and pain; in all moments."

"I remove all engrams of me suffering to find God; in all moments."

"I send all energy matrices into the light and sound that confuse God and suffering; in all moments."

" I remove all programming and conditioning that tell me I need to suffer to find God; in all moments."

"I release the belief that God could ever reject me; in all moments."

"I release the belief that God could ever abandon me; in all moments."

"I release the belief that God could ever hate me; in all moments."

"I release the belief that God could ever want me to suffer; in all moments."

"I release the belief that God could ever withdraw love from me; in all moments."

"I remove all engrams of God rejecting, abandoning or hating me; in all moments." (It wasn't God. It was man.)

"I remove all engrams of God withdrawing love from me; in all moments."

"I remove all engrams of suffering for God; in all moments."

"I release the belief that I am separate from God; in all moments."

"I release feeling unworthy of God; in all moments."

"I release the belief that others are closer to God than myself; in all moments."

"I shift my paradigm from believing God is vengeful to knowing God as pure love and kindness; in all moments."

"I shift my paradigm from pain to love; in all moments."

"I release using pain to pay homage to God; in all moments."

"I extract all the pain from my beingness that I was using to pay homage to God; in all moments."

"I make space in this world to experience the ultimate resolve of God's Love; in all moments."

"I remove all blockages to perpetually experiencing the source of love; in all moments."

"I stretch my capacity to experience and perpetuate the source of love; in all moments."

"I declare myself a sacred conduit and channel for the source of love; in all moments."

Checklist to Address Pain Issues

So many are in chronic pain. Here is a checklist to help you uncover the tipping point for yourself. The environment has gotten so toxic that it is not enough to just show up. For so many, this list is their lifeline to a pain free life.

- Do you do soaks in Epsom salt and hydrogen peroxide?
- Do you take MSM?
- Do you only wear breathable clothes?
- Have you taken all perfumes out of your diet?
- Have you removed white sugar and gluten from your diet?
- Are you using magnets, crystals and kelp to ground your energy?
- Have you removed all toxic people from your life?
- Do you use hypoallergenic products?
- Do you turn off the news?
- Have you taken all nitrates and preservatives out of your diet?
- Do you spend time during the day doing something just for you?
- Do you spend time in nature?
- Do you have any hobbies or things you enjoy doing?
- Do you have things that bring you joy?
- Do you nurture yourself?
- Does anyone else nurture you?
- Do you listen to or sing uplifting music?
- Do you open your energy system often by being grateful?
- Did you eliminate all negative words and thoughts from your thoughts and speech?
- Do you forgo talking about issues as if you own them or they define you?
- Do you forgo seeking negative attention or taking on the role of a victim?

Not doing any one of these can create physical pain.

Relief for Panic Attacks

(Say each statement three times out loud while continuously tapping on the top of your head at the crown chakra and say it a fourth time while tapping on your chest.)

"I release allowing memories to overtake the moment; in all moments."

"I release being shoved out of the moment; in all moments."

"I release allowing the parasympathetic system to bully the sympathetic nervous system; in all moments."

"I release diminishing the sympathetic nervous system's effectiveness; in all moments."

"I release being a control freak; in all moments."

"I release valuing the sympathetic nervous over the parasympathetic nervous system; in all moments."

"I release putting the sympathetic nervous system in charge; in all moments."

"I release allowing the sympathetic nervous system to create drama; in all moments."

"I release being paralyzed by the past; in all moments."

"I release allowing the parasympathetic nervous system to railroad the body; in all moments."

"I remove all engrams that the sympathetic nervous system uses to railroad the body; in all moments."

"I repair and fortify the Wei chi of my parasympathetic nervous system; in all moments."

"I repair and fortify the Wei chi of my sympathetic nervous system; in all moments."

"I balance the dance of symmetry between the parasympathetic and sympathetic nervous system; in all moments."

"I repair and fortify the Wei chi of the dance of symmetry between the sympathetic and parasympathetic nervous system; in all moments."

"I am centered and empowered in a balanced symmetry between the sympathetic and parasympathetic nervous system; in all moments."

Living Your Purpose

(Say each statement three times out loud while continuously tapping on the top of your head at the crown chakra and say it a fourth time while tapping on your chest.)

"I release subscribing to ignorance; in all moments."

"I release being deceived by ignorance; in all moments."

"I release being duped by ignorance; in all moments."

"I release being blind to ignorance; in all moments."

"I release being immersed in ignorance; in all moments."

"I withdraw all my energy and support from ignorance; in all moments."

"I release being a conduit for ignorance; in all moments."

"I remove all the pain, burden, apathy and limitations that ignorance has put on me; in all moments."

"I remove all the pain, burden, apathy and limitations I have put on all others as a conduit for ignorance; in all moments."

"I take back all the joy, love, abundance, freedom, success, health, life wholeness and enlightenment that ignorance has taken from me; in all moments."

"I give back all the joy, love, abundance, freedom, success, health, life wholeness and enlightenment that I have taken from all others as a conduit for ignorance; in all moments."

"I shift my paradigm from ignorance to enlightenment; in all moments."

"I make space in this world to share my gifts and to live my highest purpose; in all moments."

"I remove all obstacles to sharing my gifts and living my highest purpose; in all moments."

"I stretch my capacity and hone my capabilities to share my gifts and live my highest purpose; in all moments."

"I am centered and abundant in sharing my gifts and living my highest purpose; in all moments."

"I release the fear of living my purpose; in all moments."

"I release allowing outer circumstances interfere with me living my purpose; in all moments."

"I release being overwhelmed by the thought of living my purpose; in all moments."

"I release defining living my purpose with massive responsibility; in all moments."

"I release defining living my purpose as a burden; in all moments."

"I release allowing unworthiness to sabotage living my purpose; in all moments."

"I release all the confusion in figuring out what my purpose is; in all moments."

"I release allowing someone else to tell me what my purpose is; in all moments."

"I release losing touch with my purpose; in all moments."

"I make space in this world to live my purpose; in all moments."

"I remove all blockages to living my purpose; in all moments."

"I connect wholeheartedly in living my purpose; in all moments."

"I stretch my capacity to live my purpose; in all moments."

"I release any fear, doubt and hesitancy in living my purpose; in all moments."

"I now recognize how to live my purpose; in all moments."

"I am centered and empowered in living my purpose; in all moments."

"I resonate and emanate with living my purpose; in all moments."

Manifesting Your Higher Purpose

(Say each statement three times while tapping on your head and say it a fourth time while tapping on your chest.)

"I connect to my universal energy; in all moments."

"I saturate my microcosm with my universal energy; in all moments."

"I release all fear of expressing my universal energy; in all moments."

"I make space in this world to express my universal energy; in all moments."

"I remove all blockages to expressing my universal energy; in all moments."

"I stretch my capacity to express my universal energy; in all moments."

"I release the fear of living my purpose; in all moments."

"I release doubting my purpose; in all moments."

"I release receding into my microcosm; in all moments."

"I release allowing others to deter me from my purpose; in all moments.

"I am centered, empowered and imbued in my universal energy; in all moments."

Past Lovers

(Say each statement three times out loud while tapping on the top of your head at the crown chakra and say it a fourth time while tapping on your chest at the heart chakra.)

"I release being a manipulative bitch; in all moments."

"I release the fear and trauma of being abandoned; in all moments."

"I release the trauma of being betrayed; in all moments."

"I release betraying my love; in all moments."

"I recant all vows and agreements between myself and all past lovers; in all moments."

"I remove all curses between myself and all past lovers; in all moments."

"I sever all strings and cords between myself and all past lovers; in all moments."

"I dissolve all karmic ties between myself and all past lovers; in all moments."

"I remove all the pain, burden, limitations, engrams and anger that I have put on all past lovers; in all moments."

"I remove all the pain, burden, limitations, engrams and anger that I have put on all past lovers; in all moments."

"I take back all the joy, love, abundance, freedom, health, success, security, companionship, creativity, peace, life, wholeness, beauty, enthusiasm, contentment, spirituality, enlightenment, and confidence that all past lovers have taken from me; in all moments."

"I give back all the joy, love, abundance, freedom, health, success, security, companionship, creativity, peace, life, wholeness, beauty, enthusiasm, contentment, spirituality, enlightenment, and confidence that I have taken from all past lovers; in all moments."

"I withdraw all my energy from all past lovers; in all moments."

"I release resonating with all past lovers; in all moments."

"I release emanating with all past lovers; in all moments."

"I remove all past lovers from my sound frequency; in all moments."

"I remove all past lovers from my light body; in all moments."

"I repair and fortify the Wei chi of all my bodies; in all moments."

"I repair and fortify the Wei chi that I may have damaged of all past lovers; in all moments."

"I my paradigm from all past lovers to joy, love, abundance, freedom, health, success, security, companionship, creativity, peace, life, wholeness beauty, enthusiasm, contentment, spirituality, enlightenment and confidence; in all moments."

"I transcend all past lovers; in all moments."

"I am centered and empowered in divine love; in all moments."

Stop Living in the Past

(Say each statement three times while tapping on your head and then say it a fourth time while tapping on your chest.)

"I release being enslaved to the past; in all moments."

"I release dipping in the past; in all moments."

"I release pulling the past into the moment; in all moments."

"I release weaving the past into the moment; in all moments."

"I remove all vivaxes between myself and the past; in all moments."

"I remove all vivaxes between the past and the moment; in all moments."

"I remove the claws of the past from the moment; in all moments."

"I remove all tentacles between the past and the moment; in all moments."

"I remove all programming and conditioning that the past has put on the moment; in all moments."

"I remove all engrams of the past from the moment; in all moments."

"I remove the physical onslaught of the past from the moment; in all moments."

"I remove the emotional onslaught of the past from the moment; in all moments."

"I remove the hiccup of past experiences on the moment; in all moments."

"I remove the echo of past experiences from the moment; in all moments."

"I remove the mental onslaught of the past from the moment; in all moments."

"I release allowing the past to disturb the calm of the moment; in all moments."

"I release allowing the past to disturb the joy, love and abundance of the moment; in all moments."

"I release allowing the past to disturb the freedom, health or success of the moment; in all moments."

"I release allowing the past to disturb the peace, life or wholeness of the moment; in all moments."

"I release allowing the past to disturb the beauty, enthusiasm or contentment of the moment; in all moments."

"I release allowing the past to disturb the spirituality, enlightenment or confidence of the moment; in all moments."

"I release allowing the past to disturb the interconnectedness, empowerment or ability to discern of the moment; in all moments."

"I strip all illusion off of the past; in all moments."

"I remove all masks walls and armor of the past from the moment; in all moments."

"I dissolve in the light and sound all energy matrices of the past; in all moments."

"I command all complex energy matrices of the past that inflict themselves on the moment to be dissolved in the light and sound; in all moments."

"I release being pulled out of the moment by the past; in all moments."

"I release being led around by the past; in all moments."

"I nullify all contracts between the moment and the past; in all moments."

"I recant all vows and agreements between the moment and the past; in all moments."

"I remove all curses between the moment and the past; in all moments."

"I remove all blessings between the moment and the past; in all moments."

"I sever all strings, cords and wires between the moment and the past; in all moments."

"I dissolve all karmic ties between the moment and the past; in all moments."

"I withdraw all the energy of the moment from the past; in all moments."

"I remove all the pain, burden and limitations that the past has inflicted on the moment; in all moments."

"I remove all the fear, futility, and unworthiness that the past has inflicted on the moment; in all moments."

"I remove all the primal urges and archaic structures that the past has inflicted on the moment; in all moments."

"I remove all the beliefs, rituals and illusion of separateness that the past has inflicted on the moment; in all moments."

"I shatter all glass ceilings of the past from the moment; in all moments."

"I collapse and dissolve the past; in all moments."

"I release the moment resonating with the past; in all moments."

"I release the moment emanating with the past; in all moments."

"I extract all of the past from the moment; in all moments."

"I extract all of the past from the moment's sound frequency; in all moments."

"I extract all of the past from the moment's light emanation; in all moments."

"I shift the paradigm of the moment to totally in the moment; in all moments."

"The moment transcends the past; in all moments."

"I am centered, empowered and imbued totally in the moment; in all moments."

"I resonate, emanate and am interconnected with all life exponentially and perpetually in the moment; in all moments."

Release Carrying Past Life Traumas (Weakness)

(Say each statement three times out loud while continuously tapping on the top of your head at the crown chakra and say it a fourth time while tapping on your chest at the heart chakra. Say each word deliberately. They are not just words but a vibration that you are initiating to shift energy. Pause after each word. Say it in a commanding but even tone, not as a question. Forgo saying it in a singsong tone or with bravado. Say them all.)

"I release the trauma of being bashed in the head; in all moments."

"I release the trauma of losing my tail; in all moments."

"I release mourning my tail; in all moments."

"I release mourning my home planet; in all moments."

"I release the belief that I was forsaken; in all moments."

"I release trying too hard; in all moments."

"I release the trauma of being dissected; in all moments."

"I release the belief that God has abandoned me; in all moments."

"I release waiting to be saved; in all moments."

"I release dissipating my energy; in all moments."

"I release giving my energy to a false God; in all moments."

"I release the trauma of having my wings clipped; in all moments."

"I release the trauma of having my wings cut off; in all moments."

"I release the trauma of being stripped of my status; in all moments."

"I release the trauma of being born; in all moments."

"I release the trauma of being trapped in a human body; in all moments."

"I release the belief that I am being punished; in all moments."

"I remove all possible limitations in being in a human form; in all moments."

"I send all energy matrices into the light that trap me in the human form; in all moments."

"I send all energy matrices into the light that cause resistance to me; in all moments."

"I repair and fortify the Wei chi on all my bodies; in all moments."

"I release being bullied; in all moments."

"I release being inundated by a crazy person; in all moments."

"I release attracting crazy energy; in all moments."

"I release the fear of transcending; in all moments."

"I release the fear of losing everything; in all moments."

"I release the fear of losing my mind; in all moments."

"I release the fear of being separated from my consciousness; in all moments."

"I release the fear of facing myself; in all moments."

"I release being stubborn; in all moments."

"I release fighting truth; in all moments."

"I release being obtuse; in all moments."

"I release mourning my soul; in all moments."

"I release the belief that I am separate from my soul; in all moments."

"I release being attached to the illusion; in all moments."

"I remove all vivaxes between myself and the illusion; in all moments."

"I remove all tentacles between myself and the illusion; in all moments."

"I remove all programming and conditioning that the illusion has put on me; in all moments."

"I remove all engrams that the illusion has put on me; in all moments."

"I send all energy matrices into the light and sound that immerse me in illusion; in all moments."

"I send all energy matrices into the light and sound that have me believe the illusion; in all moments."

"I am centered and empowered in divine love; in all moments."

Remove the Stronghold of the Past

(Say each statement three times while tapping on your head and say it a fourth time while tapping on your chest.)

"We declare ourselves surrogates for humanity in doing these taps; in all moments."

"We release being fixated on the past; in all moments."

"We release trying to reinstate the past; in all moments."

"We pull up roots from the past; in all moments."

"We remove all vivaxes with the past; in all moments."

"We release being imbedded in the past; in all moments."

"We pluck ourselves out of the past; in all moments."

"We remove all tentacles between ourselves and the past; in all moments."

"We remove the claws of the past from our beingness; in all moments."

"We remove all programming and conditioning that the past has put on us; in all moments."

"We remove all engrams of the past; in all moments."

"We strip all illusion off the past; in all moments."

"We strip all illusion off of our attempts to reinstate the past; in all moments."

"We withdraw all our energy from the past; in all moments."

"We collapse and dissolve all portals to the past; in all moments."

"We eliminate the first cause in reinstating the past; in all moments."

"We send all energy matrices into the light that keep us connected to the past; in all moments."

"We send all energy matrices into the sound that keep us connected to the past; in all moments."

"We command all complex energy matrices that keep us connected to the past to be escorted into the light and sound; in all moments."

"We nullify all contracts with the past; in all moments."

"We recant all vows and agreements between ourselves and the past; in all moments."

"We remove all curses between ourselves and the past; in all moments."

"We remove all blessings between ourselves and the past; in all moments."

"We remove all shackles of the past; in all moments."

"We sever all strings and cords between ourselves and the past; in all moments."

"We dissolve all karmic ties between ourselves and the past; in all moments."

"We remove all the burden of the past; in all moments."

"We take back all that the past deprives us of; in all moments."

"We release resonating with the past; in all moments."

"We release emanating with the past; in all moments."

"We extract all of the past from the individual and universal sound frequencies; in all moments."

"We extract all of the past from the individual and universal light emanations; in all moments."

"We shift our paradigm from the past to the moment; in all moments."

"We transcend the past; in all moments."

"We are centered and empowered in the moment; in all moments."

"We resonate, emanate, and are interconnected with all life in the moment; in all moments."

Pets

(Say each statement three times while tapping on your head and say it a fourth time while tapping on your chest.)

"I declare myself a surrogate for (Pet's Name) in doing these taps; in all moments."

"I release that sadness of being separated from my litter; in all moments."

"I release missing my mother; in all moments."

"I release the trauma of being pulled away from my family with no understanding; in all moments."

"I release feeling like I was stolen from my family; in all moments."

"I release mourning my innocence; in all moments."

"I release the belief I was kidnapped; in all moments."

"I release being held hostage; in all moments."

"I release being ignored; in all moments."

"I release being confused; in all moments."

"I release being misunderstood; in all moments."

"I release my fear of humans; in all moments."

"I release my resentment; in all moments."

"I release the trauma of being yelled at; in all moments."

"I release the trauma of disappointing the people; in all moments."

"I release the trauma of being adopted; in all moments."

"I am assured that I am in my forever home; in all moments."

"I release the angst of a new environment; in all moments."

"I communicate clearly; in all moments."

"I open my heart to the love that is offered me; in all moments."

"I release my unwarranted mistrust; in all moments."

"I release dipping into primal mode; in all moments."

"I release the trauma of disappointing my humans; in all moments."

"I release the trauma of being potty trained; in all moments."

"I accept all members of my family; in all moments."

"I release barking out of fear; in all moments."

"I release biting at all costs; in all moments."

"I release the trauma of being forced to fight; in all moments."

"I release the trauma of being abandoned; in all moments."

"I release the trauma of being rejected; in all moments."

"I release the trauma of being laughed at or talked down to; in all moments."

"I release being treated like I don't matter; in all moments."

"I release being treated like I don't have feelings; in all moments."

"I release being humiliated; in all moments."

"I release the loneliness of being separated from my people; in all moments."

"I am reassured that my person will come home to me; in all moments."

"I am assured that I will get fed; in all moments."

"I am assured that I am loved; in all moments."

"I release all jealous or possessive behavior; in all moments."

"I release being overtaken by the issues happening in my human; in all moments."

"I release processing my human's issues within my own body; in all moments."

"I release processing care for my humans as personal disease; in all moments."

"I pass people's issues right out of my energy field; in all moments."

"I embrace the love of my people; in all moments."

"I release being aggressive in any way; in all moments."

"I release processing fear as aggression; in all moments."

"I release all primal fear; in all moments."

"I am secure and safe in my family and home; in all moments."

"I am centered and empowered in security and safety; in all moments."

"I resonate, emanate and am interconnected with my family in security and safety; in all moments."

Prepare Your Body for Surgery

(Say each statement three times while tapping on your head and say it a fourth time while tapping on your chest.)

"I release treating surgery like going to battle; in all moments."

"I release confusing the surgeon for the enemy; in all moments."

"I release betraying my body; in all moments."

"I nurture my body; in all moments."

"I release treating the procedure as if I'm going to battle; in all moments."

"I release confusing sympathy for love; in all moments."

"I release choosing sympathy over health; in all moments."

"I pour love into every cell of my beingness; in all moments."

"I release using dis-ease to connect to loved ones; in all moments."

"I release the genetic propensity to manifest dis-ease; in all moments."

"I release the belief that a disease is inevitable; in all moments."

Prisms of Power

(Say each statement three times out loud while tapping on your head and say it a fourth time while tapping on your chest.)

"We release being trapped in all prisms of power; in all moments."

"We release being diminished by all prisms of powers; in all moments."

"We release being rendered helpless by all prisms of power; in all moments."

"We release being enslaved by all prisms of power; in all moments."

"We release being manipulated by all prisms of power; in all moments."

"We recant all vows and agreements between ourselves and all prisms of power; in all moments."

"We remove all curses between ourselves and all prisms of power; in all moments."

"We dissolve all karmic ties between ourselves and all prisms of power; in all moments."

"We sever all cords and connections between ourselves and all prisms of power; in all moments."

"We withdraw all our energy from all prisms of power; in all moments."

"We shatter all prisms of power; in all moments."

"We free all souls that we have trapped in all prisms of power; in all moments."

"We remove all the fear, pain, burden, limitations, engrams, cords, ties and control devices that all prisms of power have put on us; in all moments."

"We remove all the fear, pain, burden, limitations, engrams, cords, ties and control devises that we have put on all others for all prisms of power; in all moments."

"We take back all the joy, love, abundance, freedom, health, success, security, companionship, creativity, peace, life, wholeness, beauty, enthusiasm, contentment, confidence, light, music, spirituality and enlightenment that all prisms of power have taken from us; in all moments."

"We give back all the joy, love, abundance, freedom, health, success, security, companionship, creativity, peace, life, wholeness, beauty, enthusiasm, contentment, confidence, light, music, spirituality and enlightenment that we have taken from all others for all prisms of power; in all moments."

"We release resonating with all prisms of power; in all moments."

"We release emanating with all prisms of power; in all moments."

"We remove all prisms of power from our sound frequency; in all moments."

"We remove all prisms of power from our light body; in all moments."

"We shift our paradigm from all prisms of power to joy, love, abundance, freedom, health, success, security, companionship, creativity, peace, life, wholeness, beauty, enthusiasm, contentment, confidence, light, music, spirituality and enlightenment; in all moments."

"We transcend all prisms of power; in all moments."

"We collapse and dissolve all prisms of power; in all moments."

."We repair and fortify our Wei chi; in all moments."

"We are centered imbued and empowered in divine light, love and music; in all moments."

Stop Procrastinating

(Say each statement three times out loud while continuously tapping on the top of your head at the crown chakra and say it a fourth time while tapping on your chest.)

"I release procrastinating; in all moments."

"I release the inertia of procrastinating; in all moments."

"I release being paralyzed in a stagnant stance of indifference; in all moments."

"I release choosing indifference over my own growth; in all moments."

"I release the fear of moving forward; in all moments."

"I release resisting action; in all moments."

"I release interpreting action as looming towards my own death; in all moments."

"I release the fear of making the wrong choice; in all moments."

"I release being enslaved to inaction; in all moments."

"I release choosing inaction over growth; in all moments."

"I remove all vivaxes between myself and inaction; in all moments."

"I remove all tentacles between myself and inaction; in all moments."

"I remove all engrams that paralyze me in inaction; in all moments."

"I send all energy matrices into the light that paralyze me in inaction; in all moments."

"I send all energy matrices into the light that cause me indifference; in all moments."

"I shift my paradigm from inaction to perpetual positive growth; in all moments."

"I am centered and empowered in perpetual positive growth; in all moments."

Unfinished Projects

The pattern of sabotaging one's success and not finishing what is started may indicate that you are reliving old trauma. In private sessions, it comes up once in a while that someone died when they were really enthralled with their life. In this lifetime, it shows up by not following through on accomplishments. It is heart wrenching to be so involved in living and then to die too soon. That is why people seem so helpless when they don't finish projects.

Here are taps to help: (Say each statement three times while tapping on your head, and say it a fourth time while tapping on your chest.)

"I release the trauma of premature death; in all moments."

"I release killing my own cycles of success; in all moments."

"I shift my paradigm from interruption to completion; in all moments."

Psoriasis

(Say each statement three times while tapping on your head and a fourth time while tapping on your chest.)

"I release being burned alive; in all moments."

"I release feeling unsafe; in all moments."

"I release the feeling of being unsafe from my skin; in all moments."

"I infuse security into all of the layers of my skin; in all moments."

"I replenish my skin's ceramides; in all moments."

"I replenish my skin's emollients; in all moments."

"I refurbish all my layers of skin; in all moments."

"I remove all trauma from the muscle memory of my skin; in all moments."

"I release the trauma of being a leper; in all moments."

"I release drying up in the sun; in all moments."

"I remove all engrams of drying up in the sun; in all moments."

"I return my skin to the vibrancy and resonance of a child's skin; in all moments."

"I replenish all my skin's needs; in all moments."

Psychic Control

(Say each statement three times while tapping on your head and say it a fourth time while tapping on your chest.)

"I declare myself a surrogate for humanity in doing these taps; in all moments."

"We dissipate the psychic energy of control and ignorance that happens from watching television; in all moments."

"We dissipate the psychic energy of control and ignorance that happens from following politics; in all moments."

"We dissipate the psychic energy of control and ignorance that happens from watching movies; in all moments."

"We dissipate the psychic energy of control and ignorance that happens from playing videos; in all moments."

"We dissipate the psychic energy of control and ignorance that happens from personality worship; in all moments."

"We dissipate the psychic energy of control and ignorance that happens from group sports; in all moments."

"We dissipate the psychic energy of control and ignorance that happens from owning a gun; in all moments."

"We dissipate the psychic energy of control and ignorance that happens from tribalism; in all moments."

"We dissipate the psychic energy of control and ignorance that happens from watching television; in all moments."

"We dissipate the psychic energy of control and ignorance that happens from ascribing to western medicine; in all moments."

"We dissipate the psychic energy of control and ignorance that happens from using social media; in all moments."

"We dissipate the psychic energy of control and ignorance that happens from social group affiliation; in all moments."

"We dissipate the psychic energy of control and ignorance that happens from being a member of society; in all moments."

"We dissipate the psychic energy of control and ignorance that happens from ascribing to any particular secular belief; in all moments."

"We dissipate the psychic energy of control and ignorance that happens that is fueled by need; in all moments."

"We dissipate the psychic energy of control and ignorance that happens that is administered by power mongers; in all moments."

Psychic Energy

My cousin came to visit me. He is so passionate about self-discovery and his spirituality. I have seen this in many younger people. They have the vigor, passion and health to discover their greater self and are distracted on all sides by these traps to prevent them from discovering their empowerment. He is doing amazing. He and others like him who fall through the cracks of the conditioning are the hope of humanity.

Generation after generation, young adults are awakening to their inner quest of self-realization yet are distracted on all fronts. Here are some taps to dissipate the psychic energy of the traps they fall into. Do these as a surrogate for all the seekers of something greater out there. Awaken that inner passion in yourself that you may have felt was lost along the way.

(Say each statement three times while tapping on your head and say it a fourth time while tapping on your chest.)

"We dissipate the psychic streams of energy caused and created by video games; in all moments."

"We dissipate the psychic streams of energy of passion for war; in all moments."

"We dissipate the psychic streams of energy infused in all genres of music; in all moments."

"We dissipate the psychic streams of energy of unnatural sexual stimulation; in all moments."

"We dissipate the psychic streams of energy of puritanical beliefs and judgment; in all moments."

"We dissipate the psychic streams of energy of selfish taking; in all moments."

"We dissipate the psychic streams of energy of unconscious living; in all moments."

"We dissipate the psychic streams of energy that drive cruelty; in all moments."

"We dissipate the psychic streams of energy of peer pressure; in all moments."

Psychic Policing

Morality is an inside job. The only one who can dictate integrity is our own moral compass. It is a connection with our own truth. Everything I write and share is dictated to me in energy and I transcribe it into words. I have become very proficient at listening to my Guides. It has kept me alive and has served me well. My Guides are my friends and equals. I do not sit at their feet.

All my posts are designed to free individuals from the grips of mass control. I have been writing and sharing for the last eight years daily techniques, poems, insights, taps, inspirational quotes and observations. It is all about gifting the world with higher awareness. I am a very gifted healer as well. Truth and love resonate at similar frequencies. So if there is more truth in the world, there is more love as well.

Many people have told me to stop sharing so much because it ruins my business. It meets people's needs without them needing a session with me. Good. I have watched the freedom and awareness that is blooming in the world and I sincerely know that I have initiated that with my work. I did not come here merely to provide food for my table. I have come here to empower all individuals to make space in this world for Universal peace.

(Say each statement three times while tapping on your head and say it a fourth time while tapping on your chest.)

"I declare myself a surrogate for humanity in doing these taps; in all moments."

"I dismantle the practice of psychic policing; in all moments."

"I release being a contributor of psychic policing; in all moments."

"I withdraw all my energy from psychic policing; in all moments."

"I strip all layers of illusion and authority away from all psychic policing; in all moments."

"I disarm all agents of psychic policing; in all moments."

"I collapse and dissolve all limitations or walls maintained by psychic policing; in all moments."

"I nullify all contracts with psychic policing; in all moments."

"I shift my paradigm from psychic policing to spiritual freedom; in all moments."

"I transcend psychic policing; in all moments."

Psychic Streams of Energy

Psychic energy can be the collective byproduct of individuals or it can be an intentional balm to induce onto people as a form of control. It is done through inducing fear into beings and then "collecting" the energetic byproduct of that fear to hold others in that same state.

Most people these days are not thinking for themselves. They are held in a group consensus by different psychic streams of energy. The psychic streams drive individuals similarly to how cattle are driven in a cattle drive. Thoughts that are considered absolutes are then used to pen these people in.

With many people, the great motivations of their fears are God and country. These psychic promptings have been working for so long to keep people motivated in fear. Another one that has become an old favorite is demonizing someone to the point of seeing them as the enemy. We have a great example of this in the Salem Witch Trials.

The psychic fear of being attacked is being used a lot by a present political party to see everyone who is not like themselves, even in the most abstract beliefs, as the enemy. The scary thing about this one is that the enemy is everyone who deviates from a particular agenda. The reason it is so effective is because it galvanizes the base group that is creating the psychic energy streams.

Since the normal process of evolving is to become individualized, the groups that are more susceptible to influence are being worked into a frenzy to harness their abilities to emit fear and add their energy to these psychic streams. That is why it is important to NOT banter with these people and counter them at their level. Their degree of fear is enhanced because of their susceptibility to it.

People who are more aware are not capable of emitting the same level of fear. They just aren't. They have already experienced the trials that would bring them to such fear. There is nothing left in them to induce it to the same level.

These psychic streams of energy are collected, using the grainy energy of fear, into clouds. Anything you do will be a means of extracting more fear out of them. So that is why it is not effective to address them at their level. This is actually what the power mongers do.

The way to dissipate these psychic streams is to withdraw your energy from them and to not engage others into a "them versus us mode" so they cannot be induced to fear. Some very aware or intelligent people still don't understand this concept. But think of it this way: When you are dealing with a poisonous snake, you learn not to provoke it. You maintain calm energy so it is not induced into reacting and striking out. You wait until it slithers away on its own or it is calm enough to engage.

(Say this statement three times while tapping on your head and say it a fourth time while tapping on your chest.)

"I dissipate the psychic streams of energy that hold humanity in fear; in all moments."

"I dissipate the psychic streams of energy that hold humanity in 'them versus us' mode; in all moments."

"I dissipate the psychic streams of energy that threaten hell; in all moments."

"I dissipate the psychic streams of energy that cause addiction; in all moments."

"I dissipate the psychic streams of energy that cause debauchery; in all moments."

"I dissipate the psychic streams of energy that crave war; in all moments."

"I dissipate the psychic streams of energy that crave power; in all moments."

"I dissipate the psychic streams of energy that worship perfection and beauty; in all moments."

"I dissipate the psychic streams of energy that worship power; in all moments."

"I dissipate the psychic streams of energy that worship monetary wealth; in all moments."

"I dissipate the psychic streams of energy that hold our attention with electronics; in all moments."

"I dissipate the psychic streams of energy that shackle us in need; in all moments."

"I dissipate the psychic streams of energy that create enemies out of differences; in all moments."

"I dissipate the psychic streams of energy that hold people trapped in a sect, religion or belief; in all moments."

"I dissipate the psychic streams of energy that hold anyone above others; in all moments."

"I dissipate the psychic streams of energy that cause cruelty or neglect; in all moments."

"I dissipate the psychic streams of energy that enjoy debating; in all moments."

"I dissipate the psychic streams of energy that rape the land; in all moments."

"I dissipate the psychic streams of energy that blind people to their passion and truth; in all moments."

"I dissipate the psychic streams of energy that prevent individuals from wakening; in all moments."

"I dissipate the psychic streams of energy that create schisms in the ability to love and show kindness; in all moments."

"I dissipate the psychic streams of energy that bind us to a man made God; in all moments."

"I dissipate the psychic streams of energy that separate us from truth and love; in all moments."

"I dissipate the psychic streams of energy that dampen creativity; in all moments."

"I dissipate the psychic streams of energy that put glass ceilings on us; in all moments."

"I evaporate all psychic streams of energy of rhetoric; in all moments."

"I evaporate all psychic streams of energy of all dictators; in all moments."

"I evaporate all psychic streams of energy of all governments; in all moments."

"I evaporate all psychic streams of energy of all religions; in all moments."

"I evaporate all psychic streams of energy of self righteousness; in all moments."

"I evaporate all psychic streams of energy of monetary worship; in all moments."

"I evaporate all psychic streams of energy of superiority; in all moments."

"I evaporate all psychic streams of energy of mental mazes; in all moments."

"I evaporate all psychic streams of energy of war; in all moments."

"I evaporate all psychic streams of energy that induce hatred; in all moments."

"I evaporate all psychic streams of energy that induce violence; in all moments."

"I evaporate all psychic streams of energy of patriotism; in all moments."

"I evaporate all psychic streams of energy of dysfunction; in all moments."

"I evaporate all psychic streams of energy of caste systems; in all moments."

"I evaporate all psychic streams of energy of blind faith; in all moments."

"I evaporate all psychic streams of energy of 'them versus us mode'; in all moments."

"I evaporate all psychic streams of energy of male domination; in all moments."

"I evaporate all psychic streams of energy of victimhood; in all moments."

"I evaporate all psychic streams of energy of revenge; in all moments."

"I evaporate all psychic streams of energy of poverty; in all moments."

"I evaporate all psychic streams of energy set up by all hierarchies; in all moments."

"I evaporate all psychic streams of unworthiness; in all moments."

"I evaporate all psychic streams of energy of slavery; in all moments."

"I evaporate all psychic streams of energy of servitude; in all moments."

"I evaporate all psychic streams of energy of ignorance; in all moments."

"I evaporate all psychic streams of energy of sexual deviance; in all moments."

"I evaporate all psychic streams of energy of poverty; in all moments."

"I evaporate all psychic streams of energy of demonizing truth; in all moments."

"I evaporate all psychic streams of energy of reactionary mode; in all moments."

"I evaporate all psychic streams of energy of power; in all moments."

"I evaporate all psychic streams of energy of greed; in all moments."

"I evaporate all psychic streams of energy created by electronics; in all moments."

"I evaporate all psychic streams of energy of mass media; in all moments."

"I evaporate all psychic streams of energy of despair; in all moments."

"I evaporate all psychic streams of energy of hopelessness; in all moments."

"I evaporate all psychic streams of energy of need; in all moments."

"I evaporate all psychic streams of energy of want; in all moments."

"I evaporate all psychic streams of energy of addiction; in all moments."

"I evaporate all psychic streams of energy of suicide; in all moments."

"I evaporate all psychic streams of energy of big business; in all moments."

"I evaporate all psychic streams of energy of selfishness; in all moments."

"I evaporate all psychic streams of energy of illusion; in all moments."

"I evaporate all psychic streams of energy of primal mode; in all moments."

"I evaporate all psychic streams of energy that hold humanity hostage; in all moments."

Know that your very thought that this post and these taps are too long is part of a psychic stream that you are immersed in. If you were not, you would merely be grateful for such information and such opportunity. Allow your own reaction to this post be your gauge to how much it is needed. These taps have been making a difference in the world.

Psychic Streams of Energy, II

Because these energies are so low on the frequency scale, love and truth--real love and truth--sear through them like sunshine dries up the morning mist. It is only an illusion that they are powerful. It is a trick of manipulated light shining back in the eyes of the truth seer.

(Say each statement three times while tapping on your head and say it a fourth time while tapping on your chest.)

"All psychic streams of hate are exhausted; in all moments."

"All psychic streams of war are exhausted; in all moments."

"All psychic streams of fear are exhausted; in all moments."

"All psychic streams of division are exhausted; in all moments."

"All psychic streams of sensationalizing trauma are exhausted; in all moments."

"All psychic streams of power mongering and control are exhausted; in all moments."

"All psychic streams of rhetoric are exhausted; in all moments."

"All psychic streams of ignorance are exhausted; in all moments."

"All psychic streams of linear imprisonment are exhausted; in all moments."

"All psychic streams of superiority are exhausted; in all moments."

"All psychic streams of manipulation are exhausted; in all moments."

"All psychic streams of disease are exhausted; in all moments."

"All psychic streams of addiction are exhausted; in all moments."

"All psychic streams of entitlement are exhausted; in all moments."

"All psychic streams of bigotry are exhausted; in all moments."

"All psychic streams of class shaming are exhausted; in all moments."

Stop Being Manipulated or Coerced

(Say each statement three times out loud while continuously tapping on the top of your head at the crown chakra and say it a fourth time while tapping on your chest.)

"I release being manipulated and coerced into disease; in all moments."

"I release being manipulated and coerced into problems; in all moments."

"I release being manipulated and coerced into gossip; in all moments."

"I release being manipulated and coerced into apathy; in all moments."

"I release being manipulated and coerced into depression; in all moments."

"I release being manipulated and coerced into overcompensation; in all moments."

"I release being manipulated and coerced into poverty; in all moments."

"I release being manipulated and coerced into weakness; in all moments."

"I release being manipulated and coerced into helplessness; in all moments."

"I release being manipulated and coerced into anger; in all moments."

"I release being manipulated and coerced into greed; in all moments."

"I release being manipulated and coerced into attachment; in all moments."

"I release being manipulated and coerced into vanity; in all moments."

"I release being manipulated and coerced into lust; in all moments."

"I release being manipulated and coerced into sloth; in all moments."

"I release being manipulated and coerced into self pity; in all moments."

"I release being manipulated and coerced into martyrdom; in all moments."

"I release being manipulated and coerced into servitude; in all moments."

"I release being manipulated and coerced into arrogance; in all moments."

"I release being manipulated and coerced into manipulation; in all moments."

"I release being manipulated and coerced into indifference; in all moments."

"I release being manipulated and coerced into cruelty; in all moments."

"I shift my paradigm from being manipulated and coerced to being empowered and free; in all moments."

"I am centered in freedom and empowerment; in all moments."

"I am satiated in freedom and empowerment; in all moments."

"I resonate and emanate freedom and empowerment; in all moments."

PTSD

There are predominantly two types of people: Those who have had enough conflict in their lives and those who still crave it. Those who have had enough spend their time avoiding creating more conflict by avoiding others. Those who crave conflict spend their lives drawing others in to create more conflict.

Those who have had enough conflict have been to battle many lifetimes. They have no desire left to conquer anything. They don't exude righteous anger. They recognize the futility of debate and seeing the enemy everywhere. They may see both sides of an issue, but they keep it to themselves so as not to cause a reaction in others.

This is the dance that we do in society. Some of us want peace for all. Some want conflict so bad we create it. Some feel it is imperative to expose the enemy at whatever cost. Some are not in such a rush to take a stance. No one is right, no one is wrong. It depends more on what experiences that have brought us all to the point at which we are.

Here are some taps to help:

(Say each statement three times while continuously tapping on your head. Say it a fourth time while tapping on your chest.)

"I release the trauma of war; in all moments."

"I release the trauma of killing others; in all moments."

"I release the trauma of losing innocence; in all moments."

"I release hating my enemies; in all moments."

"I release having enemies; in all moments."

"I release going to battle; in all moments."

"I release creating conflict; in all moments."

"I lay down my sword and shield; in all moments."

"I interrupt all mind loops; in all moments."

"I remove myself from hell; in all moments."

"I dry up hell; in all moments."

"I release carrying my brethren; in all moments."

"I heal all my brethren; in all moments."

"I release all the mental torment; in all moments."

"I release all the emotional torment; in all moments."

"I release all the physical torment; in all moments."

"I release all the causal torment; in all moments."

"I release dying out of habit; in all moments."

"I release being a pawn; in all moments."

"I release rejecting _____ (partner); in all moments."

"I release imploding on my family; in all moments."

"I am worthy; in all moments."

By the way, the reason so many families are in conflict is because they have been on separate sides of the battle in past lives. It may work wonders for families to do these taps together. They may help many teenagers as well. A teenager in this lifetime would be coming of age to go to battle in a past era. Perhaps some of them still have that urge to do battle. These taps may assist them in settling down.

Purifying Water

(Say each statement three times out loud while continuously tapping on the top of your head at the crown chakra and say it a fourth time while tapping on your chest.)

"I release pouring negativity and ingratitude into water; in all moments."

"I release taking water for granted; in all moments."

"I release desecrating the sacredness of water; in all moments."

"I release poisoning water; in all moments."

"I release killing the innocence of water; in all moments."

"I release stripping the goodness out of water; in all moments."

"I release violating spiritual law; in all moments."

"I release gutting water of its purity; in all moments."

"I release wasting water; in all moments."

"I release hoarding water; in all moments."

"I release violating the sacred trust of water; in all moments."

"I release pouring ignorance and waste into water; in all moments."

"I release violating a sacred trust with water and all of nature; in all moments."

"I release desecrating the sacredness of the earth by polluting the water; in all moments."

"I release condoning the systemic abuse of water; in all moments."

"I release hating myself and water; in all moments."

"I shift my paradigm to honor and appreciate the gift of water; in all moments."

"I purify all the waters of the world with my respect and gratitude; in all moments."

"I extract everything but divine love and purpose from water; in all moments."

"I infuse infinite and perpetual joy, love, abundance, freedom, life and wholeness into the sound frequency of the water of the word; in all moments."

"I imbue infinite and perpetual joy, love, abundance, freedom, life and wholeness into the light emanation of the water of the word; in all moments."

"I shift the paradigm of the water of the world into purity and the sanctity of gratitude and respect; in all moments."

"I am centered and empowered in infinite gratitude and respect for the water of the world; in all moments."

"The water of the world is centered and empowered in purity and the sanctity of its purpose; in all moments."

Raise Your Vibration

Here is a shortcut to attaining and holding the vibration of a desired intention.

(Say each statement three times while tapping on your head and say it a fourth time while tapping on your chest.)

"I remove unhappiness from my sound frequency; in all moments."

"I infuse Joy into my sound frequency; in all moments."

"I resonate with Joy; in all moments."

"I remove hate from my sound frequency; in all moments."

"I infuse Love into my sound frequency; in all moments."

"I resonate with Love; in all moments."

"I remove poverty from my sound frequency; in all moments."

"I infuse Abundance into my sound frequency; in all moments."

"I resonate with Abundance; in all moments."

"I remove enslavement from my sound frequency; in all moments."

"I infuse Freedom into my sound frequency; in all moments."

"I resonate with Freedom; in all moments."

"I remove disease from my sound frequency; in all moments."

"I infuse Health into my sound frequency; in all moments."

"I resonate with Health; in all moments."

"I remove failure from my sound frequency; in all moments."

"I infuse Success into my sound frequency; in all moments."

"I resonate with Success; in all moments."

"I remove isolation from my sound frequency; in all moments."

"I infuse Companionship into my sound frequency; in all moments."

"I resonate with Companionship; in all moments."

"I remove conflict from my sound frequency; in all moments."

"I infuse Peace into my sound frequency; in all moments."

"I resonate with Peace; in all moments."

"I remove death/depression from my sound frequency; in all moments."

"I infuse Life into my sound frequency; in all moments."

"I resonate with Life; in all moments."

"I remove fragmentation from my sound frequency; in all moments."

"I infuse Wholeness into my sound frequency; in all moments."

"I resonate with Wholeness; in all moments."

Rape

(Say each statement three times while tapping on the top of your head. Say it a fourth time while tapping on your chest.)

"I release the trauma of being raped; in all moments."

"I release blaming myself for being raped; in all moments."

"I release the guilt and shame of being raped; in all moments."

"I release the fear of being raped; in all moments."

"I release the belief that I deserved to be raped; in all moments."

"I release the belief I caused the rape; in all moments."

"I release quantifying rape; in all moments."

"I release confusing rape for intimacy; in all moments."

"I release allowing intimacy to be shrouded by the rape; in all moments."

"I release being defined by the rape; in all moments."

"I release mourning my innocence; in all moments."

"I release the belief that I am sullied; in all moments."

"I release the fear of intimacy; in all moments."

"I release the belief that I am unlovable; in all moments."

"I release the belief that I am unworthy of love; in all moments."

"I erase the rape from my energy field; in all moments."

"I remove the rape cookies from my hard drive; in all moments."

"I reboot my system to love; in all moments."

"I install intimacy software into my system; in all moments."

"I make space in this world for a loving, intimate relationship; in all moments."

"I remove all blockages to having a loving, intimate relationship; in all moments."

"I release sabotaging my love life; in all moments.

"I stretch my capacity to have a loving, intimate relationship; in all moments."

"I am centered in joy, love abundance, freedom and intimacy; in all moments."

Raynaud's Disease

(Say each statement three times while tapping on your head and say it a fourth time while tapping on your chest.)

"I release the trauma of freezing to death; in all moments."

"I release reliving freezing to death; in all moments."

"I release reacting to the cold; in all moments."

"I release reacting to the age that I died; in all moments."

"I release reacting to the way that I died; in all moments."

"I release an aversion to the cold; in all moments."

"I remove all engrams of freezing to death; in all moments."

"I release shutting down my faculties; in all moments."

"I release having hypothermia; in all moments."

"I remove all the trauma of dying from my present body; in all moments."

"I warm all my limbs; in all moments."

"I awaken the healing energy through all my limbs; in all moments."

"I am vibrant and alive; in all moments."

"I am grateful and healthy; in all moments."

Learn to Receive

Some people are great givers but they aren't very good at receiving. This robs others of the joy of giving. Here are some taps to assist with this issue: (Say each statement three times while tapping on your head and say it a fourth time while tapping on your chest.)

"I release the aversion to receiving; in all moments."

"I release being a martyr; in all moments."

"I release viewing gift giving as competition; in all moments."

"I release feeling unworthy to receive; in all moments."

"I release viewing gift exchange as manipulation; in all moments."

"I release denying the receiver; in all moments."

"I release interrupting the fluidity of exchange; in all moments."

"I release denying a gift to feel superior; in all moments."

"I accept the ebb and flow of receiving and giving; in all moments."

"I am centered in giving and receiving; in all moments."

Exonerate Yourself from All Regret

(Say this statement three times out loud while continuously tapping on the top of your head at the crown chakra and say it a fourth time while tapping on your chest)

"I release punishing myself with regret; in all moments."

"I release drowning myself in regret; in all moments."

"I release running scenarios of regret through my mind; in all moments."

"I release lamenting the past; in all moments."

"I release being gripped with regret; in all moments."

"I release the belief that I have failed; in all moments."

"I release tormenting myself over the choices I have made; in all moments."

"I release grieving missed opportunities; in all moments."

"I remove all engrams that elicit regret in me; in all moments."

"I release being paralyzed in regret; in all moments."

"I release being tethered to regret; in all moments."

"I remove all vivaxes between myself and regret; in all moments."

"I remove all tentacles between myself and regret; in all moments."

"I remove the claws of regret from my beingness; in all moments."

"I send all energy matrices into the light that cause me any regret; in all moments."

"I release confusing regret with moral integrity; in all moments."

"I recant all vows and agreements between myself and regret; in all moments."

"I release using regret to admonish myself; in all moments."

"I release cursing myself with regret; in all moments."

"I remove all curse and blessings between myself and regret; in all moments."

"I sever all strings and cords between myself and regret; in all moments."

"I dissolve all karmic ties between myself and regret; in all moments."

"I withdraw all my energy from regret; in all moments."

"I extract all regret from all the layers of my auric field; in all moments."

"I remove all the pain, burden, limitations, illusion of failure and separateness regret has put on me; in all moments."

"I take back from regret all that it has taken from me; in all moments."

"I release resonating and emanating with regret; in all moments."

"I extract all of regret from my sound frequency and light emanation; in all moments."

"I shift my paradigm from regret to acceptance of my spiritual journey; in all moments."

"I transcend all regret; in all moments."

"I am exonerated from all regret; in all moments."

"I am centered and empowered in acceptance of my spiritual journey; in all moments."

"I resonate and emanate spiritual acceptance; in all moments."

Reincarnating

Mastership is collecting all your energy from reincarnating and your experiences into the present moment.

This is how we transcend. It is not by magic. It is not through osmosis or being saved by a superhuman race. We must take the initiative. That is why we came here. To do the work. We are actually making it so much easier for others to transcend.

We eliminate the debilitating odds against humanity and allow individuals to make choices to uplift their energy instead of being stuck in the quicksand of apathy.

(Say each statement three times while tapping on your head and say it a third time while tapping on your chest.)

"I declare myself a surrogate for humanity in doing these taps; in all moments."

"I remove all vivaxes between myself and past lives; in all moments."

"I release being enslaved to past lives; in all moments."

"I sever all strings and cords between myself and all past lives; in all moments."

"I remove all tentacles between myself and all past lives; in all moments."

"I remove the claws of all past lives from my essence; in all moments."

"I remove the scars of reincarnating from my essence; in all moments."

"I free myself from reincarnating; in all moments."

"I remove the engrams of past lives from my essence; in all moments."

"I remove all programming and conditioning that past lives have put on me; in all moments."

"I deactivate all muscle memory of reincarnating; in all moments."

"I send all energy matrices into the light and sound that cause me to incarnate out of habit; in all moments."

"I command all complex energy matrices that cause me to incarnate out of habit to be escorted into the light and sound; in all moments."

"I send all energy matrices into the light and sound that keep me stuck in the cycle of reincarnating; in all moments."

"I command all complex energy matrices that keep me stuck in the cycle of reincarnating to be escorted into the light and sound; in all moments."

"I send all energy matrices into the light and sound that keep me stuck in energy loops; in all moments."

"I command all complex energy matrices that keep me stuck in energy loops to be escorted into the light and sound; in all moments."

"I send all energy matrices into the light and sound that prevent me from speaking truth; in all moments."

"I command all complex energy matrices that prevent me from speaking truth to be escorted into the light and sound; in all moments."

"I nullify all contracts with reincarnating; in all moments."

"I recant all vows and agreements between myself and reincarnating; in all moments."

"I remove all curses between myself and reincarnating; in all moments."

"I remove all blessings between myself and reincarnating; in all moments."

"I dissolve all karmic ties between myself and reincarnating; in all moments."

"I remove all the pain, burden and limitations that reincarnating has put on me; in all moments."

"I remove all the fear, futility, and unworthiness that reincarnating has put on me; in all moments."

"I remove all the apathy, indifference and illusion of separateness that reincarnating has put on me; in all moments."

"I remove all that I have put on all others due to reincarnating; in all moments."

"I remove all that I have put on others due to reincarnating; in all moments."

"I take back ALL that reincarnating has taken from me; in all moments."

"I give back ALL that I have taken from others due to reincarnating; in all moments."

"I release resonating with reincarnating; in all moments."

"I release emanating with reincarnating; in all moments."

"I extract reincarnating from my sound frequency; in all moments."

"I extract reincarnating from my light emanation; in all moments."

"I extract reincarnating from all 32 layers of my auric field; in all moments."

"I extract reincarnating from my whole essence; in all moments."

"I release the fear of being separated from my consciousness; in all moments."

"I shift my paradigm from reincarnating to exponential joy, love, abundance, and freedom; in all moments."

"I am centered and empowered in exponential joy, love, abundance, and freedom; in all moments."

"I transcend reincarnating; in all moments."

"I resonate, emanate, and am interconnected with all life in exponential joy, love, abundance, and freedom; in all moments."

Improve Your Relationships

(Put your partner, parent, child, or pet's name in all the spaces. Do all these for one subject at a time. Say each statement three times out loud while continuously tapping on the top of your head at the crown chakra and say it a fourth time while tapping on your chest at the heart chakra)

"I release being annoyed with _____ out of habit; in all moments."

"I release feeling dependent on _____; in all moments."

"I release feeling beholden to _____ ; in all moments."

"I release being enslaved to _____; in all moments."

"I recant all vows and agreements between myself and _____; in all moments."

"I remove all curses between myself and _____; in all moments."

"I sever all strings and cords between myself and _____; in all moments."

"I dissolve all karmic ties between myself and _____; in all moments."

"I remove all the pain, burden, limitations and engrams that _____ has put on me; in all moments."

"I remove all the pain, burden, limitations and engrams that I have put on _____; in all moments."

"I take back all the joy, love, abundance, freedom, health, success, security, companionship, creativity, peace, life, wholeness, beauty, enthusiasm, contentment, spirituality, enlightenment and confidence that _____ has taken from me; in all moments."

"I give back all that I have taken from _____; in all moments."

"I withdraw all my energy from arguing with _____; in all moments."

"I release resonating with arguing with _____; in all moments."

"I release emanating with arguing with_____; in all moments."

"I remove all of arguing with _____ from my sound frequency; in all moments."

"I remove all of arguing with_____ from my light body; in all moments."

"I shift my paradigm from arguing with _____ to joy, love, abundance, freedom, health, success, security, companionship, creativity, peace, life, wholeness, beauty, enthusiasm, contentment, spirituality, enlightenment and confidence; in all moments."

"I strip all illusion off of arguing with _____; in all moments."

"I transcend _____; in all moments."

"I repair and fortify the Wei chi on all my bodies; in all moments."

"I align all my bodies; in all moments."

"I am centered and empowered in divine love; in all moments."

"I make space in this world to truly understand _____; in all moments."

"I remove all blockages to truly understand _____; in all moments."

"I stretch my capacity to truly understand_____; in all moments."

"I stretch my capacity to embrace truly understanding _____; in all moments."

Your Relationship with God

Know that in doing these, you will never disconnect from the beautiful loving source of all of creation. This is to release all the bastardization of the sacred trust that has happened through the history of man speaking for God. Just like God is used in the present day to sway our political opinion, God has been used through history to manipulate the hearts and mind of man. That form of deception is what these taps are addressing.

(Say each statement three times out loud while continuously tapping on the top of your head at the crown chakra and say it a fourth time while tapping on your heart chakra.)

"I release the belief that God hates me; in all moments."

"I release the belief that I am damned; in all moments."

"I release the belief that God is punishing me; in all moments."

"I release the belief that I am a sinner; in all moments."

"I release the belief that I am forsaken; in all moments."

"I release feeling abandoned by God; in all moments."

"I release the trauma of being sacrificed to God; in all moments."

"I release confusing God for the will of the ruling power; in all moments."

"I release the guilt and confusion of killing in God's name; in all moments."

"I release diminishing others and justifying it as God's will; in all moments."

"I release defiling the sanctity of God with my interpretation; in all moments."

"I release desecrating God; in all moments."

"I release the belief that God is anything but love; in all moments."

"I release confusing God with power; in all moments."

"I release the belief that God has an ego; in all moments."

"I release cursing God; in all moments."

"I release the belief that God has cursed me; in all moments."

"I release confusing God with the interpretation of God; in all moments."

"I recant all vows and agreements between myself and God; in all moments."

"I remove all curses between myself and God; in all moments."

"I remove all blessings between myself and God; in all moments."

"I sever all strings and cords between myself and God; in all moments."

"I dissolve all karmic ties between myself and God; in all moments."

"I remove all the pain, burden, limitations and engrams that God has put on me; in all moments."

"I remove all the pain, burden limitations and engrams that I have put on all others due to God; in all moments."

"I take back all the joy, love, abundance, freedom, health, success, security, companionship, peace, life, wholeness, beauty, enthusiasm, contentment, spirituality, enlightenment, confidence and the ability to discern that God has taken from me; in all moments."

"I give back all the joy, love, abundance, freedom, health, success, security, companionship, peace, life, wholeness, beauty, enthusiasm, contentment, spirituality, enlightenment, confidence and the ability to discern that I have taken from all others due to God; in all moments."

"I infuse purity, reverence and love into my understanding of God; in all moments."

"I extract anything that is not sacred, pure love from my understanding of God; in all moments."

"I am centered and empowered in a loving God that is benevolent beyond reproach; in all moments."

"I Am that I Am; in all moments."

Relationship Worksheet

The biggest issue that people seem to lament about is getting over a relationship with another person. That is because when you are intimate with someone, you swap energy freely. But when you part, you have left an energetic aspect of yourself with them. You walk around talking about them because you are trying to get your essence back from them. Here is the protocol to do just that.

Now you never have to suffer at the hands of a past lover and be left un-whole. Now you don't have to be hesitant to give all of yourself to the next person because now you have the means to energetically regain your empowerment. In fact, because these taps include, "In all moments," you are safeguarded from being fragmented in the future as well.

This protocol is simply meant to put your fate back in your own hands where it should be. It is not merely words. Doing this protocol is you being the shaman; it is you being empowered. It is you taking back your energy and releasing the things that have been weighing you down. It is also repairing your energy field so that you are not susceptible in the future. It is you taking back your empowerment and freeing you to love as unabashedly as your truly desire without the fear of being annihilated in the process.

It may feel so freeing to do these taps for past partners that you may want to do them regarding every person in your life. You may want to untangle yourself from every family member, co-worker, boss and friend. You may even want to do this protocol with every organization or idea that has held you back. Here is to you freeing yourself in a very profound way. Maybe in releasing all entanglements, you can finally get an understanding of who you really are unhindered and free.

You can make it a practice to do this once a day with a different person. You can even do it with groups, subjects, concepts and anything else that limits your freedom.

(Say each statement three times out loud while continuously tapping on the top of your head at the crown chakra and say it a fourth time while tapping on your chest at the heart chakra.)

"I release being with _____ out of habit; in all moments."

"I release feeling dependent on _____; in all moments."

"I release feeling beholden to _____; in all moments."

"I release being enslaved to _____; in all moments."

"I remove all vivaxes between myself and _____; in all moments."

"I remove all tentacles between myself and _____; in all moments."

"I remove the claws of _____ from my beingness; in all moments."

"I remove all programming and conditioning that _____ has put on me; in all moments."

"I remove all engrams of _____ from my beingness; in all moments."

"I send all energy matrices into the light and sound that limit my freedom in regards to _____; in all moments."

"I command all complex energy matrices that limit my freedom in regards to _____; to be escorted into the light and sound by my Guides; in all moments."

"I strip all illusion off of my dynamics with _____; in all moments."

"I withdraw all my energy from _____; in all moments."

"I eliminate the first cause in regards to _____; in all moments."

"I remove all masks, walls and armor that I have worn because of _____; in all moments."

"I nullify all contracts with _____; in all moments."

"I recant all vows and agreements between myself and _____; in all moments."

"I remove all curses between myself and _____; in all moments."

"I sever all strings and cords between myself and _____; in all moments."

"I dissolve all karmic ties between myself and _____; in all moments."

"I remove all the pain, burden, limitations and engrams that _____ has put on me; in all moments."

"I remove all the pain, burden, limitations and engrams that I have put on _____; in all moments."

"I take back all the joy, love, abundance, freedom, health, success, security, companionship, creativity, peace, life, wholeness, beauty, enthusiasm, contentment, spirituality, enlightenment and confidence that _____ has taken from me; in all moments."

"I give back all that I have taken from _____; in all moments."

"I release resonating with _____; in all moments."

"I release emanating with _____; in all moments."

"I remove all of _____ from my sound frequency; in all moments."

"I remove all of _____ from my light body; in all moments."

"I shift my paradigm from _____ to joy, love, abundance, freedom, health, success, security, companionship, creativity, peace, life, wholeness, beauty, enthusiasm, contentment, spirituality, enlightenment and confidence; in all moments."

"I strip all illusion off of _____ for myself; in all moments."

"I transcend _____; in all moments."

"I repair and fortify the Wei chi on all my bodies; in all moments."

"I align all my bodies; in all moments."

"I am centered and empowered in joy, love, abundance, freedom, health, success, security, companionship, creativity, peace, life, wholeness, beauty, enthusiasm, contentment, spirituality, enlightenment and confidence; in all moments."

"I resonate, emanate and am interconnected with all life in joy, love, abundance, freedom, health, success, security, companionship, creativity, peace, life, wholeness, beauty, enthusiasm, contentment, spirituality, enlightenment and confidence; in all moments."

This opportunity to free yourself is my gift to you. The gift that you can give yourself is to recognize its value and to take this technique seriously. Devotion to a true love is noble. But many of us have spiritually outgrown blind loyalty. It is important for everyone's empowerment to know the difference.

It can also benefit you to give this to your friends and family members who are dealing with a break up. When they lament about another person, they are begging the Universe for help. This worksheet is the Universe answering their call through you.

Relationships/Cleanse your Soul

(Say each statement three times out loud while continuously tapping on the top of your head at the crown chakra and say it a fourth time while tapping on your chest.)

"I release demonizing others; in all moments."

"I release glamorizing others; in all moments."

"I release comparing myself to others; in all moments."

"I release gauging my worth against the backdrop off others; in all moments."

"I release categorizing anyone's worth using a physical syllabus; in all moments."

"I remove all engrams of jealousy; in all moments."

"I remove all engrams of competing; in all moments."

"I release the primal urge to compete; in all moments."

"I release creating hostility in my interactions; in all moments."

"I release feeling or believing that I am justified; in all moments."

"I release selling my soul for wisps of illusion; in all moments."

"I reflect the purity of my soul; in all moments."

"I express myself through the purity of my soul; in all moments."

"I deal in integrity and my language is truth; in all moments."

"I have benevolence for all; in all moments."

"I am centered and empowered in integrity and truth; in all moments."

Release the Burden of Having Enemies

(Say each statement three times while tapping on your head and say it a fourth time while tapping on your chest.)

"I remove all labels on me; in all moments."

"I shatter all glass ceilings that have been put on me; in all moments."

"I release carrying the burden of war; in all moments."

"I remove all engrams of war; in all moments."

"I release the need to defend myself; in all moments."

"I release habitually attacking others; in all moments."

"I release the burden of my enemies; in all moments."

"I release having enemies; in all moments."

"I heal all my enemies; in all moments."

"I convert all enemies to friends; in all moments."

"I lay down my sword and shield; in all moments."

"I drop all guilt; in all moments."

"I release confusing being empowered with abusing power; in all moments."

"I forgo abusing power; in all moments."

"I release the fear of my own empowerment; in all moments."

"I shift my paradigm from abusing power, to empowerment; in all moments."

"I transcend abusing power; in all moments."

"I am centered and sustained in my own empowerment; in all moments."

"I resonate, emanate, and am interconnected with all life in my own empowerment; in all moments."

"I meet all other Souls in their own empowerment; in all moments."

Release Suffering a Job

(Say each statement three times out loud while continuously tapping on the top of your head at the crown chakra and say it a fourth time while tapping on your heart chakra.)

"I release defining work as drudgery; in all moments."

"I release considering work as the polar opposite to play; in all moments."

"I release confusing work for imprisonment; in all moments."

"I release confusing work as slavery; in all moments."

"I release dreading work; in all moments."

"I release being chained to a paycheck; in all moments."

"I release perceiving work as a separation from life; in all moments."

"I release doing what I hate to please others; in all moments."

"I release relinquishing my passion to go to work; in all moments."

"I release relinquishing my life's purpose to work; in all moments."

"I release suffering in a job that I don't enjoy; in all moments."

"I release suffering in a job that doesn't feed my soul; in all moments."

"I release allowing work to break my spirit; in all moments."

"I release referring to work as the salt mines; in all moments."

"I release living a meaningless life of chasing the bills; in all moments."

"I release the fear of living my passion; in all moments."

"I release confusing living my passion with treason; in all moments."

"I release the belief that I need to choose between happiness and a vocation; in all moments."

"I release choosing a vocation out of fear; in all moments."

"I release the belief that work is giving up my freedom; in all moments."

"I release choosing apathy over work; in all moments."

"I release making myself sick to get out of work; in all moments."

"I release choosing sickness over work; in all moments."

"I shift my paradigm from work to living my passion; in all moments."

"I make space in this world to live my passion; in all moments."

"I remove all blockages to living my passion; in all moments."

"I stretch my capacity to live my passion; in all moments."

"I am centered and empowered in living my passion; in all moments."

Resentment

Resentment is a thin veneer of anger mingled with an undercurrent of feeling wronged and victimized. I am surprised when I feel a layer of it in myself. I know when it shows up. I have a photographic memory for interactions with people. So every time they promise something and forget it, I have not. Every time they say they will do something and do not, I feel it. I do not want to be resentful and wasn't aware of how prevalent it was.

Someone whom I respect told me recently that I had resistance to manifesting my book because of all the times I was killed, tortured, burned at the stake, stoned to death, etc. for sharing my gifts. So I sat down to release it. Now I realize when I was feeling resentful, it wasn't about an afterthought of people I love to help, it was about those times of life and death.

I have the conscious memory of sitting on the side of a hill and welcoming people to come and get healings. I would touch them and the pain would pass into my body and then spirit guides would pull it out of me from the other side. The people kept coming and coming. I could not get to everyone one by one. I took the all of what needed to be released into my body and went to lie down to release it all.

Those who came to see me did not understand that I was helping them and got very angry. A few of them worked up into a frenzy and stoned me to death. I crossed over with everyone's issues still with me. Those that stoned me were family members in this life. They resented me. Also, while I did the taps that I am about to share, I realized that I was gestated in a pool of resentment. I was the youngest of ten children and I was not wanted or even liked when I arrived. I have been resented most of my life.

As I did the taps, I realized that this sheath of resentment that I have felt, in myself and in other people upon meeting me, may not be so personal. It may be like a filter that withholds the light so that it does not blind those who look upon it. Maybe the resentment has been an energetic sunblock for me so that others could not read me or use me up in my willingness to please. Maybe, I don't need the veneer anymore, and maybe neither do you. If resentment has been part of your make up, and if you can be honest with yourself, stop allotting blame and just release it. These taps may be helpful in finally allowing you to be joyful, loving and free.

(Say each statement three times while tapping on your head and say it a fourth time while tapping on your chest.)

"I release harboring resentment; in all moments."

"I release being a carrier of resentment; in all moments."

"I release being pooled in an underlying current of resentment; in all moments."

"I release being captivated by resentment; in all moments."

"I release saying F#@k you to life; in all moments."

"I recant all vows and agreements between myself and resentment; in all moments."

"I remove all curses between myself and resentment; in all moments."

"I dissolve all karmic conditioning that brought resentment to me; in all moments."

"I remove all the anger that anchors the resentment; in all moments."

"I remove all the pain, burden and limitations that resentment has put on me; in all moments."

"I remove all the pain burden, limitations and anger I have put on all others due to resentment; in all moments."

"I take back all the joy, love, abundance, freedom, peace, life and wholeness that resentment has taken from me; in all moments."

"I give back all the joy, love, abundance, freedom, peace, life and wholeness that I have taken from all others due to resentment; in all moments."

"I release resonating with resentment; in all moments."

"I release emanating with resentment; in all moments."

"I remove all resentment from my sound frequency; in all moments."

"I remove all resentment from my light body; in all moments."

"I shift my paradigm from resentment to joy, love, abundance, freedom, peace, life and wholeness; in all moments."

"I am centered and empowered in divine love; in all moments."

Break Through All Resistance

(Say each statement three times out loud while continuously tapping on the top of your head at the crown chakra and say it a fourth time while tapping on your chest.)

"I release being paralyzed in resistance; in all moments."

"I release relinquishing my momentum for resistance; in all moments."

"I release succumbing to resistance; in all moments."

"I release confusing resistance as defeat; in all moments."

"I release allowing resistance to defeat me; in all moments."

"I release confusing resistance for exhaustion; in all moments."

"I release allowing resistance to exhaust me; in all moments."

"I release being overwhelmed by resistance; in all moments."

"I release allowing resistance to overwhelm me; in all moments."

"I release processing resistance as being overwhelmed; in all moments."

"I release rolling over for resistance; in all moments."

"I remove all vivaxes between myself and resistance; in all moments."

"I remove the claws of resistance from my beingness; in all moments."

"I remove all tentacles between myself and resistance; in all moments."

"I remove all engrams that are triggered by resistance; in all moments."

"I send all energy matrices into the light that cause resistance within me; in all moments."

"I break through all resistance; in all moments."

"I collapse and dissolve all resistance; in all moments."

"I shift my paradigm from resistance to enthusiasm and empowerment; in all moments."

"I transcend all resistance; in all moments."

"I am centered and empowered in enthusiasm and empowerment; in all moments."

Ridicule

Humor is such a subjective thing. It is such a pleasure to laugh when there are no victims involved. When the inner joy is able to bubble to the surface, it is a priceless exchange. It is a wonderful art worth mastering as long as there are no casualties involved. It is possible. The great Don Rickles comes to mind. He made fun of everyone and everything and did so with no malice. It is possible.

Laughter can be used as a weapon or a shield. Sarcasm, unless done with the gentlest intention, bleeds anger through to the surface. The intention to manipulate shows up in people who try too hard to get others to laugh. It becomes a power struggle. This is not the same as sharing an effortless joy that emanates from within.

(Say each statement three times while tapping on your head and say it a fourth time while tapping on your chest.)

"I release the pain and trauma of being ridiculed; in all moments."

"I release using humor as a weapon; in all moments."

"I release using humor as a shield; in all moments."

"I release using humor as a diversion; in all moments."

"I release using humor as a means of control; in all moments."

"I release confusing humor for power; in all moments."

"I release defining humor as diminishing; in all moments."

"I release using humor to exude anger; in all moments."

"I release confusing inner joy with sarcasm and ridicule; in all moments."

"I recant all vows and agreements between myself and ridicule; in all moments."

"I remove all curses between myself and ridicule; in all moments."

"I dissolve all karmic ties between myself and ridicule; in all moments."

"I remove all the pain, burden, limitations and imprints that ridicule has put on me; in all moments."

"I remove all the pain, burden, limitations and imprints that I have put on all others by using ridicule; in all moments."

"I shift my paradigm from ridicule to inner joy; in all moments."

The Sacred Blessing of the Violet Light

(Say each statement three times out loud while continuously tapping on the top of your head at the crown chakra and say it a fourth time while tapping on your chest.)

"I AM my I AM Presence and I AM One with the I AM Presence of ALL Humanity; in all moments."

"We are One Voice, One Breath, One Heartbeat, and One Energy, Vibration, and Consciousness of Pure Divine Love; in all moments."

"We invoke the most intensified frequencies of the 5th Dimensional Crystalline Solar Violet Flame that Cosmic Law will allow; in all moments."

"We ask Saint Germain and your Legions of Violet Fire Angels to assist; in all moments."

"We blaze, blaze, blaze this Violet Flame with the power and might of a thousand suns; in all moments."

"We blaze through and around every thought, feeling, word, action, memory, and belief that Humanity has ever expressed in any time frame or dimension; in all moments."

"We blaze through both known and unknown all that is reflecting anything less than Heaven on Earth; in all moments."

"We transmute this energy, cause, core, effect, record, and memory back into its original perfection and seal it in an invincible force field of God's Infinite Light; in all moments."

"We invoke the Goddess of Liberty who takes her strategic position at the Cardinal point to the North of this Planet; in all moments."

"We invoke the Goddess of Divine Justice who takes her strategic position at the Cardinal point to the East; in all moments."

"We invoke the Goddess of Freedom who takes her strategic position at the Cardinal point to the South; in all moments."

"We invoke the Goddess of Victory who takes her strategic position at the Cardinal point to the West; in all moments."

"We join these powerful Beings of Light and welcome also the Silent Watchers, the Mighty Guardians, and ALL of the Beings of Light who are assisting Humanity at this time from the Heavenly Realms; in all moments."

"We establish the patterns of perfection for the New Earth on the physical plane; in all moments."

"We welcome all blessed ones to come now and blaze forth the most powerful cleansing activity of the 5th Dimensional Crystalline Solar Violet Flame that Humanity and the Earth are capable of receiving; in all moments."

"Humanity's I AM Presence now opens the Stargate of our Heart; in all moments."

"Instantly, we are the Open Door for this unfathomable frequency of the Violet Flame; in all moments."

"This exquisite Sacred Fire pulsates through our Heart Flames and blazes in, through and around all inharmonious actions; in all moments."

"This cleansing fire flushes out all lower human consciousness and all obstructions of the Light that any person, place, condition or thing has ever placed in the pathway of Life's perfection; in all moments."

"Through the Divine Power of Liberty, Justice, Freedom and Victory, the Violet Flame transmutes this discordant energy back into Light - cause, core, effect, record, and memory now and forever; in all moments."

"The influx of this unprecedented frequency of the Violet Flame washes over every country, state, city, town, village, and hamlet on the planet; in all moments."

"I and the Silent Watchers reach out our loving arms and raise up a limitless number of Lightworkers; in all moments."

"I join with Lightworkers in every location who are willing to participate in the faithful use of the NEW 5th Dimensional Crystalline Solar Violet Flame of God's Infinite Perfection; in all moments."

"We Lightworkers understand the full importance of the sacred gift now being offered by our Father-Mother God to help free Humanity from all of our human miscreations; in all moments."

"We consciously and continuously use of this Sacred Fire from the Heart of God to establish great force fields of the Violet Flame everywhere; in all moments."

"Every being in a force field of Violet Flame is continuously bathed in it; in all moments."

"Through the presence of the I AM, every person on Earth and the Legions of Light throughout infinity, the monumental Violet Flame expands; in all moments."

"I merge the Violet Flame with the Divinity that is blazing in every person's heart, and expands into a tremendous Starburst of Light; in all moments."

"The influx of the Violet Flame increases exponentially to the intensity and might of a thousand Suns; in all moments."

"We blaze this NEW 5th Dimensional Crystalline Solar Violet Flame with the Light of a thousand Suns through the thoughts, words, actions and feelings of every being on Earth; in all moments."

"We empower a Blazing Violet Light of a thousand Suns in every individual to acknowledge and accept the Divinity within ALL Life; in all moments."

"We empower a Blazing Violet Light of a thousand Suns through all incoming babies, children, their parents, and guardians; in all moments."

"ALL youth are raised up in energy, vibration, and consciousness to carry out the directives of their I AM Presence; in all moments."

"We empower a Blazing Violet Light of a thousand Suns through all youth centers and activities, all schools, colleges and universities, all leaders, teachers, instructors, and professors; in all moments."

"We empower a Blazing Violet Light of a thousand Suns through all religious and spiritual teachings; in all moments."

"We empower a Blazing Violet Light of a thousand Suns through all doctors, nurses, healers, hospitals, insurance companies, pharmaceutical conglomerates, and every institution associated with healing; in all moments."

"We empower a Blazing Violet Light of a thousand Suns through all banking and financial institutions, all economic systems, all money and the people associated with monetary interactions of any kind; in all moments."

"We empower a Blazing Violet Light of a thousand Suns through all places of incarceration and all employed there through every correctional institution and every judge, jury, and court of law, through all police officers and every law enforcement organization; in all moments."

"We empower a Blazing Violet Light of a thousand Suns through ALL of the governments of the world and every person, place, condition, and thing associated with the governments of the world at national, state, and local levels throughout the planet; in all moments."

"We empower a Blazing Violet Light of a thousand Suns through all space activities throughout the world; in all moments."

"We empower a Blazing Violet Light of a thousand Suns through the physical, etheric, mental, and emotional bodies of Humanity; in all moments."

"We empower a Blazing Violet Light of a thousand Suns through the food and water industries and through all of the food and water used for human consumption; in all moments."

"We empower a Blazing Violet Light of a thousand Suns through and around every remaining electron of precious Life energy; in all moments."

"We are centered and empowered in a Blazing Light of a thousand Suns; in all moments."

"We are centered and empowered in KNOWing that the Violet Flame is increasing daily and hourly; in all moments."

"With every breath we realize that the sweet Earth and ALL her Life have ascended into the 5th Dimensional Realms of Light on the New Earth; in all moments."

"We resonate and emanate the Beloved I AM; in all moments."

Sciatica/Scoliosis

(Say each statement three times while tapping on your head and say it a fourth time while tapping on your chest.)

"I release being deformed; in all moments."

"I release lying in one position; in all moments."

"I release living in cramped quarters; in all moments."

"I release being shackled to a wall; in all moments."

"I release carrying my weight on one side; in all moments."

"I release all imbalances in my body; in all moments."

"I pour balance through my spine and hips; in all moments."

"I realign my spine and hips; in all moments."

"I make space in this world to stand and walk completely straight and erect; in all moments."

"I remove all blockages to standing and walking completely straight and erect; in all moments."

"I stretch my capacity to stand and walk completely straight and erect; in all moments."

"I pour flexibility and resiliency into my spine; in all moments."

"I am centered and empowered in having a straight back and spine; in all moments."

Negative Self-Talk

Your brain is a service machine ready to manifest anything you tell it. You tell it things and it manifests them. It is that simple. The reason we don't see more evidence of this is because we give it a statement to program it but then we give it another one and another one. People are so fickle that they vacillate in their commands and so change the programming. Every statement is a form of programming the mind. So at first we say, "Life is good," and it is, but then we say things like, "They are breaking my heart," or "It's killing me." These are ways that we program the mind to create these experiences for ourselves. We are breaking our own hearts in that way.

(Say each statement three times out loud while tapping on the top of your head at the crown chakra and say it a fourth time while tapping on your chest.)

"I release programming myself for negative outcomes; in all moments."

"I edit all negative self-talk; in all moments."

"I speak only kindness to myself; in all moments."

"I release manifesting negative outcomes with my words and my thoughts; in all moments."

"I prevent negative words from affecting me; in all moments."

"I release lowering the bar to what I allow for myself; in all moments."

"I release refuting my own empowerment; in all moments."

"I release the effects of telling myself that 'someone is killing me'; in all moments."

"I release the effects of telling myself that someone is breaking my heart; in all moments."

"I release 'killing myself' with my words and thoughts; in all moments."

"I release breaking my own back; in all moments."

"I release breaking my own heart; in all moments."

"I release making myself sick to death over anything; in all moments."

"I release diminishing my well-being with the drama of my words; in all moments."

"I release cursing myself; in all moments."

"I release diminishing myself; in all moments."

"I release subjugating myself; in all moments."

"I release being reckless with my words and thoughts; in all moments."

"I gear all words and thoughts to the highest manifestation of my empowerment; in all moments."

"I am centered and empowered in manifesting my empowerment; in all moments."

Self-Confidence: Boost Your Confidence

(Say each statement three times while tapping on your head and say it a fourth time while tapping on your chest.)

"I release the shame and embarrassment of being invalidated; in all moments."

"I release the need to be validated; in all moments."

"I strengthen my inner conviction; in all moments."

"I empower my own intuition; in all moments."

"I tap into direct knowing; in all moments."

"I release sitting on the sideline of life; in all moments."

"I release cheering everyone else on more than myself; in all moments."

"I release taking the backseat to everyone's happiness; in all moments."

"I release depleting my resources to help others; in all moments."

"I release the daily martyring of myself; in all moments."

"I release deferring to the empowerment of others; in all moments."

"I release being a bit player in my own life; in all moments."

"I release living unseen in the shadows of greatness; in all moments."

"I release living as if I am insignificant; in all moments."

"I release highlighting others at the cost of myself; in all moments."

"I release cringing at my own greatness; in all moments."

"I embrace my own magnificence; in all moments."

"I am centered and empowered in direct knowing; in all moments."

"I embrace my own omnipotence; in all moments."

Seeking Approval

(Say three times while tapping on the top of your head and say it a fourth time while tapping on your chest.)

"I release the fear of being judged; in all moments."

"I release the trauma of being judged; in all moments."

"I release the trauma of being bought and sold; in all moments."

"I release associating acceptance with survival; in all moments."

"I release associating rejection as a death sentence; in all moments."

"I release the need to be liked; in all moments."

"I release associating likability with good standing in the community; in all moments."

"I release trying to be good; in all moments."

"I release hiding in plain sight; in all moments."

"I release camouflaging myself; in all moments."

"I release being draped in conformity; in all moments."

"I free myself of conformity; in all moments."

"I release making myself invisible; in all moments."

"I release being good as a form of insulation; in all moments."

"I shatter all limitations of being nice; in all moments."

"I release pleasing others to be liked; in all moments."

"I release the belief I need to perform to earn love; in all moments."

"I release playing a role to protect my true self; in all moments."

"I release becoming disconnected from my true self; in all moments."

"I reconnect with my true self; in all moments."

"I release the need to earn love; in all moments."

"I release confusing approval with love; in all moments."

"I release needing approval; in all moments."

"I make space in the world to receive love through self-acceptance; in all moments."

"I remove all blockages to receiving love through self-acceptance; in all moments."

"I stretch my capacity to love myself; in all moments."

"I am centered and empowered in loving myself; in all moments."

"I align all my bodies to self-love; in all moments."

"I am a powerhouse of self-love; in all moments."

"I resonate, emanate and am interconnected to all life in self-love; in all moments."

Self-Acceptance

When you run negative scenarios in your head of what a bad person you are and all the horrible things you have done, your energy system is trying to release stagnant energy. The stagnant energy uses the thoughts and feelings to travel out on. By doing the taps that I post, it gives this energy a means to release without torturing you. Try saying these taps specifically for you and see if you get a sense of what transpires when you do them.

(Say each statement three times while continuously tapping on the top of your head and say it a fourth time while tapping on your chest.)

"I release torturing myself with my thoughts; in all moments."

"I release guilting myself; in all moments."

"I release blaming myself; in all moments."

"I release punishing myself; in all moments."

"I release cursing myself; in all moments."

"I remove all curses I have put on myself; in all moments."

"I forgive myself; in all moments."

"I exonerate myself; in all moments."

"I interrupt the mind loops; in all moments."

"I reprogram myself to self-acceptance; in all moments."

"I appreciate myself; in all moments."

"I am centered and empowered in self-appreciation; in all moments."

"I resonate, emanate and am interconnected with all life through self-acceptance; in all moments."

Self-Esteem Marathon

One of the biggest problems with people is their lack of confidence in their own ability. It is because in so many lifetimes and experiences we have been diminished, enslaved, imprisoned, used, sacrificed, tortured, humiliated, broken, beaten, abandoned and scorned. We have adopted the belief that we are born in sin so our very existence is contingent on performing great acts to overcome an innate flaw. The only way we can shine and still be acceptable is to be the best at being the most undeserving. It is a reverse play of the ego.

If one person can do something, and we are all of the same make up, it makes sense that another person can do it as well. How many times have you witnessed someone sharing their gift and thought, *I could never do that.* The first primal thought that manifests within yourself SHOULD BE, *Yes I can do that! I want to do that. It may not be the same but it will be good!* This is what young children do.

If you go into a classroom of five year olds and ask them who can draw, most will raise their hands. If you ask them who can sing or who can dance, most will raise their hands. If you do that with a group of adults, maybe one or two will come forward. That is their ego getting in the way. Being afraid to be criticized is the ego. Being afraid of not being good enough is ego. We have been taught to compete in life to win. But we are not at war with others. It has become an eternal battle that calls up unconscious memories when the battles were life and death.

(Say each statement three times while tapping on your head and say it a fourth time while tapping on your chest.)

"I release hating myself; in all moments."

"I release the belief that God hates me; in all moments."

"I release the guilt and trauma of hurting others; in all moments."

"I release the belief that God is punishing me; in all moments."

"I release the belief that I am damned; in all moments."

"I release the belief that I am a sinner; in all moments."

"I recant my vow of servitude; in all moments."

"I recant my vow of humility; in all moments."

"I recant my vow of self-deprecation; in all moments."

"I recant my vow of self-deprivation; in all moments."

"I recant my vow to not transcend; in all moments."

"I release sabotaging myself; in all moments."

"I release all the trauma of the past; in all moments."

"I release all the fear of the future; in all moments."

"I release the fear and trauma of being seen; in all moments."

"I release being invisible; in all moments."

"I release the fear of abusing power; in all moments."

"I release choosing power over love; in all moments."

"I release the fear and trauma of being separated from the herd; in all moments."

"I recant all vows and agreements I have made with myself; in all moments."

"I remove all curses that I have put on myself; in all moments."

"I remove all false beliefs I have been operating under; in all moments."

"I dissolve all karmic ties that I have tangled myself in; in all moments."

"I remove all the pain, burden and limitations I have put on myself; in all moments."

"I remove all the pain, burden and limitations that I have put on all others; in all moments."

"I take back all the joy, love, abundance, freedom, health, success, security, companionship, peace, life, wholeness, beauty, enthusiasm, spontaneity, contentment and enlightenment I have kept from myself; in all moments."

"I give back all that I have taken from all others; in all moments."

"I call back all my parts; in all moments."

"I make myself whole; in all moments."

"I repair and fortify my Wei chi; in all moments."

"I am centered and empowered in divine love; in all moments."

"I happily and unabashedly share my gifts; in all moments."

If this exercise can help you share your abilities and feel the confidence that you deserve to feel, then you will be able to own that greatness that deep down we both know you feel. If you can do it for yourself, others will learn from watching you. Here is to all finding self-empowerment.

Self-Loathing

(Say each statement three times out loud while continuously tapping on the top of your head at the crown chakra and say it a fourth time while tapping on your chest.)

"I release hating myself; in all moments."

"I release blaming myself; in all moments."

"I release feeling unworthy; in all moments."

"I release the belief that I am unworthy; in all moments."

"I release lamenting the past; in all moments."

"I release dreading the future; in all moments."

"I release sabotaging my future; in all moments."

"I release being a masochist; in all moments."

"I release having masochistic tendencies; in all moments."

"I release giving away my power; in all moments."

"I release sending mixed signals to the universe; in all moments."

"I release refusing my gifts; in all moments."

"I release refusing to be gifted; in all moments."

"I shift my paradigm to take in all the wonderment of living in abundance; in all moments."

"I draw all wonderful things to me and receive them graciously; in all moments."

"I am centered and empowered in accepting all things wonderful; in all moments."

Stop Beating Yourself Up

Powerful exercise to remove self-derision: (Say each statement three times out loud while tapping on the top of your head at the crown chakra and say it a fourth time while tapping on your chest at the heart chakra.)

"I declare myself a surrogate for humanity in doing these taps; in all moments."

"I release feeling bad about myself; all moments."

"I release hating myself; in all moments."

"I release having a self-defeating attitude; in all moments."

"I release feeling sorry for myself; in all moments."

"I release mourning my actions; in all moments."

"I release wasting energy beating myself up; in all moments."

"I release being conditioned to beat myself up; in all moments."

"I remove all vivaxes between myself and beating myself up; in all moments."

"I release torturing myself with self-derision; in all moments."

"I remove all vivaxes between myself and self-derision; in all moments."

"I pull myself out of the hell that self-derision has made; in all moments."

"I remove all tentacles between myself and self-derision; in all moments."

"I remove the claws of self-derision from my beingness; in all moments."

"I remove all programming and conditioning that self-derision has put on me; in all moments."

"I remove all engrams of self-derision from my beingness; in all moments."

"I remove all the pain, burden and limitations that self-derision has put on me; in all moments."

"I remove all the fear, futility and unworthiness that self-derision has put on me; in all moments."

"I remove all the compartmentalization, self-righteousness and paralysis that self-derision has put on me; in all moments."

"I remove all the cruelty, apathy and illusion of separateness that self-derision has put on me; in all moments."

"I send all energy matrices of self-derision into the light; in all moments."

"I command all complex energy matrices of self-derision to be escorted into the light and sound; in all moments."

"I release being enslaved to self-derision; in all moments."

"I remove the chains of self-derision; in all moments."

"I release confusing self-derision with devotion to Source; in all moments."

"I release adopting self-derision as a form of worship; in all moments."

"I recant all vows and agreements between myself and self-derision; in all moments."

"I release confusing self-derision with making myself worthy; in all moments."

"I release using self-derision to purify myself; in all moments."

"I release cursing myself with self-derision; in all moments."

"I release anointing myself in self-derision; in all moments."

"I remove all blessings of self-derision from my beingness; in all moments."

"I remove all curses of self-derision from my beingness; in all moments."

"I release using self-derision as a crutch; in all moments."

"I release using self-derision as a distraction; in all moments."

"I release the fear of being free of self-derision; in all moments."

"I sever all strings and cords between myself and all self-derision; in all moments."

"I dissolve all karmic ties between myself and all self-derision; in all moments."

"I strip all illusion off all self-derision; in all moments."

"I take back all that self-derision has taken from me; in all moments."

"I remove all masks, walls and armor of self-derision from my beingness; in all moments."

"I collapse and dissolve all self-derision; in all moments."

"I release resonating with self-derision; in all moments."

"I release emanating with self-derision; in all moments."

"I extract all self-derision from my sound frequency; in all moments."

"I extract all self-derision from my light emanation; in all moments."

"I extract all self-derision from my whole beingness; in all moments."

"I shift my paradigm from all self-derision to perpetual love and approval; in all moments."

"I transcend all self-derision; in all moments."

"I am centered and empowered in perpetual love and approval; in all moments."

"I resonate, emanate and am interconnected with all beings in perpetual love and approval; in all moments."

Stop Berating Yourself

(Say each statement three times out loud while continuously tapping on the top of your head at the crown chakra and say it a fourth time while tapping on your chest.)

"I release railroading my own greatness with the need to compete; in all moments."

"I release converting my greatness into concern over superficial beauty; in all moments."

"I release judging myself; in all moments."

"I release basing my worth on my outer appearance; in all moments."

"I release associating outer beauty with self-worth; in all moments."

"I release basing my self-worth on exterior indicators; in all moments."

"I release the need to be pretty to be loved; in all moments."

"I release needing to be successful to be worthy; in all moments."

"I release overlooking my own greatness; in all moments."

"I release overlooking my own beauty; in all moments."

"I release denying myself a lack of self-support; in all moments."

"I release berating myself; in all moments."

"I release sizing myself up in relationship to others; in all moments."

"I release diminishing myself compared to others; in all moments."

"I remove all others from their pedestal; in all moments."

"I elevate myself in equal measurable worth to all others; in all moments."

"I recommit myself to valuing myself; in all moments."

"I pour love, approval and nurturing love into myself; in all moments."

"I shift my paradigm from berating myself to loving myself; in all moments."

"I transcend berating myself; in all moments."

"I am centered and empowered in nurturing and loving myself; in all moments."

Sexual Issues

(Say each statement three times out loud while tapping on your head and say it a fourth time while tapping on your chest.)

"I release the trauma of being physically raped; in all moments."

"I release the trauma of being emotionally raped; in all moments."

"I release the trauma of being mentally raped; in all moments."

"I release confusing sex for power; in all moments."

"I release confusing sex for submission; in all moments."

"I release confusing sex for danger; in all moments."

"I release confusing sex for fear; in all moments."

"I release confusing sex for hate; in all moments."

"I release confusing sex for poverty; in all moments."

"I release selling sex for money; in all moments."

"I release confusing sex for manipulation; in all moments."

"I release confusing sex for slavery; in all moments."

"I release confusing sex for domination; in all moments."

"I release confusing sex for evil; in all moments."

"I release confusing sex for shame; in all moments."

"I release storing shame in my body; in all moments."

"I release being ashamed of myself; in all moments."

"I release making love to power; in all moments."

"I release confusing power for love; in all moments."

"I release defining sex as shameful; in all moments."

"I release defining sex as a sin; in all moments."

"I release using sex to feel worthy; in all moments."

"I release using sex to feel loved; in all moments."

"I release using sex to feel safe; in all moments."

"I release using sex to wield power; in all moments."

"I release associating pain with sex; in all moments."

"I release associating fear with sex; in all moments."

"I release confusing sex with devotion; in all moments."

"I release needing to give sex to prove loyalty; in all moments."

"I release confusing lovemaking with rape; in all moments."

"I release the belief that sex is anything but loving and wonderful; in all moments."

"I recant all vows and agreements between myself and sex; in all moments."

"I remove all curses between myself and sex; in all moments."

"I sever all strings and cords between myself and sex; in all moments."

"I dissolve all karmic ties between myself and sex; in all moments."

"I remove all the pain, fear, shame, burdens, limitations and engrams that sex has put on me; in all moments."

"I take back all the dignity, joy, love, abundance, freedom, health success, security, companionship, peace, life, wholeness, beauty, enthusiasm, contentment, spirituality, enlightenment and confidence that sex has taken from me; in all moments."

"I release all sexual perversion; in all moments."

"I remove all masks, walls and armor between myself and intimate, joyful, trusting lovemaking; in all moments."

"I infuse joy, love, intimacy, trust and play into the sexual act; in all moments."

"I am centered and empowered in joyful, intimate, trusting lovemaking; in all moments."

Shoulders

(Say each statement three times while tapping on your head and say it a fourth time while tapping on your chest.)

"I release carrying the weight of the world on my shoulders; in all moments."

"I release being a pack animal; in all moments."

"I release being a beast of burden; in all moments."

"I release being overtaxed and being underappreciated; in all moments."

"I remove the yoke from my body; in all moments."

"I release wearing heavy armor; in all moments."

"I remove all engrams of being at war; in all moments."

"I release being a grunt; in all moments."

"I release being a pawn; in all moments."

"I remove all engrams of being a pack animal; in all moments."

"I remove all engrams of going to war; in all moments."

"I remove all engrams of being enslaved; in all moments."

"I remove the useless drudgery of life; in all moments."

"I release feeling like a pawn for others; in all moments."

"I release feeling inconsequential; in all moments."

"I release feeling hopeless; in all moments."

"I release being enslaved to convention; in all moments."

"I release being enslaved to conditioning; in all moments."

"I remove all programming and conditioning that has been put on me; in all moments,"

"I shift my paradigm from enslavement to freedom; in all moments."

"I free myself; in all moments."

"I reawaken my exuberance for life; in all moments."

"I reclaim my empowerment; in all moments."

"I am centered and empowered in being free; in all moments."

"I infuse freedom into my sound frequency; in all moments."

"I imbue my light emanation with freedom; in all moments."

"I resonate, emanate and am interconnected with all life in being grateful and free; in all moments."

Simple Truth

People just don't understand the damage that they do to themselves when they post their medical issues on social media. They say they want to update the people who REALLY care about them with what is going on with them. They may be getting some attention for what they are dealing with, but it is a price to pay for what is transpiring energetically.

When one talks about their issues, they are publicly declaring themselves as married to them. Think about it. Once it is out there, it is forever a part of your identity. It is hard enough to shake something when you have identified with it. It is way more difficult to shake when everyone who knows you identifies it as part of you as well.

Did you know that the body gets cancer a few times in everyone's lifetime? The body naturally addresses it. It is when it is discovered and labeled and defined that many times it takes hold and becomes life changing. Pain is an emotional issue that becomes so heavy in the body that it shows up as weight and mass. If you can address the emotional issue, the physical issue can and does recede.

But to bring attention to an issue and to build your identity around it calcifies it in the body. Why do so few people understand this? If you want something in your life, talk about it as a reality especially with others who agree with it. This is an exacting spiritual law as concise and consistent as the law of gravity. This is what people do with illness and problems. This is what happens when people share their issues on social media. If someone wanted to improve the quality of their life, adhering to the Spiritual Law of Silence is the one thing they could do to greatly dry up many of their issues.

When you talk about being poor, sick, depressed or tired, these are very charged words. Charged means that the words are like little magnets. When you use negatively charged words to describe yourself or your life, your brain picks up on them and is programmed to give you what you want. It doesn't know you DON'T want these things. It just knows that you talk about them, so you must want to manifest them. You are programming yourself to manifest more of what you don't want. It is formula. It is how the brain works, what talking does and how manifestation works.

My seventy six year old friend easily recovered from stage four something. She is thriving after the bout. She went through traditional means yet adhered to all the suggestions I gave her to augment her treatment. One of the main points on the list of suggestions was to not converse about her ordeal, to not allow it to be a topic of conversation. A year after her total recovery, the surgeon confided in her that he had thought that she would be one that did not make it. Her recovery beat the odds. Not allowing her identity to become entwined with disease was part of the factor that made the difference in her survival. I so hope people get this point.

I love all my social media friends so much. It saddens me when I stumble upon a post where they are sharing updates on their illness, pain or other life issues. It just shows me how little understanding they have of spiritual law. They would be devastated with me if they realized what they were doing to themselves in sharing. It is not a judgment on my part. It is a twinge of *ooh...noooo...don't do this to yourself! Don't nail this issue to yourself for the payoff of a little attention.*

They would, of course, argue with me and say that their friends and family are helping them get through this. But in the energetic realms, most humans are rendered ineffective being able to assist only because of their lack of understanding spiritual law. Some humans stumble upon the formula for being able to assist but these people are rare. The general belief system for personal empowerment has gotten so watered down that people are now struggling just to exist and feel worthy to exist.

That is why I am angry with people who continuously benefit from my assistance yet are afraid to share what is possible because they are afraid of what their family and friends will think. Or they can diminish or dismiss the help as a fluke. It happens too consistently these days. The people who know what I do, know. Their family and friends are suffering with a lack of understanding. Most of the world is suffering because of a lack of understanding. The people whom I have helped should be able to let others know what is possible at this point. Otherwise they are using me as a muse.

It has never been about the payment, the validation or the appreciation. They are just a part of the snapshot. It is about getting a majority of people to collectively agree to what is consistently possible in the realm of human healing. If people deny a spiritual gift they have received with shame and embarrassment, how can the world be immersed in healing? How can we heal as a group? What I share in my posts and in my love for you as individuals is the truth that will inevitably uplift consciousness. It is not my truth. It is there for everyone to tap into.

Being ashamed or embarrassed to share what I do and how I have helped you is being in agreement with the world as it is now as opposed to an existence that is more empowering. I don't ask you to choose. You choose all the time. You are all choosing. You are empowered in this way. You are creating the world that we live in by your choices. That is how empowered you are.

Sinus Issues

In one of my private sessions, a core cause was revealed for one of my clients who had suffered from sinus headaches. He had suffered with them for years even though his diet and other triggers were eliminated.

A past lifetime opened up where he was bashed in the skull with a huge club. On some level, it left him feeling unsafe and vulnerable.

The body's ultimate job is to keep functioning so we can continue to have physical experiences. There are many orifices in the body. Since he was killed by something smashing in his skull, his physical component strives to keep him safer by filling up those orifices so it is harder to crush him when there is a blow.

I have seen past lives where people are crushed in the rib cage. Maybe people who have lung issues have past lives of drowning and being suffocated. Maybe they should look at being crushed to death as well.

Here are some taps to try for such issues:

(Say each statement three times while tapping your head and say it a fourth time while tapping your chest)

"I release the trauma of being bashed in the skull; in all moments."

"I release the trauma of being crushed to death; in all moments."

"I release storing trauma in the orifices of my body; in all moments."

"I release the belief that I am vulnerable or unsafe; in all moments."

"I release feeling vulnerable or unsafe; in all moments."

"I release bracing against a blow; in all moments."

"I release waiting for the ax to fall; in all moments."

"I release feeling fragile and breakable; in all moments."

"I release overcompensating in rigidity to protect myself; in all moments."

"I drain all the orifices of my body of all negative emotions, thoughts and experiences; in all moments."

Improve Your Skin

Your skin is doing everything it can to help you. It is protecting you, it is stretching for you, it is releasing toxins. Please don't expect it to be perfect. Please don't reject it or blame it. Show some respect to your personal boundary and sentry in this world.

"I release melting into the background; in all moments."

"I release the fear of being persecuted; in all moments."

"I release the trauma of hearing my own skin crackle; in all moments."

"I release the trauma of watching my skin melt off; in all moments."

"I release the trauma of being covered with pustules; in all moments."

"I release the trauma of being covered with bites; in all moments."

"I release the trauma of having my skin peeled off; in all moments."

"I release the trauma of being skinned alive; in all moments."

"I release the trauma of having my skin sliced up; in all moments."

"I remove all vivaxes between my skin and pain; in all moments."

"I remove all tentacles between my skin and pain; in all moments."

"I remove the claws of pain from my skin's beingness; in all moments."

"I release the trauma of being scalded; in all moments."

"I release the trauma of having my skin singed; in all moments."

"I release reliving torture; in all moments."

"I release holding back a wall of sadness; in all moments."

"I release confusing love and pain; in all moments."

"I untangle all the pain from the love; in all moments."

"I strip away all the pain; in all moments."

"I dissolve all the pain into the light and sound; in all moments."

"I remove all programming and conditioning of pain from my skin; in all moments."

"I remove all engrams of pain from my skin; in all moments."

"I remove all engrams of humiliation from my skin; in all moments."

"I remove all engrams of shame from my skin; in all moments."

"I remove all engrams of unworthiness from my skin; in all moments."

"I remove all engrams of persecution from my skin; in all moments."

"I remove all engrams of torture from my skin; in all moments."

"I remove all engrams of rejection from my skin; in all moments."

"I remove all engrams of ugliness from my skin; in all moments."

"I remove all engrams of depravity from skin; in all moments."

"I remove all engrams of futility from my skin; in all moments."

"I remove all engrams of anguish from my skin; in all moments."

"I release the trauma and helplessness of watching my skin rot; in all moments."

"I remove all engrams of putrid from my skin; in all moments."

"I release cursing my skin; in all moments."

"I release faulting my skin for doing its job; in all moments."

"I release rejecting my skin; in all moments."

"I release blaming my skin; in all moments."

"I release scapegoating my skin; in all moments."

"I nullify all contracts between my skin and pain; in all moments."

"I remove all engrams of martyrdom from my skin; in all moments."

"I send all energy matrices of pain into the light and sound; in all moments."

"I command all complex energy matrices of pain to be escorted into the light and sound; in all moments."

"I heal my skin; in all moments."

"I infuse joy, love, health, and forgiveness into my skin; in all moments."

"I infuse security into my skin; in all moments."

"I appreciate my skin; in all moments."

"I infuse gratitude and resiliency into my skin; in all moments."

"I regenerate my skin; in all moments."

Soldier's Guilt

Recently, I was able to facilitate a session on someone who has been in active duty in this lifetime. He came to me because of depression. I was able to tap into his many lifetimes of being a soldier and how it created a dichotomy in him. I was able to alleviate a great deal of angst in him. When I was imprisoned by the captor, he made me kill small animals. One in particular was a sweet squirrel that I named Butters. Butters is a naive character on the show, *South Park,* that is very endearing. This squirrel pulled at my heartstrings. It was anguish to feel such tenderness for this squirrel inside and watch my body be on autopilot and kill his sweetness. It just didn't exist anymore at my hand.

In helping the soldier, it comforted me to think that Butters maybe didn't die in vain. That maybe he helped me develop a deeper ability to understand the soldier's dilemma and help him release the guilt, trauma and confusion of his service.

(Say each statement three times while tapping on your head and say a fourth time while tapping on your chest.)

"I release the guilt and trauma of killing others; in all moments."

"I release confusing fear with being a traitor; in all moments."

"I release confusing taking orders with being a man; in all moments."

"I release the guilt and trauma of taking orders; in all moments."

"I release keeping evil as a pet; in all moments."

"I release harboring evil; in all moments."

"I release being a pawn for power; in all moments."

"I recant my vow to serve; in all moments."

"I recant all vows and agreements between myself and serving; in all moments."

"I release being enslaved to serving; in all moments."

"I dissolve all karmic ties between myself and serving; in all moments."

"I remove all the pain, burden, limitations and programming that serving has put on me; in all moments."

"I remove all the pain, burden, limitations and programming that I have put on all others through serving; in all moments."

"I take back all the joy, love, abundance, freedom, life, wholeness and peace that serving has taken from me; in all moments."

"I give back all the joy, love, abundance, freedom, life, wholeness and peace that I have taken from all others due to serving; in all moments."

"I remove all of serving from my sound frequency; in all moments."

"I remove all of serving from my light body; in all moments."

"I shift my paradigm from serving to joy, love, abundance, freedom, life, wholeness and peace; in all moments."

"I recall all my sacred parts; in all moments."

"I rebuild my fractured vessel; in all moments."

"I heal all causal wounds; in all moments."

"I am centered and empowered in divine love; in all moments."

There seemed to be a weight lifted off my client. He had a sense of being a soldier in many lives. To get a sense that he was finally free of the unconscious agreement to be a soldier in the future gave him a sense of hope that he was not feeling before the session. He felt more spacious and free. I was very grateful to be able to assist him. We shared that incredible sacred bond that soldiers share, only it was forged in our energetic connection and not through service.

Celebration Prayer/Exercise for the Winter Solstice

(Say each statement a total of four times. The first three times while tapping continuously on your head and the fourth time while tapping continuously on your chest.)

Through doing these taps, you can get a sense of your own empowerment.

"I infuse joy into the Universal Sound Frequency and the Universal Light Emanation; in all moments."

"I infuse the divinity of pure love into the Universal Sound Frequency and the Universal Light Emanation; in all moments."

"I infuse abundance into the Universal Sound Frequency and the Universal Light Emanation; in all moments."

"I infuse freedom into the Universal Sound Frequency and the Universal Light Emanation; in all moments."

"I infuse healing into the Universal Sound Frequency and the Universal Light Emanation; in all moments."

"I infuse health into the Universal Sound Frequency and the Universal Light Emanation; in all moments."

"I infuse success into the Universal Sound Frequency and the Universal Light Emanation; in all moments."

"I infuse interconnectedness into the Universal Sound Frequency and the Universal Light Emanation; in all moments."

"I infuse creativity into the Universal Sound Frequency and the Universal Light Emanation; in all moments."

"I infuse peace into the Universal Sound Frequency and the Universal Light Emanation; in all moments."

"I infuse wholeness into the Universal Sound Frequency and the Universal Light Emanation; in all moments."

"I infuse beauty into the Universal Sound Frequency and the Universal Light Emanation; in all moments."

"I infuse enthusiasm into the Universal Sound Frequency and the Universal Light Emanation; in all moments."

"I infuse contentment into the Universal Sound Frequency and the Universal Light Emanation; in all moments."

"I infuse spirituality into the Universal Sound Frequency and the Universal Light Emanation; in all moments."

"I infuse enlightenment into the Universal Sound Frequency and the Universal Light Emanation; in all moments."

"I infuse confidence into the Universal Sound Frequency and the Universal Light Emanation; in all moments."

"I infuse a sense of belonging into the Universal Sound Frequency and the Universal Light Emanation; in all moments."

"I infuse independence into the Universal Sound Frequency and the Universal Light Emanation; in all moments."

"I infuse joy into the Universal Sound Frequency and the Universal Light Emanation; in all moments."

"I infuse the ability to discern into the Universal Sound Frequency and the Universal Light Emanation; in all moments."

"I infuse enlightenment into the Universal Sound Frequency and the Universal Light Emanation; in all moments."

"I infuse empowerment into the Universal Sound Frequency and the Universal Light Emanation; in all moments."

"I infuse compassion into the Universal Sound Frequency and the Universal Light Emanation; in all moments."

"I infuse kindness into the Universal Sound Frequency and the Universal Light Emanation; in all moments."

"I infuse acceptance into the Universal Sound Frequency and the Universal Light Emanation; in all moments."

"I infuse golden self-worth into the Universal Sound Frequency and the Universal Light Emanation; in all moments."

"I infuse gratitude into the Universal Sound Frequency and the Universal Light Emanation; in all moments."

"I infuse reverence into the Universal Sound Frequency and the Universal Light Emanation; in all moments."

"I infuse conscious exponential experiences into the Universal Sound Frequency and the Universal Light Emanation; in all moments."

"I infuse being immersed in the moment into the Universal Sound Frequency and the Universal Light Emanation; in all moments."

"I infuse exhilaration into the Universal Sound Frequency and the Universal Light Emanation; in all moments."

"I infuse total awareness into the Universal Sound Frequency and the Universal Light Emanation; in all moments."

Solstice Celebration

(Say this statement three times while tapping on your head and say it a fourth time while tapping on your chest.)

"We return dignity, love, and respect back to the earth; in all moments."

"We return dignity, love and respect to Gaia; in all moments."

"We hold space for the sacred sweetness of innocence and kindness; in all moments."

"We return balance back to the earth; in all moments."

"We return to Fairy Kind all that has been taken from them; in all moments."

"We pay homage to all trees with dignity and respect; in all moments."

"We reclaim our joy; in all moments."

"Universal peace on earth; in all moments."

"We bury the dead; in all moments."

"Universal joy; in all moments."

"Universal love; in all moments."

"Universal abundance; in all moments."

"Universal freedom; in all moments."

"Universal health; in all moments."

"Universal success; in all moments."

"Universal security; in all moments."

"Universal connection; in all moments."

"Universal perpetual exponential life; in all moments."

"Universal wholeness; in all moments."

"Universal beauty; in all moments."

"Universal enthusiasm; in all moments."

"Universal contentment; in all moments."

"Universal spirituality; in all moments."

"Universal enlightenment; in all moments."

"Universal confidence; in all moments."

"Universal family; in all moments."

"Universal intellect; in all moments."

"Universal discernment; in all moments."

"Universal empowerment; in all moments."

Soul Revival

I have a client who has done some deep work with my assistance. She came to me for another session. She just wants to be free and gets frustrated when she feels like someone is inhibiting her in any way. She and I have worked on all the issues around freedom and being limited. The issues that she is feeling are hiccups from past issues that we have addressed. These beautiful taps came through to remove all residual effects of old issues.

(Say each statement three times while tapping on your head and say it a fourth time while tapping on your chest.)

"I remove all engrams; in all moments."

"I recalibrate my truth to the expansiveness of my own vortex; in all moments."

"I recast my Soul to the highest possible Truth; in all moments."

"I recast my Soul to the highest possible Joy; in all moments."

"I recast my Soul to the highest possible Love; in all moments."

"I recast my Soul to the highest possible Abundance; in all moments."

"I recast my Soul to the highest possible Freedom; in all moments."

"I recast my Soul to the highest possible Health; in all moments."

"I recast my Soul to the highest possible Success; in all moments."

"I recast my Soul to the highest possible Confidence; in all moments."

"I recast my Soul to the highest possible Companionship; in all moments."

"I recast my Soul to the highest possible Creativity; in all moments."

"I recast my Soul to the highest possible Peace; in all moments."

"I recast my Soul to the highest possible Life; in all moments."

"I recast my Soul to the highest possible Wholeness; in all moments."

"I recast my Soul to the highest possible Beauty; in all moments."

"I recast my Soul to the highest possible Enthusiasm; in all moments."

"I recast my Soul to the highest possible Contentment; in all moments."

"I recast my Soul to the highest possible Dimension; in all moments."

"I recast my Soul to the highest possible Reality; in all moments."

"I recast my Soul to the highest possible Purity; in all moments."

"I recast my Soul to the highest possible Completeness; in all moments."

"I recast my Soul to the highest possible Surrender; in all moments."

"I recast my Soul to the highest possible Moment; in all moments."

"I recast my Soul to the highest possible Awareness; in all moments."

"I recast my Soul to the highest possible Understanding; in all moments."

"I recast my Soul to the highest possible Adventure; in all moments."

"I recast my Soul to the highest possible Journey; in all moments."

"I recast my Soul to the highest possible Omniscience; in all moments."

"I recast my Soul to the highest possible Omnipotence; in all moments."

"I recast my Soul to the highest possible Omnipresence; in all moments."

"I recast my Soul to the highest possible Amalgamation of all the above qualities; in all moments."

"I dissolve and re-caste everything that is not in agreement with the highest expression of my Soul; in all moments."

"I strengthen and fortify the highest expression of my new Soul's Wei chi; in all moments."

"I am centered and empowered in the divinity of the highest loving expression of my new Soul; in all moments."

Working with the Spiritual Law of Reversed Efforts

Not everyone realizes that there are exacting laws that run the universe. They are exacting as the law of gravity. This means, they don't just happen haphazardly. They happen the same way across the board. No one is excused from the law of gravity and so it is with the spiritual laws as well.

Many people are familiar with the law of attraction and how it works. But they may not realize that there is a spiritual law of reversed efforts. You know how when you don't care about something, you can have it, and when you desperately want something, it eludes you? The law of reversed efforts is what is responsible.

People all over the world are wondering why they can't manifest money, happiness or the love of their life when they are trying as hard as they possible can. One such client came to me recently. She did the protocol of my taps, not on the item she wanted to accrue, but with the spiritual law of reversed efforts. It created a powerful release for her.

Imagine all the times you felt you were unworthy because something didn't work out for you or you blamed yourself in some way when you were trying your very best. Well, it turns out, blaming yourself for these things is as inaccurate as it would be for blaming yourself when you fall and gravity did its thing. You cannot take the blame for gravity.

(Say each statement three times out loud while continuously tapping on the top of your head at the crown chakra and say it a fourth time while tapping on your chest.)

"I am impervious to the spiritual law of reversed efforts; in all moments."

"I release being affected by the spiritual law of reversed efforts; in all moments."

"I release violating the spiritual law of reversed efforts; in all moments."

"I release blaming myself for the spiritual law of reversed efforts; in all moments."

"I release attracting the spiritual law of reversed efforts to my efforts; in all moments."

"I recant all vows and agreements between myself and the spiritual law of reversed efforts; in all moments."

"I remove all curses between myself and the spiritual law of reversed efforts; in all moments."

"I remove all blessings between myself and the spiritual law of reversed efforts; in all moments."

"I sever all strings and cords between myself and the spiritual law of reversed efforts; in all moments."

"I dissolve all karmic ties between myself and the spiritual law of reversed efforts; in all moments."

"I withdraw all my energy from the spiritual law of reversed efforts; in all moments."

"I remove all the pain, burden, limitations, engrams, blame and failure that the spiritual law of reversed efforts has put on me; in all moments."

"I take back all the joy, love, abundance, freedom, health, success, companionship, life and wholeness that the spiritual law of reversed efforts has taken from me; in all moments."

"I release resonating with the spiritual law of reversed efforts; in all moments."

"I release emanating with the spiritual law of reversed efforts; in all moments."

"I remove all of the spiritual law of reversed efforts from my sound frequency; in all moments."

"I remove all of the spiritual law of reversed efforts from my light emanation; in all moments."

"I shift my paradigm from the spiritual law of reversed efforts to joy, love, abundance, freedom, health, success, companionship, life and wholeness; in all moments."

"I transcend the spiritual law of reversed efforts; in all moments."

"I am centered, empowered and confident in joy, love, abundance, freedom, health, success, companionship, life and wholeness; in all moments."

Spiritual Teacher/Student Dynamic

It is difficult to stretch our own wings when we are bowing our head under the wings of another and supporting their flight with our enthusiasm. The best way to encourage others to grow is by stretching your own wings and showing them what is possible. It is not done by creating a breeze for their flight.

(Say each statement three times while tapping on your head and say it a fourth time while tapping on your chest.)

"I release being disillusioned by the teacher; in all moments."

"I release the pain and loneliness of outgrowing the teacher; in all moments."

"I release being diminished by the teacher; in all moments."

"I release giving my power to the teacher; in all moments."

"I release being used; in all moments."

"I recant all vows and agreements between myself and the teacher; in all moments."

"I remove all curses between myself and the teacher; in all moments."

"I dissolve all karmic ties between myself and the teacher; in all moments."

"I remove all pain, burden and limitations that the teacher has put on me; in all moments."

"I take back all the joy, love, abundance, freedom, life and wholeness that the teacher has taken from me; in all moments."

"I withdraw all my energy from the teacher; in all moments."

"I release the fear of outgrowing the teacher; in all moments."

"I release worshiping the teacher; in all moments."

Spiritual Wedding Vows

Here is a set of taps to help two people become closer with their pure intentions.

(Say each statement three times while tapping on your head and say it a fourth time while tapping on your chest. Perhaps you and your partner can do these together.)

"I declare _____ my spiritual equal and partner; in all moments."

"All other relationships were merely training to be worthy of_____; in all moments."

I convert all past angst, drama, desires and commitments to love and devotion for _____; in all moments."

"I remove all blindsides and sabotages in my commitment to loving _____; in all moments."

"I strip off all selfishness and petty pursuits that deviate from the spiritual journey of myself and _____; in all moments."

"I make no promises that I can't keep; in all moments."

"I refute all temptations and unworthy distractions that deviate from awakening to the perpetual state of being worthy of _____'s love; in all moments."

"I transcend all matter, energy, time and space to be in perpetual love with _____; in all moments."

"I sidestep all emotional, physical and mental inertia that have me doubt the perpetual state of loving _____; in all moments."

"I keep my heart open to _____ beyond matter, energy, space and time; in all moments."

"I maintain a clarity of mind that keeps me tuned into the heart beyond all tangible realms; in all moments."

"I see _____'s beauty, fortitude and resilience in loving me and our partnership; in all moments."

"Our love pierces through all doubt and cynicism, and is impervious to the unworthy intentions of others; in all moments."

"I see _____always from the most empowered vantage point; in all moments."

"I reflect to _____ all their beauty, strength, fortitude and resilience; in all moments."

"I walk, breathe and know my own empowerment through the sanctity of my and _____ love; in all moments."

"Every intention is blessed with the gratitude of loving _____; in all moments."

"Every experience is sweetened in loving _____; in all moments."

"I live, move, and have my own beingness in the sanctity of loving _____; in all moments."

"Every increment of loving _____leads me ever deeper into the heart of love; in all moments."

"I dedicate my existence to loving _____ more deeply, profoundly and effectively and in doing so, reveal all the secrets of love's beckon; in all moments."

"I carry these intentions with me clearly, in each moment of our daily pursuits; in all moments."

"Each moment captivated in love with _____ is a victory of valor; in all moments."

"I love all life and all beings more clearly and colorfully as an extension of my love for _____; in all moments."

"I uplift all humanity and hold it in the highest regards through my love for _____; in all moments."

"I beckon all to love through the purity and sanctity of loving _____; in all moments."

In all experiences, dreams, intentions and prayers, I give the highest regard for _____ and align it with my love of Source; in all moments."

"_____ is a reflection of my relationship with Source and I nurture our relationship continually with gratitude and grace; in all moments."

The Success Marathon

(Say each statement three times out loud while continuously tapping on the top of your head at the crown chakra and say it a fourth time while tapping on your chest.)

"I release placating my ego; in all moments."

"I release projecting my ego onto humanity; in all moments."

"I release projecting my ego onto a targeting audience; in all moments."

"I remove all the barriers of my own ego; in all moments."

"I remove all ego between myself and humanity; in all moments."

"I remove the ego barriers between myself and success; in all moments."

"I release backsliding in success; in all moments."

"I release choosing linear success; in all moments."

"I release opting for power; in all moments."

"I release opting for a success based on male slanted truth; in all moments."

"I release giving my power to male slanted truth; in all moments."

"I release trading in my convictions for male slanted truth; in all moments."

"I release being enslaved to male slanted truth; in all moments."

"I release using male slanted truth as a crutch; in all moments."

"I release trying to impress my father; in all moments."

"I release projecting my daddy issues onto society; in all moments."

"I release the disappointment and trauma of having an asshole for a father; in all moments."

"I release competing for the love of an asshole father; in all moments."

"I release overcompensating for having an asshole for a father; in all moments."

"I release the fear of being an asshole; in all moments."

"I release the genetic propensity to be an asshole; in all moments."

"I release being an asshole; in all moments."

"I release connecting to others on an asshole level; in all moments."

"I release making a name as an asshole; in all moments."

"I release turning empowerment into power; in all moments."

"I release converting empowerment into power; in all moments."

"I feed empowerment to others through osmosis; in all moments."

"I feed empowerment to others through sharing my gifts; in all moments."

"I release dreading the process; in all moments."

"I release confusing the process of creation with torture; in all moments."

"I release confusing the process of creation with failure; in all moments."

"I release confusing the process of creation with imprisonment; in all moments."

"I release confusing the process of creation with being a muse; in all moments."

"I release treating the public as a muse; in all moments."

"I release the need for outer validation; in all moments."

"I release sabotaging my own success; in all moments."

"I shift my paradigm from outer success to the complete empowerment of success; in all moments."

"I am centered and empowered in the complete empowerment of success; in all moments."

"I infuse the complete empowerment of success into my sound frequency; in all moments."

"I imbue the complete empowerment of success into my light emanation; in all moments."

"I resonate and emanate the complete empowerment of my success; in all moments."

Suffering

(Say each statement three times out loud while continuously tapping on the top of your head at the crown chakra and say it a fourth time while tapping on your chest.)

"I declare myself a surrogate for humanity in doing these taps; in all moments."

"We close all portals to suffering; in all moments."

"We extract all negative charge vibration out of humanity; in all moments."

"We heal all wounds; in all moments."

"We free all souls trapped in suffering; in all moments."

"We remove all vivaxes between suffering and humanity; in all moments."

"We remove all tentacles between suffering and humanity; in all moments."

"We send all energy matrices into the light and sound that keep humanity trapped in suffering; in all moments."

"We remove all engrams that suffering has put on us; in all moments."

"We collapse and dissolve all portals to suffering; in all moments."

"We recant all vows and agreements between humanity and suffering; in all moments."

"We remove all curses between humanity and suffering; in all moments."

"We remove all blessings between humanity and suffering; in all moments."

"We sever all strings and cords between humanity and suffering; in all moments."

"We dissolve all karmic ties between humanity and suffering; in all moments."

"We remove all the pain, burden and limitations that suffering has put on humanity; in all moments."

"We remove from all of humanity all the helplessness and illusion of separateness that suffering has put on us; in all moments."

"We take back for humanity all the joy, love, abundance and freedom that suffering has taken from us; in all moments."

"We take back for humanity all the health, success, security and wholeness that the anguish of suffering has taken from us; in all moments."

"We take back for all of humanity all the beauty, enthusiasm, contentment and peace that the anguish of suffering has taken from us; in all moments."

"We withdraw all our energy from suffering; in all moments."

"We strip all illusion off of suffering; in all moments."

"We remove all masks, walls and armor from suffering; in all moments."

"We collapse and dissolve all suffering; in all moments."

"We release resonating with suffering; in all moments."

"We release emanating with suffering; in all moments."

"We extract all of the anguish of suffering from humanity's sound frequency; in all moments."

"We extract all of the anguish of suffering from humanity's light emanation; in all moments."

"Humanity transcends the anguish of suffering; in all moments."

"Humanity is centered and empowered in divine love; in all moments."

"We repair and fortify the Wei chi of humanity; in all moments."

"We re-institute the health and well-being of humanity; in all moments."

"Humanity resonates and emanates divine love; in all moments."

Suicide

(Say each statement three times while tapping on your head and say it a fourth time while tapping on your chest.)

"I release the burden that causes me to want to end my life; in all moments."

"I free myself from a cesspool of drama; in all moments."

"I release being immersed in need; in all moments."

"I release neglecting myself; in all moments."

"I release abusing my spirit; in all moments."

"I release being pulled on by desperate spirits; in all moments."

"I send all energy matrices into the light and sound that immerse me in sadness; in all moments."

"I command all complex energy matrices that immerse me in sadness to be escorted into the light and sound; in all moments."

"I send all energy matrices into the light and sound that create drama; in all moments."

"I command all complex energy matrices that create drama to be escorted into the light and sound; in all moments."

"I send all energy matrices into the light and sound that deem everything hopeless; in all moments."

"I command all complex energy matrices that deem everything hopeless to be escorted into the light and sound; in all moments."

"I send all energy matrices into the light and sound that prompt me to take my life; in all moments."

"I command all complex energy matrices that prompt me to take my life to be escorted into the light and sound; in all moments."

"I withdraw all my sympathy from those who have taken their own life; in all moments."

"I release being manipulated by those who have taken their own life; in all moments."

"I repair and fortify the Wei chi of all my bodies; in all moments."

"I align all my bodies; in all moments."

"I am centered and empowered in divine love; in all moments."

"I collapse and dissolve all timelines where power abuses humanity; in all moments."

"I remove all engrams of ruthless or indifferent governing; in all moments."

"I evaporate all psychic waves of energy that pull humanity into a state of submission or defeat; in all moments."

"I instantly deactivate all power sieges in the world with the scouring efficiency of pure and divine love; in all moments."

"I return all energies back to all individuals who have been raped and plummeted over the eons; in all moments."

"I return the course of humanity back onto the track of universal joy, love, peace, health and truth; in all moments."

"I dry up all psychic sieges that hold individuals in a paralyzing grip of inaction; in all moments."

"I re-gift all individuals their innate confidence and abilities to recognize their worth, realize their gifts, awaken their awareness and share their purpose; in all moments."

Sweating the Small Stuff

(Say each statement three times out loud while continuously tapping on the top of your head at the crown chakra and say it a fourth time while tapping on your chest.)

"I release obsessing over my weight; in all moments."

"I release complaining about the weather; in all moments."

"I release the fear of the next incoming bill; in all moments."

"I release living in dread and disdain; in all moments."

"I release waking up in dread; in all moments."

"I release treating each day like the day before; in all moments."

"I release limiting my options with limiting thoughts and beliefs; in all moments."

"I release telling myself that I am getting old; in all moments."

"I release focusing on aches and pains; in all moments."

"I release the belief that disease is inevitable; in all moments."

"I release professing gloom and doom; in all moments."

"I release giving up all hope; in all moments."

"I release throwing in the towel; in all moments."

"I release the belief that I am a powerless grunt; in all moments."

"I release spinning my wheels; in all moments."

"I awaken to a positive outlook; in all moments."

"I shift my whole paradigm to positive potential; in all moments."

"I am centered and empowered in joy, love, abundance, freedom and wholeness; in all moments."

Systems of the Body

It is good to bypass the mind's permission as much as possible. That is partly why the taps are so effective. The mind takes in all the information and decides for us, just like it decides to pull our hand away from the stove automatically so we don't get burned. But without the wisdom of the heart, the body can be put on autopilot. Here is taking it off autopilot.

Another way of doing that is by giving the body commands that the body/mind agreement has put on autopilot. By overriding those instructions, one can take back the running of their own body. It is similar to the head boss coming in and firing an ineffective manager or at least retraining him. These taps are designed to do that to help the body return to ease.

(Say each statement three times while tapping on the head and say it a fourth time while tapping on your chest.)

"I release storing sadness in my lungs; in all moments."

"I release the trauma of drowning; in all moments."

"I release storing loss in my heart cavity; in all moments."

"I release the belief that my heart is broken; in all moments."

"I repair and revitalize my heart; in all moments."

"I release storing anger in my liver; in all moments."

"I remove and dissolve all the anger stored in my liver; in all moments."

"I release the trauma of being raped; in all moments."

"I release the trauma of running for my life; in all moments."

"I remove all sexual trauma stored in my pelvic bowl; in all moments."

"I balance out my systolic and diastolic pressures; in all moments."

"I balance out the pH of my body; in all moments."

"I release lining my arteries with problems; in all moments."

"I release all problems transporting through my circulatory system; in all moments."

"I release all problems transporting through my nervous system; in all moments."

"I release all problems transporting through my digestive system; in all moments."

"I release all problems transporting through my endocrine system; in all moments."

"I release all problems transporting through my immune system; in all moments."

"I release all problems transporting through my lymphatic system; in all moments."

"I release all problems transporting through my muscular system; in all moments."

"I release all problems transporting through my reproductive system; in all moments."

"I release all problems transporting through my respiratory system; in all moments."

"I release all problems transporting through my lymphatic system; in all moments."

"I release all problems transporting through my skeletal system; in all moments."

"I release all problems transporting through my urinary system; in all moments."

"I release all problems transporting through my integumentary system; in all moments." (The skin)

"I release all problems transporting through my energy system; in all moments."

"I release telling myself that I am sick; in all moments."

"I release needing excuses; in all moments."

"I release the pain and trauma of being enslaved; in all moments."

"I release using pain and illness to free myself from slavery; in all moments."

"I release using illness to get attention; in all moments."

"I release confusing being incapacitated with being nurtured; in all moments."

"I release owning pain and disease; in all moments."

"I dry up disease and illness from my world; in all moments."

"I untangle all the systems of my body; in all moments."

"I remove all the silt and issues stored in all the systems of my body; in all moments."

"I repair, fortify and recharge the entire energy system of my body; in all moments."

"I repair, fortify and recharge the entire circulatory system of my body; in all moments."

"I repair, fortify and recharge the entire digestive system of my body; in all moments."

"I repair, fortify and recharge the entire endocrine system of my body; in all moments."

"I repair, fortify and recharge the entire lymphatic system of my body; in all moments."

"I repair, fortify and recharge the entire muscular system of my body; in all moments."

"I repair, fortify and recharge the entire nervous system of my body; in all moments."

"I repair, fortify and recharge the entire reproductive system of my body; in all moments."

"I repair, fortify and recharge the entire respiratory system of my body; in all moments."

"I repair, fortify and recharge the entire skeletal system of my body; in all moments."

"I repair, fortify and recharge the entire urinary system of my body; in all moments."

"I repair, fortify and recharge the entire integumentary system of my body; in all moments."

"I align and integrate all the systems of my body; in all moments."

"I repair and recharge the working interaction of all the systems of my body; in all moments."

"I am centered and empowered in a highly efficient, totally integrated, completely operational, twelve system body; in all moments."

"Every aspect of my beingness is imbued and infused with divine love; in all moments."

"Every aspect of my beingness resonates and emanates divine love; in all moments."

When we rally around a cause like the "c" word or diabetes, we are actually giving it more mind attention. We are creating more space in the world for it. The "c" word has ruined pink for me. I used to think of it as a sweet innocent color for a baby girl's room. That was nice. But now it is identified with the "c" word. Am I the only one troubled by that?

They take our compassion for our loved ones who have struggled and twist it into rallying around a disease. The mind does not know we are fighting against it. The mind thinks we are inviting it in! So society uses our love and lack of insight to make us more entrenched with the disease. This is slavery. I hope that others start to see this.

Removing the Energetic Abscess: Taps to Release Talking Too Much

Just yesterday, I facilitated a session on a new client. A person goes into a session giving me no background information. Details just cause a distraction and I can work deeper without even knowing the drama. This one person was a real dear soul and there was an instant love for her.

Immediately, she started the introduction by being very agreeable and saying very warm things. She was nervous underneath, but I could tell immediately that she used her socials skills to handle people and situations. She was very good at it and was trying to handle me. She was unwittingly trying to stay in control of our dynamics with her social game.

I immediately switched the dynamics and took her crutch from her. "You are talking too much," I said abruptly, "It is an interference."

I felt how I had just hurt her feelings and she was taken aback. But what she didn't realize is that it needed to be done. What I saw in her was a dear woman who was very energetically savvy. She loved people and maintained an open heart. But she was unfamiliar with how to release the energetic exchange with people. She knew enough not to take it into her body but she didn't know how to dissipate it. She created a bubble over her heart chakra and stored all the issues from herself and others in this bubble.

It was infected and impacted. It was like an infected tooth. It was creating an infection down into her core and way down into her root chakra. It was creating physical issues because it was so impacted. Me taking away her ability to talk was ripping off the sheath of containment of this oozing infected energy that was poisoning her slowly. I was able then to extract the "puss" easily.

Her feelings were hurt of course. That is how it registers to the body when a layer is ripped off. It is necessary to work as effectively as I do. A less experienced soul would just stay annoyed at me and close up within themselves. But she was savvy enough to tolerate the discomfort. I explained to her how she was using talking to maintain a skin over all the stagnant energy that she was holding over her heart chakra. I then did my shamanic noises to convert the infection into sound and extract it from her energy.

Immediately, she felt all this stagnant energy extracted from her. She felt immensely lighter and free. She was amazed at the incredible shift she was experiencing in just a few moments. She explained how she had been dealing with this discomfort most of her life and did not realize that there was a way to get rid of it so easily. She explained how it was with her whole life, and it manifested by her feeling that she needed to explain herself to others.

I was able to see her Akashic records easily. It was clear that this woman used talking as a survival tool, and it indeed worked in talking her out of getting sacrificed and punished in past lives. She was still using it that way. To her, talking was her crutch to ensure that she survived, but she was missing so much by not being able to trust silence as well. Here are the taps I led her through during the session.

(Say each statement three times while continuously tapping on the top of your head and say it a fourth time while tapping on your chest.)

"I release using talking as a crutch; in all moments."

"I release using talking to validate myself; in all moments."

"I release confusing talking with existing; in all moments."

"I release the belief that I do not exist beyond the talking; in all moments."

"I release the need to validate myself through talking; in all moments."

"I release confusing my worth with talking; in all moments."

"I release using talking as a survival tool; in all moments."

"I release talking as if my life depends upon it; in all moments."

"I release using talking to manipulate circumstance; in all moments."

"I release the belief that taking is my saving grace; in all moments."

"I release the compulsion to talk; in all moments."

"I release being enslaved to talking; in all moments."

"I release dissipating my effectiveness through talking; in all moments."

"I remove all vivaxes between myself and talking; in all moments."

"I remove all tentacles between myself and talking; in all moments."

"I remove all engrams that talking has put on me; in all moments."

"I remove all programming and conditioning that talking has put on me; in all moments."

"I send all energy matrices into the light that cause me to over-talk; in all moments."

"I command all complex energy matrices that cause me to over-talk to be escorted into the light and sound; in all moments."

"I recant all vows and agreements between myself and talking; in all moments."

"I remove all blessings between myself and talking; in all moments."

"I remove all curses between myself and talking; in all moments."

"I sever all strings, cords and wires between myself and talking; in all moments."

"I dissolve all karmic ties between myself and talking; in all moments."

"I remove all the pain, burden, limitations, disconnectedness, futility and unworthiness that talking has put on me; in all moments."

"I take back all the joy, love, abundance, freedom, life and wholeness that talking has taken from me; in all moments."

"I shift my paradigm from talking to listening; in all moments."

"I transcend talking; in all moments."

"I am centered and empowered in listening; in all moments."

Perhaps you can share this post with someone who is suffering in the imprisonment of talking too much. Perhaps women talk too much with their husbands because they represent authority to them. Perhaps these taps can better an already awesome person.

Speaking Truth

(Say each statement three times out loud while continuously tapping on the top of your head at the crown chakra and say it a fourth time while tapping on your chest at the heart chakra.)

"I release the fear of speaking my truth; in all moments."

"I release the trauma of being called on my truth; in all moments."

"I release being diminished for standing for truth; in all moments."

"I release the fear of being tortured; in all moments."

"I release associating speaking my truth with being tortured; in all moments."

"I release associating living my purpose with being killed or tortured; in all moments."

"I release rejecting my truth; in all moments."

"I release hiding my truth; in all moments."

"I release living in complacency; in all moments."

"I release squelching other people's truth by association; in all moments."

"I release living a lie; in all moments."

"I release succumbing to the will of others; in all moments."

"I release associating living my truth with dying defeated; in all moments."

"I shift my paradigm to be the victor; in all moments."

"I relish in being victorious in my truth and living my purpose; in all moments."

"I release shoving opinions down others' throats in the name of living my truth; in all moments."

"I am centered and empowered in the sanctity of living my truth; in all moments."

"I am centered and empowered in the omniscience of living my purpose; in all moments."

Soften Your Words

(Say each statement three times out loud while continuously tapping on the top of your head at the crown chakra and say it a fourth time while tapping on your chest.)

"I release using words as weapons; in all moments."

"I release cursing others; in all moments."

"I release cursing myself; in all moments."

"I release wishing anything but the highest intention for others; in all moments."

"I release wishing anything but the highest intention for myself; in all moments."

"I release being paralyzed into non-action; in all moments."

"I release being paralyzed by the thoughts and words of others; in all moments."

"I release enjoying the misfortune of others; in all moments."

"I remove all vivaxes between myself and all those rooting against me; in all moments."

"I remove all vivaxes between myself and all those who wish to see me fail; in all moments."

"I remove all vivaxes between myself and all those who curse me in indifference; in all moments."

"I release consciously or unwittingly rooting against others; in all moments."

"I remove all vivaxes between myself and all those that I have rooted against; in all moments."

"I remove all vivaxes between myself and all those that I have wished to see fail; in all moments."

"I remove all vivaxes between myself and all those I have cursed; in all moments."

"I am centered and empowered in the purity and integrity of my truth; in all moments."

Regaining Our Voice

People are afraid to speak their mind. They don't do it in their everyday life so they don't do it with major life altering issues either. The people in power depend on your silence to keep the status quo and to keep energetically raping the individual of their rights.

The reason people don't speak out is because of past life traumas where they were pulled out of the crowd and tortured for their beliefs. Those traumas show up in this lifetime as being afraid of what people will think, being afraid to share being different and the fear of looking stupid. I also see it all the time with clients who have heartfelt, energy shifting sessions with me and then are afraid to mention it to anyone.

There is a way to gain a voice in the bigger picture. It is by sharing one's truth on smaller items. One can share their point of view without attacking or being attacked. One can simply state with love and conviction where they stand. If one gets upset at doing this, it is because in past lives they have been killed for doing so. So by sharing in the present and living through it, we are reprogramming ourselves to more joy, love, abundance, freedom and wholeness.

The more we share with others in a conscientious, loving way, the more we show them that it is okay to be different. It doesn't mean that we are enemies and that someone has to die. It is a great service to others to let them see what clear, loving communication looks like. Maybe that way, we can all infuse more positivity into our shared macrocosm and bring the world back to joy, love, abundance, freedom and wholeness for all!

Here are some taps to assist: (Say each statement three times while tapping on your head and say it a fourth time while tapping on your chest.)

"I recant my vow of silence; in all moments."

"I release the fear and trauma of being persecuted; in all moments."

"I release the fear of speaking my truth; in all moments."

"I release the trauma of being muted; in all moments."

"I release losing my voice; in all moments."

"I recant all vows and agreements between myself and being stifled; in all moments."

"I remove all curses between myself and being stifled; in all moments."

"I dissolve all karmic ties between myself and being stifled; in all moments."

"I remove all the pain, anguish and limitations that being stifled has put on me; in all moments."

"I remove all the pain, anguish and limitations I have put on all others by stifling them; in all moments."

"I take back all the joy, love, abundance, freedom, life and wholeness that being stifled has taken from me; in all moments."

"I give back all the joy, love, abundance, freedom, life and wholeness that I have taken from all others by stifling them; in all moments."

"I shift my paradigm from being stifled to joyful and loving expression; in all moments."

Teeth

(Say each statement three times while tapping on your head and say a fourth time while tapping on your chest.)

"I release the trauma of rotting; in all moments."

"I release degenerating; in all moments."

"I release having my skull crushed in; in all moments."

"I release having my teeth knocked out; in all moments."

"I release storing issues in my gums; in all moments."

"I release the trauma of losing my teeth; in all moments."

"I remove all fear from my gums; in all moments."

"I remove all mental imbalances from my gums; in all moments."

"I release neglecting my teeth and gums; in all moments."

"I remove all inflammation from my gums; in all moments."

"I release associating gum issues with death; in all moments."

"I infuse optimal health and well-being into my gums; in all moments."

Throat

(Say each statement three times while tapping on your head and say it a fourth time while tapping on your chest.)

"I release sucking down smoke; in all moments."

"I release holding in the sadness; in all moments."

"I release breathing in poison; in all moments."

"I vomit out the toxins; in all moments."

"I release being impaled; in all moments."

"I release tasting my own blood; in all moments."

"I release the trauma of having my throat slit; in all moments."

"I release drowning on my own blood; in all moments."

"I release drowning on my own fluids; in all moments."

"I release the trauma of sucking in water; in all moments."

"I remove all engrams of drowning; in all moments."

"I release reliving my own drowning; in all moments."

"I release reliving the trauma of having my throat slit; in all moments."

"I release the trauma of dying in a fire; in all moments."

"I release reliving the trauma of being killed in a fire; in all moments."

"I release the trauma of being burned alive; in all moments."

"I remove all the trauma stored in my throat; in all moments."

Thyroid

(Say each statement three times while tapping on your head and say it a fourth time while tapping on your chest.)

"I release the trauma of dying; in all moments."

"I release the trauma of running for my life; in all moments."

"I release the trauma of being murdered; in all moments."

"I remove all engrams of being murdered; in all moments."

"I release reliving my own death; in all moments."

"I release being trapped in a traumatic death; in all moments."

"I withdraw all my energy from reliving trauma; in all moments."

"I convert all trauma to peace; in all moments."

"I unlock my throat chakra; in all moments."

"I remove all the stagnant energy from my thyroid; in all moments."

"I reconnect my endocrine system with my chakra system; in all moments."

"I recharge my chakra system; in all moments."

"I infuse my whole endocrine system with the higher energies of healing love; in all moments."

"I am centered and empowered in the healing energies of healing love; in all moments."

"I regain all normal bodily functions; in all moments."

"I am infused with exuberance and the lifeblood of optimal joy; in all moments."

Time and Space

(Say each statement three times out loud while continuously tapping on the top of your head at the crown chakra and say it a fourth time while tapping on your heart chakra.)

"I release being distracted by time; in all moments."

"I release being beholden to time; in all moments."

"I adopt a timeless state; in all moments."

"I release being immersed in matter; in all moments."

"I release caring if I matter; in all moments."

"I release owning things to feel like I matter; in all moments."

"I validate myself in and beyond matter; in all moments."

"I release needing space; in all moments."

"I release a tight space being confused with suffocating to death; in all moments."

"I release spacing out; in all moments."

"I release all limiting references to space; in all moments."

"I exist in a spacious, grounded state; in all moments."

"I release running out of energy; in all moments."

"I release the belief that energy is in limited supply; in all moments."

"I embrace myself as an energy being; in all moments."

"I function and exist in an effortless, spacious, limitless state; in all moments."

Collapsing Time and Space

Here are some powerful taps that came out of the private group session. There is always something new that reveals itself during these sessions. We are exploring new dimensions now. We might as well explore them as the navigator.

(Say each statement three times out loud while continuously tapping on the top of your head at the crown chakra and say it a fourth time while tapping on your chest.)

"I collapse time and space to pour perpetual healing into dissolving the tortured me; in all moments."

"I collapse time and space to pour perpetual comfort into dissolving the rejected me; in all moments."

"I collapse time and space to pour perpetual security into dissolving the abandoned me; in all moments."

"I collapse time and space to pour perpetual love into dissolving the fearful me; in all moments."

"I collapse time and space to pour perpetual nurturing into dissolving the tortured me; in all moments."

"I collapse time and space to pour perpetual lightness into dissolving the angry me; in all moments."

"I collapse time and space to pour perpetual freedom into dissolving the enslaved me; in all moments."

"I collapse time and space to pour perpetual fullness into dissolving the starving me; in all moments."

"I collapse time and space to pour perpetual abundance into dissolving the impoverished me; in all moments."

"I collapse time and space to pour perpetual joy into dissolving the disheartened me; in all moments."

"I collapse time and space to pour perpetual health into dissolving the sick me; in all moments."

"I collapse time and space to pour perpetual success into dissolving the failing me; in all moments."

"I collapse time and space to pour perpetual enlightenment into dissolving the ignorant me; in all moments."

"I collapse time and space to reveal and be the loving, empowered me; in all moments."

"I am centered and empowered in perpetual love; in all moments."

Remove Limitations of Time and Space

They may not make sense, but doing these taps can harvest huge results. I encourage everyone to invest in doing these. It is a profound shift in dynamics to do so.

(Say each statement three times out loud while continuously tapping on the top of your head at the crown chakra and say it a fourth time while tapping on your chest.)

"I release the belief that matter, energy, space and time are all finite; in all moments."

"I release converting energy to time; in all moments."

"I release converting energy into space; in all moments."

"I release converting energy into matter; in all moments."

"I release 'time' dominating matter, energy and space; in all moments."

"I recant all vows and agreements between matter, energy, space and time; in all moments."

"I release the symbiotic relationship between matter, energy, space and time; in all moments."

"I remove all curses between matter, energy, space and time; in all moments."

"I remove all blessings between matter, energy, space and time; in all moments."

"I sever all strings and cords between matter, energy, space and time; in all moments."

"I dissolve all karmic ties between matter, energy, space and time; in all moments."

"I release being ganged up on by matter, energy, space and time; in all moments."

"I release being tag teamed by matter, energy, space and time; in all moments."

"I recant all vows and agreements between humanity and matter, energy, space and time; in all moments."

"I release the symbiotic relationship between humanity and matter, energy, space and time; in all moments."

"I release humanity being enslaved by matter, energy, space and time; in all moments."

"I release humanity being dependent on matter, energy, space and time; in all moments."

"I remove all curses between humanity and matter, energy, space and time; in all moments."

"I remove all blessings between humanity and matter, energy, space and time; in all moments."

"I sever all strings and cords between humanity and matter, energy, space and time; in all moments."

"I dissolve all karmic ties between humanity and matter, energy, space and time; in all moments."

"I recant all vows and agreements between matter, energy, space and time and humanity; in all moments."

"I release the symbiotic relationship between matter, energy, space and time and humanity; in all moments."

"I remove all curses between matter, energy, space and time and humanity; in all moments."

"I remove all blessings between matter, energy, space and time and humanity; in all moments."

"I sever all strings and cords between matter, energy, space and time and humanity; in all moments."

"I dissolve all karmic ties between matter, energy, space and time and humanity; in all moments."

"I remove all the pain, burden, limitations and engrams that humanity has put on matter, energy, space and time; in all moments."

"I remove all the pain, burden, limitations and engrams that matter, energy, space and time has put on humanity; in all moments."

"I give back to humanity all the joy, love, abundance, freedom, health, success, security, companionship, peace, life, wholeness, beauty, enthusiasm, contentment, spirituality, enlightenment, confidence, family, intellect and the ability to discern that matter, energy, space and time has taken from them; in all moments."

"I give back to matter, energy, space and time all that humanity has taken from it; in all moments."

"I release matter, energy, space and time resonating with humanity; in all moments."

"I release matter, energy, space and time emanating with humanity; in all moments."

"I release humanity resonating with matter, energy, space and time; in all moments."

"I release humanity emanating with matter, energy, space and time; in all moments."

"I extract all of matter, energy, space and time from humanity's sound frequency; in all moments."

"I extract all of humanity from matter, energy, space and time's sound frequency; in all moments."

"I extract all of matter, energy, space and time from humanity's light emanation; in all moments."

"I extract all of humanity from matter, energy, space and time's light emanation; in all moments."

"I shift matter, energy, space and time's paradigm from humanity to joy, love, abundance, freedom, health, success, security, companionship, peace, life, wholeness, beauty, enthusiasm, contentment, spirituality, enlightenment, confidence, family, intellect and the ability to discern; in all moments."

"I shift humanity's paradigm from matter, energy, space and time to joy, love, abundance, freedom, health, success, security, companionship, peace, life, wholeness, beauty, enthusiasm, contentment, spirituality, enlightenment, confidence, family, intellect and the ability to discern; in all moments."

"Matter, energy, space and time transcend humanity; in all moments."

"Humanity transcends matter, energy, space and time; in all moments."

"Matter, energy, space and time are centered and imbued in divine love; in all moments."

"Humanity is centered and empowered in divine love; in all moments."

"Matter, energy, space and time resonate and emanate divine love; in all moments."

"I infuse humanity's sound frequency with joy, love, abundance, freedom, health, success, security, companionship, peace, life, wholeness, beauty, enthusiasm, contentment, spirituality, enlightenment, confidence, family, intellect and the ability to discern; in all moments."

"I imbue humanity's light emanation with joy, love, abundance, freedom, health, success, security, companionship, peace, life, wholeness, beauty, enthusiasm, contentment, spirituality, enlightenment, confidence, family, intellect and the ability to discern; in all moments."

"Humanity resonates and emanates divine love; in all moments."

Tinnitus

(Say each statement three times while tapping on your head and say it a fourth time while tapping on your chest.)

"I release whining; in all moments."

"I remove all judgment; in all moments."

"I release allowing life to sour; in all moments."

"I release interpreting beauty with a negative slant; in all moments."

"I release the trauma of hearing the screams; in all moments."

"I release deducing all of life to a whiny scream; in all moments."

"I release the need to drown out the harshness; in all moments."

"I release interpreting life as a trauma; in all moments."

"I release converting beauty into an ugliness; in all moments."

"I release the need to drown out the sounds; in all moments."

"I convert all trauma back into sweetness; in all moments."

"I release all internal pressure; in all moments."

"I release being forced to perform unethical acts; in all moments."

"I hear only sweet sounds; in all moments."

"I soften my vibration to the resonance of joy; in all moments."

Releasing Torture from the Human Repertoire

I was in the shower with the water running all over my face and it occurred to me in that moment to send healing love to all the people who have ever been water-boarded. It had nothing to do with politics or being in agreement with anything on the surface. It had to do with helping them to maintain their connection with humanity.

That is why torture is so egregious. It separates an individual from humanity and creates an engram on their causal body that may take many lifetimes to undo.

Think of yourself as a 3-D old vinyl record. The grooves that are in it are all memories from all the experiences in all your lives. The ones that are less deep are the pleasant experiences. The ones that make the record skip (repeat experiences) are deeply ingrained physically, emotionally and mentally, painful experiences. These deepest ones are the ones I read in private sessions and the ones I help to rub out or fill in so that the client can return to their joy. The reason torture is so horrendous is that it carves deep grooves in all components of the human experience by combining physical, emotional and mental pain.

What the torturer doesn't realize is that they are obligated to assist that person in undoing what they have done to them. As a group, the same rule applies. Ignorance of the understanding of cause and effect does not excuse one from violating others. Denial will run out of steam as well. I have experienced torture in this lifetime and I see it in the memory banks of my clients. Doing the following taps may assist lightening the burden that such acts have put on humanity. May all feel lightness in you doing them.

(Say each statement three times while tapping on your head and say it a fourth time while tapping on your chest.)

"I release the trauma of being tortured; in all moments."

"I release the guilt and trauma of torturing others; in all moments."

"I release condoning torture; in all moments."

"I release surrendering my power to torture; in all moments."

"I recant all vows and agreements between myself and torture; in all moments."

"I release quantifying torture; in all moments."

"I dissolve the karmic pull of torture; in all moments."

"I remove all the pain, burden and limitations that torture has put on me; in all moments."

"I remove all the pain, burden and limitations I have put on all others through torture; in all moments."

"I take back all the joy, love, abundance, freedom, health, life and wholeness that being tortured has taken from me; in all moments."

"I withdraw all my energy from, and support of, torture; in all moments."

"I give back all that I have taken from others through means of torture; in all moments."

There are varying degrees of torture as well. Mental anguish and emotional upheaval in this life may be a playing out of past life torture. To a soul at the end of a leash when all those they love are in the house, this is indeed torture to them. Who is to justify it? Who is to deem one soul more or less worthy? By honoring all souls as worthy, it sidesteps the dangerous pitfalls of arrogance and control. May anyone reading this forgo the resistance and just do the technique above. In this way, they will be loving the heart of humanity.

Taps for Tourette's Syndrome

(Say each statement three times while tapping on your head and say it a fourth time while tapping on your chest.)

"I untangle my parasympathetic nervous system from the sympathetic nervous system; in all moments."

"I release involuntary sympathetic nervous system behavior; in all moments."

"I remove all emotional issues from my sympathetic and parasympathetic nervous system; in all moments."

"I release storing trauma in my nervous system; in all moments."

"I remove all the trauma that causes tics; in all moments."

"I repair and fortify the myelin sheath on my nervous system; in all moments."

"I calm all tics; in all moments."

"I eliminate the first cause in displaying tics; in all moments."
"I release the genetic propensity to have Tourette's; in all moments."

"I nullify all contracts with Tourette's; in all moments."

"I deactivate all involuntary behavior; in all moments."

"I heal all schisms between my sympathetic and parasympathetic nervous system; in all moments."

"I remove all engrams that cause me to react involuntarily; in all moments."

"I calm and heal my nerves; in all moments."

Toxic Mold

(Say each statement three times while tapping on my head and say it a fourth time while tapping on my chest.)

"I release being inundated with toxic mold; in all moments."

"I release the effects of toxic mold; in all moments."

"I release being poisoned by toxic mold; in all moments."

"I release processing toxic mold into my physical realm; in all moments."

"I extract all toxic mold from my genetic makeup; in all moments."

"I extract all toxic mold from my nervous system; in all moments."

"I release being suffocated by toxic mold; in all moments."

"I remove all vivaxes between myself and toxic mold; in all moments."

"I expose all toxic mold; in all moments."

"I dry up all toxic mold; in all moments."

"I instantaneously detox from all toxic mold; in all moments."

"I strip all illusion off of toxic mold; in all moments."

"I eliminate the first cause in creating toxic mold; in all moments."

"I collapse and dissolve all portals to toxic mold; in all moments."

"I flush all toxic mold out of existence with divine love; in all moments."

"I recant all vows and agreements between myself and toxic mold; in all moments."

"I free myself of all infirmities caused by toxic mold; in all moments."

"I release being cursed with toxic mold; in all moments."

"I released being blessed with toxic mold; in all moments."

"I remove all programming and conditioning that toxic mold has put on us; in all moments."

"I remove all engrams of toxic mold; in all moments."

"I dissolve all karmic ties between myself and toxic mold; in all moments."

"I release the dumbing down of humanity caused by toxic mold; in moments."

"I send all energy matrices into the light and sound that create toxic mold; in all moments."

"I command all complex energy matrices that create toxic mold to be escorted into the light and sound; in all moments."

"I send all energy matrices into the light and sound that perpetuate toxic mold; in all moments."

"I command all complex energy matrices that perpetuate toxic mold to be escorted into the light and sound; in all moments."

"I remove all the illness that toxic mold has put on us; in all moments."

"I release feeding toxic mold; in all moments."

"I withdraw all my energy from toxic mold; in all moments."

"I release creating a fertile environment for toxic to grow; in all moments."

"I remove all the pain, burden and limitations that toxic mold has put on us; in all moments."

"I remove all the fear, futility and unworthiness that toxic mold has put on us; in all moments."

"I remove all the anger, apathy and indifference that toxic mold has put on us; in all moments."

"I remove all the illusion of separateness that toxic mold has put on us; in all moments."

"I take back all that toxic mold has taken from us; in all moments."

"I extract all toxic mold from all 32 layers of my auric field; in all moments."

"I release resonating or emanating with toxic mold; in all moments."

"I extract all toxic mold from my sound frequency and my light emanation; in all moments."

"I transcend toxic mold; in all moments."

"I am centered and empowered in the clarity and purity of divine love; in all moments."

"I resonate, emanate, and am interconnected with all life in the clarity and purity of divine love; in all moments."

"I restore my Soul; in all moments."

"I release being trapped in the lower worlds by toxic mold; in all moments."

"I release being trapped in the mental realms by toxic mold; in all moments."

"I release being trapped in the psychic realms by toxic mold; in all moments."

"I send all energy matrices into the light and sound that trap Soul in illusion; in all moments."

"I command all complex energy matrices that trap Soul in illusion to be escorted into the light and sound; in all moments."

"I send all energy matrices that trap Soul in the lower worlds into the light and sound; in all moments."

"I command all complex energy matrices that trap Souls in the lower worlds to be escorted into the light and sound; in all moments."

"I free Souls everywhere; in all moments."

Removing Energetic Toxic Mold

I have been told that there has been such a thing as energetic toxic mold that exists at the sub-physical level. It has been the contributing element that creates diseases that scientists have not been able to distinguish a cure for. This includes such issues as muscular dystrophy, fibromyalgia, Parkinson's disease and other neuromuscular diseases.

It acts like black mold in destroying our homes and infiltrating our bodies. It has seeped into our DNA and made many diseases act as if they react to a genetic factor when they are really reacting to an environmental issue of energetic toxic mold. Just like the sunlight dries up ringworm, light and love dry up this energetic mold. Prayer used to be very effective in dissipating it until it got too systemic and corroded even our correspondences to God. That is why prayer seems less effective these days for so many.

It takes a strong energetic intention to dry up what we have all been immersed in. That is what we did in this morning's group session. Have you ever seen a family living in a house that was corroded with black mold not realizing that it was affecting them? That is what we all have been doing...until now. Here are the taps we used to dry up this energetic toxic mold. See how you feel after doing them.

(Say each statement three times while tapping on your head and say it a fourth time while tapping on your chest.)

"We declare ourselves surrogates for humanity in doing these taps; in all moments."

"We release being inundated with energetic toxic mold; in all moments."

"We release the effects of energetic toxic mold; in all moments."

"We release being poisoned by energetic toxic mold; in all moments."

"We release processing energetic toxic mold into our physical realm; in all moments."

"We extract all energetic toxic mold from our genetic makeup; in all moments."

"We extract all energetic toxic mold from our nervous system; in all moments."

"We release being suffocated by energetic toxic mold; in all moments."

"We remove all vivaxes between ourselves and energetic toxic mold; in all moments."

"We expose all energetic toxic mold; in all moments."

"We dry up all energetic toxic mold; in all moments."

"We instantaneously detox from all energetic toxic mold; in all moments."

"We strip all illusion off of energetic toxic mold; in all moments."

"We eliminate the first cause in creating energetic toxic mold; in all moments."

"We collapse and dissolve all portals to energetic toxic mold; in all moments."

"We flush all energetic toxic mold out of existence with divine love; in all moments."

"We recant all vows and agreements between ourselves and energetic toxic mold; in all moments."

"We free ourselves of all infirmities caused by energetic toxic mold; in all moments."

"We release being cursed with energetic toxic mold; in all moments."

"We released being blessed with energetic toxic mold; in all moments."

"We remove all programming and conditioning that energetic toxic mold has put on us; in all moments."

"We remove all engrams of energetic toxic mold; in all moments."

"We dissolve all karmic ties between ourselves and energetic toxic mold; in all moments."

"We release the dumbing down of humanity caused by energetic toxic mold; in moments."

"We send all energy matrices into the light and sound that create energetic toxic mold; in all moments."

"We command all complex energy matrices that create energetic toxic mold to be escorted into the light and sound; in all moments."

"We send all energy matrices into the light and sound that perpetuate energetic toxic mold; in all moments."

"We command all complex energy matrices that perpetuate energetic toxic mold to be escorted into the light and sound; in all moments."

"We remove all the illness that energetic toxic mold has put on us; in all moments."

"We release feeding energetic toxic mold; in all moments."

"We withdraw all our energy from energetic toxic mold; in all moments."

"We release creating a fertile environment for energetic toxic mold to grow; in all moments."

"We remove all the pain, burden and limitations that energetic toxic mold has put on us; in all moments."

"We remove all the fear, futility and unworthiness that energetic toxic mold has put on us; in all moments."

"We remove all the anger, apathy and indifference that energetic toxic mold has put on us; in all moments."

"We remove all the illusion of separateness that energetic toxic mold has put on us; in all moments."

"We take back all that energetic toxic mold has taken from us; in all moments."

"We extract all energetic toxic mold from all 32 layers of our auric field; in all moments."

"We release resonating or emanating with energetic toxic mold; in all moments."

"We extract all energetic toxic mold from our sound frequency and our light emanation; in all moments."

"We transcend energetic toxic mold; in all moments."

"We are centered and empowered in the clarity and purity of divine love; in all moments."

"We resonate, emanate and are interconnected with all life in the clarity and purity of divine love; in all moments."

"We restore our Soul; in all moments."

"We release being trapped in the lower worlds by energetic toxic mold; in all moments."

"We release being trapped in the mental realms by energetic toxic mold; in all moments."

"We release being trapped in the psychic realms by energetic toxic mold; in all moments."

"We send all energy matrices into the light and sound that trap Soul in illusion; in all moments."

"We command all complex energy matrices that trap Soul in illusion to be escorted into the light and sound; in all moments."

"We send all energy matrices that trap Soul in the lower worlds into the light and sound; in all moments."

"We command all complex energy matrices that trap Souls in the lower worlds to be escorted into the light and sound; in all moments."

"We free Souls everywhere; in all moments."

Release the Fear of Enlightenment

(Say each statement three times while tapping on your head and say it a fourth time while tapping on your chest.)

"I release the belief that I am alone; in all moments."

"I release the belief that I am insignificant; in all moments."

"I release the belief that I don't matter; in all moments."

"I release the belief that I am not being heard; in all moments."

"I release believing the lie that I am alone; in all moments."

"I release glazing over from all that I've seen; in all moments."

"I release confusing surgery as an assault; in all moments."

"I release confusing the surgeon with the enemy; in all moments."

"I release being blinded to truth; in all moments."

"I release being pinned down in fear; in all moments."

"I release being stuck in defense mode; in all moments."

"I release being stuck in primal mode; in all moments."

"I release deferring to primal mode; in all moments."

"I release the genetic propensity to revert to primal mode; in all moments."

"I release the trauma of being stabbed in the eye; in all moments."

"I remove all engrams in the eyes; in all moments."

"I heal my causal eyes; in all moments."

"I repair my vision; in all moments."

"I declare myself a surrogate for humanity in doing these taps; in all moments."

"I release being trapped in primal mode; in all moments."

"I release the fear of transcending; in all moments."

"I release confusing transcending with death; in all moments."

"I release fighting amongst my peers; in all moments."

"I remove myself from infighting; in all moments."

"I open my spiritual eye; in all moments."

"I awaken my subtle senses; in all moments."

"I repair all the energy systems in my beingness; in all moments."

"I recharge all the energy systems in my beingness; in all moments."

"I synchronize all the energy systems in my beingness to work in harmony; in all moments."

"I remove all the outmoded filters from my beingness; in all moments."

"I release filtering out the joy; in all moments."

"I release filtering out the love; in all moments."

"I release filtering out the abundance; in all moments."

"I release filtering out the freedom; in all moments."

"I release filtering out health; in all moments."

"I release filtering out success; in all moments."

"I release filtering out wholeness; in all moments."

"I release filtering out enlightenment; in all moments."

"I recalibrate my whole energy system to embrace joy; in all moments."

"I recalibrate my whole energy system to embrace love; in all moments."

"I recalibrate my whole energy system to embrace abundance; in all moments."

"I recalibrate my whole energy system to embrace freedom; in all moments."

"I recalibrate my whole energy system to embrace health; in all moments."

"I recalibrate my whole energy system to embrace success; in all moments."

"I recalibrate my whole energy system to embrace wholeness; in all moments."

"I recalibrate my whole energy system to embrace enlightenment; in all moments."

"I release the disconnect between the microcosm and the macrocosm; in all moments."

"I shift my paradigm from primal mode to spiritual being; in all moments."

"I shift the universal paradigm from primal mode to spiritual being; in all moments."

"I shift my paradigm from primal mode to enlightenment; in all moments."

"I shift the universal paradigm from primal mode to enlightenment; in all moments."

"I am centered and empowered in enlightenment; in all moments."

"I am universally centered and empowered in enlightenment; in all moments."

"I resonate, emanate and am interconnected with all life in enlightenment; in all moments."

"I resonate, emanate and am interconnected with all life in universal enlightenment; in all moments."

Transcendence

(Say each statement three times out loud while tapping on the top of your head at the crown chakra and say it a fourth time while tapping on your chest at the heart chakra.)

"I release being stubborn; in all moments."

"I release being diametrically opposed to anything; in all moments."

"I release switching; in all moments."

"I release confusing hate for love; in all moments."

"I release confusing love for hate; in all moments."

"I release confusing blessings for curses; in all moments."

"I release confusing curses for blessings; in all moments."

"I release confusing slavery for freedom; in all moments."

"I release confusing freedom for slavery; in all moments."

"I release confusing abundance for poverty; in all moments."

"I release confusing poverty for abundance; in all moments."

"I release confusing ugliness for beauty; in all moments."

"I release confusing beauty for ugliness; in all moments."

"I release confusing ignorance for truth; in all moments."

"I release confusing truth for ignorance; in all moments."

"I release confusing manipulation for grace; in all moments."

"I release confusing grace for manipulation; in all moments."

"I release confusing complacency for peace; in all moments."

"I release confusing peace for complacency; in all moments."

"I release confusing health for dis-ease; in all moments."

"I release confusing dis-ease for health; in all moments."

"I release confusing failure for success; in all moments."

"I release confusing success for failure; in all moments."

"I release confusing denseness for awareness; in all moments."

"I release confusing awareness for denseness; in all moments."

"I release confusing disconnectedness for connectedness; in all moments."

"I release confusing connectedness for disconnectedness; in all moments."

"I release confusing rhetoric for truth; in all moments."

"I release confusing truth for rhetoric; in all moments."

"I release confusing imprisonment for security; in all moments."

"I release confusing security for imprisonment; in all moments."

"I release confusing religion for spirituality; in all moments."

"I release confusing spirituality for religion; in all moments."

"I release confusing fragmentation for wholeness; in all moments."

"I release confusing wholeness for fragmentation; in all moments."

"I release confusing stewing for taking the higher ground; in all moments."

"I release confusing taking the higher ground for stewing; in all moments."

"I release confusing illusion for enlightenment; in all moments."

"I release confusing enlightenment for illusion; in all moments."

"I release confusing completeness for isolation; in all moments."

"I release confusing isolation for completeness; in all moments."

"I release confusing stubbornness for strength; in all moments."

"I release confusing strength for stubbornness; in all moments."

"I release confusing an open heart for weakness; in all moments."

"I release confusing weakness for an open heart; in all moments."

Transcending Power

I was facilitating a session today and it occurred to me that the issue with power is that people think it is the pinnacle of existence, that there is nothing beyond power. It was an issue I was working on with my client and we were in such an incredible place of love that we were at a vantage point where power was a lower level of consciousness. In fact in the session, we both had the experience of seeing how power is a hindrance. It was, in the experience, plugging up the pathways of love.

In contemplation, assume the vantage point of omniscient love. Look out on the horizon at an incredible world of pure love. Get a sense of the murky channels of power that run like sludge through most pure realm. Get a good look at what concentrated, unadulterated power looks like when stripped of illusion. See it as the septic stream of stagnant energy that it is. May you never look at power or even being important the same way.

(Say each statement three times while tapping on your head and say it a fourth time while tapping on your chest.)

"I release worshiping power; in all moments."

"I release looking up to power; in all moments."

"I strip off the illusion of power; in all moments."

"I release being enslaved to power; in all moments."

"I transcend power; in all moments."

"I remove all the pain, burden, illusion and limitations that power has put on me; in all moments."

"I remove all the pain, burden, illusion and limitations that I have put on all others in the name of power; in all moments."

"I take back all the joy, love, abundance, freedom, life and wholeness that power has taken from me; in all moments."

"I give back all the joy, love, abundance, freedom, life and wholeness that I have taken from all others in the name of power; in all moments."

"I am centered and empowered in divine love; in all moments."

Transcending War

There is a spiritual law that is as exacting as the Law of Attraction or the Law of Gravity. It is the Law of Opposites. It states that for every action, there is an equal and opposite action. Part of what this means is that as long as people keep reacting to and opposing any position, they are going to perpetuate, by that reaction, the exact action that they oppose.

A lack of understanding of this spiritual law is what keeps war in business generation after generation. The spiritual way to stop war is by not feeding into it but by transcending the need to react. Many of us may lack the understanding of this concept and so may still feed war as a group. But if enough individuals adopt this stance, the individuals can be the tipping point to create a change in world affairs.

(Say each statement three times while tapping on your head and say it a fourth time while tapping on your chest.)

"I release indulging in conflict; in all moments."

"I release having enemies; in all moments."

"I withdraw all my energy from war; in all moments."

"I recant all vows and agreements between myself and all enemies; in all moments."

"I remove all curses between myself and all enemies; in all moments."

"I dissolve all karmic ties between myself and all enemies; in all moments."

"I remove all the pain, burden, fear and limitations that all enemies have put on me; in all moments."

"I remove all the pain burden, fear and limitations that I have put on all enemies; in all moments."

"I take back all the joy, love, abundance, freedom, life and wholeness that all enemies have taken from me; in all moments."

"I give back all the joy, love, abundance, freedom, life and wholeness that I have taken from all enemies; in all moments."

"I release resonating with war; in all moments."

"I release emanating with war; in all moments."

"I remove all war from my sound frequency; in all moments."

"I remove all war from my light body; in all moments."

"I shift my paradigm from war to LOVE; in all moments."

There doesn't have to be a personal assault to life and limb for war to affect us all. War itself is an assault on humanity. The thing that is most intolerable for a loving parent is watching their children fight. Imagine what God must feel seeing his children at war. Being kind to others beyond all reason is a great way to express gratitude to God.

Save the Trees

(Say each statement three times while tapping on your head and say in a fourth time while tapping on your chest.)

"I declare myself a surrogate for society in doing these taps."

"I release the genocide of trees; in all moments."

"I release needing to sacrifice a tree to feel holiday joy; in all moments."

"I untangle sacrificing a tree with holiday joy; in all moments."

"I release associating cutting down a tree with Christmas; in all moments."

"I remove all engrams of cutting down trees; in all moments."

"I release the muscle memory of cutting down a tree; in all moments."

"I dissipate the psychic energy that depicts joy in cutting down a tree; in all moments."

"I strip all illusion from cutting down a tree; in all moments."

"I eliminate the first cause in cutting down a Christmas tree; in all moments."

"I release the systemic ignorance that invalidates the wonder of trees; in all moments."

"I free humanity of the systemic practice of cutting down trees; in all moments."

"I nullify all contracts with the practice of cuttings trees; in all moments."

"I recalibrate the worth of a tree to at least as valuable to society as a white human baby; in all moments."

"I remove all vivaxes between myself and cutting down trees; in all moments."

"I remove all tentacles between myself and cutting down trees; in all moments."

"I release the cultural propensity to cut down trees; in all moments."

"I remove all programming and conditioning to cut down trees; in all moments."

"I send all energy matrices of enjoying cutting down trees into the light and sound; in all moments."

"I command all complex energy matrices that enjoy cutting down trees be escorted into the light and sound; in all moments."

"I recant all vows and agreements between myself and cutting down trees; in all moments."

"I remove all curses between myself and cutting down trees; in all moments."

"I remove all blessings between myself and cutting down trees; in all moments."

"I sever all strings and cords between myself and cutting down trees; in all moments."

"I dissolve all karmic ties between myself and cutting down trees; in all moments."

"I extract cutting down trees from our holiday traditions; in all moments."

"I extract cutting down trees from our nostalgia; in all moments."

"I extract cutting down trees from our sound frequency and light emanation; in all moments."

"I release all animosity towards earth; in all moments."

"I extract cutting down trees from our akashic records; in all moments."

"I extract cutting trees from all 32 layers of our auric field; in all moments."

"I extract cutting trees from the whole existence humanity; in all moments."

"I shift our paradigm from cutting down trees to honoring and respecting trees; in all moments."

"I align all our bodies to honoring and respecting trees; in all moments."

"I am centered and empowered in honoring and respecting trees; in all moments."

"I transcend cutting down trees; in all moments.'"

"I resonate, emanate and am connected with all life in honoring trees; in all moments."

Tribalism

(Say each statement three times while continuously tapping the top of your head and say it a fourth time while tapping your chest.)

"We declare ourselves surrogates for humanity in doing these taps; in all moments."

"We release the schism between the awakened and those who are awakening; in all moments."

"We remove the ignorance from those who are still awakening; in all moments."

"We remove the crutch of hatred from those who are still awakening; in all moments."

"We pull all those in tribalism out of attack mode; in all moments."

"We dry up all psychic streams of energy of tribalism; in all moments."

"We heal all the wounds of tribalism; in all moments."

"We free all those in tribalism from primal mode; in all moments."

"We heal the exploitation that causes awakening Souls to adopt tribalism; in all moments."

"We release all Souls that have been trapped in tribalism; in all moments."

"We remove all engrams of hate from all those in tribalism; in all moments."

"We remove all engrams of fear from all those in tribalism; in all moments."

"We release the hunger of war from all those in tribalism; in all moments."

"We remove all engrams of global war from all those in tribalism; in all moments."

"We remove all muscle memory of war from all those in tribalism; in all moments."

"We hasten the awakening of all those in tribalism; in all moments."

"We nullify all contracts between global war and all those in tribalism; in all moments."

"We nullify all contracts between all those in tribalism and ignorance; in all moments."

"We nullify all contracts between all those in tribalism and fear; in all moments."

"We release being tethered to lower consciousness by all those in tribalism; in all moments."

"We release the resistance of all those in tribalism to awakening; in all moments."

"We nullify all contracts between all Souls and tribalism; in all moments."

"We remove all vivaxes between all those in tribalism and war; in all moments."

"We remove the scales from the eyes of all those in tribalism; in all moments."

"We remove all curses between all Souls and all those in tribalism; in all moments."

"We strip all illusion off of all those in tribalism; in all moments."

"We remove all masks, walls and armor from all those in tribalism; in all moments."

"We remove all tentacles between all those in tribalism and war; in all moments."

"We disarm all those in tribalism from being fed by fear or hate; in all moments."

"We eliminate the first cause of all those in tribalism being trapped in fear; in all moments."

"We repair and fortify the Wei chi of all those in tribalism; in all moments."

"We return to all those in tribalism all their missing components; in all moments."

"We remove from all those in tribalism all the devastation that primal mode has put on them; in all moments."

"We love all those in tribalism out of reactionary mode; in all moments."

"We raise the vibration on all those in tribalism; in all moments."

"We gift all those in tribalism the ability to discern; in all moments."

"We sever all strings and cords between all those in tribalism and primal mode; in all moments."

"We nurture the transcendence of all those in tribalism; in all moments."

"We infuse joy, love, abundance and freedom into all those in tribalism; in all moments."

"We dry up all want and need from all those in tribalism; in all moments."

"We infuse joy, love, abundance and freedom into all those in tribalism's sound frequency and light emanation; in all moments."

"We gift all those in tribalism with the ability to know truth; in all moments."

"We strip all illusion off of tribalism; in all moments."

"We disarm all those in tribalism from using power; in all moments."

"We command all of those in tribalism's reactions to circle back on them; in all moments."

"We render all those in tribalism ineffective of harming others; in all moments."

"We render all those in tribalism transparent; in all moments."

"We leave humanity unscathed by all those caught up in tribalism; in all moments."

"We awaken to our own empowerment; in all moments."

"We remove all those in tribalism from a position of authority; in all moments."

"We are centered and empowered in world peace; in all moments."

"We break up the power mongers that gravitate to tribalism; in all moments."

"We thwart all dictatorships from using tribalism as a means of abusing power; in all moments."

"We strip all dictatorships of power; in all moments."

"We free all citizens of humanity; in all moments."

Tribalism II

The root races are the separate races before they started traveling around the world and mixing.

(Say each statement three times while tapping on your head and say each statement a fourth time while tapping on your chest.)

"I declare myself a surrogate for humanity in doing these taps; in all moments."

"We strip all denial off of the world in identifying with a particular root race; in all moments."

"We release allowing root races to divide us; in all moments."

"We release allowing any root race to be segregated or diminished by anyone or any group; in all moments."

"We dissipate the systemic indifference that allows any root race to be deemed superior; in all moments."

"We remove all masks, walls and armor from allegiance to any root race; in all moments."

"We release allowing the superiority of any root race to be condoned by the elite; in all moments."

"We release allowing root races to poison the earth with hate; in all moments."

"We release allowing root races to be validated as superior to another; in all moments."

"We release allowing root races to gain power over another; in all moments."

"We release allowing root races to threaten our personal freedoms; in all moments."

"We release sitting by and watching root races be unloving to each other; in all moments."

"We strip all illusion off of allegiance to root races; in all moments."

"We release allowing root races to segregate us; in all moments."

"We release being indifferent or apathetic to any root race; in all moments."

"We release allowing any root races to erode our civil liberties; in all moments."

"We release being separated from our humanity by a particular root race; in all moments."

"We release being terrorized by root races; in all moments."

"We break up the power mongers of any particular root race; in all moments."

"We release being immersed in ignorance by any particular root race; in all moments."

"We prevent root races from instilling fear in the masses; in all moments."

"We release denying our responsibilities in dealing with the segregation of root races; in all moments."

"We release enabling the segregation of root races; in all moments."

"We release being stripped of our progressiveness by any particular root race; in all moments."

"We release being complacent with the segregation of root races; in all moments."

"We release allowing root races to mandate mainstream segregation; in all moments."

"We eliminate the first cause in the segregation of root races; in all moments."

"We strip all illusion and defenses off of the segregation of root races; in all moments."

"We release converting our empowerment to loyalty to one particular root race; in all moments."

"We release being enslaved to any particular root race; in all moments."

"We remove all vivaxes between ourselves and the segregation of root races; in all moments."

"We remove all tentacles between ourselves and the segregation of root races; in all moments."

"We withdraw all our energy from the segregation of root races; in all moments."

"We collapse and dissolve all of the segregation of root races; in all moments."

"We remove all programming and conditioning the segregation of root races has put on us; in all moments."

"We remove all individual and universal engrams of the segregation of root races; in all moments."

"We release allowing any particular root race to rob us of our empowerment; in all moments."

"We release allowing any root races to diminish others; in all moments."

"We send all energy matrices into the light and sound that empower the segregation of root races; in all moments."

"We command all complex energy matrices that enable the segregation of root races to be escorted into the light and sound; in all moments."

"We send all energy matrices into the light and sound that allow any particular root race to wield power; in all moments."

"We command all complex energy matrices that allow any root race to wield power to be escorted into the light and sound; in all moments."

"We send all energy matrices into the light and sound that allow any root race to diminish another; in all moments."

"We command all complex energy matrices that allow any root race to diminish another to be escorted into the light and sound; in all moments."

"We recant all vows and agreements between ourselves and all root races; in all moments."

"We remove all curses between ourselves and all root races; in all moments."

"We remove all blessings between ourselves and all root races; in all moments."

"We sever all strings, cords and wires between ourselves and all root races; in all moments."

"We dissolve all karmic ties between ourselves and all root races; in all moments."

"We remove all the pain, burden, limitations, fear, futility unworthiness and illusion of separateness that all root races have put on each other; in all moments."

"We give back to all root races all the joy, love, abundance, freedom, health, success, security, companionship, creativity, peace, life wholeness, beauty, enthusiasm, contentment, spirituality, enlightenment, confidence, the ability to discern and empowerment that all root races have taken from them; in all moments."

"We strip all root races of all their ignoble intentions; in all moments."

"We strip root races of their illusions of grandeur; in all moments."

"We crumble all constructs created by any particular root race; in all moments."

"We nullify all contracts between ourselves and all root races; in all moments."

"We eliminate the first cause in all ignoble intentions between all root races; in all moments."

"We release being locked in the sites of any particular root race; in all moments."

"We release humanity from engaging in a race war; in all moments."

"We release being targeted by any particular race; in all moments."

"We relinquish the ruthless pursuit of any root race; in all moments."

"We release resonating or emanating with any particular root race; in all moments."

"We extract all of root races from our individual and universal sound frequency; in all moments."

"We extract all of root races from our individual and universal light emanation; in all moments."

"We extract all of root races from all 32 layers of our individual and universal aura; in all moments."

"We extract all of root races from our whole beingness; in all moments."

"We shift our paradigm from root races to universal individual empowerment and peace; in all moments."

"We transcend allegiance to any root race; in all moments."

"We are centered and empowered in universal and individual freedom and peace; in all moments."

"We infuse universal and individual freedom and peace into our sound frequency; in all moments."

"We imbue universal and individual freedom and peace into our light emanation; in all moments."

"We resonate, emanate and are interconnected to all life in universal and individual freedom and peace; in all moments."

Unity and Empowerment

(Say each statement three times while tapping on your head and say it a fourth time while tapping on your chest.)

"All blocks on certain demographics are eliminated; in all moments."

"All religious rivalries are dismantled; in all moments."

"All political rivalries are dismantled; in all moments."

"All cock blocking is released; in all moments."

"All illusion is stripped off the ugly; in all moments."

"All portals of manipulation are collapsed and dissolved; in all moments."

"All systemic poisons are rendered inoperable; in all moments."

"All shunts to poisons are removed; in all moments."

"All walls are crumbled; in all moments."

"Purity is returned as the mainstay; in all moments."

"The world is transmuted through the alchemy of enlightenment; in all moments."

"All Souls are blessed with the alchemy of enlightenment; in all moments."

"All poisons are extracted from the universal sound frequency and light emanation; in all moments."

"The alchemy of enlightenment is infused in the universal sound frequency and light emanation; in all moments."

"All Souls resonate, emanate, and are interconnected with all life in the universal alchemy of enlightenment; in all moments."

Untangling the Wires

I just finished facilitating a session with a longtime client. She has really opened up in the last year and is enjoyable to work with. In her first sessions, she was asking about her love life and career, but now she is asking questions about the Universe, getting glimpses of her past lives, and she told me today that she sees energy now.

But the biggest change she described was where before she would feel love for her dog or family, now it is magnified to consume her. It is so beautiful to know that my work with her is directly related to more love being experienced in the world.

In her session, I was given the reason that people don't have a particular desire in their life. It is because they are processing certain concepts differently due to their experiences. For instance, if a small child was hit by its mother, it might process love as pain, or if someone was in love for the first time and that person they adored dumped them, they might process relationships as abandonment. The wires get crossed.

Some of the issues seemed to work in reverse. For example, one of them is confusing health for youth, but how that processes to the self is in the belief that one cannot be healthy unless they are young.

Here are the taps that I led her through at the end of the session. I love that my clients allow me to share what we encounter in their sessions. It depicts their generous nature and desire to assist others with their experiences. It is how we uplift humanity. Once a truth is thrown into the hat, it is there for all to partake of. We are all assisting the upliftment of humanity by delving into truth and sharing our findings.

(Say each statement three times out loud while tapping on you head and say it a fourth time while tapping on your chest.)

"I release processing Joy as loss; in all moments."

"I release processing Love as pain; in all moments."

"I release processing Abundance as a stockpile of things; in all moments."

"I release processing Freedom as loneliness; in all moments."

"I release processing Health as youth; in all moments."

"I release processing Success as conquering others; in all moments."

"I release processing Security as withholding my truth; in all moments."

"I release processing Companionship as giving away my power; in all moments."

"I release processing Creativity as being unstable; in all moments."

"I release processing Peace as a stagnant state; in all moments."

"I release processing Life as being difficult; in all moments."

"I release processing Beauty as a weapon; in all moments."

"I release processing Enthusiasm as a waste of energy; in all moments."

"I release processing Contentment as boredom; in all moments."

"I release processing Spirituality as being impoverished; in all moments."

"I release processing being human as superior; in all moments."

"I release processing Humility as unworthiness; in all moments."

"I release processing being human as being separate from nature; in all moments."

"I release processing feelings as reality; in all moments."

"I release processing the mind as the ultimate truth; in all moments."

"I release processing Intelligence as power; in all moments."

"I release processing being human as being encased in matter; in all moments."

"I release processing Dreams as a whim; in all moments."

"I release processing God as separate from myself; in all moments."

"I release processing the Universe as outside of myself; in all moments."

"I release processing Enlightenment as unattainable; in all moments."

"I release processing God realization as unfathomable; in all moments."

You may have different ones and you may have some not listed. It is a great exercise in self-reflection.

Unwanted Weight

(Say each statement three times while tapping on your head and say it a fourth time while tapping on your chest.)

"I release carrying around thoughts as extra weight on my body; in all moments."

"I release carrying around feelings as extra weight on my body; in all moments."

"I release carrying around memories as extra weight on my body; in all moments."

"I release carrying around traumas as extra weight on my body; in all moments."

"I release carrying around opinions and judgments as extra weight on my body; in all moments."

"I release carrying around jealousies as extra weight on my body; in all moments."

"I release carrying around unworthiness as extra weight on my body; in all moments."

"I release carrying around grudges as extra weight on my body; in all moments."

"I release carrying around regrets as extra weight on my body; in all moments."

"I release carrying around frustrations as extra weight on my body; in all moments."

"I release carrying around past lovers as extra weight on my body; in all moments."

"I release carrying around mistakes as extra weight on my body; in all moments."

"I release carrying around wrong choices as extra weight on my body; in all moments."

"I release carrying fears as extra weight on my body; in all moments."

"I release carrying self-punishment as extra weight on my body; in all moments."

"I release carrying sadness as extra weight on my body; in all moments."

"I release carrying around indoctrination or shame as extra weight on my body; in all moments."

Upgrade

(Say three times while tapping on your head and say it a fourth time while tapping on your chest.)

"I release lagging behind; in all moments."

"I upgrade my data; in all moments."

"I empty all cookies; in all moments."

"I recalibrate my processing system; in all moments."

"I remove all unnecessary data; in all moments."

"I clean all my filters; in all moments."

"I upgrade my operating systems; in all moments."

"I download greater awareness into my energy system; in all moments."

"I release living in the past; in all moments."

"I release the wear and tear on my bodies; in all moments."

"I release being locked in outmoded views; in all moments."

"I release being stodgy; in all moments."

"I recalibrate to higher truth; in all moments."

"I awaken to higher consciousness; in all moments."

"I enjoy the resiliency, buoyancy and exuberance of youth; in all moments."

"I adopt the agility and awareness of the youth; in all moments."

Upgrading

(Say each statement three times while tapping on your head and say it a fourth time while tapping on your chest.)

"I release being taken from by male energy; in all moments."

"I release giving male energy all the credit; in all moments."

"I release propping up male energy; in all moments."

"I release being fracked by male energy; in all moments."

"I release being taken for granted by male energy; in all moments."

"I release being tapped dry by male energy; in all moments."

"I unwind all my energy; in all moments."

"I release micromanaging the world that our children are inheriting; in all moments."

"I release carrying the pain of parents everywhere; in all moments."

"I release being crushed by concentrated parental responsibilities; in all moments."

"I release confusing burden with the love; in all moments."

"I untangle the burden from the love; in all moments."

"I extract and dissolve the burden; in all moments."

"I recant my vow to not transcend; in all moments."

"I transcend the lower worlds; in all moments."

"I join the vantage point of the ancient ones; in all moments."

"I release all residual lower-world bullshit; in all moments."

"I release all residual fear; in all moments."

"I remove all residual illusion of separateness; in all moments."

"I remove all residual compulsion to self-sabotage; in all moments."

"I release creating busyness to reflect my spiritual effectiveness; in all moments."

"I release confusing busyness with spiritual effectiveness; in all moments."

"I release the trauma of being born; in all moments."

"I release the trauma of the uncertainty of knowing my purpose; in all moments."

"I untangle busyness from spiritual effectiveness; in all moments."

"I extract and dissolve busyness; in all moments."

"I am centered and empowered in my spiritual effectiveness; in all moments."

"I remove all doubt; in all moments."

"I resonate, emanate and am interconnected with all life in my spiritual effectiveness; in all moments."

"I release the fear of transcending; in all moments."

"I release confusing transcending with being crucified; in all moments."

(Fill in the blank with the antagonist in your life.)

"I release blaming _____; in all moments."

"I release the belief that _____ is holding me back; in all moments."

"I forgive _____ for having me crucified; in all moments."

"I release punishing _____for holding me back; in all moments."

"I remove all that I have inflicted on _____; in all moments."

"I release being terrified of _____; in all moments."

"I remove all engrams of myself with _____; in all moments."

"I strip all illusion off of my love for _____; in all moments."

"I release clinging onto illusion; in all moments."

"I release confusing parenthood with martyrdom; in all moments."

"I untangle martyrdom from parenthood; in all moments."

"I extract and dissolve martyrdom; in all moments."

"I recant my vow of martyrdom; in all moments."

"I recant my vow of servitude; in all moments."

Vanities

(Say each statement out loud three times while tapping on your head and say it a fourth time while tapping on your chest.)

"I release abusing power; in all moments."

"I release giving my free will over to the vanities; in all moments."

"I release succumbing to the vanities; in all moments."

"I release worshiping the vanities; in all moments."

"I release being enslaved to the vanities; in all moments."

"I release wielding power for the vanities; in all moments."

"I release craving world domination; in all moments."

"I release perpetuating the vanities; in all moments."

"I release choosing the vanities over love; in all moments."

"I release the relentless pursuit for the vanities; in all moments."

"I release an allegiance with evil; in all moments."

"I release endorsing evil; in all moments."

"I release personifying evil; in all moments."

"I withdraw all my energy from evil; in all moments."

"I recant all vows and agreements between myself and the vanities; in all moments."

"I remove all curses between myself and the vanities; in all moments."

"I dissolve all karmic ties between myself and the vanities; in all moments."

"I remove all the pain, burden, limitations and engrams that the vanities have put on me; in all moments."

"I remove all the pain burden limitations and engrams that I have put on the world due to the vanities; in all moments."

"I release providing a blueprint for war; in all moments."

"I withdraw all my energy from the vanities; in all moments."

"I withdraw all my energy from war; in all moments."

"I take back all the joy, love, abundance, freedom, life and wholeness; in all moments."

"I give back all the joy, love, abundance, freedom, life and wholeness that I have taken from the world due to the vanities; in all moments."

"I release resonating with the vanities; in all moments."

"I release emanating with the vanities; in all moments."

"I remove all of the vanities from my sound frequency; in all moments."

"I remove all the vanities from my light body; in all moments."

"I shift my paradigm from the vanities to joy, love, abundance, freedom, life and wholeness; in all moments."

"I transcend the vanities; in all moments."

"I remove all masks, walls and armor; in all moments."

"I repair and fortify the Wei chi of all my bodies; in all moments."

"I am centered and imbued in divine love; in all moments."

"I emanate and resonate Divine Love to every corner of the world; in all moments."

"I dissolve everything that is not motivated by Divine Love; in all moments."

Vision

(Say each statement three times while tapping on your head and say it a fourth time while tapping on your chest.)

"I release being disheartened; in all moments."

"I release carrying the trauma of all that I have seen; in all moments."

"I release growing weary; in all moments."

"I strengthen my eye muscles; in all moments."

"I correct my vision; in all moments."

"I see with the eyes of a youth; in all moments."

"I release blurring the lines; in all moments."

"I sharpen my colors; in all moments."

"I realign my rods and cones; in all moments."

"I disintegrate all obstacles to my optimal sight; in all moments."

"I take back my empowerment; in all moments."

"I release degenerating; in all moments."

"I remove all floaters; in all moments."

"I remove all blinders; in all moments."

"I release being shortsighted; in all moments."

"I release having a narrow view; in all moments."

"I release being blinded to the truth; in all moments."

"I release being in denial; in all moments."

"I open my eyes; in all moments."

"I release having tunnel vision; in all moments."

"I release degenerating; in all moments."

"I release all conditioning to grow old; in all moments."

"I regenerate my eyesight; in all moments."

"I release the pain and trauma of all that I have witnessed; in all moments."

"I release averting my eyes from the truth; in all moments."

"I release the fear of what I may see; in all moments."

"I release un-focusing the lens of my eyes; in all moments."

"I release confusing the moral majority for truth; in all moments."

"I release being blind to the truth; in all moments."

"I release the fear of being confronted with the truth; in all moments."

"I release the fear of needing to confront truth; in all moments."

"I remove the film of indifference from my beingness; in all moments."

"I release mistrusting my own truth; in all moments."

"I release the fear of needing to defend my truth; in all moments."

"I release the fear of being rejected for my truth; in all moments."

"I release the fear of being alone with my truth; in all moments."

"I release the belief that I need to choose between truth and love; in all moments."

"I release the belief that I need to choose between truth and my social standing; in all moments."

"I shift my paradigm from denial to truth; in all moments."

"I am centered and empowered in truth and love; in all moments."

"I resonate and emanate truth and love; in all moments."

"I convert all need into being; in all moments."

"I convert all hope into knowing; in all moments."

"I convert all dreams into experiencing; in all moments."

"I convert all wants into having; in all moments."

"I convert all wishes into expressions; in all moments."

"I convert all desires into contentment; in all moments."

"I convert all conflicts into peace; in all moments."

"I convert all lamenting into joyful expression; in all moments."

"I convert all self-doubt into the manifestation of my truth; in all moments."

"I convert all procrastination into living my purpose; in all moments."

Waiting

(Say each statement three times out loud while tapping on the top of your head at the crown chakra and say it a fourth time while tapping on your chest at the heart chakra.)

"I release waiting for love; in all moments."

"I release waiting for joy, love, abundance, freedom, health, success, security, companionship, peace, life, wholeness, beauty, enthusiasm, contentment, spirituality, enlightenment or confidence; in all moments."

"I release being content to wait; in all moments."

"I release the belief that waiting is a virtue; in all moments."

"I release confusing waiting with security; in all moments."

"I release choosing waiting over action; in all moments."

"I release being paralyzed in waiting; in all moments."

"I release using waiting as an excuse; in all moments."

"I release confusing waiting as a choice; in all moments."

"I release the fear of having; in all moments."

"I release the belief that I am unworthy to have; in all moments."

"I release using waiting to martyr myself; in all moments."

"I release using waiting as a form of punishment; in all moments."

"I release using waiting as a weapon; in all moments."

"I release using waiting to gain sympathy; in all moments."

"I release living in waiting; in all moments."

"I release disappointing others through waiting; in all moments."

"I release causing the demise of others through inaction; in all moments."

"I release being imprisoned to waiting; in all moments."

"I release suffering in silence; in all moments."

"I release waiting too long; in all moments."

"I recant all vows and agreements between myself and waiting; in all moments."

"I remove all curses between myself and waiting; in all moments."

"I sever all strings and cords between myself and waiting; in all moments."

"I dissolve all karmic ties between myself and waiting; in all moments."

"I remove all the pain, heartache, burden, shackles, limitations and engrams that waiting has put on me; in all moments."

"I take back all the joy, love, abundance, freedom, health, success, security, companionship, peace, life, wholeness, beauty, enthusiasm, contentment, spirituality, enlightenment or confidence; in all moments."

"I shift my paradigm from waiting to having; in all moments."

"I shift my paradigm from waiting to having; in all moments."

"I transcend waiting; in all moments."

"I am centered and empowered in having joy, love, abundance, freedom, health, success, security, companionship, peace, life, wholeness, beauty, enthusiasm, contentment, spirituality, enlightenment and confidence; in all moments."

War Veterans

Many people are afraid of their power because they have a deep-seated memory of abusing it. That is why they avoid the moment, because they are afraid of abusing power. They prefer to take anything that life dishes out to them as long as they never hurt another being. For them, the moment is the only place to access your empowerment to NOT abuse power and yet not be at the mercy of circumstance.

(Say each statement three times out loud while continuously tapping on the top of your head at the crown chakra and say it a fourth time while tapping on our chest.)

"I declare myself a surrogate for all soldiers in doing these taps; in all moments."

"I release the fear of abusing power; in all moments."

"I release the fear of losing control; in all moments."

"I release the guilt and trauma of killing innocence; in all moments."

"I release punishing myself; in all moments."

"I release suffering in silence; in all moments."

"I release turning my anger inward; in all moments."

"I release mentally torturing myself; in all moments."

"I release berating myself; in all moments."

"I release the trauma of war; in all moments."

"I release the need to justify my actions; in all moments."

"I release the schism between man's law and God's law; in all moments."

"I release abiding by man's law over God's law; in all moments."

"I release the guilt and trauma of betraying God; in all moments."

"I release becoming a brute; in all moments."

"I heal all the emotional scars of battle; in all moments."

"I release ignoring my gut instinct; in all moments."

"I release being in hell; in all moments."

"I release justifying taking life; in all moments."

"I release diminishing life to a score card; in all moments."

"I release resenting those who are ignorant of my plight; in all moments."

"I release the anguish of being invalidated by society; in all moments."

"I release being disillusioned in life; in all moments."

"I erase all the memories of my unfavorable actions; in all moments."

"I release being depressed; in all moments."

"I release the belief that I am alone; in all moments."

"I release the belief that I am going insane; in all moments."

"I untangle all the mind loops that trap me in hell; in all moments."

"I release creating a hell for myself; in all moments."

"I release resenting my loved ones for being impervious to my pain; in all moments."

"I release having my ego stroked as a token gesture; in all moments."

"I bless and heal all those that I have afflicted; in all moments."

"I pour love and healing energy into all those that I have afflicted; in all moments."

"I clean the karmic slate between myself and all those that I have afflicted; in all moments."

"I untangle all the confusion between the present and the past; in all moments."

"I collect all my parts and return my vessel to wholeness; in all moments."

"I repair and fortify the Wei chi of all my bodies; in all moments."

"I align all my bodies; in all moments."

"I release my aversion to loud sounds; in all moments."

"I release allowing sounds to transport me into pain; in all moments."

"I squeeze out all the trauma like toothpaste out of tube and send it into the ground; in all moments."

"I dampen the inner chaos with peace; in all moments."

"I soak the inner chaos with peace; in all moments."

"I melt all the inner chaos into peace; in all moments."

"I am a neutral canvas for peace; in all moments."

"I pour joy, love, abundance, freedom, life and wholeness onto my canvass; in all moments."

"I saturate myself with joy, love, abundance, freedom, life and wholeness; in all moments."

"I shift my whole paradigm to joy, love, abundance, freedom, life and wholeness; in all moments."

"I am centered and empowered in joy, love, abundance, freedom, life and wholeness; in all moments."

"I release expecting and inviting reciprocation for my actions; in all moments."

"I release feeling like an outsider; in all moments."

"I release resenting those in denial; in all moments."

"I release the anger of being used as a pawn; in all moments."

"I release hating society for the structure that it has created; in all moments."

What to Tell Yourself

In quiet intimate moments of contemplation, here are healing things to tell yourself:

- Talk to your eyes and tell them that they're no longer responsible to release anguish through their tears.
- Tell them they never have to be burned by blinding winds, burning sun, or witness to horrendous atrocities again.
- Talk to your ears and tell them that they never have to be deafened by the cries of suffering again.
- Explain to your nose that it never has to be assaulted by the rotting acrid smell of putrid death. It will never let you down again by feeding such rotting assaults into your mouth.
- Tell your arms that they never have to raise up to strike down a life ever again.
- Tell your hands that they need never be used as weapons in battle again.
- Tell them that they need never grip any weapon that will take the life of another.
- Tell your beautiful cheeks that they never need feel or express shame again with their demure blush.
- Tell your shoulders that they never have to carry the responsibility of the world on them again.
- Tell your hips that they no longer need to be twisted and gnarled by the guilt of all the times they rode you into battle.
- Tell your legs that they never again have to march towards death for a cause that they don't believe in.
- Talk to your neck and tell it that it never has to be strung up or choked again as payment for a petty offense.
- Talk to you lips and tell them they never have to taste evil again.
- Tell your mouth that it never has to speak lies to survive ever again.
- Talk to your feet and tell them they never have to be ripped, torn or shredded in the journey again.
- Talk to your heart and tell it that it never as to be broken again. Remind it that no matter what it may perceive, it is healthy, whole, loved and appreciated.
- Talk to your stomach and tell it that it never has to be tortured with deprivation. If you don't send down food, it is merely to give it a rest.
- Tell your skin that it will never be burned off your body again because you spoke your truth.
- Talk to your beautiful form and tell it that it never has to be raped of its dignity again.
- Speak to your nervous system that it never has to endure unfathomable pain again.
- Talk to your essence and tell it that you will never be deceived into giving up your essence again.

Thank all aspects of you for their loyalty, service, integrity and strength. Validate each aspect of yourself and renew your commitment to it. Renew your commitment to you.

What's Your Shtick?

I recently facilitated a session where the client had many health concerns. But the first issue that showed up in looking through the pictures of their life was the issue of not being listened to. When I mentioned this, he didn't think it was an issue at first but then he started to think back to all the times when he was dismissed and realized it was an issue.

In his past lives, I saw layers of lifetimes where he was considered so ill that the only time he was listened to was when he had another devastating symptom. I saw a particular lifetime where he was a child in an affluent family and both arms were tied to a bedpost. His family was leaving the room after a consultation with the doctor and he was screaming for them to stay or to untie him. The father's face had such concern on it that look of concern was the only love the client was privy to. That look of concern translated to love in my client's mind.

In this life, the client unwittingly was still trying to get that look of concern from people. He didn't understand that people can only listen to problems for so long before they shut down. So the way to get that look of concern is to up the ante on the symptoms and, unfortunately, the pain and discomfort that go along with them.

Here is a tap we used. There were many but it boiled down to this:

(Say the statement three times while tapping on your head, and say it a fourth time while tapping on your chest.)

"I release using illness to be loved; in all moments."

For many people, illness is what they use to get love. Most of us use something to get our need for love met. It could be beauty, intelligence, sex, giving, drama, helping, money, laughter, skills, gossip, superiority, etc. Whatever it is, (it will be healing just knowing what it is), replace that word with illness and do the tap. You may be amazed at how good you feel.

White Supremacy

(Say each statement three times while tapping on your head and say it a fourth time while tapping on your chest.)

"I declare myself a surrogate for the world inhabitants in doing these taps; in all moments."

"We strip all denial off of the world in dealing with White supremacists; in all moments."

"We release allowing White supremacists to run amok; in all moments."

"We release allowing White supremacists to be validated by governing parties; in all moments."

"We dissipate the systemic indifference that allows White supremacists to reign; in all moments."

"We remove all masks, walls and armor from White supremacists; in all moments."

"We release allowing White supremacists to be condoned by the elite; in all moments."

"We release allowing White supremacists to poison the earth with hate; in all moments."

"We release allowing White supremacists to be validated; in all moments."

"We release allowing White supremacists to gain power; in all moments."

"We release allowing White supremacists to threaten our personal freedoms; in all moments."

"We release sitting by and watching White supremacists dismantle inalienable rights; in all moments."

"We strip all illusion off of White supremacists; in all moments."

"We release allowing White supremacists to segregate us; in all moments."

"We release being indifferent or apathetic to White supremacists; in all moments."

"We release allowing White supremacists to erode our civil liberties; in all moments."

"We release being separated from our humanity by White supremacists; in all moments."

"We release being terrorized by White supremacists; in all moments."

"We break up the cluster of power mongers that condone White supremacists; in all moments."

"We release being inundated by ignorance by White supremacists; in all moments."

"We prevent White supremacists from being allowed to instill fear in the masses; in all moments."

"We release denying our responsibilities in dealing with White supremacists; in all moments."

"We release enabling White supremacists; in all moments."

"We release being stripped of our progressiveness by White supremacists; in all moments."

"We release being complacent with White supremacists; in all moments."

"We release allowing White supremacists to mainstream; in all moments."

"We eliminate the first cause in empowering White supremacists; in all moments."

"We strip all illusion and defenses off those who use White supremacists to wield power; in all moments."

"We release converting our empowerment to loyalty to White supremacists; in all moments."

"We release being enslaved to White supremacists; in all moments."

"We remove all vivaxes between ourselves and White supremacists; in all moments."

"We remove all tentacles between ourselves and White supremacists; in all moments."

"We withdraw all our energy from White supremacists; in all moments."

"We collapse and dissolve all groups of White supremacists; in all moments."

"We remove all programming and conditioning that White supremacists have put on us; in all moments."

"We remove all individual and universal engrams of White supremacists; in all moments."

"We release allowing White supremacists to rob us of our voice; in all moments."

"We release allowing White supremacists to diminish others; in all moments."

"We send all energy matrices into the light and sound that enable White supremacists; in all moments."

"We command all complex energy matrices that enable White supremacists to be escorted into the light and sound; in all moments."

"We send all energy matrices into the light and sound that allow White supremacists to wield power; in all moments."

"We command all complex energy matrices that allow White supremacists to wield power to be escorted into the light and sound; in all moments."

"We send all energy matrices into the light and sound that prevent us from dealing with White supremacists; in all moments."

"We command all complex energy matrices that prevent us from dealing with White supremacists to be escorted into the light and sound; in all moments."

"We recant all vows and agreements between ourselves and White supremacists; in all moments."

"We remove all curses between ourselves and White supremacists; in all moments."

"We remove all blessings between ourselves and White supremacists; in all moments."

"We sever all strings, cords and wires between ourselves and White supremacists; in all moments."

"We dissolve all karmic ties between ourselves and White supremacists; in all moments."

"We remove all the pain, burden, limitations, fear, futility, unworthiness and illusion of separateness that White supremacists have put on us; in all moments."

"We give back to White supremacists all the pain, burden, limitations, fear, futility, unworthiness and illusion of separateness that they have put on us; in all moments."

"We take back all the joy, love, abundance, freedom, health, success, security, companionship, creativity, peace, life wholeness, beauty, enthusiasm, contentment, spirituality, enlightenment, confidence, ability to discern and empowerment that White supremacists have taken from us; in all moments."

"We strip all White supremacists of all their ignoble intentions; in all moments."

"We strip White supremacists of their illusions of grandeur; in all moments."

"We crumble all constructs created by White supremacists; in all moments."

"We nullify all contracts with White terrorist; in all moments."

"We eliminate the first cause in all ignoble intentions of White supremacists; in all moments."

"We release being locked in the sites of White supremacists; in all moments."

"We release the belief that White supremacists must be allowed to go unchecked; in all moments."

"We release being targeted by White supremacists; in all moments."

"We relinquish the ruthless pursuit of White supremacists' agenda; in all moments."

"We release resonating or emanating with White supremacists; in all moments."

"We extract all of White supremacists from our individual and universal sound frequency; in all moments."

"We extract all of White supremacists from our individual and universal light emanation; in all moments."

"We extract all of White supremacists from all 32 layers of our individual and Universal aura; in all moments."

"We extract all of White supremacists from our whole beingness; in all moments."

"We shift our paradigm from White supremacists to universal individual empowerment and peace; in all moments."

"We transcend White supremacists; in all moments."

"We are centered and empowered in universal and individual freedom and peace; in all moments."

"We infuse Universal and individual freedom and peace into our sound frequency; in all moments."

"We imbue Universal and individual freedom and peace into our light emanation; in all moments."

"We resonate, emanate and are interconnected to all life in Universal and individual freedom and peace; in all moments."

Command Worthiness

(Say each statement three times while tapping on your head and say it a fourth time while tapping on your chest.)

"I release the aversion to worthiness; in all moments."

"I release being invested in unworthiness; in all moments."

"I release the repulsion between worthiness and monetary value; in all moments."

"I release the aversion to allot a monetary value to my worth; in all moments."

"I release being enslaved to unworthiness; in all moments."

"I release leaving my worth in the intangible realms; in all moments."

"I release the fear of tainting my worth with physicality; in all moments."

"I release the fear that my worth will be stolen from me; in all moments."

"I release the trauma of losing my worth; in all moments."

"I send all energy matrices into the light and sound that steal my worth; in all moments."

"I command all complex energy matrices that steal my worth, to be escorted into the light and sound; in all moments."

"I send all energy matrices that negate my worth into the light and sound; in all moments."

"I command all complex energy matrices that negate my worth to be escorted into the light and sound; in all moments."

"I send all energy matrices into the light and sound that diminish my worth; in all moments."

"I command all complex energy matrices that diminish my worth to be escorted into the light and sound; in all moments."

"I take back my worth; in all moments."

"I remove all vivaxes between myself and unworthiness; in all moments."

"I remove all tentacles between myself and unworthiness; in all moments."

"I remove the claws of unworthiness from my beingness; in all moments."

"I remove all programming and conditioning that unworthiness has put on me; in all moments."

"I remove all engrams of unworthiness from my beingness; in all moments."

"I untangle myself from unworthiness; in all moments."

"I release identifying with unworthiness; in all moments."

"I release associating with unworthiness; in all moments."

"I send all energy matrices of unworthiness into the light and sound; in all moments."

"I command all complex energy matrices of unworthiness to be escorted into the light and sound; in all moments."

"I strip all illusion off of unworthiness; in all moments."

"I remove all masks, walls and armor of unworthiness from my beingness; in all moments."

"I strip all illusion of unworthiness from my beingness; in all moments."

"I withdraw all my energy from unworthiness; in all moments."

"I release using unworthiness to wield superiority; in all moments."

"I release donning unworthiness as competition; in all moments."

"I release using unworthiness to gain favor with God; in all moments."

"I release using unworthiness as leverage; in all moments."

"I release using unworthiness as a decoy; in all moments."

"I recant all vows and agreements between myself and unworthiness; in all moments."

"I remove all curses between myself and unworthiness; in all moments."

"I release deeming worthiness as unfathomable; in all moments."

"I remove all blessings between myself and unworthiness; in all moments."

"I shatter all glass ceilings on the worthiness that I will allow; in all moments."

"I release waiting to deem myself worthy; in all moments."

"I remove all repulsion between my worthiness and matter, energy, space and time; in all moments."

"I release being rendered unworthy in matter, energy, space and time; in all moments."

"I render matter, energy, space and time ineffective in affecting my worthiness; in all moments."

"I sever all strings, cords and wires between myself and unworthiness; in all moments."

"I dissolve all karmic ties between myself and unworthiness; in all moments."

"I remove all the pain, burden and limitations that unworthiness has put on me; in all moments."

"I remove all the pain, burden and limitations that I have put on all others due to unworthiness; in all moments."

"I release deeming myself or others unworthy; in all moments."

"I remove all the fear, futility and illusion of separateness that unworthiness has put on me; in all moments."

"I remove all the fear, futility and illusion of separateness that I have put on all others due to unworthiness; in all moments."

"I take back all that unworthiness has taken from me; in all moments."

"I give back to all others all that I have taken from them due to unworthiness; in all moments."

"I release resonating with unworthiness; in all moments."

"I release emanating with unworthiness; in all moments."

"I extract all unworthiness from my sound frequency; in all moments."

"I extract all unworthiness from my light emanation; in all moments."

"I extract all unworthiness from my whole beingness; in all moments."

"I shift my paradigm from unworthiness to worthiness; in all moments."

"I transcend all unworthiness; in all moments."

"I infuse worthiness into my sound frequency; in all moments."

"I infuse worthiness into my light emanation; in all moments."

"I am centered and empowered in worthiness; in all moments."

"I resonate, emanate and am interconnected with all life in worthiness; in all moments."

Releasing Deep-Seated Unworthiness

In many of my clients, there is one cause or another for deep-seated unworthiness. It doesn't just start in gym class by not getting picked for kickball. The issues are what is triggered when we are not included, or we are teased or overlooked. It is much deeper in some than in others. That is why one person can laugh off a comment and another feels excruciating offense at a similar comment. One has come by their reactions honestly.

Different cultures have different ways of subjugating their people. Some of them come up in my private sessions. Following is a list of taps that may undo some of the ingrained unworthiness of past times.

(Say each statement three times while tapping on your head and say it a fourth time while tapping on your chest.)

"I release being an untouchable; in all moments."

"I release being damned; in all moments."

"I release being enslaved; in all moments."

"I release being tortured; in all moments."

"I release the belief that I am a sinner; in all moments."

"I release the trauma of being sacrificed; in all moments."

"I release having my feet bound; in all moments."

"I release letting my people down; in all moments."

"I release being ostracized; in all moments."

"I release being an abomination; in all moments."

"I release being left for dead; in all moments."

"I release the belief that I am unholy; in all moments."

"I release the belief that God hates me; in all moments."

"I release the belief that I let God down; in all moments."

"I release the belief that I am unworthy; in all moments."

"I release identifying with garbage; in all moments."

"I release the belief I only deserve garbage; in all moments."

"I release being more comfortable with garbage; in all moments."

"I release being a throwaway; in all moments."

"I release living in squalor; in all moments."

"I release feeling like garbage; in all moments."

"I release the belief that I am garbage; in all moments."

"I release making others feel or believe they are garbage; in all moments."

"I release the belief that I am only worthy of garbage; in all moments."

"I release the pain, trauma and unworthiness of being an untouchable; in all moments."

"I recant all vows and agreements between myself and living in squalor; in all moments."

"I remove all curses between myself and living in squalor; in all moments."

"I sever all strings and cords between myself and living in squalor; in all moments."

"I dissolve all karmic ties between myself and living in squalor; in all moments."

"I remove all the pain, burden, limitations, engrams and unworthiness that living in squalor has put on me; in all moments."

"I remove all the pain, burden, limitations, engrams and unworthiness that I have put on all others by causing them to live in squalor; in all moments."

"I take back all the joy, love, abundance, freedom, health, success, security, companionship, creativity, peace life and wholeness that living in squalor has taken from me; in all moments."

"I give back all the joy, love, abundance, freedom, health, success, security, companionship, creativity, peace, life and wholeness that I have taken from all others by causing then to live in squalor; in all moments."

"I release resonating with squalor; in all moments."

"I release emanating with squalor; in all moments."

"I remove all squalor from my sound frequency; in all moments."

"I remove all squalor from my light bodies; in all moments."

"I shift my paradigm from squalor to joy, love, abundance, freedom, health, success, security, companionship, creativity, peace life and wholeness; in all moments."

"I transcend squalor; in all moments."

"I am centered and empowered in the richness of my own divinity; in all moments."

"I am imbued in divine love; in all moments."

"I shift my paradigm from unworthiness to joy, love, abundance, freedom, life and wholeness; in all moments."

"I release converting feelings of unworthiness into contempt; in all moments."

"I release converting feelings of unworthiness into disease; in all moments."

"I release converting feelings of unworthiness into problems; in all moments."

"I release converting feelings of unworthiness into gossip; in all moments."

"I release converting feelings of unworthiness into apathy; in all moments."

"I release converting feelings of unworthiness into depression; in all moments."

"I release converting feelings of unworthiness into obnoxiousness; in all moments."

"I release converting feelings of unworthiness into overcompensation; in all moments."

"I release converting feelings of unworthiness into ego; in all moments."

"I release converting feelings of unworthiness into indifference; in all moments."

"I release converting feelings of unworthiness into noise; in all moments."

"I release converting feelings of unworthiness into gaudiness; in all moments."

"I release converting feelings of unworthiness into poverty; in all moments."

"I release converting feelings of unworthiness into weakness; in all moments."

"I release converting feelings of unworthiness into helplessness; in all moments."

"I release converting feelings of unworthiness into hoarding; in all moments."

"I release converting feelings of unworthiness into anger; in all moments."

"I release converting feelings of unworthiness into lust; in all moments."

"I release converting feelings of unworthiness into greed; in all moments."

"I release converting feelings of unworthiness into attachment; in all moments."

"I release converting feelings of unworthiness into vanity; in all moments."

"I release converting feelings of unworthiness into sloth; in all moments."

"I release converting feelings of unworthiness into self pity; in all moments."

"I release converting feelings of unworthiness into martyrdom; in all moments."

"I release converting feelings of unworthiness into servitude; in all moments."

"I release converting feelings of unworthiness into arrogance; in all moments."

"I release converting feelings of unworthiness into manipulation; in all moments."

"I release converting feelings of unworthiness into indifference; in all moments."

"I release converting feelings of unworthiness into cruelty; in all moments."

"I shift my paradigm from feeling unworthy to the fullness of being loved and empowered; in all moments."

"I am centered in love and empowerment; in all moments."

"I am satiated in love and empowerment; in all moments."

"I resonate and emanate love and empowerment; in all moments."

In doing all the taps, get a sense of which ones are harder to do and which ones bring up more emotion. Use that as a clue to discovering the initial causes to some things that affect the present day. In doing so, it can help you achieve more of a sense of freedom.

Balance Your Yin and Yang

When we talk in male and female energy, some people may get defensive and believe we are talking about a battle of the sexes. It is so not true. What is being referred to is the attribute of the yin energy that gets steamrolled by yang energy. These attributes are kindness, compassion, patience, thoughtfulness, discernment, encouragement and empowerment for all.

Yang energy is single focused and single goal oriented. Yang energy is important, but it needs to be balanced by the yin energy that is equally important and necessary. Yin without yang creates a weakling. Yang without yin creates the brute. We have watched the brute energy go amok. It is up to us all to put value and purpose into the yin energy so that it doesn't so readily fold into the yang.

The balance of the two needs to be reestablished and always maintained with an overview. It is like riding a bike and having both hands on the handlebars to steer, so it is easy to stay on course. But if one hand dominates, the whole bike will go off course. It is now for humanity to maintain the overview of both hands. This is how to maintain balance. It is not the luxury of a few to be aware of such things but a necessity.

(Say each statement three times while tapping on your head and say it a fourth time while tapping on your chest.)

"I declare myself a surrogate for the Universal in doing these taps; in all moments."

"I release the systemic domination of yang energy; in all moments."

"I release yin energy from rolling itself into yang energy; in all moments."

"I dry up all psychic manipulation and control of yang energy; in all moments."

"I release the systemic belief that yin is weak; in all moments."

"I prevent yang energy from burying yin; in all moments."

"I recalibrate yin and yang energy to be balanced; in all moments."

"I return to yin what yang has taken from it; in all moments."

"I repair and fortify the Wei chi of yin; in all moments."

"I remove all masks, walls and armor that yang has built up; in all moments."

"I withdraw all of yin's empowerment from yang; in all moments."

"I prevent yang from overpowering yin; in all moments."

"I regain balance between yin and yang; in all moments."

"I maintain an overview and command of both yang and yin energy; in all moments."

"I maintain awareness to prevent yin or yang from overtaking the other; in all moments."

"I release the yang adopting actions of a bully; in all moments."

"I establish and maintain a harmony and peace between yin and yang energy; in all moments."

"I make space in the world for yin and yang energy to be co-empowered; in all moments."

"I restore yin to all those who are writhing in power and greed; in all moments."

"I restore yang to all those who fear speaking their truth or living their purpose; in all moments."

"I remove all blockages to Universal balance of yin and yang energy; in all moments."

"I stretch the capacity to maintain an overview of Universal balance of yin and yang energy; in all moments."

"We are centered and empowered in the overview of balanced Universal yin and yang energy; in all moments."

"We resonate, emanate and are interconnected with all life in the overview of balanced Universal yin and yang energy; in all moments."

Stop "Yanging" up Your Yin

There are so many people looking for love. Does it need to be so difficult? A recent session revealed a couple of issues preventing a woman from attracting a mate. It has always been obvious to me that many women who wear makeup and a power wardrobe to attract a man are doing so in male energy. It is as if they are putting on their war paint when they go out clubbing.

Recently, a client revealed two of her past lives that were interfering with her attracting a mate. One of them was a life as a Geisha. In that life, she was trained to be very submissive to men. It left her feeling vulnerable as a woman. But even more damaging to her was interpreting being female as a negative, passive experience.

From this experience and others, she defined her yin energy as passive. Being in yin energy came to feel like a very vulnerable state to her. She avoided it as much as possible. As a result, she stayed in yang energy most of the time. Even when she was interested in a man, unbeknownst to her, when she liked someone, she was engaging him in male energy. Her yang energy trying to attract a yang male would just not work. It had nothing to do with her being pretty or worthy enough. It was just a simple matter of the Law of Attraction. Yang energy will repel yang energy every time.

Another lifetime was getting in the way of her attracting a mate as well. There was a past lifetime where she was a gay male soldier. She was in love with another soldier who was her soul mate. He was NOT gay. He would have been repulsed at the thought of a romantic relationship with another man. Knowing this, the gay soldier made certain to always be a good friend to him. As painful as it was, he preferred to suffer in silence rather than risk losing a connection with the love of his life. That lifetime of innate rejection was bleeding through to this life.

Since our natural state is joy, the more devastating an experience is, the deeper it is ingrained into our Akashic records. When the woman met someone she was attracted to, she naturally went into friend mode as it was ingrained from that past experience. This woman was trying to attract a man using passive yang energy. It was still yang energy. No matter what, yang will always repel yang, regardless of whether it is in a yin body or not.

Here is why the taps are so important. Trying to rectify this would take a lot of therapy, even if it were possible. Here are the taps we used to correct this at a deep level. The shift was immediate as we could both feel it and hear it in her voice.

"I release diminishing my yin; in all moments."

"I release the belief that yin is weak; in all moments."

"I release the fear of being yin; in all moments."

"I release feeling vulnerable in yin; in all moments."

"I release confusing yin with being geisha; in all moments."

"I remove all negative engrams of being geisha; in all moments."

"I release habitually diminishing my yin; in all moments."

"I release making my yin inoperable; in all moments."

"I release being enslaved to diminishing my yin; in all moments."

"I repair and fortify the wei chi of my yin; in all moments."

"I remove all engrams of diminished yin from my beingness; in all moments."

"I remove all vivaxes between myself and diminishing my yin; in all moments."

"I remove all tentacles between myself and diminishing my yin; in all moments."

"I remove the claws of diminishing my yin from my beingness; in all moments."

"I recant all vows and agreements between myself and diminishing my yin; in all moments."

"I remove all curses between myself and diminishing my yin; in all moments."

"I remove all blessings between myself and diminishing my yin; in all moments."

"I sever all strings and cords between myself and diminishing my yin; in all moments."

"I dissolve all karmic ties between myself and diminishing my yin; in all moments."

"I remove all the pain, burden, limitations and confusion that diminishing my yin has put on me; in all moments."

"I remove all the pain, burden, limitations and confusion that me diminishing my yin has put on my partner; in all moments."

"I take back all that diminishing my yin has taken from me; in all moments."

"I give back to my partner all that me diminishing my yin has taken from them; in all moments."

"I release resonating with diminishing my yin; in all moments."

"I release emanating with diminishing my yin; in all moments."

"I extract all of diminishing my yin from my sound frequency; in all moments."

"I extract all of diminishing my yin from my light emanation; in all moments."

"I shift my paradigm from diminishing my yin to having balanced yin and yang; in all moments."

"I transcend diminishing my yin; in all moments."

"I release overcompensating in yang; in all moments."

"I release always being in yang; in all moments."

"I release using a war cry to call forth love; in all moments."

"I release feeling safe only in yang; in all moments."

"I release confusing yang with being complete; in all moments."

"I release habitually overcompensating in yang; in all moments."

"I release making my yang the controlling faction; in all moments."

"I release being enslaved to overcompensating in yang; in all moments."

"I remove all masks, walls and armor from my yang; in all moments."

"I lay down my yang's sword and shield; in all moments."

"I remove all engrams of overcompensating in yang from my beingness; in all moments."

"I remove all vivaxes between myself and overcompensating in yang; in all moments."

"I remove all tentacles between myself and overcompensating in yang; in all moments."

"I remove the claws of overcompensating in yang from my beingness; in all moments."

"I recant all vows and agreements between myself and overcompensating in yang; in all moments."

"I remove all curses between myself and overcompensating in yang; in all moments."

"I remove all blessings between myself and overcompensating in yang; in all moments."

"I sever all strings and cords between myself and overcompensating in yang; in all moments."

"I dissolve all karmic ties between myself and overcompensating in yang; in all moments."

"I remove all the pain, burden, limitations and confusion that overcompensating in yang has put on me; in all moments."

"I remove all the pain, burden, limitations and confusion that me overcompensating in yang has put on my partner; in all moments."

"I take back all that overcompensating in yang has taken from me; in all moments."

"I give back to my partner all that me overcompensating in yang has taken from them; in all moments."

"I release resonating with overcompensating in yang; in all moments."

"I release emanating with overcompensating in yang; in all moments."

"I extract all of overcompensating in yang from my sound frequency; in all moments."

"I extract all of overcompensating in yang from my light emanation; in all moments."

"I shift my paradigm from overcompensating in yang to having balanced yin and yang; in all moments."

"I transcend overcompensating in yang; in all moments."

"I am centered and empowered in balanced yin and yang; in all moments."

"I resonate and emanate balanced yin and yang; in all moments."

Testimonials

"In a few minutes after asking Jen to post taps on hiatal hernia, I experienced a hot searing pain at the uppermost left section of my abdomen near my solar plexus. It was very localized and wow it hurt! Then it stopped hurting in an instant. I was definitely relieved about that. Later in the day, I habitually massaged the hiatal hernia in vain hoping it'd quell its physical torment of my insides. It's been decades! At that moment, I realized it was GONE! I began pressing deeper and lower and...no hernia!

"I was so elated! Speechless--which is hard to do for me! I shared this occurrence immediately knowing full well Jen was (is) the conduit, the facilitator, and the healer that put in motion my healing. It can be no other! I then received the taps she wrote and, upon Jen's encouragement to still do them even though I was healed, the taps had a profound effect on me still! Even the sound of my voice changed - it was softer, less thin sounding, and I felt truly HEARD and understood inside out, not from her standpoint but my OWN!

"Each tap she wrote was my life that I held in, kept out, hid, longed for, feared, missed, was hurt by and loved. I will continue to do these taps knowing full well the power within us is of infinite proportion. Jen is clearly able to see, connect with, and help us heal. Tapping is a healing process and so is being healed by being open to it, so when she does her work, it is lovingly fulfilled in each of us."

"That was very powerful! I feel like I've needed these words for some time now. While doing the taps, one of my cats came over right away and my upper body, primarily my upper/middle back muscles, felt warm like they were being worked out. I feel now almost like I've gained some upper body strength!

"Very powerful, wow! Certainly had trouble saying some of these, felt breathless and wanted to mix up the wording in some of them."

"Thank you so much for these. The taps you shared were (are) profoundly spot on. You read me inside and out. When I did the taps this morning, I became keenly aware, not in a nervous sense at all but in a calming sense, of the change in my voice. It was not as high or thin sounding, I guess is a good way to say it. I became teary-eyed but in a good way and lighter. I will keep these taps with me and say them daily. Thank you, Jen."

"Jen, you are so helpful. A very dear friend and I were having a wonderful lunch today and she mentioned she was "quitting sugar." I shared your posts with her. She loved them. I just wanted you to know that your message is being spread far and wide. Thank you. Love from British Columbia Canada, where we are waiting with joy for springtime and new life."

About the Author

Jen Ward, LMT, is a Reiki Master, an intuitive and gifted healer, and an innovator of healing practices. She is at the leading edge of energy work, providing a loving segue for her techniques to clients, enabling them to cross the bridge of self-discovery with her. Her passion is to empower individuals in their own healing journey so that they can remain in their center every step of the way.

While attending the Onondaga School of Therapeutic Massage, she was first introduced to energy work. It soon became second nature for her to help identify and remove energy blocks from clients. She is highly proficient at tuning into individuals' specific needs to release their issues, allowing their own body to make the energetic changes necessary to return to a greater sense of ease. Her ability to pick up many different modalities as second nature is another aspect of her profound gifts.

Jen is considered a sangoma, a traditional African Shaman who channels ancestors, emoting sounds and vocalizations in ceremonies. An interesting prerequisite to being a sangoma is to have survived the brink of death. When Jen was first approached with the knowledge of being a sangoma, she had not yet fulfilled this prerequisite. However, in April 2008, when she came back to society on the brink of starvation as a result of traumatic involuntary imprisonment, the qualification had been met. She returned to the world of humanity a devout soul inspired to serve.

Her special abilities have also allowed her to innovate a revolutionary technique for finding lost pets by performing an emotional release on the animal. Using this method, she has successfully reunited many lost pets with their owners.

Jen currently works as a long-distance emotional release facilitator, public speaker, and consultant. Her special modality encompasses a holistic overview of her clients from all vantage points, including their physical, emotional, causal, and mental areas, ultimately benefiting their work, home, family, and especially spiritual lives. You can find her work at www.jenward.com, join her Facebook page, JenuineHealingwithJenWard, and find her on Twitter @jenuinehealing.

Other Books by Jen Ward

Enlightenment Unveiled: *Expound into Empowerment.* This book contains case studies to help you peel away the layers to your own empowerment using the tapping technique.

Grow Where You Are Planted: *Quotes for an Enlightened "Jeneration."* Inspirational quotes that are seeds to shift your consciousness into greater awareness.

Perpetual Calendar: *Daily Exercises to Maintain Balance and Harmony in Your Health, Relationships and the Entire World.* 369 days of powerful taps to use as a daily grounding practice for those who find meditation difficult.

Children of the Universe. Passionate prose to lead the reader lovingly into expanded consciousness.

Letters of Accord: *Assigning Words to Unspoken Truth.* Truths that the ancient ones want you to know to redirect your life and humanity back into empowerment.

The Do What You Love Diet: *Finally, Finally, Finally Feel Good in Your Own Skin.* Revolutionary approach to regaining fitness by tackling primal imbalances in relationship to food.

Emerging from the Mist: *Awakening the Balance of Female Empowerment in the World.* Release all the issues that prevent someone from embracing their female empowerment.

Affinity for All Life: *Valuing Your Relationship with all Species.* This book is a means to strengthen and affirm your relationship with the animal kingdom.

The Wisdom of the Trees. If one is struggling for purpose, they can find love, and truth by tuning into the *Wisdom of the Trees.*

Chronicles of Truth. Truth has been buried away for way too long. Here is a means to discover the truth that lies dormant within yourself.

Healing Your Relationships. This book is a means to open up communications and responsiveness to others so that clarity and respect can flourish again in society.

How to Awaken Your Inner Dragon: *Visualizations to Empower Yourself and the World.*

Collecting Everyday Miracles: *Commit to Being Empowered.* This book is a thought provoking means to recreate the moment of conception with everyday miracles. It is through gratitude and awareness. This is what this book fosters.